D0197674

Libya

Anthony Ham

LONELY PLANET PUBLICATIONS
Melbourne • Oakland • London • Paris

LIBYA

Douz • **Matmata** • **Medenine**

Ferry to Tangier (Morocco)

Ferry to Valetta (Malta)

TRIPOLI
Cosmopolitan Mediterranean city with an exceptional museum and an ancient medina

Tataouine • Ben Guerdane • Ras al-Jedir • Bu Kammash • **Zuara** • **TRIPOLI** • Al-Garabuli • **Al-Khoms** • *Leptis Magna*

SABRATHA
Wonderfully preserved ancient Roman city

LEPTIS MAGNA
One of the most magnificent and intact Roman cities anywhere in the Mediterranean

Sabratha • Surman • Aziziyah • **Tajura** • Souq al-Khums • *Leptis Magna*

Borj Bourguiba • **Sahel al-Jefara** • Bir Ayyad • **Yefren** • Gharyan • Tarhuna • Zliten • Misrata • Tauorga

TUNISIA • Wazin • Nalut • Goush • Jadu • Kabaw • **Jebel Nafusa** • Mizda • Ban Walid • *Gulf of Sirt*

JEBEL NAFUSA
Ancient villages with superb Berber architecture perched on rocky outcrops

Tiaret • Sinoun • Bir-Alagh • Fassanu • Nisma • El-Fuchia • *Tripoli-Benghazi Ferry* • **Sirt** • Medinat Sultan • Siltar

Burj el-Khadra • Burj Messouda • Deb-Deb • Ghadames • **Hamadat al-Hamrah** • Derj • Al-Qaryat • Ash-Shwareef • **Sahel as-Sirt**

GHADAMES
Evocative old town famous for its former caravan trade

Ohanet • Sokna • Waddan • Zell

In Amenas • Houn • **Jebel as-Sawda**

ALGERIA • **Idehan Ubari (Ubari Sand Sea)** • *Wadi ash-shatti* • Al-Fogaha

Ownsrik • Bargan • Brak • Ashkada • **Haruj al-Aswad**

Idri • Qardah • Samnu

Ramlat Assayef • Tekerkiba • Al-Ghoraifa • *Ubari Lakes* • **Sebha**

Ubari • Germa • Fjeaj • Zueila • Tmissah

Al-Aweinat (Serdeles) • *Wadi Methkandoush* • Murzuq • Waw al-Kabir

Kaf Ejoul (1281m) • Awiss • *Msak Settafet* • **Tassili-n-Ajjer** • Jebel Acacus • **Idehan Murzuq (Murzuq Sand Sea)** • Al-Qatrun • Waw al-Namus (538m)

Burj el-Haouses • Ghat • *Msak Mellett* • Tajarhi

Djanet • **SAHARA**

UBARI LAKES
Idyllic lakes surrounded by sand dunes in the heart of the Sahara

| 0 | 50 | 100km |
| 0 | 30 | 60mi |

JEBEL ACACUS
Spectacular desert scenery and home to prehistoric art

Tumu

ELEVATION

	1500m
	1000m
	500m
	200m
	0

NIGER

Djado • Uzu • Bardai • Zouar

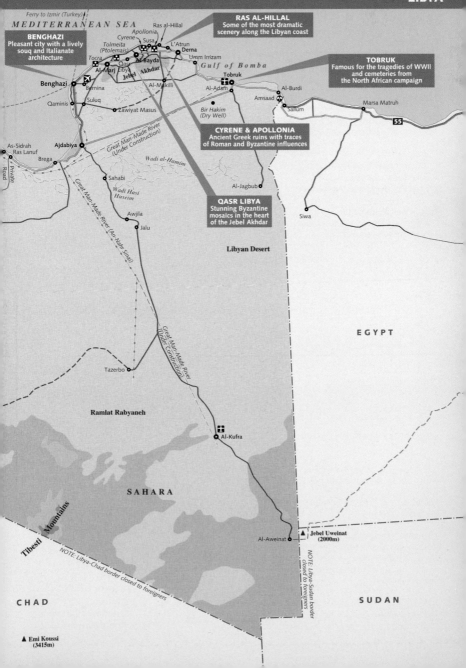

LIBYA

MEDITERRANEAN SEA

Ferry to Izmir (Turkey)

RAS AL-HILLAL
Some of the most dramatic scenery along the Libyan coast

Ras al-Hillal

BENGHAZI
Pleasant city with a lively souq and Italianate architecture

Cyrene
Tolmeita (Ptolemais)
Tocra
Al-Marj
Qasr
Al-Bayda
Jebel Akhdar
Libya

Apollonia
Susa
L'Atrun
Derna

Umm Irrizam

Benghazi
Bernina

Al-Mukili

Gulf of Bomba

TOBRUK
Famous for the tragedies of WWII and cemeteries from the North African campaign

Tobruk
Al-Adam

Qaminis
Suluq
Zawiyat Masus

Al-Burdi
Amsaad
Sallum

Marsa Matruh

55

Bir Hakim (Dry Well)

CYRENE & APOLLONIA
Ancient Greek ruins with traces of Roman and Byzantine influences

As-Sidrah
Ras Lanuf
Private
Road

Ajdabiya
Brega

Great Man-Made River (Under Construction)

Wadi al-Hamim

Sahabi

Al-Jagbub

QASR LIBYA
Stunning Byzantine mosaics in the heart of the Jebel Akhdar

Wadi Hasi Huseim

Siwa

Awjila
Jalu

Great Man-Made River (An Nahr Sinai)

Libyan Desert

Great Man-Made River (Under Construction)

Tazerbo

Ramlat Rabyaneh

EGYPT

Al-Kufra

SAHARA

Tibesti Mountains

NOTE: Libya-Chad border closed to foreigners

Al-Aweinat

▲ Jebel Uweinat (2000m)

NOTE: Libya-Sudan border closed to foreigners

CHAD

SUDAN

▲ Emi Koussi (3415m)

Libya
1st edition – March 2002

Published by
Lonely Planet Publications Pty Ltd ABN 36 005 607 983
90 Maribyrnong St, Footscray, Victoria 3011, Australia

Lonely Planet offices
Australia Locked Bag 1, Footscray, Victoria 3011
USA 150 Linden St, Oakland, CA 94607
UK 10a Spring Place, London NW5 3BH
France 1 rue du Dahomey, 75011 Paris

Photographs
Many of the images in this guide are available for licensing from
Lonely Planet Images.
W www.lonelyplanetimages.com

Front cover photograph
Graceful curves and shadows mark the crest of a sand ridge in the
Sahara. (Jane Sweeney)

ISBN 0 86442 699 2

text & maps © Lonely Planet Publications Pty Ltd 2002
photos © photographers as indicated 2002

Printed by The Bookmaker International Ltd
Printed in China

Contents – Text

Contents – Maps

The Author

Anthony worked as a refugee lawyer for three years, during which time the people of the world came to visit him in his office. After tiring of daily battles with the Australian government, he set out to see the world for himself and restore his faith in humanity. He has been travelling throughout Asia and Africa ever since, discovering unimagined uses for his Masters degree in Middle Eastern politics. He is now based in Melbourne and works as a freelance writer and photographer, with his work appearing in a range of magazines and newspapers. For Lonely Planet, Anthony has worked on *Middle East*, *Africa*, *Iran*, *India*, *North India* and *West Africa*.

FROM ANTHONY

The Libyans have a saying, *ma-arifat ar-rijaal kunz* (knowing people is a treasure) and it was my good fortune to make wonderful friends in Libya. My debt of gratitude to my dear friend Hakim is enormous. A man of unfailing patience and generosity, he taught me so much about Libya – how to navigate by the stars in the Sahara, how to dance the *kishk* (in private), boundless Libyan hospitality and everything in between. He also understood that I had to discover my own Libya; the opinions expressed in this book are entirely mine. Thank you also to Hakim's wife and children for letting me borrow him.

Also of great assistance in Libya were Mu'awia Wanis, Hussein Founi and Dr Mustapha Turjman; I am extremely grateful to each of them. In Al-Bayda, Othman al-Hama made possible a wonderful evening around the campfire on the beach near Hammamah; your *matruda* was the best I tasted. Thank you also to Sallah and Sheikh, who were my inspiring Tuareg companions in the desert, and Milod, the ultimate city boy, who brought such warmth to the journey. Thanks also to Brenda de Swaart and her crew in Cyrenaica who helped to energise me for the road ahead.

A special thank you to Michael and Claire who accompanied me for part of the journey, welcomed me so warmly to Dublin and reminded me how much I have missed them. Thanks also to Joyce and Viv Temple who were exceedingly generous during my comings and goings through London, and to Miles and Ingrid Roddis in Valencia for their hospitality, wisdom and invigorating spirit. Thanks also to Jennifer Cox for the invaluable visa information.

Back home, a massive thank you to my family and friends for their patience, understanding and warmth despite my long absences: Jan, my mother and friend for giving up so much and for teaching me to look beyond the horizon; my father Ron for being the most faithful follower of my journeys; and especially Lisa, Greg, Rachael, Ash, Thomas, Tanya, Damien, Quetta and Samantha. A special thank you to Lauren for helping me to find my wings to fly and generally being one of life's angels. And to Alexandra and Isabella: I hope that one day you will get to see the places I visit.

This Book

This first edition of *Libya* was edited in Lonely Planet's Melbourne office by Bethune Carmichael, Rebecca Turner and Lynne Preston, with additional assistance from Isabelle Young, Julia Taylor and Kerryn Burgess. Katie Butterworth coordinated the design and mapping, with assistance from Heath Comrie, Mandy Sierp, Anna Judd, Sarah Sloane and Shahara Ahmed. Thanks to Margaret Jung for the cover design, Hunor Csutorus for the climate charts, Brigitte Ellemor and Brett Moore for their insights and advice, and Quentin Frayne and Emma Koch for the Language chapter.

Last but not least, thanks to author Anthony Ham for his hard work, admirable patience and exceptional enthusiasm.

THANKS
Many thanks to the travellers who used the last edition and wrote to us with helpful hints, advice and interesting anecdotes. Your names appear in the back of this book.

Foreword

ABOUT LONELY PLANET GUIDEBOOKS

The story begins with a classic travel adventure: Tony and Maureen Wheeler's 1972 journey across Europe and Asia to Australia. There was no useful information about the overland trail then, so Tony and Maureen published the first Lonely Planet guidebook to meet a growing need.

From a kitchen table, Lonely Planet has grown to become the largest independent travel publisher in the world, with offices in Melbourne (Australia), Oakland (USA), London (UK) and Paris (France).

Today Lonely Planet guidebooks cover the globe. There is an ever-growing list of books and information in a variety of media. Some things haven't changed. The main aim is still to make it possible for adventurous travellers to get out there – to explore and better understand the world.

At Lonely Planet we believe travellers can make a positive contribution to the countries they visit – if they respect their host communities and spend their money wisely. Since 1986 a percentage of the income from each book has been donated to aid projects and human rights campaigns, and, more recently, to wildlife conservation.

Although inclusion in a guidebook usually implies a recommendation we cannot list every good place. Exclusion does not necessarily imply criticism. In fact there are a number of reasons why we might exclude a place – sometimes it is simply inappropriate to encourage an influx of travellers.

UPDATES & READER FEEDBACK

Things change – prices go up, schedules change, good places go bad and bad places go bankrupt. Nothing stays the same. So, if you find things better or worse, recently opened or long-since closed, please tell us and help make the next edition even more accurate and useful.

Lonely Planet thoroughly updates each guidebook as often as possible – usually every two years, although for some destinations the gap can be longer. Between editions, up-to-date information is available In our free, quarterly *Planet Talk* newsletter and monthly email bulletin *Comet*. The *Upgrades* section of our website (Ⓦ www.lonelyplanet.com) is also regularly updated by Lonely Planet authors, and the site's *Scoop* section covers news and current affairs relevant to travellers. Lastly, the *Thorn Tree* bulletin board and *Postcards* section carry unverified, but fascinating, reports from travellers.

Tell us about it! We genuinely value your feedback. A well-travelled team at Lonely Planet reads and acknowledges every email and letter we receive and ensures that every morsel of information finds its way to the relevant authors, editors and cartographers.

Everyone who writes to us will find their name listed in the next edition of the appropriate guidebook, and will receive the latest issue of *Comet* or *Planet Talk*. The very best contributions will be rewarded with a free guidebook.

We may edit, reproduce and incorporate your comments in Lonely Planet products such as guidebooks, websites and digital products, so let us know if you don't want your comments reproduced or your name acknowledged.

How to contact Lonely Planet:
Online: Ⓔ talk2us@lonelyplanet.com.au, Ⓦ www.lonelyplanet.com
Australia: Locked Bag 1, Footscray, Victoria 3011
UK: 10a Spring Place, London NW5 3BH
USA: 150 Linden St, Oakland, CA 94607

Introduction

Stretching from the Mediterranean to the Sahara, Libya presents travellers with a wealth of possibilities. The great civilisations of the Middle East – Roman, Greek, Byzantine, Arab-Islamic and the indigenous empires of the Sahara – have all left their footprints and monuments of grandeur on Libyan soil.

As a crossroads of empires, Libya has a treasure-trove of monuments amassed over 12,000 years of human history.

Along the Mediterranean coastline stand some of the best-preserved cities of the ancient world. Leptis Magna is one of the finest Roman sites in existence, and Greek/Roman Cyrene is alive with the echoes of titanic struggles between the gods.

The Libyan desert is home to landscapes of rare beauty, with oceans of sand dunes, enchanting oases and galleries of prehistoric rock art; in few places of the world can you swim so easily in palm-fringed lakes surrounded by towering mountains of sand. Here you will also find the dignified Tuareg,

the indigenous people of the Sahara. The desert of Libya may just be the desert you thought only existed in the imagination.

Between the Mediterranean and the Sahara are the mountain homelands of the Berber people, whose long-standing occupation of the land and resistance to foreign rule has bred a resilient and independent spirit. Like those battling for supremacy around them, Berber history has left unique architectural signposts and fascinating insights into traditional ways of living.

It all meets in cosmopolitan Tripoli, the white city of the Mediterranean, the gateway to the Sahara. The call to prayer has been drifting out over the rooftops of the medina since the 7th century and it can still be heard, yet to be drowned out by Libya's rush to embrace the modern.

The buffeting by the shifting winds of history has made the Libyans a modern people in the very best sense of the word. Outward-looking and with strong connections to Europe, Africa and the Middle East, Libya

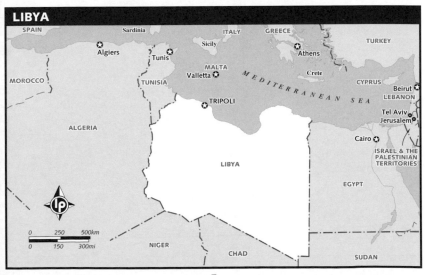

is also a land whose present is enriched by the constant awareness of its heritage. Oil platforms and ambitious development projects coexist easily with the traditional inhabitants and ancient sites.

For so long maligned by a myopic Western media as a pariah state at odds with the world, Libya surprises almost everyone who sets foot in the country. For most people who haven't visited, Libya means Colonel Gaddafi and Lockerbie. For those who've spent any time here, the friendliness and hospitality of the Libyan people are likely to be their most enduring memories, alongside a wealth of superb sights. Forget the myths about Libyan hostility to the outside world; most Libyans make a mockery of the stereotype, with their generosity and willingness to engage with the peoples of the world.

The fact that tourism is a relatively new industry in Libya has not stopped the Libyan people from catching on fast.

Buoyed by the lifting of the United Nations embargo in 1999, Libya has rapidly become a popular destination.

Tourism in Libya is constantly evolving, ensuring that careful planning is required for any visit. Visa regulations change frequently and, at the time of writing, a journey to Libya had to be arranged as part of a group tour, ostensibly to minimise tourism's impact upon what was for years a quite isolated society – history has taught Libya to be wary of foreign invasions. That said, the adaptable Libyans permit a significant degree of flexibility to enable you to get the best from this rewarding country.

Despite its modern facilities, Libya has preserved something of an old-world quality (there are no hustlers). It is quite possibly the last unspoiled outpost in North Africa. Whether you're a desert enthusiast or an aficionado of the ancient world, now is the perfect time to visit.

Facts about Libya

HISTORY

Until the second half of the twentieth century, Libya was cursed by its geography, which put it in the path of the invading empires of Europe and the Middle East. As a result, Libya has too often been an unwilling outpost of a far-distant capital.

Libya's three regions – Tripolitania (north-western Libya), Cyrenaica (northeast and south-east) and the Fezzan (southwest) – rarely formed a single entity.

Prehistory

Two distinct races appeared in North Africa between about 15,000 and 10,000 BC – the Oranian and then the Capsian – although the origins of both are virtually unknown.

The integration of the Oranians and the Capsians with indigenous peoples resulted in the spread of Neolithic (New Stone Age) culture and the introduction of farming techniques. The earliest evidence of lasting and semipermanent settlements in Libya dates from this time (8000 BC). Rock paintings in the Jebel Acacus and Wadi Methkandoush areas in Libya (as well as in the Tassili mountains in Algeria) are the greatest source of knowledge about this time of abundant wildlife, rainfall and vegetation (see the special section 'Rock Art of the Libyan Sahara' in the Fezzan & the Sahara chapter).

It is from these Neolithic peoples that the Berbers (the indigenous peoples of North Africa) are thought to be descended. Taking into consideration regional variations and the lack of hard evidence, they appear to have been predominantly nomadic pastoralists, although they continued to hunt and occasionally farm. By the time of contact with the first of the outside civilisations to arrive from the east, the Phoenicians, these local tribes were already well established.

The Phoenicians in Tripolitania (1000–201 BC)

The Phoenician empire, with its origins and base in the Levantine ports of Tyre, Sidon and Byblos (all in modern-day Lebanon), were a seafaring people renowned for their trading activities. By the 12th century BC, Phoenician traders were active throughout the Mediterranean, arriving regularly on the Libyan coast by 1000 BC.

After around 700 BC, their need for permanent settlements to facilitate their trade in gold, silver, raw metals, ivory and even apes and peacocks saw them establish the colonies of Lebdah (Leptis), Oea (Tripoli) and Sabratha. Other ports were later built at Macomades-Euphranta (near modern Sirt) and Charax (Medinat Sultan). Each was a small but essential link in a chain of safe ports stretching from the Levant to Spain. The strategic importance of the Libyan coast was not the only reason for Phoenician interest in Libya – the ports also provided a base for Phoenician merchants to trade with the Berber tribes of the interior, with whom they signed treaties of cooperation.

Phoenician civilisation in North Africa came to be called 'Punic', a derivation of both the Latin *Punicus* and Greek *Phoinix*. The colonies were governed from the city of Carthage (in modern Tunisia), a city whose dominance of North Africa represented the pinnacle of Punic civilisation.

Carthage was founded in 814 BC. Long politically dependent on the mother culture in Tyre, Carthage eventually emerged as an independent, commercial empire. By 517 BC, the powerful city-state was the leading city of North Africa and by the 4th century BC, Carthage controlled the North African coast from Tripolitania to the Atlantic.

Ultimately, ongoing tension with the nascent Roman Empire weakened Carthage and spelled the death-knell for Carthaginian rule. In what was to become a recurring theme in Libyan history, the Carthaginian empire governed Tripolitania from afar. There were few material benefits for Libya's indigenous inhabitants, yet the province was not spared the devastation caused by the Punic Wars with Rome (264–241 BC,

218–201 BC and 149–146 BC). The wars reduced Carthage to a small, vulnerable African state. It was razed by the Romans in 146 BC, the site symbolically sprinkled with salt and damned forever. Tripolitania was left to fend for itself.

The Garamantian Empire of the Fezzan (900 BC–AD 500)

The ancient historian Herodotus (5th century BC), in one of the earliest written references to Libya, spoke of the Garamantes people who lived 'in the part of Libya where wild beasts are found'. As part of the first indigenous empire of significance in Libya, the Garamantes have become a people of legend, seen alternately as a wild, warlike and ungovernable nomadic people or a sophisticated, urban community which made the desert bloom. There is undoubtedly a kernel of truth in both assessments.

The Garamantes may have descended in part from the Neolithic peoples of the region, although there is little doubt that some migrated from the oases to the east, carrying with them a knowledge of cultivation. The community, a loosely connected confederation of tribes, was centred on Garama (now Germa) in the Wadi al-Hayat in the Fezzan. Archaeologists have found evidence to suggest that these cities were more than mere desert outposts. Rather, they were thriving urban centres with markets and forums for public entertainment.

In spite of the competing claims about the nature of Garamantian society, most historians agree that the Garamantes were one of the most advanced and forward-thinking peoples of their time. They are attributed with introducing writing, horses, wheeled-transport and, finally, camels to the Sahara. Due to its location in the central Sahara, the Garamantian civilisation exercised significant control over the ancient caravan routes across the desert with strong links to Egypt and sub-Saharan Africa. Salt (a means of preserving meat and other foods) was exchanged for gold and slaves in a lucrative trade. The Garamantes also led successful raids on the cities of the coast, including Lebdah.

Most remarkably of all, the Garamantes empire thrived because of its agricultural prowess, even though they lived far from recognised water sources. Herodotus spoke of the Garamantes as 'a very numerous tribe of people who spread soil over the salt to sow their seed in'. Archaeologists have discovered the remains of hundreds of underground channels. These channels, known as *foggara*, enabled a boom in farming activity in the oases of the wadi. Ultimately, however, this innovative approach to scarce water resources, an approach adopted nearly 2500 years later by the modern Libyan state (see the boxed text 'The Great Man-Made River Project' later in this chapter), sowed the seeds of the Garamantian decline. By AD 500 the last of the Garamantes people had either died or abandoned Garama, as underground water supplies dried up as a result of overexploitation.

The Greeks in Cyrenaica (631–75 BC)

Legend has it that the inhabitants of the Greek island of Thera were ordered by the oracle of Delphi to migrate to North Africa. In 631 BC, they established the city of Cyrene. Within 200 years, during the period of great Hellenic colonisation, the Greeks had established four more cities – Barce (Al-Marj), Tocra, Ptolemais (Tolmeita) and Apollonia (the port for Cyrene). These semi-autonomous city-states came to be known as the Pentapolis (Five Cities). North Africa became so significant that by around 500 BC the Greeks divided the world into three parts – Asia, Europe and Libya.

In 331 BC, the armies of Alexander the Great made a triumphant entrance to Cyrenaica from Egypt, though the great man himself stopped at the border after the Cyrenaicans greeted him with promises of loyalty. Upon his death in 323 BC, Alexander's empire was divided among his Macedonian generals. Egypt, along with Cyrene, went to Ptolemy. Again, the cities of the Pentapolis retained a significant degree of autonomy, although Greek influence was limited to the coastal areas, with minimal penetration of the Berber hinterland.

Despite significant political turmoil throughout the years of the Pentapolis, Cyrene, in particular, flourished. In the economic sphere, the fertile slopes of the Jebel Akhdar provided Greece with valuable grain, wine, wool, livestock and a herb from the silphium plant (see the boxed text 'Silphium' in the Cyrenaica chapter), which was unique to Cyrenaica. Cyrene also became one of the Greek world's premier intellectual and artistic centres, producing and exporting some of the finest scholars of the age. The city was famed for its medical school, its learned academics and for being home to some of the finest examples of Hellenistic architecture anywhere in the world. The Cyrenians also developed a school of philosophy with a doctrine of moral cheerfulness that defined happiness as the sum of human pleasures. Such a philosophy was undoubtedly made easier by the temperate and altogether pleasant climate.

The halcyon days of Greek rule could not last forever. With Greek influence on the wane, the last Greek ruler, Ptolemy Apion, finally bequeathed Cyrenaica to Rome.

Roman Period

After the final defeat of Carthage in the Punic Wars, the Romans assigned Tripolitania to their ally, the Berber king of Numidia. In 46 BC, Julius Caesar deposed the final Numidian king, Juba I, who had sided with Pompey, a general in the Roman army and rival of Caesar in the Civil Wars of Rome. Tripolitania was thereafter incorporated into the new province of Africa Nova (later called Africa Proconsularis). In the east, Cyrenaica was formally annexed as part of the Roman Empire in 75 BC.

Communications between Tripolitania and Cyrenaica were hampered by rebellions along the southern coast of the Gulf of Sirt, although, by the end of the 1st century AD, Rome had completed the pacification of Sirtica and the two provinces were united under one administration.

The era that followed was one of Libya's finest. The Pax Romana saw Tripolitania and Cyrenaica become prosperous Roman provinces, part of a cosmopolitan and sophisticated state with a common language, legal system and identity. Many of the towns along the coast enjoyed the full range of urban amenities for which Roman cities were famous – a forum, markets, amphitheatres and baths. Traders and artisans flocked to the Libyan coast from throughout the empire. Tripolitania was a major source of olive oil for Roman merchants and also operated as an entrepot for gold and slaves brought to the coast by Berbers and the Garamantians. Cyrenaica was equally prized, as it had been under Greek rule, as a source of wine, silphium and horses.

A Libyan even became emperor of the Roman Empire. Septimus Severus (who ruled between AD 193 and 211) was known as the 'Grim African' (see the boxed text 'Septimus Severus – The Grim African' in the Coastal Tripolitania chapter). It was under his tutelage that Leptis Magna was transformed into an important cultural and commercial centre second only to Rome.

The thinly populated territory of Libya enabled the Romans to maintain control with little more than a locally recruited legion of 5500 men. The Roman army succeeded in penetrating the Saharan provinces of the Fezzan, yet made no attempt to wield administrative power (they had decided that it was not worth the effort).

Despite the relative peace that accompanied Roman rule, the region was not immune to the political instability beyond its borders. In AD 115, a Jewish revolt among settlers from Palestine began and was not quelled until AD 118, after Jewish insurgents had laid waste to Cyrene and destroyed much of Cyrenaica.

In AD 300, the Roman emperor Diocletian separated Cyrenaica from the province of Crete, dividing the region into Upper and Lower Libya – the first time the name 'Libya' was used as an administrative designation. By the 4th century AD, however, Rome was in decline and the fate of the Libyan colonies was sealed by a massive earthquake in AD 365 (see the boxed text 'The Earthquake of AD 365' in the Cyrenaica chapter) from which Roman influence in Africa never recovered.

Vandals & Byzantines

In AD 429, a rebellious Roman official invited the Vandals, a Germanic tribe, to Libya in an attempt to gain leverage with the authorities in Rome. The Vandals, with as many as 80,000 settlers in tow, quickly set about conquering Libya, a feat they achieved in 431 under their leader Genseric (Gaeseric). Faced with little choice, the Romans recognised the Vandal ascendancy as long as Libya's civil administration remained, nominally at least, in Roman hands. In 455, the Vandals sacked Rome. The last vestiges of Roman prosperity in Libya quickly evaporated and the Vandals, more adept at pillage and overseas conquests than in administering their colonies, fortified themselves in armed camps. The outlying areas fell once again under the rule of tribal chieftains.

In 533, the Byzantine army general Belisarius captured Libya for the emperor Justinian. Byzantine control was limited to the cities of the coast, Berber rebellions in the hinterland reduced the area to anarchy and the potential prosperity of the provinces was squandered. Byzantine rule was deeply unpopular, not least because taxes were increased dramatically in order to pay for the colony's military upkeep while the cities were left to decay.

The Coming of Islam

With tenuous Byzantine control over Libya restricted to a few poorly defended coastal strongholds, the Arab horsemen who first crossed into Cyrenaica in 642 encountered little resistance. Under Amr ibn al-As, the armies of Islam conquered Cyrenaica. By 643 Tripoli had also succumbed. It was not until 663, when Uqba bin Nafi invaded the Fezzan, however, that Berber resistance in Libya was overcome. By 712 the entire region from Andalucía to the Levant came under the purview of the Ummayad caliph of Damascus.

Despite the rapid success enjoyed by the forces of Islam in religious and military terms, the social character of Libya remained overwhelmingly Berber. While largely accepting the arrival of the new religion, the Berber tribes resisted the Arabisation of the region. Although Arab rule flourished in coastal areas, the enmity between the Berbers (who saw their rulers as arrogant and brutal) and the Arabs (who scorned the Berbers as barbarians) ensured that rebellions plagued much of Libya's hinterland.

In 750 the Abbasid dynasty overthrew the Ummayad caliph and shifted the capital to Baghdad, with emirs retaining nominal control over the Libyan coast on behalf of the far-distant caliph. In 800 Caliph Harun ar-Rashid appointed Ibrahim ibn al-Aghlabid as his governor. The Aghlabid dynasty effectively became independent of the Baghdad caliphs, who nevertheless retained ultimate spiritual authority. The Aghlabid emirs took their custodianship of Libya seriously, repairing Roman irrigation systems, restoring order and bringing a measure of prosperity to the region.

In the last decade of the 9th century, the Ismailis (a branch of Shiism) launched an assault on the strongholds of the Sunni Aghlabids. The movement's spiritual leader, Grandmaster Ubaidalla Said of Syria, was installed as the imam of much of North Africa, including Tripolitania. The Berbers of Libya, always happy to thumb their noses at the orthodox Sunni aristocracy, accepted the imam as the Mahdi (Promised One).

The Shiite Fatimid dynasty conquered Egypt in 972 and set up the caliphate in Cairo. The difficulty of maintaining control over Libya plagued the Fatimids, as it had almost every authority before them. At the beginning of the 11th century, Bulukkin ibn Ziri was installed as the Fatimid governor but he quickly returned Libya to orthodox Sunnism and swore allegiance to the Abbasid caliphs of Baghdad.

The Fatimid anger at what they considered an act of gross betrayal would profoundly alter the fabric of Libyan society. Two tribes from the Arabian Peninsula – the Bani Hilal and the Bani Salim (or Bani Sulaim) – were co-opted into migrating to the Maghreb. The Bani Salim settled in Libya, particularly in Cyrenaica, while the Bani Hilal (who numbered as many as 200,000 families) spread across North Africa. The destruction of Cyrene and Tripoli by this unstoppable mass migration was symptomatic of arguably the most effective conquest Libya had seen. The Berber tribespeople were displaced from their traditional lands, their farmland converted to pasture and the new settlers finally cemented the cultural and linguistic Arabisation of the region.

In 1158, the supporters of the Almohad dynasty arrived in Tripolitania from Morocco and established their authority. An Almohad viceroy, Muhammad bin Abu Hafs, ruled Libya from 1207 to 1221 and established the Hafsid dynasty, which outlived the Almohads. The Hafsids ruled Tripolitania for nearly 300 years. There was significant trade with the city-states of Europe and the Hafsid rulers encouraged art, literature and architecture, and gave scholarship priority.

Meanwhile, in the Fezzan in the 13th century, King Danama of Kanem (near Lake Chad) annexed territories as far north as the Al-Jufra oases. His Toubou viceroy founded the autonomous Bani Nasr dynasty, which ruled the Fezzan until the 14th century. They were followed by the theocratic kingdoms of Kharijite sectarians, including the Bani Khattab in the Fezzan. In the early 16th century, the Libyan Sahara fell under the sway of Muhammad al-Fazi from Morocco who, early in the 16th century, founded the Awlad Suleiman dynasty in Murzuq.

Ottoman Rule

By the start of the 15th century, the Libyan coast had little central authority and its harbours were havens for unchecked bands of pirates. Hapsburg Spain occupied Tripoli in 1510, but the Spaniards were more concerned with controlling the port than with the inconveniences of administering a colony. Charles V entrusted the territory to the Knights of St John of Malta in 1524. Fourteen years later, Tripoli was reconquered by a pirate king called Khair ad-Din (known more evocatively as Barbarossa, or Red Beard). It was then that the coast became renowned as the Barbary Coast.

When the Ottomans arrived to occupy Tripoli in 1551, they saw little reason to reign in the pirates, preferring to profit from the booty. The French, Dutch and British navies all bombarded Tripoli to warn off further robbery on the high seas, but the Turks saw the pirates as a second column in their battle for naval supremacy. As long as they continued to control the ports of Algiers, Tripoli and Tunis, the Turks were happy to turn a blind eye to the anarchy there.

Under the Ottomans, the Maghreb was divided into three provinces, or regencies: Algiers, Tripoli and Tunis. After 1565, administrative authority in Tripoli was vested in a pasha appointed by the sultan in Constantinople. The sultan provided the pasha with a corps of janissaries (professional soldiers committed to a life of military service). This corps was in turn divided into a number of companies under the command of a junior officer with the title of bey (literally 'maternal uncle'). The janissaries quickly became the dominant force in Ottoman Libya. As self-governing military guilds answerable only to their own laws and protected by a divan (a council of senior officers who advised the pasha), the janissaries soon reduced the pasha to a largely ceremonial role. The sultan, whose forces were stretched to the limits in this vast empire, was in no position to argue.

In 1711, Ahmed Karamanli, an Ottoman cavalry officer and son of a Turkish officer and Libyan woman, seized power and founded a dynasty which would last 124 years. Again, while the Ottomans wielded ultimate authority from afar, power was vested in a local leader acting well beyond his original brief. The founder of the Karamanli dynasty was described by British explorer Hugh Clapperton as 'a cruel and unprincipled tyrant'.

One of the primary preoccupations of the Karamanli dynasty was an attempt to bring the Fezzan (and hence trans-Saharan trade routes) under its control. The sultans of the Awlad Suleiman based in Murzuq resisted the Ottoman army. Periods of stability were due more to expedience than any mutual feelings of brotherhood – they tolerated the presence of each other unless their interests directly clashed. In 1810 the Ottomans dispatched troops to Ghadames to regain control and, soon after, the Ottomans overthrew the Awlad Suleiman by killing the last of its sultans, Ahmed, and re-annexed the Fezzan.

On the coast, Western powers followed the American lead (see the boxed text 'Round One to Libya' in the Cyrenaica chapter) and refused to pay any further protection money to the Karamanli-controlled pirates. England and France began to ask for the repayment of debts incurred by the Karamanli regime. Tripoli's economy collapsed and Yusuf Karamanli – who had fought and won a civil war against his father and brother in 1795 and always made a point of defying his Ottoman overlords – tried to make up the financial shortfall by increasing taxes. Rebellions broke out across Libya and the countryside soon descended into civil war. Yusuf finally succumbed to the pressure and abdicated in favour of his son Ali in 1835. When Ali asked the Ottoman sultan Mohammed II for assistance in repelling a European takeover of Tripoli, the Ottomans took the opportunity to rein in their troublesome offspring and brought the rule of the Karamanli dynasty to a close. With full Ottoman authority restored, the Turks once again relegated Libya to the status of a neglected outpost of a decaying empire.

Less than a decade after the hated Ottoman authority was resumed, the indigenous Sanusi Movement, lead by Islamic cleric Sayyid Mohammed Ali as-Sanusi, called on the Cyrenaican countryside to resist Ottoman rule. The Grand Sanusi established his headquarters in the oasis town of Al-Jaghbub while his *ikhwan* (followers) set up *zawiyas* (religious colleges or monasteries) across North Africa and brought some stability to regions not known for their submission to central authority. In line with the express instruction of the Grand Sanusi, their gains were made largely without coercion.

The highpoint of Sanusi influence was to come in the 1880s under the Grand Sanusi's son, Mohammed al-Mahdi, who was a skilled administrator and a charismatic orator. With 146 lodges spanning the length and breadth of the Sahara, Mohammed al-Mahdi moved the Sanusi capital to Al-Kufra. Harsh Ottoman rule only fuelled the appeal of the

The Grand Sanusi

Sayyid Mohammed Ali as-Sanusi was born in 1787 in what is now Algeria. A descendant of the Prophet Mohammed and a Sufi, he studied in Morocco and then at Cairo's prestigious Al-Azhar University. This pious scholar was forceful in his criticism of the Egyptian ulema for what he perceived as their timid compliance with the Ottoman authorities and their spiritual conservatism. He also argued that all learned Muslims had the right to disregard the four classical schools of Islamic law and Quranic interpretation, and themselves engage in *ijtihad* (individual interpretation of sacred texts and traditions). Not surprisingly, this upstart from a North African backwater was denounced by the religious scholars of Cairo as a heretic and they issued a fatwa against him.

As-Sanusi removed himself to Mecca, where he found greater support for his radical ideas. There he was influenced by the Wahhabi movement, which called for a return to the purity of Islam. In Mecca he founded his first *zawiya* (a religious college or monastery), before returning to North Africa. He settled in Cyrenaica (near Al-Bayda) in 1843 where he found fertile ground among a people known for their dislike of authority.

Sanusi Movement's call to repel foreign occupation. Remarkably, Mohammed al-Mahdi succeeded where so many had failed before him, securing the enduring loyalty of the Berber tribes of Cyrenaica.

Over a 75-year period the Ottoman Turks provided 33 governors – not one of them distinguished themselves enough to be remembered by history.

Italian Occupation

With Ottoman control tenuous at best, the Italian government saw an opportunity to join, albeit belatedly, the scramble for African colonies. On 3 October 1911, the Italians attacked Tripoli, claiming somewhat disingenuously to be liberating Libya from Ottoman rule. The Libyan population was unimpressed and refused to accept yet another occupying force. A major revolt against the Italians followed, with battles near Tripoli, Misrata, Benghazi and Derna.

The Ottoman sultan had more-important concerns and ceded Libya to the Italians by signing the 1912 Treaty of Lausanne. Tripolitania was largely under Italian control by 1914, but both Cyrenaica and the Fezzan were home to rebellions led by the Sanusis. Throughout WWI, with the Turks and Germans supplying arms to the Sanusi rebels, the Italians in Cyrenaica could lay claim to controlling only a few ports. Meanwhile, Libyan notables began agitating for self-rule.

The Italian government failed to heed the unrest of a people tired of foreign occupation. In 1921 the government appointed Governor Giuseppe Volpi. The following year, Mussolini announced the *Riconquista* of 'Libya' (a name not used as an administrative entity since Roman times). Marshal Pietro Badoglio, who commanded the Italian army under Volpi, waged a punitive 'pacification' campaign. Badoglio was succeeded in the field by Marshal Rodolfo Graziani. Graziani only accepted the commission from Mussolini on the condition that he was allowed to crush Libyan resistance unencumbered by the inconvenient restraints imposed by Italian and international law. Mussolini reportedly agreed immediately and Graziani intensified the oppression.

The Libyans rebelled, with the strongest voices of dissent coming from Cyrenaica. Omar al-Mukhtar, a Sanusi sheikh, became the leader of the uprising.

After a much-disputed truce in 1929 descended into claim and counter claim, Italy's Libya policy reached new depths of brutality. A barbed-wire fence was built from the Mediterranean to the oasis of Al-Jaghbub to sever supply lines critical to the resistance's survival. Soon afterwards, the colonial administration began the wholesale deportation of the people of the Jebel Akhdar to deny the rebels the support of the local population. The forced migration of more than 100,000 people ended in concentration camps in Suluq (south of Benghazi) and Al-'Aghela (west of Ajdabiya) where tens of thousands died in squalid conditions. It's estimated that the number of Libyans who died – killed

The Lion of the Desert

Omar al-Mukhtar was born in Cyrenaica in 1858. His education through the Sanusi school system invested him with a passionate faith in Islam and a belief that it was the obligation of every Libyan to resist all forms of foreign domination. He distinguished himself in the first campaign against the Italians (1911–17). With Italian rule being increasingly extended through the use of terror, he again took up the call of freedom for his people. In addition to a number of unlikely successes against the better-resourced Italian army, Al-Mukhtar's greatest achievement was to unite Libya's disparate tribes into an effective fighting force. For almost ten years, he and his fighters held out, frustrating the Italians at every turn. In 1931 Al-Mukhtar was still fighting at the age of 73, which earned him the sobriquet of 'Lion of the Desert'. When supplies for the resistance movement ran out later that year, Al-Mukhtar was captured by the Italian army and on 15 September 1931 he was hanged in Benghazi in front of his followers (see boxed text 'The Capture & Trial of Omar al-Mukhtar' in the Cyrenaica chapter). A likeness of Al-Mukhtar appears on 10LD banknotes.

either directly (military campaigns) or indirectly (starvation and disease) – could be a minimum of 80,000 or even up to half of the Cyrenaican population. Up to 95% of the local livestock was also killed. That this was no accident is demonstrated by the Italian determination to win 'even if the entire population of Cyrenaica has to perish'. After Al-Mukhtar's capture, the rebellion petered out. The wholesale massacring of civilians fleeing Al-Kufra was the final outrage of a ruthless occupation.

By 1934 Italian control extended into the Fezzan, and in 1937 Mussolini cynically declared himself the 'Protector of Islam', in the process appointing compliant and conservative Sunni clerics. In 1938–39 Mussolini sought to fully colonise Libya, introducing 30,000 Italian settlers which brought their numbers to more than 100,000 (proportionally more than French settlers in neighbouring Algeria). These settlers were shipped primarily to Sahel al-Jefara (Jefara Plain) in Tripolitania and the Jebel Akhdar in Cyrenaica, and given land from which the indigenous inhabitants had been forcibly removed. Throughout almost three decades of Italian occupation, a quarter of Libya's population died.

In July 1999 the Italian government offered a formal apology to Libya. The next year reports circulated that Italy had agreed to pay US$260 million as compensation for the occupation.

WWII & the Road to Independence

Just when the Italians had beaten the Libyan resistance into submission, WWII broke out and Libya once again became a major theatre for somebody else's war. From 1940 until late 1942, the Italians and Germans, led by Lieutenant-General Erwin Rommel, waged a devastating war for the territory between Benghazi and El-Alamein (Egypt), with much of the fighting centred on Tobruk (see the boxed text 'The Rats of Tobruk' in the Cyrenaica chapter for more details). In October 1942 General Montgomery's army broke through the German defences at El-Alamein. In November the Allied forces retook Cyrenaica; by January 1943 Tripoli was in British hands and by February the last German and Italian soldiers were driven from Libya.

The British administered Tripolitania and Cyrenaica from 1943. The initial military presence became a caretaker administration while the victorious powers decided what to do with Libya. In the meantime, the French were, with British acquiescence, occupying the Fezzan, with their headquarters at Sebha. Ghat was attached to the French military region of Algeria, while Ghadames was subject to French control in southern Tunisia.

The country was hardly a lucrative prospect for potential occupiers: Libya was impoverished and had become renowned for its fierce resistance to colonial rule. The Libyan countryside and infrastructure had been totally devastated – it was estimated that at the end of WWII there were 11 million unexploded mines on or under Libyan soil – and prevailing education levels presented a damning indictment of Italy's colonial neglect.

The Four Powers Commission, comprising France, the UK, USSR and USA, was set up to decide Libya's fate. After the customary squabbling and distrust among the Great Powers, it emerged that Sayyid Idris as-Sanusi (the grandson of the Grand Sanusi) had received promises of independence from the British in return for Sanusi support during WWII. Among Libyans, who found themselves finally being listened to, the notion of independence quickly gathered momentum. Libyan nationalists raced against the clock to prevent France from detaching the Fezzan from the provinces of Cyrenaica and Tripolitania. The United Nations General Assembly approved the formation of an independent state in November 1949, by 53 votes to one (Ethiopia) with five (Soviet bloc) abstentions, which paved the way for Libyan independence

Tripolitanian representatives pushed for a unitary, centralised state, while the leaders of the Fezzan and Cyrenaica, fearful of being overwhelmed by a more populous and economically powerful Tripolitania, argued strongly for a federal state. The latter option was chosen as the most effective means of preserving Libyan unity. Members of the first National Assembly were appointed by the Mufti of Tripolitania, Emir of Cyrenaica and the Chief of the Fezzan.

On 24 December 1951 the independent United Kingdom of Libya, with King Idris as its monarch, was finally, and unanimously, proclaimed by the National Assembly.

Post-Independence Period (1951–69)

The Libya of the 1950s was largely preoccupied with building state institutions and rebuilding its shattered economy. In 1952 the first elections for the National Assembly were won by conservatives. The only party of note at the time, the National Congress Party of Tripolitania, opposed the dilution of Tripolitania's influence in a federal system and agitated for a unitary state. The party was quickly outlawed.

In 1953, the Libyan government signed a treaty with the British government which allowed Britain to maintain military bases on Libyan soil for 20 years in return for annual aid of around UK£1 million. The following year, a similar agreement was signed with the Americans who agreed to pay US$40 million over the same period. Libya also forged links across the Mediterranean, signing a friendship pact with France in 1955 and a trade agreement with Italy in 1957.

In June 1959 an oilfield was discovered at Zelten in Cyrenaica. By early 1960, 35 wells had been sunk nationwide and international oil companies clamoured to obtain exploration rights in Libya. Over the decade which followed, Libya was transformed from an economic backwater into one of the world's fastest-growing economies. Private wealth and urban migration increased, creating social upheaval with which the political process was ill-equipped to deal.

From 1960–63, a succession of Libyan governments ruled and then fell; all struggled to adjust to the new and radically different reality of being the custodians of an oil-rich state. In March 1963, a new cabinet was formed under the progressive leadership of Dr Mohi ad-Din Fekini. The federal system was abolished and Libya was proclaimed a unitary state. Officially, this was to increase the efficiencies of the new economy. However, the move fostered unease in Cyrenaica and the Fezzan with Tripolitanian dominance. A bicameral parliamentary system was introduced, with an upper house consisting of 24 senators appointed by the king; the executive power of the three regional administrative councils was handed over to a council of ministers. In a move which outraged the conservative religious establishment, women were granted the vote.

Dr Fekini's reforms did not bring stability and he resigned less than a year after taking office. He was replaced as prime minister by Mohammed Muntasser, whose preoccupation was less with electoral reform than with

championing Arab resistance to imperialism (at the time, the charismatic Gamal Abdel Nasser was at the height of his popularity in neighbouring Egypt and his anti-imperialist, Arab nationalism won great support in Libya). Muntasser announced that his government did not intend to renew the military bases agreements with the UK and US governments. The British largely accepted the decision and by March 1966 had withdrawn most of its forces. The Americans held out and their Wheelus Air Base remained the largest in the world outside the US.

After the crushing defeat suffered by the Arab armies in the June 1967 war against Israel, there was widespread unrest in Libya, especially in Tripoli and Benghazi. After attacks on Western embassies and Libya's Jewish population, Libyans soon turned their anger towards their own government, which was accused of failing to send assistance against Israel and being half-hearted in its commitment to the Arab cause. The government and monarchy were caught unawares by this paradigmatic shift in the political landscape and their inability to respond effectively saw their popularity spiral downwards. Their days were numbered.

September Coup

On 1 September 1969, an obscure group of military personnel seized power in Libya. Their planning was exemplary. They waited until all senior military figures were in the country and King Idris was in Turkey receiving medical treatment, thereby denying the government a figurehead around which to rally. They reportedly even postponed their coup by a day to avoid a clash with a concert by the popular Egyptian singer Umm Kolthum. There was little opposition to the coup and very few deaths. Among the Libyan population, there was considerable curiosity, as few people knew anything about the shadowy Revolutionary Command Council (RCC) which claimed responsibility. It was not until almost a week later that a young colonel by the name of Mu'ammar Gadaffi emerged as the country's charismatic leader.

Gadaffi's Libya

The revolutionary ripples of the coup soon began to transform almost every corner of Libyan society.

Riding on a wave of anti-imperialist anger, the new leader made his first priorities the closing of British and American military bases, the expansion of the Libyan armed forces, the exile or arrest of senior officers with connections to the monarchy and the closure of all newspapers, churches and political parties. In the mosques, Sanusi clerics were replaced by compliant religious scholars. Banks were nationalised and foreign oil companies were threatened with nationalisation. All assets in Libya belonging to Italians and nonresident Jews were expropriated and close to 30,000 Italian settlers were deported. The rounding-up of political opponents saw Libya gain the unenviable prize of having the highest prison population in the world per head of population.

On the plus side, the Revolutionary Command Council injected massive new funds into agriculture and long-overdue development programs, and there was an accompanying rise in the standard of living of ordinary Libyans. Ambitious social reforms were also implemented to redress the entrenched inequalities present under the monarchy (see The Role of Women under Society & Conduct later in the chapter).

In the mid-1970s, Colonel Gadaffi became the self-appointed visionary of the revolution when he retreated to the desert for a period of reflection and writing. What emerged was his Third Universal Theory, spelled out in *The Green Book* (see the boxed text 'The Cult of *The Green Book*' in the Facts for the Visitor chapter). While his much-touted alternative to capitalism and communism has always been characterised by confusing implementation in the economic sphere (for more details, see Economy later in this chapter), his political reforms endure. In 1976, the General People's Congress replaced an earlier parliamentary body (the Arab Socialist Union). It had the express aim of political participation by all Libyans rather than a representative system.

His dream of 'committees everywhere' soon became a reality. In yet another stamp of his vision on Libyan society, he renamed the country the Socialist People's Libyan Arab Jamahiriya (SPLAJ); *jamahiriya* has no direct translation but is generally taken to mean 'a state of the masses'. This was formalised on 2 March 1977.

The new government's secular reforms involved walking a fine line between its revolutionary program and placating conservative Islamic critics of the regime's liberalising streak. Gadaffi's unique style of leadership and revolutionary ideals have ensured that assassination and coup attempts have been regular features of the Libyan political landscape from the mid-1970s until the most recent reports of unrest in 1998. While some of this instability derives from disagreements within the revolutionary leadership over the direction of revolution, the greatest threat has increasingly come from militant Islamic groups.

Some of the less-savoury institutions of revolutionary Libya have been the Revolutionary Committees, which were at the height of their powers in the mid-1980s. Officially set up as conduits for raising political consciousness, they quickly evolved into the zealous guardians of the revolution and the enforcers of revolutionary orthodoxy. Their membership consisted increasingly of members of the Al-Qaddhafa tribe. They were the inspiration for the assassination squads set out to liquidate opposition Libyans living in exile. Assassinations were carried out in Athens, Bonn, London, Milan and Rome, among other cities of Europe.

The activities of these groups reached their nadir in 1984, when members of the revolutionary committees took over the Libyan People's Bureau in London. In April, with Libyan exiles protesting outside, a shot was fired from inside the embassy killing WPC Yvonne Fletcher. After a 10-day siege by the British authorities, the diplomats were allowed to return to Libya but the British government severed diplomatic relations with Tripoli. With the US having done likewise in 1981, Libya's status as a pariah state was confirmed.

Mu'ammar Gadaffi – The Man with Many Names

Mu'ammar Gadaffi is many things to many people. Leaving aside the fact that the transliteration of his name from Arabic into English can reportedly be done in over 600 different ways, the self-proclaimed 'Leader of the Masses' has been called just about every name under the sun. Ronald Reagan decided that the Libyan leader was a 'mad dog' while Yasser Arafat dubbed him the 'knight of the revolutionary phrases'. In more recent times, African diplomats have been known to call him the 'father of African unity' while Western media analysts prefer 'Libya's ageing *enfant terrible*'. To trendy young Libyans in Tripoli, their leader is known simply as 'the man', while many travellers visiting Libya are told to give their best regards to 'the Colonel'.

Everyone seems to have an opinion about Mr Gadaffi but very few know anything about the man himself. He was born in 1942 in the Libyan desert near Sirt. As with many things about him, the exact place of Gadaffi's birth is shrouded in mystery, although the homeland of the Al-Qaddhafa tribe is the area around Al-Jufra. Much political mileage has been made from the fact that he was born in a tent. His father, Mohammed Abdul Salam bin Hamed bin Mohammed (Abu Meniar), and his mother, Aisha, were poor Bedouins. By all accounts, the future leader of the revolution was a serious, pious child. He attended primary school in Sirt until the age of 14 and became the first member of his family to learn how to read and write. His childhood was a difficult one, with reports that he was ridiculed by his classmates because of his impoverished background and that he slept in a mosque during the school week, returning home on weekends.

Stung by these experiences and caught up in the Arab nationalist fervour of the day, Gadaffi was politically active from an early age. After attending secondary school for a time in Sebha, he was expelled because of his political activities. He completed his schooling in Misrata and his heroes were Omar al-Mukhtar and the Egyptian president Gamal Abdel Nasser. In 1961, he organised a demonstration against Syria for breaking the unity agreement with Egypt and proceeded to a military academy in Benghazi, from which he graduated in 1965. In 1966, he was sent to England for further training, including four months at Beaconsfield learning English, then with the Royal Armoured Corps at Bovington in Dorset. It was a difficult experience for the young Libyan and he became angry at the racial discrimination and prejudice he suffered.

When he seized power in 1969, at the age of just 27, few expected him to last the distance, a prediction he has proven wrong by outliving many of his critics. Indeed, it is for his survival – and his alternately eccentric and revolutionary behaviour – that Gadaffi will be most remembered. His capacity to recover from bitter defeats (domestic opposition, the war with Chad and the obsessive vilification by the West) and reinvent himself (eg, as the saviour of Africa) is central to his endurance. For all his transformations, he has remained steadfast on a number of fronts: his implacable opposition to Israel, support for revolutions against conservative regimes, his pursuit of unity with Arab and African neighbours, and his visceral hatred of imperialism.

In 1986, the US accused Libya of involvement in Palestinian attacks at Rome and Vienna's airports in December 1985 in which 20 people were killed; Gadaffi had labelled the attacks as heroic and the assailants were reportedly travelling on Libyan passports. In an act of considerable provocation and without the sanction of the UN, the US Sixth Fleet conducted military exercises off the Libyan coast with a number of skirmishes resulting. With typical restraint, then–US President Ronald Reagan labelled the Libyan leader as 'the most dangerous man in the world'. The spiral into conflict was inevitable.

On 5 April, a bomb went off in a Berlin nightclub frequented by US soldiers, killing two and injuring more than 200. Convinced of Libyan involvement, the US, using aircraft based in the UK and aircraft carriers in the Mediterranean, fired missiles into Tripoli and Benghazi on 15 April. The targets were officially the Aziziyah barracks (Gadaffi's

residence in Tripoli) and military installations, but residential areas were also hit.
Up to 100 people were killed in Tripoli and
around 30 in Benghazi. Two of Gadaffi's
sons were injured and his adopted daughter,
Hanna, was killed. A defiant Gadaffi renamed his country the Great SPLAJ.

Libya was also under siege on other
fronts, with a debilitating war with neighbouring Chad. A 1935 protocol between
France and Italy granted 111,370 sq km of
modern Chadian territory, including the
uranium-rich Aouzou Strip, to the Libyans,
although all other treaties granted the area
to Chad. Libya's support for armed opposi-

Looking for Someone to Love

You can't fault Colonel Gadaffi for his persistence. Since 1969 he has pursued unity between Libya and its neighbours, including
Egypt and Syria (1969 and 1971), Egypt
(1972), Tunisia (1974), Syria (1980), Chad
(1981), Morocco (1984), Algeria (1986) and
Sudan (1991). Most attempts foundered because the ideals of Arab brotherhood were no
match for the realities of incompatible governments; revolutionary and republican Libya
was never really likely to remain happily married to the conservative monarchy of Morocco. It also hasn't helped that Libyan troops
and money have been regularly dispatched to
support opposition movements or to promote
destabilisation. Indeed, frontier clashes with
Egypt in July 1977 came critically close to de-
scending into all-out war.

In light of this history of fraught relations, it
is somewhat remarkable that Libya remains at
peace with (and even good friends with) most
of its neighbours. The most cogent reason for
this is that most face domestic unrest from
militant Islamic groups and would have more
to fear from Gadaffi's removal than his (these
days) relatively benign eccentricities. Or perhaps they are simply grateful for his moments
of generosity. The most bizarre manifestation
of this came on 20 January 1989, when Libya
cancelled a World Cup soccer match (thereby
handing the result to Algeria) because the two
teams 'are in fact one team'.

tion movements inside Chad also didn't
help. The conflict saw the Libyan army
briefly occupy the Chadian capital, N'Dja-
ména, in 1980 before French intervention
drove it north again. It was not until 1987
that the Libyan army was finally driven
back across the border.

At the end of the 1980s, the Libyan government was under considerable pressure
and took steps towards greater openness by
releasing the majority of political prisoners.
But repression again intensified in the early
1990s, a decade which was to prove one of
Libya's, and Gadaffi's, most difficult.

Lockerbie In November 1991, the US and
UK governments accused two Libyans –
Abdel Basset Ali Ahmed al-Megrahi and
Ali Amin Khalifa Fhimah – of the 1988
bombing of Pan Am flight 103 over the
Scottish town of Lockerbie, which killed
270 people. Libya was also suspected of in-
volvement in the 1989 bombing of a French
UTA airliner over the Sahara in which 171
people were killed.

In January 1992, the UN Security Council ordered that the two men be extradited
and the International Court of Justice
rebuffed Libyan attempts to stop the move.
The US and UK rejected a Libyan offer to
hand over the suspects for trial in a neutral
country. UN sanctions came into effect on
15 April 1992, six years to the day after the
US air strikes on Tripoli and Benghazi.

As early as 1994 Gadaffi accepted The
Hague as an appropriate venue for any trial
and also Libya's 'general responsibility' for
the 1984 death in London of WPC Fletcher.
All of these overtures were rejected. At the
same time reports began to emerge of tensions between the Libyan leadership and the
Al-Megraha tribe, one of the most powerful
in Libya and which was holding out against
any deal (Abdel Basset Ali Ahmed al-
Megrahi belongs to the Al-Megraha tribe).
A key powerbroker and member of the original Revolutionary Command Council,
Major Abd as-Salam Jalloud, also of the
Al-Megraha tribe, reportedly clashed with
Gadaffi over the Lockerbie issue. To com-
plicate matters, Basset Ali Ahmed Ali is the

Lockerbie – Conspiracy or Justice?

The Lockerbie trial in The Hague raised more questions than answers. The Scottish judges acquitted Fhimah but found Al-Megrahi guilty, sentencing him to life imprisonment in a Scottish jail.

To Western governments, the verdict was justification for their isolation of Libya. From the Libyan perspective, the whole process was a show trial, part of an international conspiracy to apportion blame to a country and leader who had already been tried in the world's media. All eyes are on the outcome of Al-Megrahi's appeal. Regardless of the outcome, Libyans and others in the Arab world remain convinced that double standards apply.

Professor Robert Black, the Scottish legal expert who devised the unusual trial (unusual because it was the first time that a country handed its citizens over for trial, outside of UN tribunals, by a foreign court and because that court was set up outside Scottish territory) confessed to being 'absolutely astounded' at the outcome, which he claimed was based on a 'very weak, circumstantial case' which couldn't convict anyone, 'even a Libyan'. Even some of the grieving families of the victims expressed doubts over the verdict.

Syria was the original suspect. But when Syria supported the Allies in the Gulf War against Iraq, suspicion shifted to Libya. One of the most credible theories was that the bombing had been ordered by Iran in retaliation for the shooting down of an Iran Air airbus by a US warship in the Persian Gulf on 3 July 1988. The story goes that the bombing was carried out by members of the Palestinian Front for the Liberation of Palestine–General Command (PFLP–GC) who have sheltered in Syria since the bombing. Also yet to be refuted are the claims that the flight was being used to courier drugs for a US-backed international operation, meaning that security checks of the aircraft were waived. Immediately after the crash US investigators instantly secreted away an unidentified body which crash investigators were never allowed to see.

One sobering footnote on this matter appeared in February 2001, when Bassam and Saniya al-Ghussein, a Palestinian-Lebanese couple, went public with their attempts to bring the US government to court for the death of their 18-year-old daughter, Rafaat, who was killed by the US raid on Tripoli in 1986. The parents had a question for the international community: 'Just a simple admission...Or is it that the US government has a licence to kill?'.

For the full text of the Lockerbie verdict, go to Ⓦ www.ltb.org.uk.

son of one of Gadaffi's deputies. In October 1993, according to some accounts, there were small-scale army rebellions around Misrata and Tobruk in which sections of the army split along tribal lines.

In 1995, and again in 1998, assassination attempts were made on Gadaffi by militant Islamic groups based in Cyrenaica. The government's edginess was also brought to the fore on 9 July 1996 when the bodyguards of Gadaffi's son fired on a crowd reportedly chanting anti-government slogans at a football match in which he was playing; up to 50 people were killed.

In 1997, with international support for the embargo waning, cracks began to appear in the facade of international unity. South African President Nelson Mandela flew into Libya in defiance of the ban and a number of African leaders followed suit. In early 1999 a deal was brokered, with the international community accepting the procedural proposals that Libya had effectively been making since 1992. The suspects were then handed over and UN sanctions were immediately lifted, although unilateral US sanctions still remained in place at the time of writing.

European governments made a beeline for Tripoli, keen to re-establish diplomatic and economic ties. In March 2001, a French court finally shelved all attempts to pursue Colonel Gadaffi and Libya over the 1989 UTA bombing. By this stage, Libya was well on the road to rejoining the international community.

Libya Today There are two public preoccupations that dominate Libya today. One is the Lockerbie verdict, unfinished business that takes some of the gloss off Libyan efforts to rebuild the economy and international reputation. It's an issue that continues to trouble the national soul.

The other is Gadaffi's shift in attention from pan-Arab ideals to a messianic crusade to unify the disparate nations of Africa (see the boxed text 'Turning Towards Africa').

Another question simmers beneath the surface of Libyan society, one that Libyans are only willing to express unease over: What happens after Gadaffi? No-one knows the answer, and many of the surrounding states seem to believe that, for all his faults, the Libyan leader has provided stability and been a defence against the spread of Islamic fundamentalism. Fearful of the alternative, most are quite happy for the Libyan leader to stay in power for the foreseeable future.

Turning Towards Africa

Having spent a lifetime trying to forge unions with Arab countries who could never quite bring themselves to share his vision of a united pan-Arab nation, Colonel Gadaffi shifted his focus to Africa. In 1999, the Libyan leader hosted Conference of African Heads of State at a cost of some US$30 million. Officially the reason was to thank the African nations for their support during the embargo but, never one to miss an opportunity, Gadaffi unveiled his plans for a United States of Africa. In February 2001, 41 nations signed the Constitutive Act of African Union and 13 ratified it. The agreement replaces the troubled and politically fractured Organisation of African Unity (OAU) and paves the way for a future Africa-wide federation similar to the European Union. Possible outcomes include an African army, a single currency and parliament, and even a single African passport – although such ideas are a long way from being realised.

In July the gains were cemented and Colonel Gadaffi has been revelling in the accolades. It is the acclaim for which he has been searching for much of his life.

GEOGRAPHY

Libya is the fourth-largest country in Africa. With a total area of 1,759,540 sq km, Libya is twice the size of neighbouring Egypt and over half the size of the European Union. The country has one of the longest Mediterranean coastlines (1770km in length), yet this vast territory also cuts into the heart of Saharan Africa, with over 93% of Libya covered by desert. Libya is also part of the great North African Plateau, which stretches from the Atlantic to the Red Sea. Libya shares borders with six countries – Egypt to the east, Sudan to the south-east, Chad and Niger to the south and Algeria and Tunisia to the west.

There are no permanent rivers in Libya, only wadis (watercourses, or dry riverbeds), which catch the infrequent run-off from rainfall. Only 1% of the country's land can support agriculture and less than 1% contains any form of forest (in the Jebel Nafusa of Tripolitania and the Jebel Akhdar in Cyrenaica).

Tripolitania (approximately 285,000 sq km) in the north-west of the country contains the fertile Sahel al-Jefara (Jefara Plain) along Tripoli's narrow strip of Mediterranean coast. The plain rises to the formerly volcanic hills of the Jebel Nafusa with an average elevation of 600m to 900m.

The hills give way to a series of east-west depressions that lead into the Fezzan (approximately 570,000 sq km). Close to 20% of Libya is covered by sand dunes. The *idehan* or sand seas (vast areas of sand dunes) are interspersed with oases, lakes and wadis. The most dominant features of the Libyan Sahara include *hamada* (plateaus of rock scoured by wind erosion) and *sarir* (basins, formed by wadis, in which salt is deposited after evaporation). Southern Libya is also home to small mountain ranges such as the Jebel Acacus in the south-west and the larger massifs of the Tibesti along the border with Chad. In the Tibesti in the south-eastern corner of the country lies Libya's highest point – Tarsu Musa at 3376m – although most maps show it within Chadian territory.

In Cyrenaica (with an area of about 905,000 sq km), the low-lying terrain of the

Sahara is separated from Libya's north-east-ern coastline by the fertile Jebel Akhdar (Green Mountains), which drop steeply into the Mediterranean from a height of around 600m. In the far east, the terrain descends more gradually towards the Egyptian border.

CLIMATE

Due to the lack of natural barriers, the Sa-hara Desert and the Mediterranean Sea both affect the climate. Summer is generally very hot, with average temperatures on the coast of around 30°C and often accompanied by high humidity. In the south temperatures can reach a sweltering 50°C; temperatures of 57°C and 55°C have been recorded at Al-Aziziyah and Brak, respectively.

Around 2500 years ago, the historian Herodotus claimed that 'in the upper parts of Libya, it is always summer'. And, yet, in winter the weather can be cool and rainy on the coast between October and March, even snowing occasionally in the mountains. Most rain falls in the Jebel Nafusa and Jebel Akhdar. Desert temperatures can drop to subfreezing at night and, in a good year, Libya's desert regions receive less than 100mm of rain for the whole year.

During the spring in northern Libya, you may encounter the ghibli, a hot, dry, sand-laden wind which can raise the temperature in a matter of hours to between 40°C and 50°C. The ghibli can last from just a few hours to several days. In Cyrenaica there is less of a sandstorm quality to the ghibli, as the sand there is harder; here it simply becomes a hot, unpleasant wind.

ECOLOGY & ENVIRONMENT

With over 95% of Libyan territory covered by desert, water is not surprisingly the major environmental issue. Much of the Sahara is believed to have once been covered in for-est, scrub and savanna grasses and to have teemed with animal life. The last decent, regular rainfalls are thought to have oc-curred around 6000 BC, after which grass-lands began to give way to regular desert.

Since then, underground water reserves have been Libya's only reliable water sources. The oldest rocks in Libya, in the

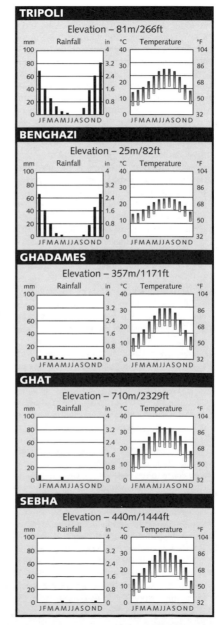

southern mountainous regions of Tibesti and the Jebel Acacus, are believed to be over 2800 million years old. During the Paleozoic period (around 600 million years ago), volcanic and earthquake activity set in train a process of erosion and rock formation. At the end of the Mesozoic era, shifting tectonic plates (which created the Red Sea, the Atlas Mountains of Morocco and the Alps of Europe) yielded the Jebel Nafusa and Jebel Akhdar in Libya. At the same time, the lands of the Sirt Basin in northern and central Libya subsided. As the land rose and fell, sedimentation occurred and massive underground basins with sandstone shelves came into existence. In the process, many of the aquifers (layers of rock which hold water and carry them in channels) and under-

The Great Man-Made River Project

An-Nahr Sinai, or the Great Man-Made River (GMR), is one of the most ambitious development projects attempted anywhere in the world and is certainly the most expensive. Put simply, the underground water of the Sahara is to be piped from hundreds of desert wells to Libya's thirsty coastal cities. Opponents of Colonel Gadaffi's brainchild see the project as little more than an attempt to upstage the Israelis or to mimic the Aswan Dam in Egypt, which will forever be associated with the vision of Gamal Abdel Nasser. According to Gadaffi, the GMR is 'the eighth wonder of the world'.

Whomever you believe, this complex project is breathtaking, both in its conception and the scale of its ambition. Traditionally, a major problem with water resources in Libya has been the high level of evaporation from marshy, low-lying coastal saltpans (sabkhas) where underground water is very close to the surface. Tapping the underground wells far below the earth's surface (as deep as 2km) farther inland in southern Libya enables the extraction of water before it evaporates.

The project, which consists of five stages, will not be completed in a hurry. Stage one is finished and connects two wells in the Tazerbo and Sarir Basins (with a storage capacity of 10,000 cu kilometres) with the coastal area from Benghazi to Sirt, transporting two million cu metres of water per day. Stage two will provide the Sahel al-Jefara of Tripolitania and Tripoli with 2.5 million cu metres a day from the Murzuq Basin (over 450,000 sq km in size, with a storage capacity of 4800 cu kilometres). Stage three brings the massive Al-Kufra Basin (capacity of 20,000 cu kilometres) into play as the source for 1.6 million cu metres of water per day added to the areas watered by stage one. Stages four and five envisage no further water extraction but rather an extension of the pipelines east, as far as Tobruk, and west to join up with those of Tripolitania in a massive national water grid. By the end, there will be over 4000km of prestressed concrete pipes crisscrossing the country, many up to 4m in diameter and buried in trenches nearly 7m below the ground, and with a daily capacity of six million cu metres. Tripoli received its first supplies of GMR water in September 1996 amid much fanfare.

Away from the hype, the project has attracted serious criticism, including the fear that a process of water storage which has taken thousands of years to form could be dried up in fifty. Already there is evidence to suggest that the GMR has begun to lower the ground-water table in north-western Libya with potentially disastrous consequences for agriculture. Others point to the fact that the amount of money spent on the first stage of the project alone could have been used to fund five desalinisation plants. Neighbouring Sudan and Egypt have weighed in, concerned over the threat to their own underground water supplies. Overpumping has also resulted in saltwater seepage into freshwater supplies along the coast.

If the GMR succeeds, it will be hailed as one of the most visionary feats of modern engineering. If it fails, the GMR promises to leave Libya without any fresh water supply at about the same time as its other underground resource, oil, runs out – a prospect which doesn't bear thinking about. However, it wouldn't be the first time it has happened (see The Garamantian Empire of the Fezzan in the History section earlier in this chapter).

ground basins on which Libya has come to rely so heavily were formed. This process continued during the Ice Age of northern Europe, when the North African climate became more temperate and higher rainfalls were absorbed into the ground, thereby filling the underground basins with fresh water.

These reservoirs of fresh, underground water were stored for millennia, preserved in porous rocks between impermeable layers. Recent radiocarbon dating suggests that the water currently stored beneath the Saharan sands has been there for between 14,000 and 38,000 years, with smaller deposits from 7000 years ago. Both of these periods are known to have been eras of increased rainfall.

Compounding concerns over the depletion of Libya's resources and the damage caused to the environment is the fact that Libya depends completely on fossil fuels for its power needs. Some new tourist developments are being designed with solar power as their energy source, but this doesn't go far in terms of addressing the whole nation's energy imbalance.

For more information about environmental issues in Libya, contact the Society for Friends of the Environment and Heritage (☎ 04-72245; postal address: PO Box 66758, Nalut), although it's geared more to recreational activities than providing serious information on the environment.

FLORA & FAUNA

Along the coast of Libya, the usual array of Mediterranean flora thrives, with large areas given over to the cultivation of olives and citrus fruit. You may also come across the occasional eucalyptus, bougainvillea and oleander. Inland, the only vegetation is largely confined to the oases, where the date palm reigns supreme, along with figs, tamarisk and oleander trees. Outside the oases, *Acacia arabica* (acacia) provides the only shade in the middle of the desert wilderness. Alfalfa grass and salt bushes often appear as if by miracle after rains.

The prehistoric rock-paintings of the southern Sahara suggest that leopards, elephants and wolves once roamed the region. Even 2500 years ago elephants, lions, horned asses and bears were reported in Cyrenaica. Not surprisingly, none remain and Libya has few surviving species of mammal.

In the desert regions, the camel is the most common animal that visitors will come across, but there are still a few herds of gazelle in remote areas, and the nocturnal fennec (a small fox with large ears) can be glimpsed if you're lucky. Lizards, snakes (the striped sand snake and the Saharan sand snake) and scorpions are also quite common. You might also come across gazelle on the plains or waddies of the Sahara, while the waddan – a large goat-like deer – can sometimes be seen hiding on the rocky ledges of the Jebel Acacus.

Libya is on the migratory route of many species of bird, although most sightings are restricted to the coast. Birds that you may come across include the Lanner falcon, desert sparrow, Egyptian vultures (in Cyrenaica), shrikes, larks, crows, turtle doves and bulbul. Farther south, you may come across the occasional migratory species blown into the desert.

GOVERNMENT & POLITICS

The government of Libya comprises the unique system of people's committees introduced by Colonel Gadaffi in *The Green Book*. The system swept away all previous administrative structures and replaced them with a pyramidal committee system. The lowest of these are the basic people's committees or congresses, to which every citizen over the age of 16 belongs under the principle, as expounded in *The Green Book*, that 'true democracy exists only through the participation of the people, not through the activity of their representatives'. They act as sounding boards and organs of power for local issues and decisions.

At last count, Libya had 25 administrative districts. Once or twice a year the General People's Congress (set up in 1976) meets, usually in September; this congress is the equivalent of a national parliament. There are approximately 1000 members, including chairpersons of the basic people's committees, and university-student and trade-union representatives. The affairs of state are carried out by general people's committees (equating to a cabinet or council of ministers). The system outlaws political parties or activity outside the committees. Revolutionary committees operate outside (or parallel to) the elected committees.

Voting for representatives is not carried out by secret ballot and, as a result, people tend to vote according to their tribal allegiances, giving rise to some disgruntlement by the weaker factions.

Interestingly, under this system there is no formal head of state, though Gadaffi has adopted the title of Leader of the Revolution. He has held this powerful position for nearly 30 years and little is done without his approval, compounding the issue of bureaucratic delays and working against efficient decision making. The formal head of state is, at least in theory, the speaker of the General People's Congress and the post of prime minister is usually held by the secretary of the General People's Committee.

ECONOMY

At the conclusion of WWII, Libya's people were among the poorest in the world. Apart from income derived from the military bases of the USA and UK, Libya's primary source of income was from scrap metal converted from the considerable stockpile of war debris scattered around the country. As a result of the discovery of oil, they now boast the highest per-capita incomes anywhere in Africa.

Despite this astonishing movement from poverty to relative riches in the course of two decades, Libya's economic growth has never fulfilled its considerable potential. The Libyan government has maintained a high level of control over the economy. All forms of private sector activity were discouraged from the outset and most businesses were either state-run and strictly regulated or caught up in often incomprehensible bureaucratic procedures. And yet, at times seemingly upon a whim, the private sector has found itself encouraged to expand its private activities. Gadaffi's Third Universal Theory has become increasingly difficult for Libyan businesses to decipher. For

Libya's Shifting Capital

It seems that just about every major city in Libya has been, at one time or another, the capital of Libya. As part of its belief in a united Libya, the Libyan government has awarded the title of national capital to Al-Bayda, Derna, Sirt (see the boxed text 'Winning Hearts & Minds' in the Tripoli chapter), Benghazi, Tripoli and, most ambitiously in January 1987, Al-Jufra. In 1993 the Libyan authorities struck fear into the heart of foreign diplomats with the announcement that all embassies would be moved from Tripoli to the bleak oil town of Ras Lanuf. For the moment, the embassies remain in Tripoli, which has the strongest claim to be the national capital, closely followed by Sirt.

example, in March 1981 all private retail licences were officially suspended, although this was never fully implemented. By the end of the same decade Gadaffi was publicly proclaiming the benefits of a rapid expansion in private enterprise.

While some of these changes made people hesitant about private investment and the full realisation of Libya's economic potential, there was another, more coherent rationale behind the changes. Under the monarchy, the new-found oil wealth was concentrated in the hands of traditional elites. It was one of the fundamental precepts of the leaders of the revolution that the unequal distribution of wealth be redressed in their pursuit of an egalitarian society with few class differences. In 1978 ownership of property was limited to one house or apartment per nuclear family. Like most economic pronouncements, this law was later reversed although its existence did help to draw attention to the prevailing disparities of wealth.

Another reason why Libya's economy stalled was the squandering of resources in pursuit of its largely unsuccessful foreign-policy goals. The stalemate in Chad for over a decade as well as failed merger projects with Arab and African countries all drained resources.

The news for the Libyan economy is not all bad. Despite the strictures imposed by sanctions, a study by the UN Development Program in 2000 listed Libya in the top third of countries in the world on its Human Development Index – a study based on economic and social data. Libya ranked easily the highest in Africa and above Saudi Arabia, Turkey and Russia. Per capita income stands at a respectable US$7900, Libya's budget has returned to surplus and Libyan oil exports continue to flourish as world oil prices rise ever higher.

Sanctions didn't prevent Libya from maintaining healthy trade relations with Western European countries – Italy, Spain and Germany accounted for almost 75% of Libya's exports while the UK, one of the primary sponsors of the sanctions resolutions, was quite happy to provide nearly 10% of Libya's imports. In 1999 the Italian ENI Energy Corporation concluded two years of negotiations by announcing an investment of US$5 billion in Libya's oil and natural-gas sectors, including an ambitious plan to pump natural gas under the Mediterranean to Italy via a 600km-long pipeline. A new five-year plan was announced in 2001 – it emphasises private-sector activity and attempts to diversify the economy.

In spite of the promising news, unemployment has remained a serious problem, hovering at around 30% (considered a conservative estimate) and inflation, while not rampant, stood at a worrying 18% at the end of the 1990s.

Oil

When oil was discovered in 1959, most multinational oil companies won contracts which enabled them to exploit Libya's natural resources on exceedingly favourable terms. That changed in September 1969, when Gadaffi and his fellow revolutionaries sought to redress this fundamental imbalance. While governments in the Persian Gulf sought 25% interests in the oil companies' activities, Libya boldly demanded at least 50% stakes as part of its program of nationalisation. By threatening to shut down oil production in Libya if he didn't get his

way, Gadaffi won the battle; by 1982 the Libyan government held majority interests in all of the major oil companies operating in Libya. The economic good sense of this move, quite apart from the imperatives of sovereignty over Libya's own resources, soon paid dividends. As a result of the OPEC oil crisis in the 1970s, Libya's annual oil revenues shot from US$2.2 billion in 1973 to US$8.8 billion in 1978; they again enjoyed a windfall in the aftermath of the Gulf War. Gadaffi has repeatedly taken the lead in calling for an equal sacrifice between oil-producing and oil-consuming countries.

Libya's oil is highly sought-after. The Libyan blends – Amna, Brega, as-Sidr, Sarir, Sirtica and Zuetina – attract high premiums on world markets as they are high-quality, light crudes, relatively free of sulphur and therefore well suited to refining.

Libya's reserves are the eleventh largest in the world and the largest in Africa, a continent for whom Libya reserves 4% of output. Proven reserves amount to a healthy 30 billion barrels and in mid-2000 the ratio of output to known reserves stood at 56 years. These reserves included a discovery in 1998 in the Murzuq Basin of the Fezzan, which may prove to be the largest discovery in the country since the early 1980s. Oil regularly, and problematically, accounts for over 95% of Libya's export income.

Agriculture

The economic dominance of oil over the Libyan economy is hardly surprising given that only 1% of Libyan territory can support agriculture. Ongoing efforts to diversify the economy away from its reliance on oil have prompted successive Libyan governments alike to dedicate huge resources to developing the agricultural sector. Despite as much as one-fifth of the labour force being involved in agricultural production, Libya still has to import more than three-quarters of its total food requirements. The great aim of the Great Man-Made River was to enable the setting up of 37,000 model farms and increase wheat cultivation in the north by an extra 180,000 ha. The massive investment has so far failed to increase agricultural production to anywhere near these levels – a source of significant concern for a country whose oil resources will not last forever.

Most agricultural activity is concentrated on Sahel al-Jefara in Tripolitania and in the Jebel Akhdar in Cyrenaica. Major crops include barley, wheat, olives and oranges. Smaller holdings of almonds, peanuts, groundnuts, tomatoes and potatoes also exist, while the fertile oases of the Sahara are known for their dates and smaller crops of wheat and millet.

Sanctions

On 15 April 1992 UN sanctions against Libya came into effect. The sanctions, while not as strict as those imposed on Iraq, prohibited all international flights to Libya, stopped arms and aircraft sales (including spare parts) and froze all Libyan assets (except those necessary for oil transactions).

Initially the sanctions appeared to impact more heavily upon oil companies doing business in Libya than the Libyan economy itself. As the 1990s wore on, however, the sanctions started to bite. Although major development projects like the Great Man-Made River were relatively unaffected, smaller projects slowed, including the construction of desalination plants. The government was also forced to cut agricultural subsidies, thereby stalling its efforts to boost the agricultural sector. A critical shortage of spare parts became a major problem, imposing serious limitations upon Libya's industrial infrastructure. Income from tourists also plummeted and Libya's rapidly growing economy was becalmed, growing at less than an average of 0.8% annually between 1992 and 1999. Negative growth of 7% was recorded in both 1993 and 1994, and there were massive lay-offs of workers as a result. To make matters worse for ordinary Libyans, prices rose to unprecedented levels.

The Libyan government has estimated that, prior to the suspension of sanctions in 2000, the UN restrictions had cost Libya over US$30 billion in lost revenues and production capacities. It also attributed the deaths of 21,000 Libyans to the air embargo, claiming that critically ill Libyans

had been unable to leave for urgent medical attention.

POPULATION & PEOPLE

In mid-2000 Libya's population was estimated to stand at 5,115,450, but official figures are notoriously unreliable; this number is thought not to include large numbers of expatriate workers. The real figure may be closer to six million. Libya's population density is one of the lowest in the world, its vast territory inhabited by less than three people per square kilometre. When you consider that over 70% of the population live in urban centres (some put the figure closer to 90%), chances are that you'll see very few people when you venture off the beaten track. This highly urbanised figure is a marked contrast to Libya's pre-oil days, when less than 25% lived in cities.

One potential problem facing Libya is its rapidly expanding (and hence increasingly youthful) population. The estimated rate of population growth as at 2000 was 2.4% per annum. While this may not sound like much, an annual growth rate of 3% will double the population every twenty years. Almost half the population is under 15 years of age and only 3% recorded in 1999 as being over 64. Among the significant implications of this situation is the imperative that the Libyan economy generate growth levels capable of creating employment for an increasingly large and educated workforce. The overwhelming majority of Libyans have never known a life other than under the revolutionary government, with the result that the old catchcries of the early 1970s are no longer a sufficient antidote to political disaffection.

Given the fact that Libya has been in the path of conquering armies and mass migrations over the centuries, Libya's demographic mix is remarkably homogenous. Although detailed census figures are hard to come by, it is believed that 97% of the population are of Arab or Berber origin. Some figures list the Berber community at 5% of the total population. Many within this number claim mixed Arab and Berber ancestry due to intermarrying between the two communities. Many Arabs are migrant workers from Tunisia and Egypt.

In the 11th century, with the large-scale migration of the Bani Hilal and Bani Salim (see History earlier in this chapter), the country became linguistically and, to a lesser extent, culturally 'Arabised'. For this reason, the inhabitants of Cyrenaica have a reputation for being the most purely Arab society outside the Arabian Peninsula.

Berbers

Many Berbers claim to be the descendants of Libya's original inhabitants. Some historians claim that the Berbers are descended from the remnants of the great Garamantian empire, which flourished in the Fezzan from around 900 BC–AD 500 (see History earlier in this chapter). Otherwise, little is known about their origins.

The name 'Berber' has been attributed to a collection of communities by outsiders, although, rarely until recently, by the Berbers themselves. The name is thought to derive from the Latin word *barbari*, the word used in Roman times to classify non-Latin speakers along the North African coast. The related name of Barbary was used to describe the region.

These days, the key touchstones of Berber identity are language and culture. 'Berber' is used as a loose term for native speakers of the various Berber dialects. In fact, many Berbers do not even use a word that unites them as a community, preferring instead to define themselves according to their tribe. These days, apart from some centres in Cyrenaica (especially Awjila, south of Ajdabiya), most Berbers are bilingual, speaking their native language and Arabic.

Within the Berber community, loyalty is primarily to the family or tribe. Households are organised into nuclear family groups, while dwellings within a village or town are usually clustered in groups of related families. The majority are located in Tripolitania (primarily in the Jebel Nafusa, the Sahel al-Jefara and a few enclaves along the coast).

In keeping with their centuries-long resistance to foreign domination and to the imposition of religious orthodoxy, the majority of Berbers belong to the Kharijite sect (see Religion later in this chapter). Because of the small size of their community, young Libyan Berbers sometimes visit Tunisia or Algeria in search of a Khariji bride. True to their religious beliefs, Berber communities have long prided themselves on their egalitarianism. The traditional Berber economy consists of farming and pastoralism, meaning that most people live sedentary lifestyles, while a small minority follow seminomadic patterns, taking flocks to seasonal pasturelands.

It is also worth noting that Berber leaders played a significant role in the battle for Libyan independence.

Tuareg

The Tuareg (singular Targui) are the indigenous people of the Sahara, the bearers of a proud desert culture whose members stretch across international boundaries into Algeria, Niger, Mali and Mauritania. In Libya, this once-nomadic people are concentrated in the south-western desert, particularly the oases around Ghadames, Ghat and Murzuq.

Their origins are not fully understood, but they are thought to be the descendants of the Lemta people of northern Libya, although until the 11th century historical records made little differentiation between the Tuareg and Moors. The similarities between the Berber and Tuareg languages also point to a strong historical link. Either way, the ancestors of the modern Tuareg made a fiercely independent living by raiding sedentary settlements, participating in long-distance trade and exacting protection money from traders passing across their lands. The majority of Tuareg in Libya (said to number no more than 17,000) have close relationships with their fellow Tuareg across the border in Algeria and Niger.

Like 'Berber', the name 'Tuareg' is a designation given to the community by outsiders and it is only recently that the Tuareg have called themselves by this name. The name is thought to be an adaptation of the Arabic word *tawarek*, which means 'abandoned by God' – a reference to their reputation for free-wheeling independence, their inhospitable surrounds and the widely held suspicion among urban communities of their nomadic lifestyle. The Tuareg themselves have always defined themselves as 'Kel Tamashek' (literally 'speakers of the Tamashek language'). Another name which the Tuareg sometimes call themselves is 'Imashaghen' – the 'noble and the free'.

The Tuareg adhere to a form of Sunni Islam, although many have incorporated non-Orthodox elements traceable to ancient folk religions. In recognition of the harsh dictates of a desert environment and nomadic lifestyle, some Tuareg do not observe Ramadan. Unusually, it is the men, not women, who wear veils. The famed indigo cloth, which stains the skin, has earned the Tuareg the romantic epithet of the 'blue people of the Sahara'. Tuareg women enjoy a high status within the community. Inheritance is through the female line and, historically, only the women were able to read and write. Marriage is also monogamous.

Toubou

The south-east of Libya is home to another nomadic community – the Toubou, a Muslim people who were strongly influenced by the Sanusi Movement during the 19th century. Numbering as few as 2600 in Libya,

this community has links with a larger population across the border in Chad. Their basic social unit is the nuclear family, with each community divided into patrilineal clans. Although they display considerable cultural and linguistic similarities, many Toubou speak related but mutually incomprehensible dialects of Tebu, which fosters a high level of independence for each community.

Hugh Clapperton described the Toubou as 'few in number but extraordinarily diffuse, lacking political or social coherence – the principle of freedom raised almost to the level of anarchy'. If the Toubous have a definable home, it is the Tibesti Mountains, which Clapperton again described as 'less a homeland than a centre of attraction'. They are viewed by other Libyans as a tough and solitary people. Their economy is a blend of pastoralism, farming and date cultivation.

Black Africans

Libya is home to a large number of migrant workers, with the largest source countries being Mali, Sudan and Niger. Travellers throughout West Africa will be familiar with the sight of huge lorries lumbering northwards towards Morocco or Libya, drawn by per-capita incomes the envy of sub-Saharan

The Testing Ground of African Unity

When Colonel Gadaffi turned his attention away from pursuing a Greater Arab Homeland to seeking a United Africa, there was great acclaim across the continent. Inside Libya itself, there was a certain unease. The lifting of visa requirements for many African nationals saw an already large population of sub-Saharan African immigrants flocking to Libya, primarily from Cameroon, Chad, Ghana, Guinea, Mali, Niger, Nigeria and Sudan. Libya's small population has always benefited from, and indeed required, additional workers, especially in its oil industry and to perform menial jobs. Gadaffi's exhortation for Libyans to marry black Africans was met by the population with a certain degree of bemusement rather than any great rush to the altar.

And, yet, most visitors who travel in Libya will encounter grumbling about the open-door policy. Mostly, it is little more than that, but an incident in 2000 indicated that the experiment is not without its problems. Clashes broke out between rival gangs in Az-Zawiya, just west of Tripoli, where the official death toll was six but independent reports put the figure closer to 100. Gadaffi labelled the protagonists (from within both the Libyan and immigrant communities) as opponents of African unity and, within months of his very public conversion to the African cause, he was forced to carry out a mass repatriation of African workers. In January 2001 the trial of some 331 suspects (including some Libyans) was postponed, this time to avoid difficult questions at a Conference of African Heads of State in Sirt designed to cement moves towards unity. The irony was not lost on some Libyans.

Africa, before finally crossing Libya's remote desert borders with Niger and Algeria. With economic growth intermittent at best throughout the 1990s and unemployment growing, resentment has grown towards the migrant workers. This tension erupted into violence in November 2000.

Although the greatest concentrations of migrant workers are in Tripoli and surrounding areas, where they are employed as menial workers, many also work as farmers and sharecroppers in the Fezzan.

Another less prominent group among Black Africans is the *harathin* (ploughers and cultivators). This small but distinct group has lived in the oases of the Sahara for centuries. The people's origins are obscure, but it is generally thought that their ancestors were servants of Tuareg nobles. Their status has traditionally been low.

Europeans

By far the largest European group in Libya is the Italians. In the 1960s, they numbered around 30,000, although the confiscation of land in the zealous early days of the 1969 revolution saw their population dwindle. A surprising amount have remained, with the majority concentrated in Tripoli, Benghazi and on the farms of the coastal hinterland. In addition to the Italians, there are small populations of Greeks and Maltese.

In 1986, there were approximately 40,000 Europeans in Libya, mostly expatriate workers involved in the oil industry. Their numbers fell after the attack on Libya by US planes in April 1986 and again as sanctions curtailed much business activity, but large numbers of workers are again taking up lucrative contracts in Libya.

EDUCATION

Libyan children attend six years of primary school (starting at age six), followed by six years of secondary school, which includes some instruction in English. The second three years of secondary school involves a choice between preparing for university or trade school. University education is free for all Libyan citizens and the Libyan government routinely pays for students to study at overseas institutions; this applies to both men and women, although lone women studying overseas is sometimes seen as less socially acceptable.

The first university in Libya was opened in Benghazi in 1958 and the largest university in the country is now Al-Fatah University in Tripoli, followed by Qar Yunis University in Benghazi. There are also universities in Al-Bayda, Az-Zawiya, Gharyan, Sebha and Zuara (plus Nasser University in Tripoli), although the line between a college and a university is not always clearly defined. Classes are coeducational in primary school and at university, and single-sex in secondary school.

Literacy levels are among the highest in the region with 1995 figures putting the overall rate at 76.2% of the population, including 63% of women and 87.9% of men. In 1971, soon after Gadaffi came to power, 72% of the population were illiterate.

Men who do not continue to university after secondary school must do two years' military service. Although this is rarely enforced, all men between 18 and 55 must complete one month's military service every year. Women must complete an initial four months' military service or work in an approved industry, for which they are paid 50LD per month.

ARTS
Architecture

Most of Libya's architecture has been shaped by the dictates of climate and geography. The ancient Berbers built structures that utilised the natural fortifications of the mountains they inhabited, while the peoples of the Sahara used building materials that protected them from the harsh desert climate. Libya also inherited a rich array of architectural gems left by the invading armies who occupied Libyan soil. The superb examples of Roman, Greek and Byzantine architecture are discussed at length throughout this book.

Berber The most stunning examples of indigenous Libyan architecture are the *qasrs* (literally castles, but more like fortified

Libya's Finest Architecture

Leptis Magna
The finest surviving monuments to Roman civilisation in North Africa (see Leptis Magna in the Tripolitania chapter for more details)

Cyrene
Superbly located Greek and Roman city in the foothills of the Jebel Akhdar (see Cyrene in the Cyrenaia chapter for more details)

Old City of Ghadames
Arguably the best-preserved caravan town in the entire Sahara Desert (see Ghadames in the Tripolitania chapter for more details)

Ghat Medina
An enchanting, crumbling and compact mud-brick medina deep in the heart of the central Sahara (see Ghat in the Fezzan & the Sahara chapter for more details)

Tripoli Medina
The Ottoman heart of Libya's cosmopolitan capital, with richly decorated mosques and whitewashed homes (see Medina in the Tripoli chapter for more details)

Qasr al-Haj, Nalut & Kabaw
Fairytale Berber troglodyte *qasrs* (fortified granaries) with cave-like doors (see Qasr al-Haj, Nalut and Kabaw in the Jebel Nafusa chapter for more details)

Mausoleum & Mosque of Sidi Abdusalam
Libya's most dazzling example of modern Islamic architecture (see Zliten in the Coastal Tripolitania chapter for more details)

granaries) of the Jebel Nafusa. The finest qasrs, most of which date from the 12th century AD, are at Qasr al-Haj, Kabaw and Nalut. They once operated as storage banks for local farmers, and were central to village life. While they were occasionally used as refuges for the villagers in times of external threat, their role in the protection of grain highlights the critical importance of agriculture for a community's survival. Local building materials such as rock and gypsum ensured that the storage areas, sealed with doors made of palm trunks, remained cool and kept insects at bay. Each storage pen belonged to a particular family or group of families and were carved like caves into the enclosed walls to dramatic effect. Grains like barley and wheat were kept in the rooms above the ground (they are still used for their original purpose in Qasr al-Haj), while olive oil was stored in underground chambers.

The other highlight of Berber architecture are the underground houses in Gharyan and the Jadu area. Built to protect against fierce summers, cold winters and invading armies, a circular pit up to three storeys deep and around 10m in diameter was dug into the earth. The rooms were cut into the base of the walls around the sunken courtyard and they were reached via a tunnel that ran from the upper level (ie, normal ground level) down through the earth to the base of the pit. The surprisingly spacious living quarters included living rooms, a kitchen, bedrooms and storage areas.

Saharan Architecture The mud-brick dwellings of the Fezzan were well suited to the harsh dictates of desert life. In Ghadames, the ancient building methods are still sufficiently intact for some of the inhabitants to move from their new air-conditioned houses into the old city during summer. Most of the medinas of the Sahara have been abandoned for modern housing and are rapidly deteriorating. The decaying mud-brick structures can be quite evocative of the ancient caravan towns; the medina at Ghat is arguably the finest example. The most common building materials are animal dung, sun-dried clay and mud brick that contains straw and a high concentration of salt. Reinforcements (and doors) were usually made from the wood of palm trunks.

In smaller settlements, many traditional flat-roofed Fezzani houses have been neglected to the point of dereliction as a result of the relocation of their residents. Part of the problem lies in the fact that many are roofed with palm beams and fronds, which in the absence of regular maintenance are liable to collapse on the rare occasions when it rains.

Hotel built in the Italianate style, Tripoli

The former cathedral, now a mosque, Tripoli

Mosque of Sidi Abdusalam, Zliten, one of Libya's most impressive modern Islamic buildings

Towering Berber *qasr* (fortified granary), Kabaw

Ancient ruins at Tolmeita, Jebel Akhdar

Palm-trunk door and rising sands, Ghat

Courtyard of a troglodyte Berber house, Gharyan

ALL PHOTOGRAPHS BY ANTHONY HAM

Ghat, an ancient Saharan oasis town with a mud-brick medieval medina still in good condition

Italian Architecture One of the few legacies of the era of Italian colonial occupation for which Libyans are grateful is the Italian Modernist architecture of the northern coast. With a decidedly Mediterranean feel, many of the elegant whitewashed facades around Tripoli's Green Square (especially east along the waterfront and the Galleria De Bono) and the Old Town Hall in Benghazi provide a most attractive complement to the Ottoman and modern Libyan architecture elsewhere in the cities. All along the coast, particularly between Tripoli and Misrata and around Gharyan, you will also come across abandoned Italian churches and farmhouses.

Islamic & Ottoman Architecture Most of Libya's mosques and madrassas date from the Ottoman era. They have typically narrow, pencil-thin minarets, sometimes octagonal in shape. The Ottoman mosques of the Tripoli medina, especially those of Ahmed Pasha Karamanli, Draghut and Gurgi, showcase Libya's finest collection of tile mosaics and woodcarvings. These mosques, built in the North African or Maghrebi style, often have superbly decorated small domes surrounding a larger dome above the prayer hall, which is often surrounded by closely packed pillars. There is also a strong Andalusian influence in many mosques evidenced by the use of elegant arches.

Modern Islamic architecture in Libya is not that much different from elsewhere in the Arab world with extensive use of marble, sandstone, lavish tile work and cavernous prayer halls rising several stories high. The finest examples include the Mausoleum & Mosque of Sidi Abdusalam in Zliten and the New Mosque in Ghadames.

The oldest surviving examples of Islamic architecture in Libya are generally to be found in the desert regions. The unusual sandstone tombs of the followers of the Prophet Mohammed in Awjila sport conical, pyramidal domes not found elsewhere. The vernacular-style mosques of the Fezzan usually do not have a courtyard, and above the prayer hall rises a squat, almost triangular minaret built in the Sudanic

Out with the Old

Soon after coming to power, Libya's revolutionary government decided that Libya was to be transformed into a modern nation. Entire communities from Saharan oases were moved wholesale into new accommodation, encouraged by free, modern housing with electricity, air-conditioning and integrated sewage systems. The most obvious examples are in Ghadames, Ghat, Murzuq and Gebraoun. Some of the aims of the program were laudable and few could resist the lure of modern amenities. Officially the moves were to be voluntary, but reports of discontent among the communities of the Ubari Lakes suggest that not all went freely. Many would argue that the benefits of such a move outweigh the loss of traditional ways of life and that a romantic attachment to vernacular architecture is something only outsiders can benefit from. Yet, the characterless, modern houses to which the inhabitants moved and the subsequent rapid deterioration of the old towns suggest that a rich desert heritage is being lost.

style, sometimes with protruding wooden struts. The best examples are in Murzuq and Ghat.

See under Medina in the Tripoli chapter for extensive descriptions of the Ottoman residential architecture of Tripoli's medina.

Modern Architecture Most modern constructions in Libya display a certain uniformity, which distinguishes it little from trends elsewhere in the Arab world. One stunning exception is the Burj al-Fateh tower complex in Tripoli, which extensively uses glass.

Dance

Libya is not known for its artistic heritage or world-famous performers, but it does have a diversity of traditional dance, all strongly influenced by Berber and Tuareg folklore. There are no organised dance troupes other than those which perform at private Libyan parties or weddings. You are most likely to come across these perfor-

mances at the festivals in Germa, Ghadames, Ghat, Kabaw and Zuara (see the relevant sections for details), but the most
enjoyable are when a traveller is invited to
a local wedding celebration. For more information about Tripolitanian weddings,
see Music.

In Ghadames, Funduq al-Waha regularly
stages local dances, which are strongly tied
to significant aspects of local life. These
include re-enactments of farming and harvesting, with up to eight dancers laying the
seeds and then harvesting them in a series
of evocative movements. The music is provided by a tight-knit circle of musicians
around a fire. Some play drums, warming
the skins of their instruments by the flames,
while someone plays a high-pitched flute.

If you do get invited to a wedding, dances
to watch out for include:

Az-Zlabin (Tripolitania) The groom circles a
group of men and when one of them gives him
money, the groom returns to the centre of the
circle and publicly lauds the giver. Accompaniment is on the *zukra* (see Music later in this
section).
Cuzca (Tripolitania) Dancers parade in circles of
two lines, with each dancer holding a small
piece of wood, which is tapped against those of
other dancers in time to the music.
Kishk (Cyrenaica) This involves rhythmical,
repetitive chants, which a group of men standing in a circle repeats after a designated leader.
A woman, adorned with henna and a brocaded
dress, dances around the circle in a series of increasingly small and mesmeric steps while the
men, also in traditional costume, vie for her attention with large, open handclaps. She then
chooses one to dance with her, a decision which
is always greeted by great acclaim.
Majruda (Cyrenaica) This is similar to the kishk,
but this time with very small, fast, alternating
handclaps.

In the oases of the south, the dances are either oasis or nomadic Tuareg in origin.
Although you may find it difficult to imagine now, European explorers were quite
taken by the Fezzani proclivity for dancing:

The women of Fezzan generally have a great
fondness for dancing and every amusement, and
the wanton manners and public freedoms which,
although Mahometans, they are permitted, aston-

ishes the Muslim traveller. They dance publicly
in the open places of the town, not only in the day
time, but even after sunset.
Frederick Hornemann
Journal of Frederick Hornemann's
Travels from Cairo to Mourzouk 1797–98

One Tuareg dance which you may see in
Ghat during its new year festival involves
seated women playing the *tende* (a drum
made of skin stretched over a mortar) and
singing ballads glorifying Tuareg figures,
while men circle around the women on their
finest camels.

Music
Traditional Music Traditional Libyan
music is often performed in conjunction
with the ritualistic dances mentioned earlier. Important musical instruments include
the clarinet-like *gheeta* (in the north-west,
especially Ghadames, and south), the *nay* (a
soft, emotion-laden flute) and the *zukra*,
which is similar to bagpipes, in the south
and west. In the east, the zukra is smaller
and without the attached bag.

One of the most famous music forms in
Libya is the *mriskaawi*, which came from
Murzuq and forms the basis for the lyrics of
many Libyan songs. It has since been mod-
ernised and is played on the accordion at a
party on the Wednesday night before a wedding, especially in Tripoli and the north-
west. During celebrations on the wedding
night (Thursday), music known as *malouf* is
played. With its origins in Andalucía, malouf
involves a large group of seated revellers
singing, reciting poetry of a religious nature
or about love; groups capable of performing
the malouf are highly sought-after. Another
form of traditional music is *'alaam*, which is
often performed by two people. The first
makes a short heartfelt statement to which
the other makes a similarly meaningful
reply, and so it continues.

Modern Music The Libyan pop-music industry is generally drowned out by the noise
of its Egyptian cousin across the border. You
are far more likely to hear Libyans listening
to music from elsewhere in the Maghreb
(Tunisia, Algeria or Morocco) or the late

Egyptian diva Umm Kolthum. In fact, so popular is the music of Umm Kolthum that some reports suggest that the coup in 1969 was delayed by a day so as not to interrupt an Umm Kolthum concert in Benghazi, which would have been a deeply unpopular move.

Libya's best known singer of long standing is Mohammed Hassan, a native of Al-Khoms who has become something of a Libyan institution. His music carries all the heartfelt passion of Arab music elsewhere, but it is the subject matter, rather than the style, which marks him out as distinctively Libyan. His better known songs include the love song 'Laysh butar musarakan' (literally, 'Don't stop your love'), 'Salaam aleik' (a cry of lament for a distant love) and 'Adi meshan' (a rousing song lauding Colonel Gadaffi). Another male singer of note is Mohammed Sanini. Libya's best-loved female singer is Salmin Zarou. Examples of their work are available in cassette stores in the larger Libyan towns or on the Web at W www.libyana.org or W www.libyaonline.com.

Literature

Libya has a strong literary tradition and one that has always been highly politicised. Sadly, very little has been translated from the Arabic, although many of the writers listed below are represented in *Libyan Stories* (see Books in the Facts for the Visitor chapter).

The first signs of a literary movement came in the early 20th century. During the Italian occupation, Libyan writers went underground and became the voice of a discontented people, with many doubling as resistance leaders. Among the best known was Suleiman al-Baruni, a resistance figure who published what is thought to have been the first book of Libyan poetry as well as a newspaper called *The Muslim Lion*. Other well-known poets born of the Libyan resistance include Al-Usta Omar (who was born in 1908 in Derna and was later a parliamentarian for Cyrene until he drowned in 1950), Ahmed Qunaba and Alfagi Hassan.

After WWII the focus of Libyan writers shifted to the country's independence, as many Libyans returned from abroad and took part in lively political debates about the country's future direction. Important works from this time include Ali Sidgi's *Dreams and Revolutions,* Ali Raque's *Thirsty Nostalgia,* Khalid Zaghbia's *The Great Wall* and Hassan Saleh's *After the War.* Of the classical Arabic poets, Ahmed ash-Sharif is the best known. In style, there was a shift away from rhyming poetry, but a weighty consideration of social issues and the political winds of the day remained at the heart of all Libyan writing.

In the 1960s, a theme of great political angst emerged as Libya underwent huge social change. Typical of the era are the short stories by Khalifa Takbali in a collection called *Rebellion*, with the title story about a Libyan worker who defies his American boss. Also symptomatic of this generation of writers was Yusuf ash-Sharif, who cast light on the unfair distribution of Libya's new-found oil wealth. Other important writers of the time included Bashir al-Hashemi, Ali Mustapha al-Misrati, Kamel al-Maghor and the playwright Abdullah al-Gwiri. This sense of political and national struggle culminated in the sense of bitterness after the 1967 Arab defeat at the hands of Israel.

The 1969 revolution brought about a sea change in Libyan writing. After literature had spent decades on the margins, the government-sponsored Union of Libyan Writers was founded by Ahmed Ibrahim al-Fagih and new publishing houses were established. A new relationship with the state transpired, moving writers from a position of rebellion to the chief advocates of the revolution. With government sanction, writers became seen as among the primary intellectuals of Libyan society, with Mohammed az-Zawi of particular significance.

Arguably Libya's best-known writer throughout the Arab world continues to be Ibrahim al-Kouni. Born in 1948 in the town of Ghadames, he studied in Moscow and was in charge of the Libyan People's Bureau in Warsaw. He now writes full-time and his fascination with the desert sees him living there for part of each year. He has published eight volumes of short stories, a number of novels, including Nazif al-Hajjar (Bleeding Rock; 1991) and Al-Majus (The Magians; 1991), as well as essays of literary criticism. Perhaps his most famous short story is the Drumming Sands, a tale of death in the desert near Ubari that is filled with a strong element of creeping menace.

A younger generation of Libyan writers has emerged in recent years. Of the novelists, Khalifa Hussein Mustapha has come to prominence, while poetry is increasingly the preserve of voices like Gillani Trebshan and Idris at-Tayeb. Libya's literary heritage is clearly dominated by men, but the voice of women is slowly coming to the fore in the short stories of Lutfiah Gabaydi and the poetry of Mariam Salame and Khadija Bsikri. Bsikri's published collections of poetry include *Woman for all Possibilities* and *I Put My Hand on My Heart*. One of her poems, *Ghat*, transforms the faces of past invaders of Libya into those of Amazonian Libyan women.

Painting

Libyan painters are little-known outside Libya. Some of the more famous painters working at the moment include Ali al-Abani (from Tarhuna), who specialises in landscapes; Ali Zwaik (from Az-Zawiya), whose paintings are more abstract; and Ramadan Abu Ras (from Sabratha), who moves between abstracts and landscapes. Other fine artists, whose work can be seen on the Internet, include Mohammed Zwawi (cartoons), Afaf al-Somali (a female painter specialising in watercolours), Taher al-Maghrabi, Ali Gana (oil paintings) and Bashir Hammoda (abstracts). There are two good Web sites with examples of paintings by Libyan artists: W www.libyana.org and W www.libyanet.com.

Cinema

Libya generates few locally produced films and film-makers' efforts are restricted by a lack of government funding or dwarfed by the blockbusters emanating from Egypt. Occasionally, documentary films are produced, but these rarely rise above their purpose of propaganda.

SOCIETY & CONDUCT
Traditional Culture

Before the arrival in Libya of large numbers of Europeans in the early years of the 20th century, Libyan social organisation was layered with concentric circles of loyalty and community solidarity. The primary units of allegiance and belonging were the extended family, clan or tribe. These family-based units were the centre of the most people's lives, including their social and economic activity, education and, in times of trouble, protection.

Within the Arab family, kinship and inheritance are determined patrilineally. The typical household consisted of a man and wife, their single sons, married sons (whose family also resided within the paternal home) and unmarried daughters. Upon the death of the father, each son was expected to establish his own household and it was simply expected that all children would marry by an appropriate age. Marriage was an important rite of passage to the extent that boys were only considered to have reached manhood upon the date of their marriage. In more traditional communities, the conferring of adult status did not arrive until the birth of their first child, preferably a son.

Tribes in Libya

Traditionally, the tribes of Libya operated both as communities of support and de facto mini-states. Each tribe's existence was inextricably tied to a homeland of farms, grazing land and wells over which the tribe exercised effective ownership. These strong ties to the land were the cause of intertribal disputes, with the identity of each tribe defined on the basis both of lineage and geography.

In Tripolitania and Cyrenaica, most tribes trace their origins to the Bani Hilal and Bani Salim. Tribes with this lineage are known as *saadi*, or dominant tribes. In Cyrenaica, where tribal loyalties remain the strongest, the two main saadi are the Jebana and the Harabi. Other tribes that fall outside this designation are known as Marabatin – most of these claim mixed Arab and Berber descent.

Reflecting the importance of the family in social life, marriage was seen within each clan as more important for the family than the individual. Taboos restricting any interaction between men and women of marriageable age meant that most marriages were unions arranged by the bride and groom's family. The family of the groom was responsible for bringing a dowry to the wedding, often up to the equivalent of US$10,000 for marriages between urbanised families of noble blood. Marriage to a member of a different tribe was most unusual, though not unheard of, and there was frequently a preference for unions between children of brothers. In this way, family became entrenched as centrepiece of community life over the generations.

Within Tuareg society, the small size of the community, matrilineal lines of kinship and the harsh exigencies of nomadic life all combined to ensure that young men and women were given a much greater freedom of choice and scope for courtship than their peers in Arab tribes farther north.

While family loyalties remained primary in urban centres, close bonds of solidarity grew up around various quarters of Tripoli and Benghazi in particular. These quarters organised their own social services and appointed leaders who were able to represent the quarter in its dealings with the city authorities. Lineage, wealth and religious piety were highly valued and the ability to wield influence on a wider stage and generate the patronage of other important leaders was seen as a measure of leadership skills.

The arrival of the Italians prompted some moves among the elites of Tripoli and Benghazi to mimic European-style dress and customs. Italian-style housing replaced traditional forms of architecture and many wealthy families moved away from the quarters around which their social existence had revolved. The older parts of town became neighbourhoods of the poor, thereby complicating the previously tight bonds of community loyalty by injecting class distinctions into the mix. That said, Italian culture never really penetrated Libyan social life to the extent of other European colonies in Africa.

By the time Libya gained its independence, the chiefs, or sheikhs, of the major tribes maintained control over the countryside while wealthy families or religious figures held sway in the cities. The monarchy – with its reliance upon traditional lines of authority, social inequities and patronage – was therefore a reflection of the society over which it ruled.

Modernisation

Within 20 years of independence, a number of profound changes had combined to radically shift the centre of Libyan society.

After the discovery of oil in 1959, an impoverished population suddenly became awash with money and an accompanying rise in expectations which the old structures of society struggled to contain or fulfil. Technocrats with a stake in the new boom industry began to challenge the influence of traditional leaders whose significance had derived from inherited privilege. Suddenly, opportunities began to open up for profitable careers in the nascent military for those born into poor families. The Libyan oil boom also spawned other changes that threatened the old order, including a population shift to the cities in a search for lucrative employment. In 1964 there were believed to be 364,000 tent-dwellers in Libya; by the mid-1970s, this had shrunk to 200,000, or less than 10% of the total population. These social transformations were rounded out with greater opportunities and resources for education, ensuring that young people increasingly married outside the tribe.

Throughout the same period, the youth of Libya were being politicised. The charismatic speeches of Egyptian president Gamal Abdel Nasser were being broadcast from Cairo across the Arab world on 'Voice of the Arabs' radio. His call to challenge the inaction of traditional Arab elites struck a chord within Libyan society, increasing pressure upon a monarchical order creaking under the weight of its own inability to adapt to the winds of change.

When the revolutionary government took power in September 1969, many of these changes became institutionalised. Pan-Arab nationalism became the ruling ideology, and, officially at least, tribal loyalties came under suspicion, being seen as obstacles to modernisation and the forging of national identity. Libya was divided into administrative zones which were deliberately drawn to cross traditional tribal boundaries. The values of the old order – lineage, piety and wealth – were replaced by a campaign to trumpet the values of education and social progress based on competence. In reality, it was not quite so clear-cut, with the new leaders often forced to perform a delicate balancing act to retain the loyalty of powerful tribal leaders who continued to enjoy widespread support. This was often done in the form of massive agricultural subsidies and the appointing of tribal notables to important bureaucratic positions.

Nonetheless, the official campaign enjoyed a measure of success and the backbone of the revolution came from a new class of youthful revolutionaries. Many were promoted in spite of their humble social origins and some came from smaller tribes. Despite deeply rooted traditional loyalties, an overarching modern Libyan identity has been forged.

Changes also occurred in the social relationship between men and women, although traditional elements remain. Men generally marry later than women (often not until they are 30 years old) and arranged marriages still frequently take place between the children of male cousins. Some courting couples are allowed to go out alone, depending on the attitude of the respective families. Most couples go out for two years, followed by up to two years' engagement before the actual marriage. Weddings usually take place in summer because guest lists often run into the hundreds (and last for days) and outdoor areas are often the only spaces capable of accommodating the crowds.

The Role of Women

One of the more radical social changes introduced after the coup was in the role of women in society. In spite of the reforms of the 1960s, which gave women the vote, the role of women remained restricted to the private domain in what was still a deeply patriarchal society. As in many traditional societies, the honour of the family or tribe was vested in women – any perceived public dishonour, whether real or imagined, was avenged, with women having to pay the price for restoring honour.

Three months after coming to power, the revolutionary government granted women equal status with men under the law. In practice, one of the most significant reforms was in the laws governing marriage. The minimum age for marriage was set at 16 for women and 18 for men. Marriage by proxy was outlawed. In 1972 a law was passed decreeing that a woman could not be married against her will. Were a father to prohibit the wedding of a woman under 21 to a man of her choice, she had the right to petition the court for official permission. Divorce rights for women were also strengthened and women have since been granted the right to own and dispose of property independently of any male relatives. The principle of equal pay for equal work and qualifications has also been sanctioned under the law.

In addition to the legal changes, government policies since the early 1970s have encouraged women to seek employment or membership in what were long considered bastions of exclusively male activity. In the early 1980s, Gadaffi founded what became known as the 'Nuns of the Revolution', a

Gadaffi's Female Bodyguards

One of the most enduring images of Colonel Gadaffi's rule has been his phalanx of formidable female bodyguards dressed, not surprisingly, all in green. Western reporters, keen for any opportunity to trivialise the eccentricities of Libya under Gadaffi, referred to them as the 'Amazon Women'. Whether or not they were intended for show, they represented a bold step for the Libyan leader, placing his personal security in the hands of women in a region where a combination of machismo and Islamic conservatism would normally preclude such a step.

special police force attached to revolutionary committees and whose membership was drawn from female conscripts who attended military academies.

Other fields of employment were also opened up to women and an increasing number of girls attended secondary schools. Social safety nets, such as free medical care and education, were provided by the state in the form of free medical care and education. Consequently, traditional family arrangements became less common, with many young couples choosing to live in smaller nuclear family groups.

In spite of these changes, restrictions upon women remained, with the government often unwilling to jeopardise the support of powerful traditional constituencies by granted women more rights. Polygamy, although practised by only a small proportion of men, has remained legal, though a man is not permitted to marry a second spouse without the permission of the first. The patrilineal hierarchy of society is also entrenched in the law that grants Libyan citizenship to a child born abroad to a Libyan father, but not to the child of a Libyan mother.

By 1987 only one woman had been promoted to the position of cabinet minister and by the end of the 1980s women still accounted for only 7% of the national workforce. Women's groups, though encouraged, were seen as secondary submovements of the national cause. The Jamahiriya Women's Federation (founded in 1977) draws all women's groups under the national banner.

Perhaps contrary to most people's expectations, social segregation remains strongest in some of the cities. Both Bedouin and Tuareg women have long enjoyed greater rights and roles in public society than their Arab counterparts.

Dos & Don'ts

If you hear a Libyan saying 'kull bilaad wa azaaha' (every country has its own customs) chances are that they're not celebrating the world's diversity, but very politely suggesting that you're in danger of offending local sensibilities. The most obvious things to remember are never to receive or pass items

(especially food) with your left hand (although the taboos are less strict in Libya than other Arab countries) and make sure you dress appropriately for the situation (see Women Travellers in the Facts for the Visitor chapter). Be careful when swimming, as skimpy bathing costumes offend. Always try to find a secluded spot away from families, as more liberal Libyans themselves do. This is not Saudi Arabia, but nor is it Tunisia.

Other things to remember – but it's less a taboo and more a gesture which will be appreciated – is to take a small gift for the host if you're invited to someone's home. Where possible, don't refuse offers of food or drink. Bargaining or haggling is also not the done thing in most places and trying to do so with *any* aggression will earn you few friends.

As free as Libya can appear at times, always be wary about entering into political discussions. Only instigate political conversations with Libyan friends once you have got to know them and never raise such issues when other people are around; to do so would cause them considerable discomfort and, in the wrong company, potential danger.

Treatment of Animals

You're unlikely to come across many animals in Libya. Most of Libya's wildlife (see Flora & Fauna earlier in this chapter) has been wiped out by a changing climate and population growth. With the damage already done, it is little surprise to find that the Libyan government has not made animal welfare one of its priorities. One disturbing area is the eastern end of Sharia ar-Rashid in Tripoli, where cats, macaws and even gazelles are offered for sale. Some roadside truckstops along the country's highways have wild animals, such as gazelles and even monkeys, tethered in cramped conditions for the entertainment of passing motorists. Then again, you're unlikely to encounter the instances of cruelty to domestic livestock (other than the fact, of course, that many are eaten!) that you might see in neighbouring Egypt. In the Sahara, camels are well treated and revered as essential to human survival. Very few Libyans keep domestic pets.

RELIGION

More than 95% of Libya's population are Sunni Muslims. The country has small communities of Kharijites and Christians (Roman Catholics, Coptic Orthodox and Anglicans), who number around 50,000.

Islam

Islam shares its roots with the great monotheistic faiths that sprang from the unforgiving and harsh soil of the Middle East – Judaism and Christianity – but is considerably younger than both. Muslims believe in the angels who brought God's messages to humans, in the prophets who received these messages, in the books in which the prophets expressed these revelations and in the last day of judgement. The Quran (the holy book of Islam) mentions 28 prophets, 21 of whom are also mentioned in the Bible; Adam, Noah, Abraham, David, Jacob, Joseph, Job, Moses and Jesus are given particular honour, although the divinity of Jesus is strictly denied.

For Muslims, Islam is the apogee of the monotheistic faiths, from which it derives so

The Five Pillars of Islam

To live a devout life and as an expression of their submission to Allah, the Muslim is expected to carry out the Five Pillars of Islam.

Profession of Faith (Shahada)

This is the basic tenet of Islam: 'There is no God but Allah and Mohammed is his prophet' *(La illaha illa Allah Mohammed rasul Allah)*. It is commonly heard as part of the call to prayer and at other events such as births and deaths.

Prayer (Sala)

Ideally, devout Muslims will pray five times a day when the muezzins call upon the faithful, usually at sunrise, noon, mid-afternoon, sunset and night. Although Muslims can pray anywhere (only the noon prayer on Friday should be conducted in the mosque), a strong sense of community makes joining together in a mosque preferable to elsewhere. The act of praying consists of a series of predefined movements of the body and recitals of prayers and passages of the Quran, all designed to express the believer's absolute humility and God's sovereignty.

Alms-giving (Zakat)

Alms-giving to the poor was, from the start, an essential part of Islamic social teaching and was later developed in some parts of the Muslim world into various forms of tax to redistribute funds to the needy. The moral obligation towards one's poorer neighbours continues to be emphasised at a personal level, and it is not unusual to find exhortations to give alms posted-up outside some mosques. Traditionally Muslims are expected to give one-fortieth of their annual income as alms to the poor.

Fasting (Sawm)

Ramadan, the ninth month of the Muslim calendar, commemorates the revelation of the Quran to Mohammed. In a demonstration of a renewal of faith, Muslims are asked to abstain from sex and from letting anything pass their lips from sunrise to sunset every day of the month. This includes smoking.

Pilgrimage (Haj)

The pinnacle of a devout Muslim's life is the pilgrimage to the holy sites in and around Mecca. Every Muslim capable of affording it should perform the haj to Mecca at least once in their lifetime. The reward is considerable – the forgiving of all past sins. Ideally, the pilgrim should go to Mecca in the last month of the year. The returned pilgrim can be addressed as Haji. In simpler villages at least, it is not uncommon to see the word Al-Haj and simple scenes painted on the walls of houses showing that its inhabitants have made the pilgrimage.

The Mosque

Embodying the Islamic faith, and representing its most predominant architectural feature, is the mosque, or *masjed* or *jama'a*. The building was developed in the very early days of Islam and takes its form from the simple, private houses where believers would customarily gather for worship.

The house belonging to the Prophet Mohammed is said to have provided the prototype for the plan of the mosque. The original setting was an enclosed, oblong courtyard with huts (housing Mohammed's wives) along one wall and a rough portico providing shade. This plan developed with the courtyard becoming the *sahn*, the portico the arcaded *riwaqs* and the haram the prayer hall. The prayer hall is typically divided into a series of aisles; the centre aisle is wider than the rest and leads to a vaulted niche in the wall called the mihrab – this indicates the direction of Mecca, which Muslims must face when they pray.

Islam does not have priests as such. The closest equivalent is the mosque's imam, a man schooled in Islam and Islamic law. He often doubles as the muezzin, who calls the faithful to prayer from the tower of the minaret – except these days recorded cassettes and loudspeakers do away with the need for him to climb up there. At the main Friday noon prayers, the imam gives a *khutba* (sermon) from the minbar, a wooden pulpit that stands beside the mihrab. In older, grander mosques, these minbars are often beautifully decorated.

Before entering the prayer hall and participating in the communal worship, Muslims must perform a ritual washing of their hands, forearms, face and neck. For this purpose, mosques have traditionally had a large ablutions fountain at the centre of the courtyard, often carved from marble and worn by centuries of use. These days, modern mosques just have rows of taps.

The mosque also serves as a kind of community centre, and often you'll find groups of children or adults receiving lessons (usually in the Quran), people in quiet prayer and others simply dozing – mosques provide wonderfully tranquil havens from the chaos of the street.

Visiting Mosques

With few exceptions, non-Muslims are quite welcome to visit mosques at any time other than during noon prayers on Friday. You must dress modestly. For men that means no shorts; for women that means no shorts, tight pants, shirts that aren't done up, or anything else that might be considered immodest. Shoes have to be removed. In Libya, women visitors are generally as free to enter mosques as men and often no headscarf is required. Increasingly, local women attend prayers at the mosque although the majority still pray at home.

much. Muslims traditionally attribute a place of great respect to Christians and Jews as *ahl al-kitab*, 'the people of the Book', and it is usually considered to be preferable to be a Christian or Jew than an atheist. However, the more strident will claim Christianity was a new and improved version of the teachings of the Torah and that Islam was the next logical step and therefore 'superior'.

Mohammed, born into one of the trading families of the Arabian city of Mecca (in present-day Saudi Arabia) in AD 570, began to receive the revelations in AD 610 from the Archangel Gabriel and after a time began imparting the content of Allah's message to the Meccans. The revelations continued for the rest of Mohammed's life and they were written down in the Quran (from the Arabic word for 'recitation') in a series of *suras* (verses or chapters). To this day, not one dot of the Quran has been changed, making it, Muslims claim, the direct word of Allah. The essence of it was a call to submit to God's will ('islam' means submission). By Mohammed's time, religions such as Christianity and Judaism had become complicated by factions, sects and bureaucracies, to which Islam offered a simpler alternative. The new religion did away with hierarchical orders and complex rituals, and instead offered believers a direct relationship with God based only on their submission to God.

Islam & the West

Unfortunately, Islam has been much maligned and misunderstood in the West in recent years, due in large part to media sound bites and Western demonisation. Any mention of Islam brings to mind for many in the West one of two images: the 'barbarity' of some aspects of Islamic law such as flogging, stoning or the amputation of hands; or the so-called fanatics out to terrorise the West.

These practices represent one strand of Islamic activity and undoubtedly speak for a very small minority of Muslims. Most are as appalled by religious violence as anyone. Many Muslims are keenly aware, if not dismayed, that they are seen as a threat by the West and rightly point to the fact that the sectarian madness of Northern Ireland is rarely portrayed as a symbol of Christian 'barbarism' in the way political violence in the Middle East is summed up as simple Muslim fanaticism. It is worth remembering that while the Christian West tends to view Islam with disdain, if not contempt, Muslims accord Christians great respect as believers in the same God.

Further, and not without justification, some Libyan Muslims regard the West's policies, especially those towards Libya, Iraq and the Palestinians, as aggressive, even akin to the medieval Crusades. If the West is offended by the anti-Western rhetoric of the radical minority, the majority of Muslims see the West and its policies, including its support for Israel, as a direct challenge to their independence. These feelings were especially keen during the embargo.

The mutual distrust between the West and the Muslim world remains strong. As long as this situation persists, Islam will continue to be seen in the West as a backwards and radical force bent on violent change, rather than as simply a code of religious and political behaviour that people choose to apply to their daily lives, and which makes an often difficult life tolerable for them.

It is worth remembering that any hostility is overwhelmingly directed at Western governments; individuals are more likely to be overwhelmed by hospitality. Rarely (if ever) are Western visitors to Libya judged on the basis of their nationality or religion.

Not all Meccans were terribly taken with the idea. Mohammed gathered quite a following in his campaign against Meccan idolaters and his movement especially appealed to the poorer levels of society. The powerful families became increasingly outraged and, by AD 622, had made life sufficiently unpleasant for Mohammed and his followers to convince them of the need to flee to Medina, an oasis town some 300km to the north and now Islam's second-most holy city. This migration – the Hejira – marks the beginning of the Islamic calendar, year 1 AH (AD 622).

In Medina, Mohammed continued to preach and increase his supporter base. Soon he and his followers began to clash with the Meccans, possibly over trade routes. By AD 630 they had gained a sufficient following to return and take Mecca. In the two years until Mohammed's death, many of the surrounding tribes swore allegiance to him and the new faith.

Upon Mohammed's death in AD 632, the Arab tribes spread quickly across the Middle East with missionary zeal, quickly conquering what makes up modern Jordan, Syria, Iraq, Lebanon, Israel and the Palestinian territories. By AD 643 Libya had been conquered.

The initial conquests were carried out under the caliphs, or Companions of Mohammed, of whom there were four. They in turn were followed by the Umayyad dynasty (AD 661–750) in Damascus and then the Abbasid line (AD 749–1258) in the newly built city of Baghdad (in modern Iraq). Given that these centres of Islamic power were so geographically removed from Libya, the religion of Islam may have taken a hold, but the political and administrative control which accompanied Islamic rule elsewhere was much more tenuous in Libya.

The occasion of breaking the fast at the conclusion of Ramadan (when the moon is sighted) is a time of great celebration. In the

1930s, the Danish traveller Knud Holmboe described the scene in Tripoli:

'It ought to be tonight,' said a young Arab who stood next to me, as he scanned the sky eagerly. Hour after hour passed, and it was beginning to look as if Ramadan would have to be continued over the next day when suddenly the cry went up: 'El Ahmar, el Ahmar!' (The moon, the moon!) The festival began. The long month of fasting was over. All night they danced and ate to their heart's content in the Medina.

Knud Holmboe, *Desert Encounter*

The orthodox Sunnis divided into four schools *(madhab)* of Islamic law, each lending more or less importance to various aspects of religious doctrine. In Libya, the Maliki rite of Sunni Islam predominates. Founded by Malik ibn As, an Islamic judge who lived in Medina from AD 715–95, it is based on the practice which prevailed in Medina in the 8th century. The Maliki strand of thought preaches the primacy of the Quran (as opposed to later teachings). In this sense, orthodox Islam in modern Libya bears strong similarities to the teachings of the Sanusi sect, which ruled Libya for a number of centuries.

There is also a small population of Kharijites, a sect whose name literally means 'seceders' or 'those who emerge from impropriety'. Their doctrine that any Muslim could become caliph (they believed that only the first two caliphs were legitimate), which questioned the Arab monopoly over Muslim legitimacy, naturally appealed to the Berbers when Islam arrived in Libya.

Islamic Customs In everyday life, Muslims are prohibited from drinking alcohol and eating pork (as the pig is considered unclean), and must refrain from fraud, usury, slander and gambling.

Judaism

Libya was once home to a thriving Jewish community. Their presence in the country can be traced back to the 3rd century BC and they prospered under the Romans. This prosperity was, however, largely dependent upon their continued submission to Roman

rule. After Jewish revolts in AD 73 and AD 115 in Cyrenaica, the Roman response was brutal, with the leaders murdered and many wealthy Jews being put to the sword.

Because of their status as ahl al-kitab, the Jews of Libya coexisted peacefully with Muslims after the arrival of Islam in the 7th century. The community lived in relative security under successive Islamic dynasties until the 20th century when the rise of fascism in Europe and the creation of Israel threatened their continued presence.

When the Italians first arrived in Libya in 1911, there were about 21,000 Jews in Libya, with the overwhelming majority living in Tripoli. Despite persecution by the Italian authorities, Jews made up more than one-quarter of Tripoli's population, according to some reports. When the Germans occupied the Jewish quarter of Benghazi in 1942, Jewish businesses were destroyed and many Jews were forcibly marched across the desert with great loss of life. In Tripoli, members of the Jewish community were herded into forced labour camps.

When the state of Israel was declared in 1948, many Jews fled Libya as recriminations rippled across the Middle East, even though emigration was officially illegal. When the Allied administration legalised emigration for Jewish Libyans, there was a mass exodus of over 30,000 to Israel.

By the time of the 1969 coup, there were less than 500 Jews left in Libya. Keen to showcase his pan-Arab credentials and his empathy for the Palestinians, Colonel Gadaffi and his revolutionary committees announced the cancelling of all debts owed to Jews and sequestered Jewish property rights. In 1974 it was estimated that there were less than 20 Jews left in the country. Officially, there are no Jews left in Libya today. Although some attempts have reportedly been made at restoring some synagogues in Tripoli, almost all tangible signs of the heritage of Libya's Jewish community have disappeared.

LANGUAGE

Arabic is the national language of Libya and all signs are in Arabic – not even motorway signs are translated. English signs have been declared illegal in a bid to safeguard against the diluting of Arab culture, although signs in English are springing up in some parts of the country. Nevertheless, these are rare and some knowledge of Arabic is extremely helpful, especially if you're navigating on your own. We have included the names of most Libyan towns covered in this book in Arabic script to make this easier.

The Arabic spoken in Libya has some similarities to the Bedouin Arabic spoken in southern Tunisia; it is, however, more closely akin to Egyptian Arabic. Most published writing and speeches are delivered in Standard Arabic, which is understood throughout the country.

See the Language chapter at the back of this book for some important Arabic words and phrases. Lonely Planet's *Egyptian Arabic phrasebook* has all you'll need for a longer stay.

Outside the main cities, where some English or Italian is spoken, few people speak a foreign language. The exception is Ghadhames or Ghat, where some French is spoken. Unusually (but helpfully) for an Arab country, numbers are almost always written in Western script, even if the rest of the sign is in Arabic.

In the Jebel Nafusa and parts of Cyrenaica, many Berbers speak their own Berber language (eg, Mazir). Berber languages represent a series of related dialects. All stem from the Afro-Asiatic language family and are distantly related to Arabic but most Berber dialects have not developed a written form. The Tuareg of the south speak Tamashek, which is related to Berber and with many of the same words. The Toubou language is Tebu, which belongs to the Nilo Saharan language family although in keeping with the diffuse nature of Toubou society, there are many different dialects. In Libya, however, these are all secondary languages and with all publications and broadcasts in Arabic, it is very rare to find someone who is not fluent in Arabic.

Facts for the Visitor

HIGHLIGHTS

You should try to see as many of Libya's five Unesco World Heritage sites as you can. The country's major highlights fall into two distinct categories: the superb ruined cities which showcase Greek and Roman civilisation; and the spectacularly diverse charms of the Sahara.

No visitor to Libya should miss the extraordinary ruined city of **Leptis Magna**, once one of the greatest cities in the Roman Empire and still one of the best-preserved examples anywhere around the Mediterranean. Not far away, the city of **Sabratha** is also superb, while in north-eastern Libya the ancient Greek-Roman city of **Cyrene** disappoints no-one who visits.

The oasis town of **Ghadames** is home to arguably the finest surviving old city anywhere in the Sahara, with echoes of the days when it was one of the most significant places on the ancient trans-Saharan caravan routes. In Libya's far south-western corner is the **Jebel Acacus**, a stunning mountain range, which is home to the indigenous Tuareg people and magnificent rock art dating back to up to 12,000 years, and the similarly ancient carvings of **Wadi Methkandoush**.

Also in the Sahara are the enchanting **Ubari Lakes**, nestling improbably among the breathtaking sand dunes of the **Idehan Ubari (Ubari Sand Sea)**, while to the south the remote **Idehan Murzuq (Murzuq Sand Sea)** is similarly magnificent. The ancient trading town of **Ghat**, gateway to the Acacus Mountains, has a charming mud-brick medina.

Libya's cosmopolitan capital, Tripoli, is the sort of place where it is easy to spend a few days visiting its whitewashed **medina** and world-class **Jamahiriya Museum**.

The mountains of Libya's coastal hinterland also contain some hidden gems. In the west, old Berber villages contain otherworldly examples of ancient Berber architecture, such as intriguing *qasrs* (fortified granaries, though the term literally means castles) of **Qasr al-Haj, Nalut** and **Kabaw**.

In the north-east, the coastline at **Ras al-Hillal**, the coastal ruins of **Apollonia** and the exceptional mosaics of **Qasr Libya** should definitely not be missed if you're in the area.

SUGGESTED ITINERARIES

Until visa regulations change, your itinerary may be determined by the length of the tour organised by the company arranging your visit. Even when the rules change, independent travellers will need to select carefully what they want to see, as they will spend a long time waiting for public transport and have difficulties getting an internal flight. Independent travellers will still need to organise their desert expedition through a tour company.

One Week

With just seven days in Libya, you will probably be restricted to exploring the northern coast, with one possible side trip to the desert, although this latter option will be difficult if you're not part of a tour group. Plan to spend a minimum of two days in Tripoli to see the medina and the Jamahiriya Museum, at least one day exploring Leptis Magna and another visiting Sabratha. If you want to pack in as much as possible, a hectic itinerary would see you exploring the Berber villages of Al-Jebel Al-Nafusa (one day) en route to Ghadames. A desert alternative is to fly to/from Sebha for a side trip to the Ubari Lakes and Idehan Ubari.

Two Weeks

Two weeks will enable you to see the best of Tripoli, Leptis Magna and Sabratha, and spend five or six days exploring the Sahara, including Ghat, the rock art of the Jebel Acacus and Wadi Methkandoush, the isolated sand dunes of the Idehan Murzuq and the Ubari Lakes. Your time in the desert will be more leisurely if you fly between Tripoli and Sebha. You could also visit Ghadames, which is well worth the long drive to get there.

If you have no interest in the desert, consider instead spending the second week visiting Benghazi, Cyrene, Apollonia (the ancient port of Cyrene) and the mosaics of Qasr Libya. As more than 1000km separates Tripoli and Benghazi, consider flying at least one way.

Three Weeks

An extra week would allow you to visit all of the above sites with more time to explore the Berber villages of the Jebel Nafusa between Ghadames and Tripoli or the Jebel Akhdar of Cyrenaica. It would also give you time to devote to Apollonia with a possible visit to Tolmeita.

One Month

Four weeks would enable you to see most places covered in this book. In addition to the sites mentioned above, this could include the WWII sites of Tobruk, the superb scenery of the Jebel Akhdar (especially Wadi al-Kuf and Ras al-Hillal), the ancient churches at L'Atrun and the archaeological site at Tolmeita. It would also enable you to spend longer in the desert, possibly exploring the remote, fortified farms at Ghirza in Tripolitania. Another alternative would be a desert expedition, either from Ghadames to Al-Aweinat (three to four days) or from Zueila to Waw al-Namus (three to four days).

PLANNING
When to Go

The most pleasant time to visit Libya is from October to March. It can actually get surprisingly cold in winter, even in the desert. The temperatures in April are still relatively mild, although the month is known for its unpredictable weather, with strong winds not unusual. In April you could easily encounter the ghibli (see Climate in the Facts about Libya chapter), rain, blazing sun, glorious mild and clear days, and sandstorms. May is similar, although few travellers set out for the desert after the end of April. By September, the worst of the summer heat has passed, although if you can wait until October to travel, do so. In summer, Libya is fiercely hot and temperatures along the coast can hover in the mid-40°Cs with searing regularity. One traveller offered the following advice:

I can really recommend going to Libya, especially in winter. In October it cools down in the south so you can go to the desert. It makes no sense going down there in summer time, when you should travel along the northern coast and visit the ancient ruins instead.

Karl Heinz Krawinkler, Austria

The other thing to factor into your decision about when to go is the timing of the annual fast of Ramadan, which is almost universally observed in Libya. Many restaurants simply don't open during Ramadan, but the bigger hotels in Tripoli, Benghazi and other places that get lots of tourists will usually have at least one restaurant open. As one traveller noted:

If you go in Ramadan, as I did, resign yourself to not finding many restaurants open. They can't open during the day. Then between 6pm and 8pm people break their fasts, but the point is they do it at home, never in public. If a restaurant does open it will be after 8pm, but many don't bother, as I discovered to my cost, since after 9pm and until around 1am or even later everyone goes off walking and talking and shopping with their friends. You're supposed to have eaten by then…It should be plain by now that Ramadan is not a good time to go to Libya.

Anonymous

During Ramadan it's a good idea to stock up on self-catering items and head away from the crowds for a picnic, especially as eating in public can be insensitive to locals. If you're lucky, you may get invited by a Libyan friend to a post-sunset feast. Surprisingly, travelling in the desert at this time can be less onerous, as Islam permits Muslims to fast at alternate times if they are travelling during Ramadan.

What Kind of Trip

At the time of writing, all foreign visitors travelling to and within Libya had to travel as part of an organised and escorted tour. Before this requirement was introduced at the end of 2000, backpackers and other travellers reported few difficulties in travelling independently. This is likely to be the case when visas for independent travel are reintroduced.

While making for a more expensive trip, travelling as part of a tour group is also more flexible than it may appear. Most tour operators are willing to arrange programs for groups as small as three, and many demonstrate great flexibility in allowing you to follow the itinerary of your choice. If you have enough time, try to arrange some free days to explore a city on your own.

For desert enthusiasts travelling with their own vehicles, the official requirement demands little more than an escort by a Libyan representative of a private tour company and a guide on some routes.

Another option, albeit rarely utilised, would be to join an archaeological dig. As a starting point, check the Web site of the Society for Libyan Studies at **W** www.britac3.britac.ac.uk/institutes/libya/index.html. The society's postal address is: c/o The Institute for Archaeology, 31–34 Gordon Square, London WC1H OPY, United Kingdom.

Maps

The maps throughout this book should be enough to satisfy most travellers, although more-detailed maps may be necessary for desert expeditions in remote areas.

The most reliable map is Michelin's Map No 953, *Afrique Nord et Ouest (Africa North and West)* at 1:4,000,000. The best map available inside Libya is published by Malt International and entitled *Map of the Socialist People's Libyan Arab Jamahiriya* (1:3,500,000); it's also available in Arabic. This map is available from Fergiani's Bookshop in Tripoli and from gift shops in most major hotels in Tripoli or Benghazi.

Other decent maps are Cartographia's *Libya* (1:2,000,000) and *Libya* (1:1,650,000) by Cartes de Voyage Internationale.

For exploring the desert, no maps are comprehensive enough to be sufficient as a sole resource, as none encompasses all topographical features or desert trails. They can be near-impossible to track down, but

the best maps are Russian-produced maps (1:200,000) from the 1970s, which are still considered to be the best for Saharan navigation although all labels are in Cyrillic. Try Stanfords in the UK (☎ 020-7240 3611, **W** www.stanfords.co.uk/), at 12–14 Long Acre, London WC2E, or Darr Expeditions service Gmbh in Germany (☎ 089-28 20 32, fax 28 25 25, **e** info@daerr.de), Theresien Strasse 66, Munich. See Maps in the Fezzan & the Sahara chapter for more information.

What to Bring

Toiletries (like toothpaste, soap and tissues) and food stuffs are widely available in Libya in the well-stocked supermarkets of Tripoli and Benghazi, as well as from the small grocery stores found in virtually all Libyan towns. Toilet paper is becoming more widely available in most towns of any size, although it's always worth carrying a couple of spare rolls in case of an emergency off the beaten track. Shaving gear is also available, although there is never a barber too far away. For women, tampons (around 6.5LD per packet) are available in most towns, although it can take a little time tracking them down; you'd be better off bringing your own. Bringing your own medical kit (see Health later in this chapter for more details) is always a good idea.

Small gifts from your home country can also be a nice way to reward the generous hospitality or assistance you're likely to receive from Libyans.

Practical items that are always worth the space they occupy in your bag include a Swiss-army knife, torch (flashlight), a small magnifying glass (for examining the detail of mosaics or ancient facades) and a universal sink plug. Also handy is a length of cord to hang drying clothes on. Given the almost complete absence of evening entertainment in Libya, a short-wave radio, portable cassette player and plenty of reading material is worth the extra weight.

A sleeping bag suitable for low temperatures is a must if you're travelling in the desert, which can get bitterly cold once the sun goes down. Most tour companies will provide them, but you can only rely on ones from the better companies. Independent travellers should consider bringing a tent.

We did hear of one group that took an Ascot picnic set to Libya, but that's getting a little excessive.

Clothing In summer, carry lightweight, loose-fitting clothing, which is especially appropriate in the desert. In winter, carry a couple of sets of warm clothing. At all times, a warm jacket or sweater is essential, as evenings can get quite cool, especially in desert or mountain areas. A hat is a must and most travellers will appreciate a pair of sunglasses. A swimming costume should also be included for beaches or the lakes of the Sahara. A towel is also worthwhile although, to minimise weight, a sarong can serve the same purpose. If you can fit them in your bag, sandals and sturdy walking shoes are a good idea. Even on hot days, consider wearing shoes or boots to explore archaeological sites, as there are invariably exposed, sharp stones ready to cut the unwary.

RESPONSIBLE TOURISM

As with any country you visit, you should be sensitive to local cultural and religious sensibilities. Libya is one of the region's more liberal and tolerant societies, but you should still try to minimise your impact. Dress for both men and women should be modest, particularly when swimming, when you should avoid ostentatious displays of flesh (see Women Travellers later in this chapter for more information on how to dress). Public displays of affection are usually tolerated, but can cause discomfort.

Libya's human-rights situation has improved in recent decades, but many Libyans are still understandably reticent about participating in political discussions (see Dos & Don'ts under Society & Conduct in the Facts about Libya chapter). If you would like to find out more about the human-rights situation in Libya, consult the resources of Amnesty International (W www.amnesty.org/ailib/index).

When exploring the desert or camping in the great outdoors, there are some general rules to keep in mind:

- Carry out all your rubbish. If you've carried it in, you can carry it out.
- Never bury your rubbish. Digging disturbs soil and ground cover, and encourages erosion. Buried rubbish will more than likely be dug up by animals, who may be injured or poisoned by it. It may also take years to decompose.
- Minimise the waste you must carry out by taking minimal packaging and instead take reusable containers or stuff sacks.
- Don't rely on bought water in plastic bottles. Disposal of these bottles is creating a major problem.
- Sanitary napkins, tampons and condoms should also be carried out despite the inconvenience. They burn and decompose poorly.
- Where there is no toilet, bury your waste. Dig a small hole 15cm (6 inches) deep. Cover the waste with soil and a rock. Use toilet paper sparingly and bury it with the waste.
- If you light a fire don't surround it with rocks, as this creates a visual scar.
- Don't assume animals around desert camp sites to be nonindigenous vermin and attempt to exterminate them.

TOURIST OFFICES
Local Tourist Offices

Libyan government tourist offices operate as overseers of the tourism industry and tour companies rather than sources of practical information. That may change as tourism grows in Libya, but most of the information you'll need is available elsewhere. The office in Tripoli is, however, useful if you want to pick up one of the excellent series of posters on Libya. The General Secretariat of Tourism (☎ 021-3603405, 3604006, fax 3603400) is on Sharia al-Corniche; its postal address is PO Box 207, Tripoli.

Tourist Offices Abroad

There simply aren't any at present. The best source of information about Libya (apart from this guidebook, of course) is the Internet (see Digital Resources later in this chapter) or Libyan tour companies.

VISAS & DOCUMENTS

Getting a Libyan visa is not that difficult if you follow the right steps, but for the forseeable future this involves arranging your visit through a Libyan tour company. Israeli citi-

Colonel Muammar Gaddafi, leader since 1969

Old meets new: rush hour in Tripoli's medina

Revolutionary reading: *The Green Book* for sale

Assai al-Hamra (Red Castle) on Tripoli's waterfront; home to a chilling and violent history

Student at a Quranic school, Zliten

Shaded alley within Tripoli's medina

Pedestrians beneath an arch, Tripoli's medina

Conversation at the Gurgi Mosque, Tripoli

The Day the Vandals Came to Libya

The restrictive change in visa regulations at the end of 2000 is largely the fault of a small minority of tourists who have spoiled it for the rest of us.

The story goes that a group of free-wheeling European visitors visiting the Jebel Acacus of southwestern Libya decided that the region's famous rock art would make a wonderful souvenir of their time in Libya. Using silicone gel to take copies from the rock in the Awiss region of the Acacus, they vandalised priceless art that had survived untouched for thousands of years. The thieves were caught with their shameful booty by government officials in Tripoli, detained for a couple of weeks, fined and then deported.

This incident was not the first, but it confirmed to the government that tourists were responsible for the increasing damage to ancient sites, and it shut down the independent travel option. Ever since, the Libyan government has insisted that you be accompanied by a Libyan escort from a tour company. The timing of this incident was unfortunate, coming as it did in the post-sanctions period when Libya was opening up to tourism. We hope the tourists in question are happy with their handiwork.

zens will not be issued with a visa under any circumstances, nor will those with Israeli stamps in their passport.

Passport

Obviously you must have a valid passport to visit Libya. Part of the visa application process requires that the essential details of your passport be translated into Arabic. There are agencies throughout Europe that can arrange the translation (cost around US$30), although the company organising your visa and itinerary can point you to the agent it usually uses in your country of application. One reliable agency in the UK is Khalifa Hamed Visa & Translating Services (☎ 020-8748 9898, fax 8748 2450, 0860 620 078, e hamed@btinternet.com) in Britannia House at 1–11 Glenthorne Rd, Hammersmith, London W6.

Inside Libya, hotels require you to leave your passport in a secure reception area for the duration of your stay. There is usually no problem in getting your passport if you need it to, for example, change money at the bank or register your passport with the authorities. If you do leave your passport with the hotel, don't forget to retrieve it when you leave. It can be a long way back to collect it, as we discovered to our cost.

Visas

Nationals of most African and Arab countries don't require visas. Everyone else does.

Apply for your visa before leaving home. It is only possible to apply for and pick up your visa from the Libyan People's Bureau (embassy) in your country of nationality, although very occasionally you may be able to pick it up in a neighbouring country. Only if your country doesn't have a Libyan embassy (such as Australia or New Zealand) can you pick up your visa elsewhere; Europe is undoubtedly the best place to arrange your visa.

Before Ramadan (November to December) in 2000, it was possible to obtain a visa for independent travel in Libya. It was almost always necessary to arrange the visa through a Libyan tour company and sometimes one or two services within the country, but once inside the country, you were free to travel as you wished. At the time of writing, visits to Libya are only possible as part of an organised tour.

Getting a Visa The process for getting a visa involves contacting a Libyan tour company (see Organised Tours in the Getting Around chapter) or an international tour company (see Organised Tours in the Getting There & Away chapter). You need to do this at least six weeks before you decide to go. You must then agree on an itinerary with the company and provide it with your passport details, occupation, date of arrival (and departure) and other details, depending on current regulations. The company will then arrange for the invitation and itinerary to be approved by the Libyan government (one to two weeks). Your details will then be forwarded, along with a visa or invitation number, to the Libyan People's Bureau, from where you can pick up your visa. Before lodging your passport with the embassy, it is necessary to get your passport details translated into Arabic (see Passports earlier in this section). It usually takes a week from the date of lodgement at the embassy to picking up your visa.

This may sound like an onerous process but, once you've reconciled yourself to travelling on a group tour and followed the above procedure, there is little reason why your visa won't be issued. If you turn up at the border without a visa already in your passport, you *will* be turned back.

Visas are valid for 30 days from the date of entry and you must enter Libya within 30 days of the visa being issued.

Throughout this book, we have provided information for travellers visiting as part of a tour and those travelling independently, as it is possible that the situation will change during the life of this book. In the meantime, some Libyan tour companies will arrange itineraries for lone travellers, although this is unusual (and expensive, given the economies of scale). Your itinerary is more likely to be approved if you can arrange a group, even one as small as three people, although European companies will rarely run a tour for such a small group. Libyan companies will also usually accept payment (in US dollars) upon your arrival in the country.

The situation for American citizens is the most complex. Since December 1981 the US government has ruled that its citizens' passports are not valid for travel to, in or through Libya without special validation. The only people who will receive this validation will be approved journalists on assignment, members of Red Cross missions or those who can provide compelling humanitarian reasons (usually connected with family unification). You can also travel if your visit is in the US's national interest, but these circumstances are not defined. If you fit the bill, validation requests can be forwarded in writing to the deputy assistant secretary for Passport Services, Office of Passport Policy and Advisory Services, US Department of State at 2401 E Street NW, 9th floor, Washington, DC 20522. You can contact the office by phone on ☎ 202-663 2662 or by fax at 202-663 2654. Consult the Web site at W www.travel.state.gov/libya .html to check whether the situation has changed. All US citizens, permanent resident aliens and anyone physically located in the USA also remain subject to the unilateral US sanctions regulations, which are outlined at W www.treas.gov/ ofac/.

The Libyan government seems to have no such hang-ups. To get around the US laws, many Libyan embassies will issue visas to US citizens on a separate piece of paper so that no record of the visit exists in their passport.

Visa Extensions If you wish to stay in Libya longer than one month, extensions (15LD; no photo) are possible, though rare. Applications are handled by the *jawazzat*, or passport office – there is one in most towns. Extensions are usually no problem if you can provide reasons (eg, places you still haven't visited or Arabic language classes) and can produce a ticket showing when you will leave the country. Remember that you will probably not be issued with a tourist visa in the first place if your original departure date is more than one month after your arrival. If you plan on staying for longer than one month, check with the airline or travel agency that issued the ticket that the small print doesn't contain conditions precluding a change of travel date.

You're much more likely to be granted a visa extension if you allow a local tour operator to make the application on your behalf for a small fee (around 10LD). They understand the process and can also help out with the Arabic application form.

Registration All holders of tourist visas must register with the Libyan authorities at any jawazzat within seven days of arrival in the country. Those who don't do this by the end of the 7th day face a minimum fine of

50LD. In this era of organised tourism, the process will invariably be completed by the tour company responsible for you during your stay and the fee is usually included in your overall tour cost. If it's not included in the cost, tour companies or hotels will charge around 10LD to take care of it for you. If you must complete the process yourself, most jawazzats are only open in the morning. It's better if you can find an Arabic-speaker to go with you as few officers speak English and the forms are in Arabic.

The procedure involves filling out two forms, which need to be stamped when you've paid the fee (5LD to 7LD depending on the office). In the larger offices in Tripoli or Benghazi, you then queue to submit it for approval and collect it from a different counter. It really is little more than a formality, although it can take time to negotiate your way to the right counters.

Visas for Onward Travel Try to arrange all your visas for onward travel before you arrive in Libya, as getting them there can be time-consuming or downright impossible. Contact details are provided under Embassies & Consulates later. But if you want to get visas in Libya, here are the particular requirements.

Algeria The consulate in Tripoli issues tourist visas within 21 days, although this may depend on whether you have Algerian diplomatic representation in your country of nationality. You will need two passport photos and 30LD.

Chad Tourist visas of up to one month's duration are issued for 20LD from the Chad embassy in Tripoli. You'll need a letter of recommendation from your embassy or government and two passport photos.

Egypt Visas are issued within a couple of days from Egyptian consulates in Tripoli and Benghazi. Visas cost 20LD and require two passport photos. Double-entry visas are sometimes issued if you ask. In Benghazi, there are two consulates; applications are lodged at the new consulate and picked up the following day at the old consulate. Alternatively, getting a visa at the border involves much less hassle.

Tunisia Visas are issued by the Consulate-General in Bin Ashour (which is, incidentally, just around the corner from the embassy). The process takes 21 days, costs 30LD and requires passport photos. If there is no Tunisian embassy in your home country (eg, Australia and New Zealand) you can get a visa at the border.

Travel Permits
Travel permits are required for trips to the Jebel Acacus and to Waw al-Namus. For the Jebel Acacus, permits can be arranged in Ghat or Germa (the situation in Al-Aweinat was unclear when we visited) at the police station or jawazzat. For permits to Waw al-Namus, go to Zueila or Sebha. If you're on a tour, the permit should be included in the cost. The permit costs 120LD for each minimum two-car convoy. In the Jebel Acacus, a guide is also compulsory (30LD to 40LD per day).

Onward Tickets
In most cases, an onward air ticket is required before a visa will be granted. This does not have to be a ticket from Tripoli as some travellers fly into Tunisia and out of Egypt. If your itinerary is fixed in advance and the authorities are satisfied that you will leave Libya before the expiry of your visa, then they may forgo the requirement of producing an onward ticket. They are more likely to do this if you can provide a plan of your movements after leaving Libya and have the requisite visas for the relevant countries. Your onward ticket will rarely be checked after your visa has been issued.

Travel Insurance
A travel insurance policy to cover theft, loss and medical problems is a good idea. There is a wide variety of policies available, so check the small print. Some policies specifically exclude 'dangerous activities', which can include scuba diving, motorcycling and even trekking. In Libya, you'll have to pay

for medical care on the spot and claim later so make sure you keep all documentation. Some insurance companies ask you to call back (reverse charges) to a centre in your home country where an immediate assessment of your problem is made. Check that the policy covers ambulances or an emergency flight home.

Also check that your policy covers travel to Libya and any adjacent countries you intend to visit. Some insurers still consider the region a 'danger zone' and either exclude it altogether or demand you pay exorbitant premiums.

Driving Licence & Permits

An international driving licence is required for any foreign visitor who intends to drive a car in Libya, although it's rarely checked. See Car & Motorcycle in the Getting There & Away chapter for information on documents needed to bring a car into Libya.

Hostel Cards

Hostel cards can come in handy in Libya as there are internationally affiliated youth hostels throughout the country. In most cases, a card will save you no more than 2LD per night so, if you don't already have one, you'll need to work out whether it will be worth your while paying to register. Some travellers have reported obtaining a card at the central youth hostel in Tripoli, but when we were there nobody seemed interested in selling us one. Remember also that any card you purchase in Libya may not be recognised at hostels outside the country.

Student & Youth Cards

Before the UN embargo, students could get a 50% discount on entry into most archaeological sites as well as on domestic airline tickets. These days everyone pays the same, except children under 12 years of age. There is no harm in bringing your student card in case the situation changes in the post-embargo period.

Vaccination Certificates

Vaccination certificates are rarely checked on entry to Libya and there are few re-

quirements for Libya. The only exception is if you're arriving from an area infected with yellow fever.

Copies

It's also worth carrying multiple copies of the relevant pages of your passport with you if you're travelling independently in Libya. If you're travelling in your own vehicle, you should also copy your carnet. Soldiers or police may request them or the original at checkpoints, which are everywhere in Libya (see Checkpoints in the Getting Around chapter). Keep a spare copy separate from the originals.

EMBASSIES & CONSULATES
Libyan People's Bureaus & Consulates

Libyan embassies are known as Libyan People's Bureaus; their locations include:

Austria (☎ 01-367 7639) Balaasstrasse 33, 1190 Vienna
Belgium (☎ 02-649 15 03) Ave Victoria 28, B-1050 Brussels
Denmark (☎ 45-35 26 36 11) Rosenvængets Hovedvej 4, 2100 Copenhagen
Egypt (☎ 02-735 1864, fax 735 0072) 7 Sharia Salah ad-Din, Zamalek, Cairo
France (☎ 01 47 04 71 60) 2 Rue Charles Lamoureux, 75116 Paris
    Consulate in Marseille: (☎ 91 71 67 02) 6 Blvd Rivet, Marseille 13008
Germany (☎ 0228-822 00 90, fax 36 42 60) Beethovenalle 12a, 53173 Bonn 0228
Greece (☎ 01-674 1843, fax 647 2122) Vironoz 13, 152–154 Psychikon, Athens
Italy (☎ 06-86 32 09 51) Via Nomentana 365, Rome 00 162
    Consulate in Milan: (☎ 02-86 46 42 85) Via Barrachini 7, Milan 02
Malta (☎ 349 47), Dar Tarek, Tower Rd, Sliema
Netherlands (☎ 020-355 8886) Parkweg 15, 1285 GHS-Gravanhaga, Amsterdam
Spain (☎ 01-915 644 675) Pisuerga No 1/2, 28002 Madrid
Switzerland (☎ 031- 351 3076) Travelweg 2 CH-3006, Bern
Tunisia (☎ 01-780 866) 48 Bis Rue due 1er Juin, Tunis 01
    Consulate in Tunis: (☎ 01-793 785) 74 Ave Mohammed V, Tunis
    Consulate-General in Sfax: 35 Rue Alexander Dumas, Sfax

UK (☎ 020-7486 8250 or 7589 6120) 54 Ennismore Gardens, London SW7 1NH
USA *Consulate in New York:* (☎ 212-752 5775, fax 593 4787, **e** lbyun@undp.org) 309 East 48th St, New York 0201
Libyan Interests Section, Embassy of United Arab Emirates (☎ 202-338 6500, fax 337 7029) Suite 740, 500 New Hampshire Ave NW, Washington DC 20522

Embassies & Consulates in Libya

An increasing number of countries are opening diplomatic offices in post-embargo Libya. The offices are usually open from 9am to 11am Sunday to Thursday, although they often open for their nationals or for visa collections in the afternoon.

Most embassies and main diplomatic missions are in Tripoli; there are also some consulates in Benghazi.

Algeria (☎ 021-4440025) 12 Sharia Kairaoun
Consulate-General in Bin Ashour, Tripoli: (☎ 3610877) Off Sharia Jama'a as-Saqa'a, Tripoli
Belgium (☎ 021-3350115, fax 3350116) Dhat al-Ahmat Tower 4, Level 5, Tripoli
Chad (☎ 021-4443955) 25 Sharia Mohammed Mossadeq, Tripoli; postal address: PO Box 1078
Egypt (☎ 021-6605500, fax 4445959) Sharia al-Fat'h, Tripoli
Consulate in Tripoli: (☎ 021-4448997) Sharia Omar al-Mukhtar, Tripoli
Consulate (old) in Benghazi: Off Sharia Jamal Abdul Nasser, Benghazi
Consulate (new) in Benghazi: Off Sharia al-Andalus, Benghazi
France (☎ 021-4774892, fax 4778266) Sharia Beni al-Amar, Hay Andalus (Gargaresh), Tripoli; postal address: PO Box 312
Germany (☎ 021-3330554, fax 444896) Sharia Hassan al-Mashai, Tripoli; postal address: PO Box 302
Greece (☎ 021-3336978, fax 4441907) 18 Sharia Galal Bayar, Tripoli; postal address: PO Box 5147
Consulate-General in Benghazi: (☎ 9093064) 4km south-east of city centre; ask a taxi driver to take you there.
Italy (☎ 021-3334131, fax 3331673) 1 Shara Uaharan, Tripoli; postal address: PO Box 912
Consulate-General in Tripoli: (☎ 021-3331222, fax 3331673) Sharia al-Fat'h, Tripoli
Consulate-General in Benghazi: (☎ 9093484, fax 99806) Sharia Amr ibn al-Ass, Tripoli

Your Own Embassy

It's important to realise what your own embassy can and can't do to help you if you get into trouble. Generally speaking, it won't be much help in emergencies if the trouble you're in is remotely your own fault. Remember that you are bound by the laws of Libya. Your embassy will not be sympathetic if you end up in jail after committing a crime locally, even if such actions are legal in your own country.

In genuine emergencies you might get some assistance, but only if other channels have been exhausted. If you need to get home urgently, a free ticket home is exceedingly unlikely – the embassy would expect you to have insurance. If you have all your money and documents stolen, it might assist with getting a new passport, but a loan for onward travel is out of the question.

Japan (☎ 021-3350056, fax 3350055) Dhat al-Ahmat Tower 4, Level 1, Tripoli; postal address: PO Box 3265
Netherlands (☎ 021-4441549, fax 4440386) 20 Sharia Galal Bayar, Tripoli; postal address: PO Box 3801
Niger (☎ 021-4443104) postal address: PO Box 2251, Tripoli
Spain (☎ 021-3336797, fax 4443743) Sharia al-Amir Abd al-Kader al Jezayir, Garden City, Tripoli; postal address: PO Box 2302
Sudan (☎ 021-75387, fax 74781) Sharia Mohammed Mossadeq, Tripoli
Tunisia (☎ 021-3331051, fax 4447600) Off Sharia al-Jrabah, Bin Ashour, Tripoli; postal address: PO Box 613
Consulate-General in Bin Ashour, Tripoli: Off Sharia al-Jrabah, Tripoli
UK (☎ 021-3351084, emergency 091-2147316, fax 3351425) Burj al-Fateh, Level 24, Tripoli. Open for British citizens 8am to 3pm Sunday to Thursday.
USA c/o US Interests Section, Belgian embassy. Open 9am to 11am Saturday to Wednesday.

CUSTOMS

Libyan customs checks on arrival are pretty cursory – there seems to have been a directive to facilitate the quick passage of tourists. The major focus of any search is alcohol, which is strictly forbidden in Libya. There are the usual prohibitions against (and stiff penalties for) importing firearms and illicit drugs. Laptop computers used to arouse suspicion and were on occasion confiscated, but this attitude appears to have relaxed. These days, you're more likely to have these and other expensive electronic items (including, possibly, video cameras) noted in your passport and checked upon departure to ensure that you haven't sold the item inside Libya.

Customs inspections tend to be more rigorous. If you're leaving by air, avoid storing sharp items in your cabin baggage, as they could be mistaken for weapons during checks and X-rays at customs and upon entering the departure lounge. The main items about which customs officials are concerned are antiquities, particularly fragments from the Saharan rock art of southern Libya.

MONEY
Currency
The official unit of currency is the Libyan dinar. Notes include 0.25LD, 0.5LD, 1LD, 5LD and 10LD. The dinar is divided into 100 piastres, or 1000 dirhams (also known as *mileem*), although the latter is less used these days. There are coins for 10 piastres, 25 piastres, 50 piastres and 1LD. Don't be surprised to find 5LD or 10LD notes of different colours – all are legal tender.

Exchange Rates
Depending on whether you got the official bank-exchange rate or the black-market rate, Libya used to be either one of the most expensive or cheaper countries in the world in which to travel. These days, the official and black-market rates are all but identical. When this equalisation process was adopted in 2000, the value of US$1 was set at 3.2LD. The government's intention was to bring the value of the dinar in line with the US dollar by the end of 2001, and while it was unlikely to meet this deadline the rate had already hit US$1 to 1.6LD by May 2001. By the time we visited, the black-market rate was 1.65LD. Always change money as soon as possible as exchange rates (and the value of your money) can drop overnight and without warning. Rates at the time of publication were as follows:

country	unit	Libyan dinar (LD)
Australia	A$1	0.32
Egypt	E£1	0.15
Euro zone	€1	0.58
Switzerland	SFF1	0.39
Tunisia	1TD	0.45
UK	UK£1	0.93
USA	US$1	0.64

There is still an official (and considerably less generous) commercial rate, which is only used for bank-to-bank transactions.

Exchanging Money
The simple rule is to bring all of your money in US-dollars cash, preferably in large denominations (US$100). It is possible to change other currencies, but some banks will be reluctant, especially outside Tripoli or Benghazi. Your best chance is with pounds sterling or euros, but don't come with these alone.

Officially, any bank is able to change money, although some are reluctant to do so if the amount is large (eg, US$500; some will claim that they have enough foreign currency already!). To change money at a bank, you must produce your passport (or at the very least you must give your passport number).

Before crossing into Libya, you can change money on the Egyptian or Tunisian side of the land borders. If arriving by air, Libya's two international airports have a foreign exchange counter, although it's not always open in the early hours of the morning. Once you're inside Libya, if you can't find a bank that will take your money (which is rare), an alternative is the small black market, which still functions in markets like Souq al-Attara in Tripoli's medina or, more openly, at the southern entrance to Souq al-Jreed in Benghazi. To avoid getting both yourself and anyone else in trouble, be discreet and, where possible, go with a Libyan friend. Otherwise, the gold shops of the souqs are the best place to start asking.

At the time of writing, Libyan customs officials were not asking for evidence that you have changed your money in recognised banks. In case they do, or if regulations change, you should keep receipts.

Travellers Cheques Travellers cheques were not being accepted by any Libyan banks at the time of research. If you are completely stuck, some shops in the souqs of Tripoli or Benghazi may be able to help out, but you'll need to take whatever exchange rate you're given.

ATMs Although you may see the occasional ATM in Libya, it will be a long time before they are linked to international financial systems, enabling you to withdraw money.

Credit Cards As should already be apparent, Libya is very much a cash society and almost no businesses will accept credit cards as a means of payment. Cash advances against credit cards are not possible. The only use for your plastic is paying the international airlines that accept payment by credit card (some won't accept cash). This doesn't apply to Libyan Arab Airlines, nor does it work if you're buying an international ticket through a local travel agency. When paying by credit card, ask for the price to be credited in US dollars; if it appears in Libyan dinars, the banks will use the official rate used for commercial transactions, which can double the price.

International Transfers It's only possible to make an international transfer if you open a foreign currency account with a local bank, a process so fraught with bureaucratic obstacles as to render it unworkable. Even if you have such an account, you can only receive your money in Libyan dinars at the poor official exchange rate for commercial transactions (where US$1 is equal to 1LD). Many Libyan companies don't even bother with the nightmare and instead set up accounts in neighbouring countries like Tunisia or Malta. If you're going to be in Libya for a while, consider doing the same.

Security

Libya is generally a safe country for travel and we have had no reports of theft from tourists. The only areas where some travellers (and Libyans) have reported feeling a little uneasy are in the Sharia ar-Rashid district of Tripoli or the Funduq Market area of Benghazi. Ever-increasing numbers of foreign travellers are arriving in Libya, most of whom have paid thousands of dollars for the privilege, so incidents inspired by an appreciation of the wealth of tourists are not beyond the realms of possibility. Always keep your valuables locked in a secure place (eg, a hotel safe or in a moneybelt under your clothes) and avoid ostentatious displays of wealth.

Costs

Libya is an expensive destination by Middle Eastern standards (and especially compared to neighbouring Egypt) if only because visas are being issued only to visitors travelling as part of an organised tour. Costs of tours vary widely between companies and tours can range from accommodation in youth hostels (3LD to 6LD per night) to five-star hotels (40LD to 120LD). Most tours are also inclusive (daily rates in brackets) of the following: entrance fees to archaeological sites and museums (3LD per person), transport (private car up to 150LD, micro 150LD, 4WD 90LD to 200LD and large bus 300LD to 700LD, depending on size and quality), guides for major sites (50LD to 65LD), tour leaders (30LD to 40LD), travel permits (120 LD for the minimum two 4WD vehicles) and meals (full-board or half-board from 5LD to 25LD). Costs that are not included are photography/video charges (5/10LD) at archaeological sites and museums, and any souvenirs you decide to take home. European and other international tour companies charge considerably more for tours than Libyan companies.

If you're travelling independently, staying in youth hostels (with an HI card), eating only at cheap restaurants, travelling by shared taxi or micro and being very selective about the sites you visit, you could survive on 15LD to 25LD per day. By staying in slightly better accommodation and eating at least one sit-down meal in a decent restaurant every day, you're likely to go through 40LD to 50LD daily. By staying in comfortable accommodation, eating well, visiting every site and paying for a camera or video permit at each one, you won't get much change from 80LD to 100LD a day although you could conceivably spend much more. Not included in this assessment are desert expeditions, where the individual cost depends entirely on how many people you can get together for a tour.

Tipping & Bargaining

Tipping is increasingly common in Libya, but there is rarely any pressure to do so. For simple tasks, like asking the caretaker to open a mosque, 1LD to 3LD is appropriate, while for most other services you'd rarely need to give more than 5LD. The only time when larger tips are appropriate are for guides (eg, in the desert) or tour leaders. In this case, it is entirely up to you, but any amount will generally be appreciated. Some guides to the archaeological sites do tend to linger just in case. A good starting point is 15LD per person for a few days, up to 50LD if the help has been exceptional over a couple of weeks.

Don't come to Libya all primed to hone your bargaining skills; this is definitely not Egypt. For most purchases the price is fixed and you'd be lucky to get a 10% reduction at the end of hours of effort. There are always exceptions (some shops in the souqs of the Tripoli's medina and some in Ghadames), but to make ridiculously low offers may simply insult your host. You're more likely to get a discount if you develop a friendly rapport with the vendor and if you go on your own, rather than as part of a group.

POST & COMMUNICATIONS
Post

Almost every town has a post and telephone office, always easily recognisable by the tall telecommunications tower rising above the building. Libya does not have a system of postal deliveries to street addresses, only post-office boxes. Make sure that you write the post-office-box number and city on the envelope. In the Fezzan, many addressees use the French equivalent, BP, followed by the number of the box and the town.

Collecting Libyan Stamps

Philatelists will find old Libyan stamps hard to come by, but scouring the old shops of the souqs in Tripoli's medina can yield some rewarding results. You may come across postage stamps that were used in Ottoman times (purely Turkish stamps with no Libyan subject matter). More likely, though still rare, are the Italian stamps from 1909 on which the word 'Italy' was overprinted with 'Tripoli di Barbaria' or 'Benghazi di Barbara'. After 1912, the name 'Libia' began to appear on stamps, along with Tripolitania, Cyrenaica and Fezzan, although the subject matter was still Italian. It was not until 1951 that Libyan subjects started to appear.

Postal Rates It costs 30 piastres (0.3LD, or 300 dirhams) to send a postcard to most places, including Europe and Australia. Sending letters is similarly cheap, generally between 50 piastres and 1LD. Sending parcels is unfortunately not so economical, with 1kg boxes costing 12LD to send to Europe and 40LD to Australia – and it only gets worse from there. DHL and other courier rates are prohibitive (148/188LD to send 1kg to Europe/Australia). The bottom line is, buy a cheap bag to carry any souvenirs out of the country, at least until you get to a neighbouring country.

Sending Mail The Libyan postal system is slow but reliable. Every year, we hear of a few postcards or letters that go astray, so if the letter is an important one always make a copy before putting it in the box. Postcards and letters sent from the central post offices in Tripoli or Benghazi usually reach their destination within a couple of weeks, while sending from a post office in a small town could take a lot longer – one we sent from Susa took five weeks to reach London. Always hand your mail to a post-office worker (never leave it in a post box), and write the address details as clearly as possible; if you can, write the name of the country in Arabic.

There are suspicions among travellers that mail never reaches its destination because it has been vetted by the Libyan authorities. We have absolutely no evidence to support this claim, but it probably is best to avoid saying anything controversial. Sending cash in the mail is never a good idea.

Receiving Mail There are generally reliable poste restante services (letters only) at the central post offices in Tripoli (Maidan al-Jezayir) and Benghazi (Sharia Omar al-Mukhtar). Address mail to:

Your Name
Poste Restante
Main Post Office
Tripoli (or Benghazi)
Libya (GSPLAJ)

Having your mail sent to your hotel or the tour company organising your trip is likely to be more reliable. Make sure you let them know that you're expecting mail, and get the sender to post it up to a month ahead and with your date of arrival written on the envelope. If you're only in Libya for a couple of weeks, it is probably not worth trying to organise this. If something's urgent, a fax is more certain to reach you.

Telephone

Libya's phone system has improved dramatically in recent years, and stories of waiting hours for a connection are a thing of the past. All phone calls, whether international or domestic, are best made at the government telephone offices attached to any post office.

Calls within Libya invariably receive instant connections and are quite cheap (around 0.25LD, or 25 piastres).

To make an international call, go to the counter, write out the number in full for the clerk who will make the connection, and then take the call in the allocated private booth. After completing the call, you pay at the counter. Connections are usually fast and rarely cost more than 1LD per minute to anywhere in the world. Only at the main telephone office in Tripoli are you likely to have to wait in line. There are also private telephone offices around most towns, but the only reason you're likely to need them is when the government telephone office is

closed. Calls at these private offices are more expensive (sometimes 2LD per minute) than at the government offices and there is often a three-minute minimum. Avoid making international phone calls from hotels, where the rates can be ridiculous.

You're unlikely to get coverage for your mobile phone in Libya.

Fax

The best places from which to send faxes are also the government telephone offices. For international faxes, the cost depends on how long the fax takes to go through (ie, the number of pages and how much writing is on the page). An international fax will rarely cost more than 2LD and 0.5LD for a fax within Libya. Again, avoid sending a fax from your hotel. If you're stuck, your tour company may be willing to help out.

The main post office in Tripoli, on Maidan al-Jezayir, provides a very handy fax restante service (fax 021-3331199, 3340040). For a small fee (no more than 1LD), staff will hold faxes for up to one month. It's in the main hall of the post office (not the telephone office) – look for the 'Fax Service' sign in English.

Email & Internet Access

Libya has joined the Internet revolution with cybercafes present in, at the time of writing, Al-Bayda, Al-Khoms, Benghazi, Gharyan, Misrata, Tobruk, Tripoli and Ubari; more are likely to spring up by the time you read this. Costs range from 2LD to 5LD per hour and the connections are generally pretty fast.

If you intend to rely on cybercafes and you don't have a Web-based email address (eg, Hotmail or Yahoo), you'll need to carry three pieces of information with you to enable you to access your Internet mail account: your incoming (POP or IMAP) mail server name, your account name and your password. Your Internet service provider or network supervisor will be able to give you these. Armed with this information, you should be able to access your Internet mail account from any Internet-connected machine in the world, provided it runs some kind of email software. It pays to become familiar with the process for doing this before you leave home.

Unless you're travelling in Libya for a prolonged period, taking a portable computer is not worth the hassle. Customs officials are often still suspicious of computers. Once you're inside the country, most international servers do not have reciprocal arrangements with servers in Libya, even those with global roaming facilities.

If you plan to carry your notebook or palmtop computer with you, remember that the power supply voltage in Libya may vary from that at home, risking damage to your equipment. The best investment is a universal AC adaptor for your appliance, which will enable you to plug it in anywhere without frying the innards. You'll also need a plug adaptor for Libya – buy it before you leave home. For more information on travelling with a portable computer, see W www.teleadapt .com or W www.warrior.com.

DIGITAL RESOURCES

The World Wide Web is a rich resource for travellers. You can research your trip, hunt down bargain air fares, book hotels, check on weather conditions or chat with locals and other travellers about the best places to visit (or avoid). There's no better place to start than the Lonely Planet Web site (W www.lonelyplanet.com). Here you'll find succinct summaries on travelling to most places on earth, postcards from other travellers and the Thorn Tree bulletin board, where you can ask questions before you go or dispense advice when you get back.

You can also find travel news and updates to many of our most popular guidebooks, and the subWWWay section links you to the most useful travel resources elsewhere on the Web.

Some of the better Libya-specific Web sites include:

153 Club Named after the original Michelin map of the Sahara, this club runs a high quality Sahara Web site.
  W www.manntaylor.com/153.html
Libya Net Most of the links are in Arabic, but there are some excellent sections on music,

painting and literature.
  W www.libyanet.com
Libya Online Another good directory devoted to music, business and travel.
  W www.libyaonline.com/
Libya Our Home Arguably the most extensive range of links on Libya, with sections on history, the arts, sport, human rights and travel.
  W http://ourworld.compuserve.com/homepages/ dr_ibrahim_ighneiwa
Libya Resources on the Internet This is a broad-ranging site, with a focus on business and links to other relevant sites.
  W www.geocities.com/LibyaPage/
Libyana Another excellent site devoted to Libyan arts, especially music and poetry.
  W www.libyana.org
More about Libya Download *The Green Book*, hear speeches by Colonel Gaddafi and visit the Leptis Magna virtual museum.
  W www.geocities.com/athens/8744/my links1.htm
Sahara el-Kebira Italian-language site devoted to the Sahara.
  W www.sahara.it
Sahara Info German-language site devoted to the Sahara.
  W www.sahara-info.ch
Sahara Overland A good site for desert enthusiasts, with up-to-date travel reports and news.
  W www.sahara-overland.com
Society for Libyan Studies Useful for researchers and those interested in the archaeological work being undertaken in Libya.
  W www.britac3.britac.ac.uk/institutes/libya/ index.html

BOOKS

There is an excellent range of books about Libya, ranging from old travelogues by intrepid travellers to those dissecting Libya's modern political history. The best place to start looking for some of these is Darf Publishers Ltd (☎ 020-7431 7009, fax 020-7431 7655), 277 West End Lane, West Hampstead, London NW6. It specialises in books on Libya. Although some of its titles are available in its bookshop (West End Lane Books), first ask for a copy of its comprehensive catalogue.

Librarie du Maghreb (☎ 020-7388 1840), 45 Burton St, London WC1H, is run by friendly Mohamed Ben Madawi and stocks an excellent selection of hard-to-find books on Libya, North Africa and Islam. Another good place to try is Al-Hoda (☎ 020-7240 8381, fax 020-7497 0180), 76–78 Charing Cross Road, London WC2H. Check out its Web site at Ⓦ www.alhoda.com.

Inside Libya, there are small selections of books in the gift shops of the larger hotels, but undoubtedly the best bookshop is Fergiani's in Tripoli (see the Tripoli chapter for details), which publishes many of the titles offered under the Darf Publishers imprint.

Lonely Planet

Lonely Planet has *Egypt* and *Tunisia* guides. For coverage of the entire Middle East from Egypt to Iran, Lonely Planet's *Middle East* contains the most comprehensive coverage, while for the African continent, pick up *Africa on a shoestring*.

Lonely Planet also publishes an *Egyptian Arabic Phrasebook*, which is equally useful in Libya.

Guidebooks

If you're planning a major expedition in the Sahara with your own vehicle, *Sahara Overland – A Route & Planning Guide* by Chris Scott provides comprehensive information as well as five route descriptions (including GPS coordinates) within Libya. For non–English speakers, German company Reisehandbuch publishes *Libyen* (4th edition). There are some good specialist publications in Italian published under the Polaris or Appunti di Viaggio imprint. These include *Libia del sud-ovest: Il Fezzan* and *Libia del sud-est*, both of which provide GPS coordinates for the serious desert expeditioner.

Travel

Around the Shores of the Mediterranean by Eric Newby. Entertaining account of the writer's visit to Libya before the tourists arrived.

Desert Encounter by Knud Holmboe. Classic and sympathetic account of a journey across Libya and one of the few first-hand accounts of the Italian occupation of Libya in the early 1930s.

Difficult & Dangerous Roads – Hugh Clapperton's Travels in Sahara & Fezzan 1822–25 by Hugh Clapperton. Sometimes cranky, but a highly readable account of Clapperton's journeys through the Libyan Sahara.

Journal of Frederick Horneman's Travels from Cairo to Mourzouk 1797–8 by Frederick Horneman. Interesting glimpse of a caravan journey in the Fezzan through European eyes.

Narrative of a Ten-Years Residence at Tripoli in Africa from the correspondence of the family of the late Richard Tully. Fascinating, if eccentric, insights into Libya in the 1780s with unparalleled access to the court of the Turkish Pasha.

South from Barbary by Justin Marozzi. Account of an epic journey by camel from Ghadames to Al-Kufra containing a wealth of historical detail, though it reads a little like a boy's own adventure at times.

Tripoli the Mysterious by Mabel Loomis Todd. Alternately fascinating and quaint account of Libya in the early 20th century.

History

Fazzan under the Rule of the Awlad Muhammad by Habib Wada'a El-Hesnawi. Hard-to-find text which is the most comprehensive study of Fezzani history.

The Garamantes of Southern Libya by Charles Daniels. The ancient history of the Garamantian desert empire.

Historical Dictionary of Libya (3rd edition) by Ronald St Bruce. Good reference for information on everything from the Abbasid dynasty to Libya's relationship with the United States.

Libya – A Modern History by John Wright. Detailed and accessible account of the revolution and Gaddafi's rise to power.

Omar al-Mukhtar – The Italian Reconquest of Libya by Enzo Santarelli et al. One of the few European histories to cast light on the brutality of colonial rule; contains a transcript of Omar al-Mukhtar's trial.

A Travellers' History of North Africa by Barnaby Rogerson. Authoritative and readable history of the region.

With Rommel's Army in Libya by Laszlo Almasy. Recent analysis of the WWII North African campaign.

Archaeology

African Rock Art by David Coulson & Alec Campbell. Beautifully illustrated study with a section on Libya's rock art.

Libia arte rupestre del Sahara published by Polaris. Useful Italian-language study of the rock art of the Jebel Acacus.

Libya – The Lost Cities of the Roman Empire by Robert Polidori et al. Superb book describing Libya's Greek and Roman sites, rich with detailed research and great photography.

Libyan Studies Periodical published by the Society for Libyan Studies dealing primarily with archaeological themes.

Sabratha, Leptis Magna and Cyrene & Apollonia by Polaris. Detailed, pocket-sized series in English, Italian and French, which is a great companion for visiting the ancient cities.

The Secret of the Desert: The Rock Art of Messak Settafet and Messak Mellet, Libya by Rudiger & Gabrielle Lutz. Another worthwhile explanation of the Fezzan's rock art.

Politics

The Green Book by Mu'ammar Gaddafi. Lays out the philosophical basis that underpins Colonel Gaddafi's Libya.

Libya Since Independence – Oil & State-Building by Dirk Vanderwalle. Interesting for its examination of the impact of oil on Libya's rapid transformation since independence.

Libya – The Struggle for Survival by Geoff Simons. A critical look at the American obsession with Colonel Gaddafi as well as providing a detailed historical background.

Libya's Qaddafi – The Politics of Contradiction by Mansour O El-Kikhia. One of the more penetrating and readable accounts of Libya under Colonel Gaddafi.

The Maverick State by Guy Arnold. Looks at Libya's relations with the rest of the world against the backdrop of *The Green Book*, Cold War politics and the Lockerbie affair.

Qaddafi and the Libyan Revolution: The First

Full Length Biography by David Blundy & Andrew Lycett. Outdated, but considered the most authoritative biography of the Libyan leader's early years.

Women at Arms – Is Ghadafi a Feminist? by Maria Graeff-Wassink. Intriguing look at the Libyan government's policies towards women.

Fiction

Ismailia Eclipse: Poems by Khaled Mattawa. Important contribution to the literature of Libyan exile by Benghazi-born poet who left Libya at age 15.

Libyan Stories – Twelve Short Stories from Libya edited by Ahmed Fagih. One of the few collections available in English, with an excellent introduction to some of Libya's best-known writers.

A Visa for Ahmed: Escape from Libya by Charles E Gustafson. Marginally the best of the sensationalist novels written about Libya.

Wildlife

Libyan Mammals by Ernst Hufnagle. Difficult to find and in need of an update, but the only comprehensive look published in English on Libya's wildlife.

FILMS

The most famous film *said* to have taken place in Libya, *The English Patient*, was actually filmed in Tunisia. The most informative movie about Libya (and it was actu-

---

The Cult of *The Green Book*

When Colonel Gaddafi re-emerged from the desert in the mid 1970s, he literally dismantled the entire structure of the Libyan state at one stroke. Even his closest revolutionary partners didn't know what was coming. He had withdrawn to the desert for months on end, thinking and writing. The product of this labour was the slender volume *The Green Book*. Between its covers was the blueprint for Gaddafi's vision of 'a peoples' power', or a Jamahiriya (a 'state of the masses'). Not capitalist and not communist, it was the 'Third Universal Theory', as he modestly called it; the solution not only to Libya's, but also the world's, problems.

The Green Book, with a strong underpinning of nationalism and religion, offers guidance, not only in the economic and political spheres, but also in the areas of sport, men and women, and the home and family. Sayings from *The Green Book* can be seen everywhere in Libya such as: 'Partners not wage-workers' and 'Committees everywhere'.

The Green Book has been translated into 84 languages (including Hebrew). Reports in the 1980s from London told of bookshops giving the books away after mass deliveries by the Libyan People's Bureau. *The Green Book* has spawned thousands of studies, theses and commentaries, enough to fill the library at *The Green Book* Studies Centre. Centres like this, known as *matabas*, dissect and promote the Colonel's volume. The mataba also plays the role of a 'party' meeting hall in this no-party state. Just for something different, these buildings are partly green in colour – easily recognisable.

ally filmed in the country) is *Lion of the Desert*, dating from 1979 and starring Anthony Quinn. It features some good footage of the Cyrenaican countryside, especially Wadi al-Kuf, and is generally historically accurate. Also worth a look is *A Yank in Libya*.

NEWSPAPERS & MAGAZINES

There is only one locally produced English-language newspaper, the fortnightly *Tripoli Post* (0.5LD), in Libya and it can be almost impossible to find. It only started up at the beginning of 2001, so distribution may become more widespread than the newsagent on Sharia Mohammed Megharief in Tripoli, where we found it. It's not exactly a riveting read – it can only get better. Top-heavy on propaganda, it nonetheless contains some interesting articles on African unity, as well as reasonable coverage of Libyan business, politics, sports and the arts. It also has a fledgling classified section, which could also be useful.

Surprisingly, given that they're also largely devoted to propaganda, the most recent issues of *Time* and *Newsweek* (1.5LD each) can be found for sale in the lobbies of some of the more upmarket hotels in Tripoli, Benghazi and Sebha, as well as a few stalls around Tripoli.

In Arabic, there are plenty of locally produced newspapers and magazines; all are government-run. *Ash-Shams* (The Sun) was started by Colonel Gaddafi before the revolution and is still in print. It contains sections on government, sport and social events and costs 0.25LD.

Other prominent newspapers include: *Al-Fajr Al-Jadid* (New Dawn), a daily that specialises in sport; *Az-Zahf Al-Akhdar* (The Green March), also published daily as the ideological journal of the Revolutionary Committees; and *Al-Jamahiriya*, a weekly publication that has broad political and social coverage and is also published by the Revolutionary Committees.

Each city also has its own local newspapers. Magazines that might be of interest include *La* (No), which is aimed at women and deals with social issues, while *Al-'Amt*

is a children's magazine devoted to cartoons and games. *Al-Amal* (Hope) is also for children (monthly).

Other than that, there's little more than specialist industry magazines, which must be exciting for someone.

RADIO & TV

Like all media in Libya, radio and television stations are government-owned and content is strictly controlled. As the sign says in Tripoli airport: 'Democracy means popular rule not popular expression'.

Radio

At last count, Libya had 17 AM stations and four FM channels. Each station does a mix of news (including sport) and music; however, there are no dedicated music channels. There are also some local radio stations for specific towns. All programs are in Arabic. Libya's Voice of Africa broadcasts in a number of languages across Africa.

The BBC World Service and most European international radio services can be heard in most locations in Libya if you have your own short-wave radio.

TV

Libyan television is nothing to write home about. Recurring themes include highlights of the Colonel receiving the praises of the people in a tent. As one of our readers observed, 'Libyan TV must be high on the list of the world's dreariest'.

The only reason to watch local television is for the nightly news at 9pm, which is delivered in Arabic and then directly interpreted into English and then French. It can be an interesting way of viewing the world through the eyes of the Libyan government. There is also a Libyan satellite channel, Al-Fa'adiya al-Jamahiriya.

Most Libyans have satellite dishes (which are legal) and are free to watch what they want. Visitors are generally restricted to watching local programs on the principle that they have much to learn about Libya. It seems lost on government planners that their dreary television broadcasts are a poor advertisement for the country. Some of the more upmarket hotel rooms have televisions that access CNN, BBC and other international television channels.

PHOTOGRAPHY & VIDEO
Film & Equipment

Tripoli and, to a lesser extent, Benghazi, has some high-quality photo shops and studios, with some having been set up by representatives of the international film companies Fuji, Konica and Agfa. Apart from film from these specialised stores, the most commonly available print film is Konica – a roll of 36 costs about 3LD or up to 5LD in out-of-the-way places such as Ghat. Slide film is much more expensive and only available in Tripoli. Expect to pay 15LD to 18LD for a roll of 36-exposure Konica slide film. When buying slide film, make sure you open the canister to check you've received what you paid for, as we've had some reports of print film being sold inside Konica slide film packaging. For professional Fuji slide film, you could pay up to 50LD, so bring your own.

There are makeshift studios for developing print film in many towns throughout the country, although the quality is variable and you'd be better off waiting until you return to Tripoli, Benghazi or, better still, back home. The cheapest rate we found for developing print film was in Tripoli: 1.5LD to get 36 negatives processed plus 0.25LD for each 10cm by 15cm print. Processing generally takes a couple of days, but always check that the films will be processed at the shop and not sent away, as that can add considerably to developing times.

There are a few places that develop slide film. One is Mamer Seriya (see Film & Photography in the Tripoli chapter for details), which charges 20LD for a 36 unmounted slides. Most photo studios will also do a set of four passport photos for around 3LD.

If you have a video camera, you should also bring your own video film. You may get lucky at one of the better photo studios or an electronics store in one of Tripoli's more upmarket shopping centres, but don't count on finding what you need.

Technical Tips

Lonely Planet publishes *Travel Photography – A guide to taking better pictures* by renowned travel photographer Richard I'Anson; it's filled with useful tips.

For most of the year, lighting conditions during the day are good, so you can usually afford to use very low-speed film. If anything, the clear Libyan light can result in many first-time photographers over-exposing their photos. One of the main problems is that the strong sunlight throws reflections on the lens (preventable with a lens hood) or casts high-contrast shadows, which can spoil an otherwise good photograph. For most shots, however, the bright light around noon can make photos look washed out and lacking in depth; usually the best light conditions are just after sunrise and in the last hours before sunset.

Many mosques, museums and other buildings are poorly lit inside so you'll need a long exposure, a powerful flash or faster film to take decent pictures. A portable tripod can be very useful.

These days video cameras have amazingly sensitive microphones and you might be surprised by how much sound is picked up. This can be a problem if there is a lot of ambient noise: be careful in noisy streets. One good rule for beginners is to try to film in long takes without moving the camera around too much. Make sure you keep the batteries charged and bring the necessary charger, plugs and transformer.

Restrictions

You're likely to end up under temporary arrest and your film confiscated if you point your camera at military installations of any description, police stations, checkpoints and major ports. Most of these are easy to avoid, although police stations are often poorly signposted – ask if you're not sure.

One traveller told us about his experiences of the restrictions:

Towards the end of the trip I realised that I had very few photos of the giant posters of the 'great leader' (Colonel Gaddafi), which are all over the coast regions. At a roadblock I chanced my luck by getting my guide to ask if I could photograph a good one depicting the 'hero' of the Great Man-Made-River Project. The officer in charge said (as I well knew) that photography was forbidden near road blocks, but then went back into his office, ripped off the wall a large cardboard-backed picture of Gaddafi addressing the masses and presented it to me as a consolation prize!

David Boyall, Australia

Still and video photography is permitted in all museums, archaeological sites and the medinas of the Saharan oasis (eg, Ghadames and Ghat), but you must buy a ticket for 5LD for still cameras and 10LD for a video camera. Ticket-sellers usually loiter near the entrance, with the exception of the old Saharan towns – where word will get around that you're there and the ticket man will come to find you.

Photographing People

You should always ask permission before taking anyone's photo in Libya and never simply point your camera at someone. Most men are perfectly happy to have their photo taken, although you should still ask permission, especially in rural areas. Male travellers should never take photos of local women without first being granted express permission; this may be refused even for women photographers. Be particularly careful in crowded public areas where you may come across people in the crowd who object to you taking a photo, although this is rare. Places where this happened to us included Tripoli's medina and the open-air souq in Ghat.

Airport Security

All airports (and some upmarket hotels in Tripoli) have X-ray machines for checking luggage, but the guards are usually happy to inspect bags separately – always carry your films in your hand luggage. If you are leaving Libya by air, your bags will have to undergo two X-rays – one at customs and another to gain entry to the departure lounge. That said, we've had no reports of travellers' films being damaged by Libyan X-ray machines.

TIME

Despite its size, Libya has only one time zone – it's two hours ahead of Greenwich Mean Time (GMT). Until relatively recently, Libyans moved their clocks forward one hour during summer. Now offices and their employees simply adjust their attendance times to suit climatic conditions.

When it's noon in Tripoli, the time elsewhere is:

Cairo	noon
London	10am
New York	5am
Paris	11am
Sydney	8pm
Tunis	11am

ELECTRICITY

The electricity current in Libya is 220V to 240V AC, 50Hz. Most of the country operates at 220V but cities like Al Marj, Benghazi, Derna, Sebha and parts of Tripoli sometimes use 230V or 240V at 50Hz. Bring along an adaptor (the same as for continental Europe) and transformer, if necessary, because they are hard to find in Libya. Power blackouts are rare in Libya.

WEIGHTS & MEASURES

Libya uses the metric system. There is a standard conversion table inside the back cover of this book.

LAUNDRY

There are reliable laundries in most Libyan cities, although they are rarely signposted. Your tour leader can usually point you in the right direction, or ask any local for *ash-sharouk maasella* or *launderie*. Standard washing costs include 1.5LD each for shirts and pants, and 0.5LD per pair of socks and underwear. That may seem expensive, especially if you want to get a whole load done, but the chances are that your clothes will be dry-cleaned and ironed (sometimes even your underwear!). To get a suit dry-cleaned costs around 2.75LD. Hotel laundry services in the larger hotels tend to be expensive. It is usually no problem to wash your underwear and socks in your hotel room; soaps and detergents are available in most grocery stores.

In the Fezzan, washing your clothes (and yourself) at the desert well of Imenineh in the Jebel Acacus rates as one of life's best washing experiences.

TOILETS

Libya is in desperate need of public toilets – there simply aren't any. If you're out and about, ask at a restaurant, teahouse, mosque or hotel if you can use the toilet. Ask for *al-hammam*, *mirhab* or *tuvalet*. One place where this option doesn't exist is in the old city of Ghadames, where going to the toilet in the ancient city is forbidden.

Most hotels have sit-down flush toilets – in the better ones you may even be presented with a choice between a toilet and a bidet! In cheaper hotels and in some mosques or restaurants (especially in the Fezzan), there are usually squat toilets. In all but the budget hotels, toilet paper is provided. Remember that some toilets are not designed for paper. If you're not sure, use the rubbish bin.

HEALTH

Libya is generally a healthy country in which to travel and we receive very few reports of travellers falling ill. Standards of hygiene are usually high and the main risk to most travellers is exhaustion from overdoing it in the sun. The information that follows is included in case you're the unlucky, rare person who goes down with something worse.

Predeparture Planning

Immunisations Plan ahead for getting your vaccinations: You may require more than

---

Everyday Health

Normal body temperature is up to 37°C (98.6°F); more than 2°C (4°F) higher indicates a high fever. The normal adult pulse rate is 60 to 100 per minute (children 80 to 100, babies 100 to 140). As a general rule, the pulse increases about 20 beats per minute for each 1°C (2°F) rise in fever.

Respiration (breathing) rate is also an indicator of illness. Count the number of breaths per minute: Between 12 and 20 is normal for adults and older children (up to 30 for younger children, 40 for babies). People with a high fever or serious respiratory illness breathe more quickly than normal.

---

one injection and some vaccinations should not be given together. Note that some vaccinations should not be given during pregnancy or to people with allergies – discuss this with your doctor. It is recommended that you seek medical advice at least six weeks before travel. Be aware that there is often a greater risk of disease with children and during pregnancy.

Discuss your requirements with your doctor, but vaccinations you should consider for Libya include the following:

Diphtheria & Tetanus Vaccinations for these two diseases are usually combined and are recommended for everyone. After an initial course of three injections (usually given in childhood), boosters are necessary every 10 years.

Hepatitis A Hepatitis A vaccine (eg, Avaxim, Havrix 1440 or VAQTA) provides long-term immunity (possibly more than 10 years) after an initial injection and a booster at six to 12 months. Alternatively, an injection of gamma globulin can provide short-term protection against hepatitis A – two to six months, depending on the dose given. It is not a vaccine, but is ready-made antibody collected from blood donations. It is reasonably effective and, unlike the vaccine, it is protective immediately. However, because it is a blood product, there are current concerns about its long-term safety. Hepatitis A vaccine is also available in a combined form, Twinrix, with hepatitis B vaccine. Three injections over a six-month period are required, the first two providing substantial protection against hepatitis A.

Hepatitis B Travellers who should consider vaccination against hepatitis B include those on a long trip, especially as blood transfusions may not be adequately screened or where sexual contact or needle-sharing is a possibility. Vaccination involves three injections, with a booster at 12 months.

Polio Everyone should keep up to date with this vaccination, which is normally given in childhood. A booster every 10 years maintains immunity.

Rabies Vaccination should be considered by those who will spend a month or longer in Libya – especially if they are cycling, handling animals, caving or travelling to remote areas – and for children (who may not report a bite). Pretravel rabies vaccination involves having three injections over 21 to 28 days. If someone who has been vaccinated is bitten or scratched by an animal, they will require two booster injections of vaccine; those not vaccinated require more.

Typhoid Vaccination against typhoid may be required if you are travelling for more than a couple of weeks in Libya. It is now available either as an injection or as capsules that are taken orally.

Malaria Medication Discuss with your doctor whether you will require antimalarial medication, although the risk in Libya is extremely small. Antimalarial drugs do not prevent you from being infected, rather they kill the malaria parasites during a stage in their development and significantly reduce your risk of becoming very ill. Expert advice on medication should always be sought before you depart.

Health Insurance Make sure that you have adequate health insurance. See Travel Insurance under Visas & Documents earlier in this chapter for details.

Travel Health Guides Lonely Planet's *Healthy Travel Africa* is a handy, pocket-sized book packed with useful information including pretrip planning, emergency first aid, immunisation and disease information and what to do if you get sick on the road. *Travel with Children* from Lonely Planet also includes advice on travel health for younger children.

There are also some excellent travel health sites on the Internet. From the

Medical Kit Check List

Following is a list of items you should consider including in your medical kit – consult your pharmacist for brands available in your country.

☐ **Aspirin or paracetamol (acetaminophen in the USA)** – for pain or fever

☐ **Antihistamine** – for allergies, eg, hay fever; to ease the itch from insect bites or stings; and to prevent motion sickness

☐ **Cold and flu tablets, throat lozenges and nasal decongestant**

☐ **Multivitamins** – consider for long trips, when dietary vitamin intake may be inadequate

☐ **Antibiotics** – consider including these if you're travelling well off the beaten track; see your doctor, as they must be prescribed, and carry the prescription with you

☐ **Loperamide or diphenoxylate** – 'blockers' for diarrhoea

☐ **Prochlorperazine or metaclopramide** – for nausea and vomiting

☐ **Rehydration mixture** – to prevent dehydration, which may occur, for example, during bouts of diarrhoea; particularly important when travelling with children

☐ **Insect repellent, sunscreen, lip balm and eye drops**

☐ **Calamine lotion, sting relief spray or aloe vera** – to ease irritation from sunburn and insect bites or stings

☐ **Antifungal cream or powder** – for fungal skin infections and thrush

☐ **Antiseptic (such as povidone-iodine)** – for cuts and grazes

☐ **Bandages, Band-Aids (plasters) and other wound dressings**

☐ **Water purification tablets or iodine**

☐ **Scissors, tweezers and a thermometer** – note that mercury thermometers are prohibited by airlines

☐ **Sterile kit** – in case you need injections in a country with medical hygiene problems; discuss with your doctor

Lonely Planet home page there are links at **W** www.lonelyplanet.com/weblinks/wlheal .htm to the World Health Organization and the US Centers for Disease Control & Prevention.

Other Preparations Make sure you're healthy before you start travelling. If you are going on a long trip, make sure your teeth are OK. If you wear glasses, take a spare pair and your prescription. If you require a particular medication, take an adequate supply, as it may not be available locally. Take part of the packaging showing the generic name rather than the brand, which will make getting replacements easier. It's a good idea to have a legible prescription or letter from your doctor to show that you legally use the medication, to avoid any problems.

Basic Rules

Food Generally, if a place looks clean and well run, and the vendor also looks clean and healthy, then the food is probably safe. In general, places that are packed with travellers or locals will be fine, while empty restaurants are questionable. The food in busy restaurants is cooked and eaten quite quickly with little standing around so it is probably not reheated.

Water Tap water in Libya is generally safe to drink, although most people choose to drink bottled water because the tap water tends to be salty and not particularly pleasant. Bottled water is universally available in the small grocery stores in just about every Libyan town. When you're in the desert, the water your guide gets from underground wells is likely to be of similar quality to bottled water.

Medical Problems & Treatment

Self-diagnosis and treatment can be risky, so you should always seek medical help. An embassy, consulate or five-star hotel can usually recommend a local doctor or clinic. Although we do give drug dosages in this section, they are for emergency use only. Correct diagnosis is vital.

Note that antibiotics should ideally be administered only under medical supervision. Take only the recommended dose at the prescribed intervals and use the whole course, even if the illness seems to be cured earlier. Stop immediately if there are any serious reactions and don't use the anti-

biotic at all if you are unsure that you have the correct one. Some people are allergic to commonly prescribed antibiotics such as penicillin; carry this information (eg, on a bracelet) when travelling.

Most Libyan medicines are labelled only in Arabic; if you do purchase anything be careful to check the expiry date and that correct storage conditions have been followed. If you're looking for a particular medicine over the counter, ask the pharmacist using the generic name (used throughout this section) rather than its Western brand name, which may not be recognised in Libya.

Medical Facilities If you are mildly sick, the best place to start is with a representative of your tour company who will be able to take you to a reputable doctor or arrange for one to visit you at your hotel; they can also help with the necessary interpretation if the doctor only speaks Arabic. If your situation is serious, contact your embassy, which should be able to recommend a good doctor or hospital. If the illness or injury is life-threatening, contact your embassy immediately and consider flying home (assuming you have insurance to cover the cost).

The standard of medical facilities is quite high in Libya, with many of the doctors having been educated at overseas institutions. Even many small towns have well-equipped clinics, although in serious cases the best place to be is Tripoli or Benghazi.

Environmental Hazards

Sunburn It is very easy to get sunburned in Libya, especially in summer. Always use a sunscreen, a hat and a barrier cream for your nose and lips. Calamine lotion or a commercial after-sun preparation is good for mild sunburn. Protect your eyes with good quality sunglasses.

Heat Exhaustion There is a high risk of heat exhaustion (caused by dehydration and salt deficiency) if you're travelling in Libya, especially in summer. Take time to acclimatise to high temperatures, drink sufficient liquids and do not do anything too physically demanding.

Salt deficiency is characterised by fatigue, lethargy, headaches, giddiness and muscle cramps; salt tablets may help, but adding extra salt to your food is better.

Heatstroke This serious, occasionally fatal, condition can occur if your body's heat-regulating mechanism breaks down and your body temperature rises to dangerous levels. Long, continuous periods of exposure to high temperatures and insufficient fluids can leave you vulnerable to heatstroke.

The symptoms are feeling unwell, not sweating very much (or at all) and a high body temperature (39°C to 41°C or 102°F to 106°F). Where sweating has ceased, the skin becomes flushed and red. Severe, throbbing headaches and lack of coordination will also occur, and the sufferer may be confused or aggressive. Eventually the victim will become delirious or convulse. Hospitalisation is essential, but in the interim get victims out of the sun, remove their clothing, cover them with a wet sheet or towel and fan continually. Give fluids if they are conscious.

Prickly Heat Excessive perspiration trapped under the skin can cause prickly heat, an itchy rash. It usually strikes people who have just arrived in a hot climate. Keeping cool, bathing often, drying the skin and using a mild talcum or prickly heat powder may help, as may renting an air-conditioned room.

Motion Sickness Eating lightly before and during a trip will reduce the chances of motion sickness. If you are prone to motion sickness try to find a place that minimises movement – near the wing on aircraft, close to midships on boats, near the centre on buses. Fresh air usually helps; reading and cigarette smoke don't. Commercial motion-sickness preparations, which can cause drowsiness, have to be taken before the trip commences. Ginger (available in capsule form) and peppermint (including mint-flavoured sweets) are natural preventatives.

Infectious Diseases

Diarrhoea Simple things like a change of water, food or climate can all cause a mild bout of diarrhoea, but a few rushed toilet trips with no other symptoms is not indicative of a major problem.

Dehydration is the main danger with any diarrhoea, particularly in children or the elderly, as dehydration can occur quite quickly. Under all circumstances *fluid replacement* (at least equal to the volume being lost) is the most important thing to remember. Weak, black tea with a little sugar, soda water, or soft drinks allowed to go flat and diluted 50% with clean water are all good. With severe diarrhoea a rehydrating solution is preferable to replace minerals and salts lost. Commercially available oral rehydration salts (ORS) are very useful; add them to boiled or bottled water. In an emergency you can make up a solution of six teaspoons of sugar and a half teaspoon of salt to a litre of boiled or bottled water. Your urine is the best guide to the adequacy of replacement – small amounts of concentrated urine suggest that you need to drink more fluids. Keep drinking small amounts often and stick to a bland diet as you recover.

Gut-paralysing drugs such as loperamide or diphenoxylate can be used to bring relief from the symptoms, although they do not actually cure the problem. Only use these drugs if you do not have access to toilets, eg, if you *must* travel. Note that these drugs are not recommended for children under 12 years.

Medical Treatment In certain situations antibiotics may be required: diarrhoea with blood or mucus (dysentery), any diarrhoea with fever, profuse watery diarrhoea, persistent diarrhoea not improving after 48 hours and severe diarrhoea. These suggest a more serious cause and in these situations gut-paralysing drugs should be avoided.

In these situations, a stool test may be necessary to diagnose what bug is causing your diarrhoea, so seek medical help urgently. Where this is not possible the recommended drugs for bacterial diarrhoea are norfloxacin 400mg twice daily for three days or ciprofloxacin 500mg twice daily for five days. These are not recommended for children or pregnant women. The drug of choice for children would be co-trimoxazole with dosage dependent on weight. A five-day course is given. Ampicillin or amoxycillin may be given in pregnancy, but medical care is necessary.

Persistent Diarrhoea Two other causes of persistent diarrhoea in travellers are giardiasis and amoebic dysentery.

Giardiasis is caused by a common parasite, *Giardia lamblia*. Symptoms include stomach cramps, nausea, a bloated stomach, watery, foul-smelling diarrhoea and frequent gas. Giardiasis can appear several weeks after you have been exposed to the parasite. The symptoms may disappear for a few days and then return; this can go on for several weeks.

Amoebic dysentery, caused by the protozoan *Entamoeba histolytica*, is characterised by a gradual onset of low-grade diarrhoea, often with blood and mucus. Cramping abdominal pain and vomiting are less likely than in other types of diarrhoea, and fever may not be present. It will persist until treated and can recur and cause other health problems.

You should seek medical advice if you think you have giardiasis or amoebic dysentery, but where this is not possible, tinidazole or metronidazole are the recommended drugs. Treatment is a 2g single dose of tinidazole or 250mg of metronidazole three times daily for five to 10 days.

Fungal Infections Occurring more commonly in hot weather, fungal infections are usually found on the scalp, between the toes (athlete's foot) or fingers, in the groin and on the body (ringworm). You get ringworm (which is a fungal infection, not a worm) from infected animals or other people. Moisture encourages these infections.

To prevent fungal infections, wear loose, comfortable clothes, avoid artificial fibres, wash frequently and dry yourself carefully. If you do get an infection, wash the infected area at least daily with a disinfectant or medicated soap and water, and rinse and dry well. Apply an antifungal cream or powder like tolnaftate. Try to expose the infected area to air or sunlight as much as possible and wash all towels and underwear in hot water, change them often and let them dry in the sun.

Hepatitis This is a general term for inflammation of the liver. It is a common disease worldwide. There are several different viruses that cause hepatitis and they differ in the way that they are transmitted. The symptoms are similar in all forms of the illness, and include fever, chills, headache, fatigue, feelings of weakness, and aches and pains, followed by loss of appetite, nausea, vomiting, abdominal pain, dark urine, light-coloured faeces, jaundiced (yellow) skin and yellowing of the whites of the eyes. People who have had hepatitis should avoid alcohol for some time after the illness, as the liver needs time to recover.

Hepatitis A is transmitted by contaminated food and drinking water. Seek medical advice, though there is not much you can do apart from resting, drinking lots of fluids, eating lightly and avoiding fatty foods.

Hepatitis E is transmitted in the same way as hepatitis A; it can be particularly serious in pregnant women.

There are almost 300 million chronic carriers of **hepatitis B** in the world. It is spread through contact with infected blood, blood products or through body fluids, for example, by sexual contact, unsterilised needles and blood transfusions, or contact with blood via small breaks in the skin (eg, shaving). The symptoms of hepatitis B may be more severe than type A and the disease can lead to long-term problems such as chronic liver damage, liver cancer or a long-term carrier state. **Hepatitis C and D** are spread in the same way as hepatitis B and can also lead to long-term complications.

There are vaccines against hepatitis A and B, but there are currently no vaccines against the other strains. Following the basic rules about food and water (to prevent hepatitis A and E) and avoiding risk situations (hepatitis B, C and D) are important preventative measures.

HIV & AIDS Infection with the human immunodeficiency virus (HIV) may lead to acquired immune deficiency syndrome (AIDS), which is a fatal disease. Any exposure to blood, blood products or body fluids may put the individual at risk. The disease is often transmitted through sexual contact or dirty needles – vaccinations, acupuncture, tattooing and body piercing can be potentially as dangerous as intravenous drug use. HIV/AIDS can also be spread through infected blood transfusions. If you do need an injection, ask to see the syringe unwrapped in front of you, or take a needle and syringe pack with you.

Fear of being infected with HIV should never preclude medical treatment for life threatening conditions.

Malaria This serious and potentially fatal disease is spread by mosquito bites. Up until the early 20th century, malaria was rife in some of the oases of the Fezzan, especially Murzuq and Wadi ash-Shatti. These days, the risk (restricted to a few lakes in the Sahara) is miniscule to the point that few doctors prescribe malaria medication for travel to Libya (a good repellent is preferable). However, you should obtain expert advice on malaria prevention before travelling to Libya.

Symptoms range from fever, chills and sweating, headache, diarrhoea and abdominal pains to a vague feeling of ill-health. Seek medical help immediately if you suspect you might have malaria. Without treatment malaria can rapidly become more serious and can be fatal.

If medical care is not available, malaria tablets can be used for treatment. You need to use a malaria tablet which is *different* from the one you were taking when you contracted malaria. The standard treatment dose of mefloquine is two 250mg tablets and a further two six hours later. For Fansidar, it's a single dose of three tablets. If you were previously taking mefloquine and cannot obtain Fansidar, then other alternatives are Malarone (atovaquone-proguanil; four tablets once daily for three days), halofantrine (three doses of two 250mg tablets every six hours) or quinine sulphate (600mg every six hours). There is a greater risk of

side effects with these dosages than in normal use if used with mefloquine, so medical advice is preferable. Be aware also that halofantrine is no longer recommended by the WHO as an emergency standby treatment, because of side effects, and should only be used if no other drugs are available.

You're advised to prevent mosquito bites at all times. The main messages are:

- Wear light-coloured clothing.
- Wear long trousers and long-sleeved shirts.
- Use mosquito repellents containing the compound DEET on exposed areas (prolonged overuse of DEET may be harmful, especially to children, but its use is considered preferable to being bitten by disease-transmitting mosquitoes).
- Avoid perfumes or aftershave.
- Use a mosquito net impregnated with mosquito repellent (permethrin) – it may be worth taking your own.
- Impregnating clothes with permethrin effectively deters mosquitoes and other insects.

Cuts, Bites & Stings

Cuts & Scratches Wash well and treat any cut or scratch with an antiseptic such as povidone-iodine. Where possible avoid bandages and elastic plasters, which can keep wounds wet.

Bedbugs & Lice Bedbugs live in various places, but particularly in dirty mattresses and bedding, evidenced by spots of blood on bedclothes or on the wall. Bedbugs leave itchy bites in neat rows. Calamine lotion or a sting relief spray may help.

All lice cause itching and discomfort. They make themselves at home in your hair (head lice), your clothing (body lice) or in your pubic hair (crabs). You catch lice through direct contact with infected people or by sharing combs, clothing and the like. Powder or shampoo treatment will kill the lice and infected clothing should then be washed in very hot, soapy water and left in the sun to dry.

Bites & Stings Bee and wasp stings are usually painful rather than dangerous. However, in people who are allergic to them severe breathing difficulties may occur and require urgent medical care. Calamine lotion or a sting relief spray will give relief and ice packs will reduce the pain and swelling. Scorpion stings are notoriously painful and can actually be fatal. Scorpions often shelter in shoes or clothing and are prevalent in the rocky *wadis* (dry river beds) of the Libyan Sahara.

See Less Common Diseases later for details of rabies, which is passed through animal bites.

Jellyfish Avoid contact with these sea creatures, which have stinging tentacles – seek local advice. A dousing in vinegar will deactivate any stingers which have not 'fired'. Calamine lotion, antihistamines and analgesics may reduce the reaction and relieve the pain.

Ticks You should always check all over your body if you have been walking through a potentially tick-infested area, as ticks can cause skin infections and other more serious diseases. If a tick is found attached, press down around the tick's head with tweezers, grab the head and gently pull upwards. Avoid pulling the rear of the body as this may squeeze the tick's gut contents through the attached mouth parts into the skin, increasing the risk of infection and disease. Smearing chemicals on the tick will not make it let go and is not recommended.

Snakes To minimise your chances of being bitten, always wear boots, socks and long trousers when walking through undergrowth or the rocky nooks and crannies of Wadi Methkandoush or the Jebel Acacus, where snakes may be present. Don't put your hands into holes and crevices, and be careful when collecting firewood.

Snake bites do not cause instantaneous death. Wrap the bitten limb tightly, as you would for a sprained ankle, and then attach a splint to immobilise it. Keep the victim still and seek medical help, if possible with the dead snake for identification. Don't attempt to catch the snake if there is a possibility of being bitten again. Tourniquets and sucking out the poison are now comprehensively discredited treatments.

Women's Health

Gynaecological Problems Antibiotic use, synthetic underwear, sweating and contraceptive pills can lead to fungal vaginal infections, especially when travelling in hot climates. Fungal infections are characterised by a rash, itch and discharge and can be treated with a vinegar or lemon-juice douche, or with yogurt. Nystatin, miconazole or clotrimazole pessaries or vaginal cream are the usual treatment. Maintaining good personal hygiene and wearing loose-fitting clothes and cotton underwear may help to prevent these infections.

Sexually transmitted infections are a major cause of vaginal problems. Symptoms include a smelly discharge, painful intercourse and sometimes a burning sensation when urinating. Medical attention should be sought and male sexual partners must also be treated. Besides abstinence, the best thing is to practise safer sex using condoms.

Pregnancy Pregnant women should think carefully about travelling to south-western Libya, as malaria (albeit a very small risk in Libya) may increase the risk of a stillborn child. Some vaccinations normally used to prevent serious diseases are not advisable during pregnancy.

Most miscarriages occur during the first three months of pregnancy. Miscarriage is not uncommon and can occasionally lead to severe bleeding. The last three months should be spent in reasonable distance of good medical care. A baby born as early as 24 weeks stands a chance of survival, but only in a good modern hospital. Pregnant women should avoid all unnecessary medication, although vaccinations and malarial prophylactics should still be taken where needed. Additional care should be taken to prevent illness and attention should be paid to diet and nutrition. Alcohol and nicotine, for example, should be avoided.

Less Common Diseases

The following diseases pose a small risk to travellers in Libya, and so are only mentioned in passing. Seek medical advice if you think you may have any of these diseases.

Leishmaniasis This is a group of parasitic diseases transmitted by sandflies, which are found in many parts of Africa, including Libya, and elsewhere. Cutaneous leishmaniasis affects the skin tissue, causing ulceration and disfigurement, and visceral leishmaniasis affects the internal organs. Seek medical advice, as laboratory testing is required for diagnosis and treatment. Avoiding sandfly bites is the best precaution. Bites are usually painless, itchy and a good reason to cover up and apply repellent.

Rabies This fatal viral infection is found in many countries. Many animals can be infected (such as dogs, cats, bats and monkeys) and it is their saliva which is infectious. Any bite, scratch or even lick from an animal should be cleaned immediately and thoroughly. Scrub with soap and running water, and then apply alcohol or iodine solution. Medical help should be sought promptly to receive a course of injections to prevent the onset of symptoms and death.

Tetanus This disease is caused by a germ that lives in soil and in the faeces of horses and other animals. It enters the body via breaks in the skin. The first symptom may be discomfort in swallowing, or stiffening of the jaw and neck; this is followed by painful convulsions of the jaw and whole body. The disease can be fatal. It can be prevented by vaccination.

Tuberculosis (TB) A bacterial infection usually transmitted from person to person by coughing, TB may also be transmitted through the consumption of unpasteurised milk. Milk that has been boiled is safe to drink, and the souring of milk to make yogurt or cheese also kills the bacilli. Travellers are usually not at great risk, as close household contact with the infected person is usually required before the disease is passed on. You may need to have a TB test before you travel as this can help diagnose the disease later if you become ill.

WOMEN TRAVELLERS
It is important for women travellers arriving from Tunisia or Egypt to remember that Libya is more conservative than either of those two countries, although it is far from the most conservative country in the region.

The influence of large numbers of tourists in Libya, and the surprising number of Libyans travelling to Europe for their holidays or business, has fostered a greater degree of latitude. This should not, however, be abused. Remember that Libyans are generally very discreet and, that if you step over the line, most will be too polite to say anything.

Trousers are perfectly OK to wear as long as they are loose-fitting. The same applies to T-shirts and other tops, although these should have sleeves to cover the upper arm. There is no need to cover your head,

---

Nutrition

If your diet is poor or limited in variety, if you're travelling hard and fast and therefore missing meals or if you simply lose your appetite, you can soon start to lose weight and place your health at risk.

Make sure your diet is well balanced. Cooked eggs, tofu, beans, lentils (dhal in India) and nuts are all safe ways to get protein. Fruit you can peel (bananas, oranges or mandarins, for example) is usually safe and a good source of vitamins. Melons can harbour bacteria in their flesh and are best avoided. Try to eat plenty of grains (including rice) and bread. Remember that although food is generally safer if it is cooked well, overcooked food loses much of its nutritional value. If your diet isn't well balanced or if your food intake is insufficient, it's a good idea to take vitamin and iron pills.

In hot climates make sure you drink enough – don't rely on feeling thirsty to indicate when you should drink. Not needing to urinate or voiding small amounts of very dark yellow urine is a danger sign. Always carry a water bottle with you on long trips. Excessive sweating can lead to loss of salt and therefore muscle cramping. Salt tablets are not a good idea as a preventative, but in places where salt is not used much, adding salt to food can help.

except when entering a mosque, although even in mosques it is not always required.

Swimsuits (and not bikinis) should definitely be worn only on the beach. Shorts (again, nothing too skimpy) are fine for desert expeditions when the only people around are other members of your party, but elsewhere even men in shorts will attract disbelieving looks.

For information on the availability of sanitary products such as tampons, see What to Bring under Planning earlier in this chapter.

Attitudes Towards Women

Libyan government policies in relation to women have, since the revolution, contributed to a less-misunderstood view of Western women than in some other countries of the region (see The Role of Women, under Society & Conduct in the Facts about Libya chapter). As a result, most female travellers, including those travelling on their own, have reported being treated with respect, with few incidents of unpleasant behaviour. When foreign visitors are introduced to Libyan men, men will in most circumstances shake hands with Western women as readily, and without hesitation, as with Western men. This is especially true of Libyans with any connection to the tourism industry.

Most Libyan restaurants do not have a segregated family area where women are expected to eat. Unlike many countries in the region, there is no need for single women to wear a wedding ring or carry a photo of their 'children' – most Libyans understand that Western societies have different rules – although travelling with a male friend can reduce further the small risk of problems. We haven't heard of unmarried couples encountering difficulties in getting accommodation or in other situations, although you should always be discreet.

On public transport, cramped shared taxis put travellers in closer proximity to other passengers than they would like and the occasional woman traveller has reported some wandering hands. On buses, the drivers will often take it upon themselves to make sure that space is made for you.

That said, some sectors of Libyan society remain traditional in both a religious and cultural sense. This can be difficult to predict, but, unusually, the cities can be more conservative, as one traveller reported:

The Libyan people are very curious and friendly, but as a woman I find Tripoli a little bit difficult, as the Libyan men can be a little too curious sometimes.

Anna Norman, Sweden

You are far more likely to come across women wearing the *burnous* (a white robe that covers the entire body with only one eye exposed) in Tripoli than you are elsewhere. Balancing the liberal and conservative strands of Libyan society is an inexact science, but one that causes few difficulties for the overwhelming number of female visitors to Libya.

Safety Precautions

The risk of serious assault in Libya is virtually nonexistent. Nonetheless, you should take the precautions of always locking your hotel room and never attempting to hitch if you are on your own. Lone female travellers will most likely feel uncomfortable staying in the really cheap hotels, especially those around city bus stations. This does not apply to most *buyut ash-shabaab* (youth hostels), where there are often designated sections for women.

If you are harassed, tell your unwanted friend firmly, but politely, to desist and try to enlist the support of other Libyans, most of whom will be appalled enough to shame the man responsible. If you scream blue murder, the situation could get out of hand. If he persists, mentioning the police will most likely have the desired effect.

GAY & LESBIAN TRAVELLERS

Homosexuality is illegal in Libya, but it's an issue that rarely makes it into the public domain. Occasionally, you may see groups of Libyan men holding hands, but this is not an indication of homosexuality, merely friendship. Gay and lesbian travellers should experience no difficulties in Libya, especially as questions relating to sexual preference by ordinary Libyans are extremely rare and nonexistent in dealings with officialdom. If you're travelling with a partner, the rules are the same as for heterosexual couples; discretion is the key and public displays of affection are almost never appropriate.

DISABLED TRAVELLERS

As long as you are healthy, there is no reason why people with a disability shouldn't enjoy travelling in Libya. If you're going as part of a group, notify your tour company well in advance of any special requirements you may have. Most of the better hotels have entrances at ground level and functioning lifts. Most group tours involve transport to all sites which relieves the process (for all travellers) of negotiating public transport. Even in the desert, transport is usually by 4WD, rather than camel. Depending on your disability, you may find it difficult exploring some of the archaeological sites where paths are uneven and access for wheelchairs can be difficult. However, Ghadames, Tobruk and the major cities are generally no problem. Discuss the possibilities with your tour company before travelling.

You should bring your own medications and prescriptions with you, although medical facilities in Tripoli and Benghazi are quite good.

SENIOR TRAVELLERS

Age should be no barrier to travelling in Libya, provided you are healthy and reasonably fit. While in Libya, we met travellers of all ages, none of whom reported any special difficulties as a result of their age. Older people in Libya are generally treated with the utmost respect.

TRAVEL WITH CHILDREN

In Libya, foreign children are treated with a good-natured mixture of amusement and curiosity. Many Libyans live with, or have close ties to, their extended families and you'll find that most are terrific in dealing with children. Nappies (diapers), powders and most simple medications are available at pharmacies and grocery stores in most cities (especially Tripoli and Benghazi) although you may want to bring your own to save you searching all over town.

The difficulty you're most likely to encounter is keeping your children entertained during all the long journeys. Also remember that most sites in Libya (entry 1LD for children under 12) are more 'adult' in their appeal. Alternatively, if you get to spend time with a Libyan family it will likely be a rewarding experience. It's worth discussing with your tour company the possibilities of having a meal with a Libyan family; this would only be an option for small groups.

Anyone travelling with their children to Libya should read *Travel with Children* by Lonely Planet's Maureen Wheeler. She has travelled around the world with her kids and has lived to tell the tale.

DANGERS & ANNOYANCES

Contrary to what media reports may have taught you, Libya is a very safe country in which to travel. Well and truly gone are the days when Libyan hotel lobbies were filled with security agents trying to be discreet and monitoring your movements. Open hostility towards foreigners is practically nonexistent and countless travellers have told us of being overwhelmed by the kindness and hospitality shown by ordinary Libyans, an experience summed up by the following statement:

Nowhere up to now have we come across so many nice and friendly and helpful and hospitable people.
Oliver Becker & Christine Ungruh, Germany

If you do your best to adhere to local customs, this is likely to be your experience.

As a relatively wealthy country, it is also rare in the post-embargo period to find Libyans hassling you for information about getting a visa to your country. Libya is also not a country that operates a dual-pricing system for locals and foreigners, and overcharging of foreign visitors is also rare.

Security

Keen to develop their tourism industry, the Libyan government has advocated a hands-off approach to tourists by police or soldiers.

The only occasions on which you may encounter difficulties is if you point your camera at a restricted site (see Restrictions in the Photography & Video section earlier in the chapter). Far more rarely, the pervasive concern for national security may cause police to ask for your papers if you are in unusual proximity to a security or military building. Checkpoints are little more than a time-consuming formality (see Checkpoints in the Getting Around chapter) and incidents of corruption are almost unheard of.

The only time when you may want to be especially careful is whenever Libya makes an appearance on the world stage. During the Lockerbie affair, public demonstrations of support for the Libyan position often took place, especially in Tripoli (where the British embassy was targeted). Such outpourings of anger are best avoided.

It is always a good idea to check the latest Foreign and Commonwealth Office travel advice on W www.fco.gov.uk/travel/ or Australia's Department of Foreign Affairs and Trade consular travel advice at W www.dfat.gov.au/consular/advice/advices_mnu.html. Alternatively, if you're concerned, consult your embassy for the latest situation before setting out from Tripoli. Remember that government sources necessarily err on the side of caution.

Crime

Petty crime does occasionally occur. Be particularly careful with your belongings on beaches while you're out in the water. If you're on a group tour, it is usually safe to leave your bags in the company's vehicle provided someone (preferably a direct employee of the company) will be keeping a watch over them. Valuables should either be carried with you in a moneybelt under your clothing or locked in the hotel safe.

In recent years there have been very occasional, but disturbing, reports of robberies around Waw al-Namus and on the remote stretches of road between Ubari and Ghat. These serious incidents have involved vehicles being stolen and, while only a couple of such reports have been made, vigilance is very important.

Traffic

Driving in Libya can be hazardous with people driving at high speed the major danger. Police enforcement of transgressions is marked by a decided lack of enthusiasm. For more details of the potential dangers of driving in Libya, see Car & Motorcycle in the Getting Around chapter.

EMERGENCIES

There is a nationwide emergency telephone number for police, ambulance and fire services throughout Libya; for most medical emergencies, Libyans prefer to make their own way to hospital. A problem can also be that few telephone operators speak any language other than Arabic.

For the record, the general emergency number is ☎ 121.

LEGAL MATTERS

Since the days of the revolution, Libya's judicial system has been heavily influenced by Islamic precepts, although modern laws are a mixture of religious and secular tenets. There are both civil and religious courts, but foreign visitors are highly unlikely to have need of the latter. Judges are appointed by the General People's Congress, and judicial independence and due process are largely observed. Special People's Courts and ad-hoc military tribunals handle crimes against the state. All proceedings are conducted in Arabic with interpreters provided for non-Arabic aliens.

Generally, the same activities that are illegal in your own country are illegal in Libya. Foreigners will simply be deported for committing most minor crimes. Remember that alcohol is forbidden in Libya and drug offences carry stiff penalties. If you flout these laws, don't expect your embassy to get you out, although it should be your first port of call in arranging legal representation.

BUSINESS HOURS

All Libyan businesses and government offices are closed on Friday, but some Internet cafes and shops are open on Friday afternoons; few restaurants are open lunchtimes on Friday, but most open Friday evening. Government offices (including post offices) are open from 7am to 2pm from Saturday to Thursday April to September and 8am to 3pm October to March. The mornings are the best time to find the relevant officials at their desks. Private businesses are usually open from 9am to 2pm and again from 4.30pm (sometimes 5.30pm) to 6.30pm (or as late as 8.30pm) Saturday to Thursday.

Banks have their own specific hours – from 8am to 1pm Sunday to Tuesday and Thursday, and from 8am to 12.30pm and 3.30pm to 4.30pm (or 4.30pm to 5.30pm) on Wednesday and Saturday.

CALENDARS

With the exception of some government departments, everyone follows the Western calendar. Even visas and visa extensions are calculated on this basis.

The Islamic calendar gives the year as After Hejira (AH), the flight of the Prophet Mohammed from Mecca to Medina on the Western equivalent of 16 July 622. Although Gaddafi decided that the Libyan calendar should date from AD 570, the year of birth of Mohammed, the idea never really stuck.

PUBLIC HOLIDAYS & SPECIAL EVENTS

There are both religious and national holidays that are worth remembering as most businesses will be closed on these days.

National Holidays

National holidays include:

March
Declaration of the People's Authority Day A school holiday and a day of speeches and rallies on 2 March commemorate the founding of the Jamahiriya in 1977.

Evacuation Day A holiday on 28 March commemorates the evacuation of British forces from Libyan soil.

June
Evacuation Day Anti-imperialist speeches and military parades on 11 June celebrate the evacuation of foreign military bases.

September
Revolution Day Held on 1 September, this is the biggest nonreligious holiday in the Libyan calendar. Green Square in Tripoli is often the scene of a big rally with speeches by Colonel Gaddafi, and there are military parades on the coastal highway east of the centre (though they are sometimes held in Benghazi for variety).

October
Day of Mourning Held on 26 October this commemorates Libyans killed or exiled during the Italian occupation. Everything closes (including borders for a few minutes) and international telephone and telex lines are cut.

Islamic Holidays

Islamic holidays vary in date according to the lunar calendar. For details of the observance of Ramadan, see When to Go under Planning earlier in this chapter and the boxed text 'The Five Pillars of Islam' under Religion in the Facts about Libya chapter. See the table 'Islamic Holidays' for dates of major holidays.

Festivals

There are annual festivals in Ghadames, Zuara, Ghat, Germa, Kabaw and Houn. They celebrate local culture and usually reflect the essential character of each town. Check with any Libyan tour company for exact dates.

Islamic Holidays

Hejira Year	New Year	Prophet's Birthday	Ramadan Starts	Eid al-Fitr	Eid al-Adha
1422	26.03.01	03.06.01	16.11.01	16.12.01	23.02.02
1423	15.03.02	25.05.02	10.11.02	05.12.02	12.02.03
1424	04.03.03	14.05.03	30.10.03	24.11.03	31.01.04
1425	22.02.04	03.05.04	19.10.04	13.11.04	20.01.05
1426	11.02.05	20.04.05	03.10.05	02.11.05	10.01.06

March

Germa Festivities here showcase local ceremonies and dance.

Houn The coming of spring in the Fezzan is welcomed by a decadent round of sweet-making in keeping with the oasis' reliance upon the seasons.

April

Kabaw The Qasr Festival pays tribute to the ancient Berber traditions of the Jebel Nafusa and centre around its evocative qasr, or granary.

August

Zuara The Awussu Festival takes place on the beach or in the water.

October

Ghadames Held in the old city, this festival centres on a celebration of traditional culture and ways of living.

December–January

Ghat The Acacus Festival celebrates the town's Tuareg heritage.

ACTIVITIES

Libya is more for seeing than for doing. There are no organised trekking routes, although both the Jebel Nafusa in the northwest and the Jebel Akhdar in the north-east would be good places to explore on foot.

Similarly, the shallows of the Mediterranean along the northern Libyan coast offer some enticing if undeveloped snorkelling possibilities, especially at Apollonia (Libyan authorities are understandably hesitant about allowing travellers to get too close to the submerged ruins). A few shops in Tripoli sell snorkelling equipment and a few of the tourist villages have some on hand. For the time being, however, swimming at one of Libya's beaches (tourist villages charge nonguests 0.5LD to swim at their beaches) is about all that you're likely to be able to do. The best beaches are from Sabratha to Bu Kammash (especially around Zuara), west of Al-Khoms and north of Al-Bayda.

If you're keen to organise a holiday that includes trekking, snorkelling, caving or cycling components, there are some Libyan tour companies that can arrange them. Companies to try include Robban Tourism Services, Azar Libya Travel & Tours Co,

Winzrik Tourism Services and Wings Travel & Tours (see Organised Tours in the Getting Around chapter).

Desert safaris, either by 4WD or camel, are big business in Libya. See the Fezzan & the Sahara chapter for guidance on the best places to visit. At Gebraoun Lake in the Idehan Ubari, there is a single set of skis if you want to try your hand at dune skiing.

COURSES

If you're in Libya for a prolonged period, the Islamic Call Society runs Arabic language courses. The three- to six-month programs are free, although a small donation is appreciated. Its office is on Maidan al-Jezayir in Tripoli, near the former cathedral.

WORK

Many expatriates work in Libya. European newspapers often carry advertisements for engineers or other positions requiring particular technical expertise to work in Libya's oil industry. Beyond that, work in other industries can be hard to come by and is almost impossible to arrange from inside Libya while on a tourist visa. An increasing number of European tour companies are running tours to Libya and you may be able to pick up work as a tour leader, although these jobs are much sought after.

ACCOMMODATION

Libya has a decided shortage of accommodation and tour companies often book out the best places weeks in advance; this would make it difficult for independent travellers. Some towns have no hotels at all. Mindful of the shortfall, the government is planning new hotels for Al-Jufra, Al-Kufra, Bsees, Derna, Germa, Ghadames, Ghat, Idri, Misrata, Murzuq, Ras al-Hillal, Sebha, Sirt, Susa, Tobruk, Tolmeita, Yefren and Zueila, as well as a number of major projects in Tripoli.

Existing options vary widely in quality and, in some places (eg, Nalut), formerly grand hotels have been allowed to fall into disrepair. Budget travellers have the hardest time and the situation for them would be critical were it not for Libya's quite extensive network of youth hostels. The situation is worst for women as the real cheapies are guaranteed to make female travellers (and many men) feel decidedly uncomfortable. Fortunately, many youth hostels have areas set aside for women. At the upper end of the market, there are some hotels of outstanding quality as well as a few mid-range gems.

Hotels, youth hostels and tourist villages throughout Libya are very rarely signposted in English. For this reason, we have listed the hotels under their Arabic name – *funduq* means hotel, *buyut ash-shabaab* indicates a youth hostel, while *qaryat as-siyahe* refers to a tourist village, except in Ghadames where English signs are used.

Camping

When visa regulations change to allow independent travel in Libya, budget travellers should seriously consider carrying a tent with them. While there are few, if any, camping grounds in the cities along Libya's coast, it's generally not a problem if you pitch a tent on a patch of open ground. This can be essential in those towns with no hotels, particularly in the small settlements of the Jebel Nafusa, the Jebel Akhdar and the Fezzan. Never simply set up your tent *(khayma)* without asking permission from the nearest landowner or local police. It is always a good idea to notify the police even if you already have permission from elsewhere.

Some hotels and youth hostels will allow you to set up tents in their compound for 5LD or 10LD and are usually happy for you to use their shower and toilet facilities. It is also possible to set up your tent in Car Park No 1 at the entrance to Leptis Magna. In the Fezzan, there are a few dedicated camping grounds that contain huts, but the owners will also allow you to pitch a tent inside the compound for the usual fee. For desert expeditions, tents are provided by most tour companies, but dozing off in your sleeping bag on the sand under the stars is better.

Youth Hostels

In Tripolitania, there are youth hostels in Tripoli (two), Sirt, Sabratha, Ghadames, Nalut, Al-Khoms, Misrata, Yefren, Zuara and Gharyan, although the last three were closed for renovations when we visited. In Cyrenaica, there are youth hostels in Benghazi and Shahat (for Cyrene), while the Fezzan is home to three youth hostels (four, if the one in Murzuq has re-opened), in Sebha, Fjeaj and Houn.

Youth hostels usually charge 3LD per night if you have a Hostelling International (HI) membership card; if you don't have one, you'll probably be charged 5LD. This gets you a bed in a dormitory with shared toilets and showers. The hostels are pretty basic, but most are clean, friendly and well run. Some have very cheap meals available and can arrange breakfasts for larger groups.

The headquarters for youth hostels in Libya is the Libyan Youth Hostel Association (☎ 021-4445171, fax 3330118) at 69 Sharia Amr ibn al Ass in Tripoli; its postal address is PO Box 8886, Tripoli. The office is in Tripoli's Central Youth Hostel and sells youth hostel membership cards (around 10 LD). It can be difficult to find anyone in the office so ring ahead if you're making a special trip.

Hotels

Libya has some fine hotels and some that fall way short of that description. The real cheapies (5LD to 10LD per night) are best avoided if you can afford to. Invariably, in the seedy areas of town, around the bus stations, they are often noisy, dirty and sometimes even filled with customers who pay by the hour. These places are not set up for tourists; their main clients are immigrant workers from Tunisia, Egypt or sub-Saharan Africa. There are exceptions to the rule, but not many.

In the mid-range category (15LD to 35LD), quality is highly variable and some places charge top-end prices for rooms that have been shoddily maintained. Although the situation has improved, some hotels have plumbing that can be downright unreliable. In the mid-range category, you should get a private bathroom, including a sit-down flush toilet. The quoted room price almost always includes a breakfast (usually bread and spreads), although you generally pay an extra 10LD if you want a more substantial buffet.

The better mid-range hotels might also have air-conditioning, a TV and balcony. Many hotels advertise suites, which can range from spacious with a sitting room to simply a slightly larger room; always have a look before forking out the extra money. Some rooms in this category have room service and, in some places, are cleaned daily.

If you're willing to pay top dollar (40LD to 120LD), top-end hotels can be excellent value with beautifully appointed rooms, good service and five-star facilities.

One thing to remember is that you'll get the best value out of your hotel if you only treat it as a place to sleep and have breakfast. Most other services (eg, laundry, barbers, lunch or dinner) come at a grossly inflated price and, in the case of restaurants, are rarely as good as you can get elsewhere. Preferring blackmail to improving the quality, some hotels have taken to threatening to evict paying customers who choose not to eat in the hotel restaurant in the evening. This is not an idle threat and if you refuse to play the game, some hotel managers will announce, bare-faced, that they are booked out for the following (or even the same) night. Once shackled to your table, you pay through the nose (up to 30LD) for a meal of generally low quality. Stay elsewhere.

If you want to make a reservation in advance, many mid-range and top-end hotels insist on payment up front to hold the room so high is the demand. The only way to do this is to make an arrangement through a Libyan friend or tour company; if you do, don't fail to reimburse them.

Tourist Villages

Libya's tourist villages are not really set up for foreign tourists, but rather locals who flock to the coast in summer. Outside peak period (mid-May to mid-September), getting a room is usually no problem. In the warmer months, forget it. Libyan families frequently block-book the rooms or villas for up to four months and bookings must be made many months in advance. The only exception to this practice is Qaryat Al-Asfar as-Siyahe at Al-Khoms where the owner claims to keep a quota of rooms for foreign visitors. Accommodation is usually right on the beachfront in self-contained, air-conditioned rooms or villas (with a fridge and kitchen) and the standard of maintenance in most is quite high. There is invariably a restaurant in the complex where breakfast is served; some even have games rooms, an on-site bakery, tennis courts, a laundry and grocery store. Some also have travel agencies.

FOOD

Libya does not have a reputation for the finest cuisine in the Middle East. If you're on a budget, the staple tourist diet consists of couscous and chicken in Tripolitania and the Fezzan, with rice replacing couscous in Cyrenaica. For a little variety, there are also macaroni-based dishes inspired by the Italians; vegetable stews and potatoes might be a recurring theme if you're lucky. You'll usually get bread with your meal, although often it's not Arabic bread but Western-style. There are also snack bars or cheap restaurants in most towns that can make chicken *shwarma* (meat sliced off a spit and stuffed in a pocket of pita-type bread with chopped tomatoes and garnish), pizza or sandwiches; if you don't like liver, ask for *bidoon kibdeh* (without liver). Some travellers have given Libyan cuisine the unenviable title of the dullest cuisine in North Africa.

If you're willing or able to spend more, eating better is all a matter of knowing where to look. Tripoli, Benghazi and a few other cities have some wonderful restaurants serving dishes of great variety. Particular highlights are the seafood dishes at specialist fish restaurants in Tripoli, although these dishes are available anywhere along the coast. International dishes (pasta and even steak) of reasonable quality are also available in Tripoli and Benghazi.

Many restaurants will assume that you will have a banquet-style meal. These can be excellent value (10LD to 25LD) and you'll rarely leave hungry. The first dish is usually soup, with some restaurants offering a choice that invariably includes 'Libyan soup' (spiced minestrone broth with lamb and pasta). Next (or at the same time) comes a salad followed by entrees (sometimes

Libyan Food

Local Specialties
Libyan cuisine includes a number of local specialities worth seeking out.

Osban A Sheep's stomach cleaned out and filled with rice, herbs, liver, kidney and other meats, and steamed or boiled in a sauce – it's only for the adventurous.
Rishda Delicately spiced vermicelli-style pasta noodles with chickpeas, tomatoes and caramelised onions.
Tajeen A lightly spiced lamb dish with a tomato and paprika-based sauce.

Home Cooking
It is also worth remembering that the vast majority of Libyans eat at home. In this context, there is a whole range of delicious local foods that you'll never see in a restaurant. To get a taste, you'd need to eat with a Libyan family or ask your tour company to arrange a picnic with some typical dishes. Some to consider include:

Aysh This is an unleavened bread similar to bazin (see following) but softer.
Bazin Unleavened bread made from barley and flour but without sugar. A staple of Tripolitanian families, it's eaten with the hands (often served with soup) and is good with fish – a speciality of Zuara.
Bseesa Bread made from seeds crushed to a flour-like consistency and mixed with oil and eaten for breakfast or with tea in western Libya.
Fitaat Lentils, mutton and buckwheat pancakes cooked together in a tasty sauce in a low oven and eaten with the hands from a communal bowl. It's served in some of the old houses of Ghadames.
Matruda Thick, oven-baked bread chopped into small pieces and then, while still warm, added to milk, butter, dates and finally honey and a home-made butter (like ghee) called *samel*. A delicacy of the Jebel Akhdar, this is one of our favourites and is designed for warming the heart in winter.
Zumeita Bread made from wheat and small yellow seeds.

One final dish worthy of special mention is Tuareg bread or *Taajeelah* (also known as sand or desert bread). See the boxed text '*Taajeelah* (Tuareg Bread)' in the Fezzan & The Sahara chapter for details.

dips), a selection of meat (or fish) dishes, rice or couscous, a few vegetables, soft drink and tea or coffee. Throughout this book, the price given for meals refers to these banquets.

Vegetarians should always specify their requirements as soon as they arrive in the restaurant (tour companies should also be told in advance to help with planning). Vegetarians will need to ask for *bidoon laham* (without meat). Many soups are pre-cooked and include meat as a matter of course, often no substitute is available. Instead of meat in the main course, most restaurants can cook up an omelette or french fries. Remember that vegetarianism is rare in Libya, but most restaurants are obliging and keen to make sure you don't leave hungry.

DRINKS
There's not a lot of choice when it comes to beverages. Soft drink and, to a lesser extent, bottled water are available in even the smallest towns. One drink that breaks the monotony in some Tripoli restaurants is the *masabiyah jamaica*, a cocktail of 7-Up, Mirinda and Coke. Libyan tea is very strong and is sometimes served with mint (*shay na'ana*) or peanuts. Coffee-drinkers can choose between instant *(nescafe)* or the thick Arab coffee *(qahwa)*, in which you could stand your spoon without fear of it falling.

Alcohol is illegal in Libya, although in trusted company you may be offered *bokha*, a potent home-brew that could start your car; it's also known as 'Libyan tequila'. Nonalcoholic beers include Crown, a malty brew from Morocco (1LD to 2LD), and the less widely available Libyan equivalent, *Ma'sharia*, another malt beer sold in brown bottles for 1LD. If you're lucky, you might also come across the occasional bottle of Becks nonalcoholic beer.

ENTERTAINMENT

Bring a good book. There are no nightclubs and most of your evening entertainment will not extend beyond passing the time in pleasant conversation at a restaurant or teahouse. The only guaranteed music or dance performances are those performed at weddings or festivals. Occasional performances are put on by larger hotels if there are enough tourists around; ask your tour company to see if anything's happening. For drama, Al-Kashaf Theatre, adjacent to the Libyan Arab Airlines office in Tripoli, stages occasional plays by one of the theatre groups in Tripoli. Hussein Founi of Robban Tourism Services (see Organised Tours in the Getting Around chapter) is a good man to ask for details.

SPECTATOR SPORTS

Football (soccer) is the number-one sport in Libya but, perhaps stung by a singular lack of success by Libyan sides, it rarely arouses the passions as it does elsewhere in Africa. The two largest club sides are Al-Ahly and La'tihad, both based in Tripoli. With one notable exception (see the boxed text 'The Best Player in the World'), Libya's most famous players are Jihad al-Muntasser, who plies his trade in the lower divisions in Italy, and Tariq at-Taib, who plays in Tunisia.

The highpoint of Libya's football history came in 1982, when it hosted the African Nations Cup and made it through to the final stages, finally losing to Ghana on penalties. The Libyan Football Association has also announced its candidacy to host the 2005 World Youth Cup tournament.

Games (3LD) take place in winter and you should check local newspapers or ask at

---

The Best Player in the World

Colonel Gaddafi's son, As-Sa'adi al-Gaddafi, is the ambitious captain of both Al-Ahly and the Libyan national team. His aim to become the best player in the world saw him attempt to bring the great players of the world (including Maradona, Pele and famous players from Italy) to Libya in 2000 as his personal coaches. It is not for us to judge whether it worked.

---

your hotel for exact times and locations. The country's two major stadiums are in: Tripoli, at the Sports City (Al-Medina ar-Riyaddiyat), 5km south-west of the parliament building and not far off the road to Sabratha; and Benghazi, on the eastern side of the harbours.

Other sports that attract a following (and are played in the two main Sports Cities in Tripoli and Benghazi) include handball, basketball and volleyball. Women's sport is not big in Libya, though volleyball and table tennis are the main games.

Racing enthusiasts have a few outlets, although remember that gambling on the outcome is forbidden. Horse racing takes place from time to time in Surman, 60km west of Tripoli, and in Tripoli itself. There is an annual show-jumping competition in Tripoli to coincide with Revolution Day celebrations; it usually takes place during the first week of September. For something different, there are occasional camel races in the south, especially around Germa; ask your tour company for details.

SHOPPING

Libya does not have markets of the calibre of those in Cairo; nor does it have a high concentration of tourist kitsch. The best place in Libya to do your shopping is in the souqs of Tripoli's medina, which have the largest selection of goods. Ghadames also has a decent variety but, unashamedly, at tourist prices – which is unusual in Libya. For Tuareg items, many Tuareg in the Fezzan spread out their items for sale on a rug alongside the lakes and a few camping grounds. For more details of Tuareg jewellery and leather items, see the boxed text 'Tuareg Handicrafts' in the Fezzan & the Sahara chapter.

Carpets & Rugs
The better Libyan (primarily Berber) rugs consist of high-quality, flat-weave kilim cushions and larger rugs, although in most places you'll mostly come across heavy-woven Berber rugs with simple, almost child-like animal motifs. The rugs on offer in the Misrata souq are noted for their bright colours.

Ceramics & Pottery
Gharyan is the undisputed pottery capital of Libya. The road into town from Tripoli is lined with stalls offering colourful bowls decorated with swirling designs in different sizes. The quality is high and surprisingly reasonable in price. In Tripoli or the Jebel Nafusa, you may see the more subtle, but attractive Berber pottery in the form of vases or food receptacles (minimalist designs on a cream background).

Clothing
The long, loose-fitting overshirt and pants worn by many Libyan men, the *galabiyya,* makes ideal summer wear. Libyan women don't wear them, but some Tripoli shopkeepers claim that their best customers are foreign women. These are available just about anywhere that there's a market, including ones suitable for small children. On an entirely different tack, Tripoli is a good place to buy good-quality men's suits in a range of fabric blends.

Jewellery
There is an astonishing range of jewellery on offer in Libya. The gold shops of Tripoli and Benghazi specialise in wedding attire for Libyan brides. Most of it is quite ornate and struck to suit Libyan tastes, although simpler (and cheaper) items are available. When we were in Libya, gold was selling for 15LD to 17LD per gram, but check prices when you arrive. The other mainstay of the Libyan jewellery trade (and one that is aimed squarely at the foreign visitor) is silver Tuareg jewellery.

Of course, no self-respecting tourist leaves Libya without a Colonel Gaddafi watch.

Leather
In Ghadames, the now-famous leather shoes in rich colours with attractive designs were for a time Ghadames' only local product of note. Although cheap imitations abound, Ghadames' famous shoe-making family, the Jeddar, still keeps the traditional craft alive. Some of its wares are on display in the Ghadames Museum or can be bought from the family store not far away.

Palm Products
Palm-woven products such as mats, baskets and bowls are the speciality of the coastal Tripolitanian towns of Tauorga and Ghadames. They are lightweight but bulky.

Getting There & Away

You can enter Libya by air, land or sea. Land borders with Egypt, Tunisia, Niger and Algeria are open. If you're arriving as part of a group, tour company representatives can meet you at the relevant entry point. It is generally much cheaper to fly to Tunisia or Egypt than directly to Tripoli (At-Tarablus).

AIR
Airports & Airlines
The airports at Tripoli and Benghazi are Libya's only airports currently servicing international flights.

Libyan Arab Airlines is Libya's national airline and its planes serve a surprising (and increasing) number of destinations. It has not taken long for the airline to recover from the exile imposed on it by United Nations sanctions and it flies to destinations throughout Europe, Africa and the Middle East. In-flight service has an Islamic flavour, with neither pork nor alcohol on offer. Women are not required to wear headscarves.

Other airlines that provide services to Libya include: Air Malta, Alitalia, Austrian Airlines, British Airways, EgyptAir, Emirates, Lufthansa Airlines, Malev-Hungarian Airlines, Olympic Airways, Royal Jordanian, Swissair, Syrianair, Tunis Air and Turkish Airlines. See Getting There & Away in the Tripoli or Cyrenaica (for Benghazi) chapters for their contact details.

To get to Libya from the USA, Canada, Australia and New Zealand, it is necessary to first fly to the UK, Continental Europe, Africa or the Middle East and then get a connecting flight to Libya.

Point Afrique operates planes from Paris and Marseilles to some of the oasis towns of the Sahara, which for a time included Sebha. These flights were suspended at the time of research, but check the company's French-language Web site in case they have now resumed (W www.point-afrique.com).

Occasionally, flights are delayed, turned back or even cancelled altogether when the hot ghibli wind starts to blow. Airlines will usually make alternative arrangements for a new flight a few days later.

Buying Tickets
With a bit of research – ringing around travel agents, checking Internet sites, perusing the travel ads in newspapers – you can often get yourself a good travel deal. Start early as some of the cheapest tickets need to be bought well in advance and popular tickets can sell out.

Full-time students and people under 26 years have access to better deals than do other travellers. You have to show a document proving your date of birth or a valid International Student Identity Card (ISIC) when buying your ticket and boarding the plane.

Generally, there is nothing to be gained by buying a ticket direct from the airline, although the situation in Libya is slightly different (see Buying International Tickets in Libya later). Discounted tickets are released to selected travel agents and specialist discount agencies, and these are usually

---

Warning

The information in this chapter is particularly vulnerable to change: Prices for international travel are volatile, routes are introduced and cancelled, schedules change, special deals come and go, and rules and visa requirements are amended. You should check directly with the airline or a travel agent to make sure you understand how a fare (and ticket you may buy) works and be aware of the security requirements for international travel.

The upshot of this is that you should get opinions, quotes and advice from as many airlines and travel agents as possible before you part with your hard-earned cash. The details given in this chapter should be regarded as pointers and are not a substitute for your own careful, up-to-date research.

the cheapest deals going. The other exception is booking on the Internet. Many airlines – both full-service and no-frills – offer some excellent fares to Web surfers.

Many travel agencies around the world have Web sites, which can make the Internet a quick way to compare prices. There is also an increasing number of dedicated online agents. Internet ticket sales work well if you are doing a simple one-way or return trip on specified dates. However, on-line fare generators are no substitute for a travel agent who knows all about special deals, has strategies for avoiding lay overs and can offer advice on everything from which airline has the best vegetarian food to the best travel insurance with your ticket.

You may find the cheapest flights are advertised by obscure agencies. Most such firms are honest and solvent, but there are some rogue fly-by-night outfits around. Paying by credit card generally offers protection, as most card issuers provide refunds if you can prove you didn't get what you paid for. Similar protection can be obtained by buying a ticket from a bonded agent, such as one covered by the Air Travel Organiser's Licence (ATOL) scheme in the UK. Agents who accept only cash should hand over the tickets straight away and not tell you to 'come back tomorrow'. After you've made a booking or paid your deposit, call the airline and confirm that the booking was made. It's generally not advisable to send money (even cheques) through the post unless the agent is very well established – some travellers have reported being ripped off by fly-by-night mail-order ticket agents.

If you purchase a ticket and later want to make changes to your route or get a refund, you need to contact the original travel agent. Airlines issue refunds only to the purchaser of a ticket – usually the travel agent who bought the ticket on your behalf. Many travellers change their routes halfway through their trips, so think carefully before you buy a ticket that is not easily refunded.

Buying International Tickets in Libya

Make sure you have a return ticket before arriving in Libya – this will continue to be a requirement for visa applications if you're arriving by air.

Although most European airlines in Libya will sell tickets direct to customers, discounts are difficult to come by, especially if you book only a couple of weeks before your departure date. The good news is that most such airlines will accept payment by Visa and MasterCard and some, like British Airways, will insist on such payments by non-Libyans. Malev is one airline that is particularly helpful.

If buying a ticket through a travel agent in Libya, you will come up against one of the quirks of Libyan commercial regulations. At the time of writing, all Libyan travel agencies could only sell outgoing international air tickets through Libyan Arab Airlines. Payment must be in Libyan dinars (cash only) and the first leg of any itinerary must be flown on Libyan Arab Airlines. Hence, if you wish to fly to a destination to which the Libyan carrier does not fly, you must fly to one which it does and then connect with an onward flight. Tickets are most often available in economy class, although excursion fares to more popular destinations can sometimes be arranged. This system usually works out cheaper than buying direct through the airline. Mediterranean Travel & Tourism Co (☎ 021-4440837, fax 4446966, Sharia 1st September, Tripoli) is arguably the best travel agency in the country that specialises in air tickets.

You are therefore faced with two choices: You can buy through the airline of your choice and have the convenience of being able to use your credit card, or go through a travel agent (or Libyan Arab Airlines direct) and pay a little less.

Travellers with Special Needs

If they're warned early enough, airlines can often make special arrangements for travellers, such as wheelchair assistance at airports or vegetarian meals on the flight. Children under two years old travel for 10% of the standard fare (or free on some airlines) as long as they don't occupy a seat. They don't get a baggage allowance. 'Skycots', baby food and nappies should be provided by the airline if requested in advance. Children aged between two and 12 can usually occupy a seat for half to two-thirds of the full fare, and do get a baggage allowance.

For further information, the disability oriented Web site W www.everybody.co.uk has a directory of facilities offered by various airline companies.

Departure Tax

Most tickets bought either in Libya or internationally include departure taxes for all the airports you'll pass through en route to Libya, but not for leaving Libya itself. Just before passing through customs and immigration on your departure, you must pay 6LD.

The UK

Discount air travel is big business in London. For those under 26 years, a popular travel agency with branches throughout the UK is STA Travel (☎ 020-7361 6262, W www.sta travel.co.uk). This agency concentrates on dealing with young people and students, but it also sells tickets to all travellers. One company with some experience of flights to Libya is Benz Travel (☎ 0207-462 0000, fax 462 0033), 83 Mortimer St, London W1N 7PV.

During peak season (October to April), the cheapest return fares to Tripoli at the time of writing were on Malev-Hungarian Airlines via Budapest for UK£235. With other airlines, quoted fares range from UK£325 up to UK£450. It is generally cheaper to pick up a flight to Tunis or Jerba (Tunisia) with one of the charter airlines, although you are usually tied into a one- or two-week turnaround.

Continental Europe

In the Netherlands, good agencies include Budget Air (☎ 00-627 1251) and Holland International (☎ 070-307 6307).

In Germany, recommended agencies include STA Travel (☎ 030-311 0950) and Usit Campus (call centre ☎ 01805 788336, Cologne ☎ 0221 923990, W www.usitcampus.de). Return flights to Tripoli from either Amsterdam or Frankfurt generally cost around US$400.

In France, a recommended travel agency with branches throughout the country is OTU Voyages (☎ 01 40 29 12 12, W www .otu.fr). This company specialises in student and youth fares. Other recommendations include Voyageurs du Monde (☎ 01 42 86 16 00), 55 rue Ste-Anne, 75002 Paris, and Nouvelles Frontières (nationwide number ☎ 08 25 00 08 25, Paris ☎ 01 45 68 70 00, W www.nouvelles-frontieres.fr). Flights to Tripoli from Paris cost approximately €564 return.

In Italy, try CTS Viaggi (☎ 06-462 0431) and Passagi (☎ 06-474 0923). Flying from Rome (about US$275 return) or Milan (around US$220) is considerably cheaper than from elsewhere in Europe.

If you're in Spain, try Usit Unlimited (☎ 91-225 25 75, W www.unlimited.es); Barcelo Viajes (☎ 91-559 1819); and Nouvelles Frontières (☎ 91-547 42 00, W www .nouvelles-frontieres.es).

In Switzerland, two recommended agencies are SSR (☎ 022-818 02 02, W www .ssr.ch) and Nouvelles Frontières (☎ 022-906 80 80).

The USA & Canada

Discount travel agents in the USA and Canada are usually known as consolidators. San Francisco is the ticket-consolidator capital of America, although good deals can also be found in Los Angeles and New York.

Council Travel, America's largest student travel organisation, has around 60 offices in the USA; its head office (☎ 800-226 8624) is at 205 E 42 St, New York, NY 10017. Call it to ask about the office nearest you or visit its Web site at W www .ciee.org. For STA Travel, call the toll-free number (☎ 800-777 0112) for office locations around the country or visit its Web site at W www.statravel.com.

Travel CUTS (☎ 800-667 2887) is Canada's national student travel agency and has offices in all the country's major cities. Its Web site can be found at W www.travel cuts.com.

Australia & New Zealand

Getting to Libya from Australia or New Zealand will often involve purchasing a ticket to Europe, Africa or the Middle East and then a separate ticket to Libya. For the Libya leg, you are better off buying through a European travel agency because Australian companies tend not to have access to most discounts – we were quoted A$9000 return for a flight from Melbourne to Tripoli! Cheap flights from Australia or New Zealand to Europe generally go via South-East Asian capitals or the Middle East.

Two well-known agencies for cheap fares are STA Travel and Flight Centre. STA Travel (☎ 1300 360 960 Australiawide, W www.statravel.com.au) has offices in all major cities, as does Flight Centre (☎ 131 600 Australiawide, W www.flightcentre .com.au).

In New Zealand, Flight Centre (☎ 09-309 6171) has many branches throughout the country, while STA Travel (☎ 09-309 0458, W www.statravel.co.nz) has offices in Auckland and the major cities.

Africa

Nairobi and Johannesburg are probably the best places in East and Southern Africa to buy tickets. Getting several quotes is a good idea as prices are always changing. One of the best agencies in Nairobi is Flight Centres (☎ 02-210024, e fcswwat@arcc .or.ke) on the 2nd floor of Lakhamshi House on Biashara St.

The main hubs in West Africa are Abidjan, Accra, Bamako, Dakar and Lagos. It is usually better to buy tickets in West Africa through a travel agency rather than from the airline. One-way/return flights (mostly Libyan Arab Airlines) to Tripoli were operating from the following destinations at the time of research: Tunis (US$60/110), Algiers (US$110/210), Casablanca (US$200/365), Ndjamena (US$310/580), Niamey (US$310/575) and Khartoum (US$180/350).

Middle East

Usually the best travel deal in the Middle East is an airline's official excursion fare, although finding one of these to Libya involves shopping around.

In İstanbul there are lots of travel agencies on the northern side of Divan Yolu in Sultanahmet, all of them specialising in budget air tickets. Orion-Tour (☎ 212-248 8437), Halaskargazi Caddesi 284/3, Marmara Apartimani, Sisli, is highly recommended. Check out its Web site at W www.oriontour.com for more information.

The area around Midan Tahrir in Cairo is teeming with travel agencies but don't expect any amazing deals. One of the best agencies in Cairo, though it's way down in Ma'adi, is Egypt Panorama Tours (☎ 02-359 0200, e ept@link.net), just outside the Ma'adi metro station.

Quoted one-way/return fares to Tripoli include: Cairo (US$120/220); İstanbul (US$200/375); Dubai (US$305/555); and Amman (US$150/280).

LAND

The most commonly used land borders for travellers are the coastal frontiers with Tunisia (Ras al-Jedir) and Egypt (Al-Burdi). The border with Sudan is open, although not for non-Libyans or non-Sudanese; the frontier with Chad is currently closed. The little-used border crossing with Niger is open, as is the Algerian border post in the extreme south-west of Libya connecting Ghat (Libya) with Djanet (Algeria). In all cases, make sure you have checked out the prevailing official position with the relevant embassy and the Libyan authorities in Tripoli before setting out, and make sure you have the necessary visas firmly ensconced in your passport – it's a long way to back track if there's some kind of problem.

There are no Libyan departure taxes payable on land departures.

Car & Motorcycle

Drivers of cars and riders of motorbikes will need the vehicle's registration papers, liability insurance and an international drivers' permit in addition to their domestic licence. You will also need a *carnet de passage en douane,* which is effectively a passport for the vehicle and acts as a temporary waiver of import duty. The carnet may also need to specify any expensive spare parts that you're planning to carry with you, such as a gearbox. This is designed to prevent car-import rackets. Contact your local automobile association for details about all documentation.

Entering Libya in your own vehicle involves completing a few additional formalities. Upon entering the country, you must pay US$105 (in US dollars cash) for a four wheel drive and most other vehicles, in return for a Libyan licence plate that is valid for one month; it's worth bringing some wire to attach the plates to your vehicle. Some travellers have reported being able to negotiate this price, but this appears to have been a function of exchange rates in the old black-market days. When you leave the country you must return the plates and collect the 50LD you get back from your original payment (paid in local currency), although some travellers have convinced the guards to let them keep their licence plates as a souvenir by forfeiting their refund money.

Liability insurance also has to be bought when crossing the border. The US$105 that you pay upon entering Libya also includes two weeks of car insurance and membership of the Automobile & Touring Club of Libya. If you are staying longer, you can either arrange additional insurance (approximately US$50 per two-week block) at the border, through your tour operator or the Automobile & Touring Club of Libya (☎ 3605 986/7 or 3605802, fax 3605866), Sharia Sayedy, Tripoli.

Lead-free petrol is not available in Libya, and neither are many car parts.

Border Crossings

Crossing the main land borders into or out of Libya is a lot easier than it used to be. Keen to encourage foreign tourists, the Libyan authorities have done away with many of the bureaucratic absurdities that could leave you lingering for up to eight hours in the hot sun. These days, you'd be unlikely to spend more than 1½ hours completing the whole procedure.

On the Libyan side of both the Egyptian and Tunisian borders, designated tourist police are often present to facilitate the speedy passage of tourists, although most only speak Arabic. If you're travelling as part of an organised tour and the company through whom you've organised your trip is experienced at that particular border crossing (and knows the border guards), the whole process can be finished with and you on your way within half an hour.

A major problem, especially at the Libyan-Egyptian frontier, used to be crossing no-man's land between the two border posts, but now the offices are within walking distance.

At both the Egyptian and Tunisian borders, most of the offices at which you'll need to complete immigration and customs formalities are on the right-hand side of the road. After completing all procedures, there is one final checkpoint to make sure that everything has been done properly.

Customs formalities are usually pretty cursory when entering Libya, especially if you are polite. The main item that officials will be looking out for is alcohol, which is forbidden in Libya. On the way out, searches are stricter, with rock art souvenirs the main target.

Libyan immigration cards are printed in Arabic only. If you are not accompanied by a Libyan tour-company representative, it's a matter of finding someone who can translate the questions for you (the answers can usually be written in English). If you're lucky, you may also receive a lift into the nearest town with your new-found friend.

Each page of your passport, including the page containing the mandatory Arabic translation, will usually be scrutinised in search of Israeli stamps.

Tunisia

The Tunisian border crossing is located at Ras al-Jedir, 169km west of Tripoli, and border officials on either side are generally quite friendly. Get there as early in the day as you can to avoid traffic congestion.

Bus There are a number of buses each day that run between Tripoli and Tunis; they cost 45LD from the Libyan side. The disadvantage with these long-distance buses is that you're only as fast in completing the formalities as your slowest fellow passenger.

Shared Taxi It is generally cheaper to take a shared taxi only as far as the border and change to new public transport on the other side.

If you're coming from the Tunisian side, many Libyan tour companies will meet you at the airport in Tunisia and arrange the necessary transport to Libya on your behalf. A shared taxi from Jerba airport costs about US$4 to the border (131km). You may have to change in Ben Guerdane, 33km short of the border. A number of Libyan taxis (black-and-white with a green sign) hover around the airport (and in the Tunisian town of Sfax) offering to take you to Tripoli. Chances are that you'd need to pay for the whole taxi, which would cost at least 100LD and probably more. From Sfax, take a shared taxi to Ben Guerdane (11TD) then another to the border (3TD). A shared taxi from the border to Tripoli shouldn't cost more than 10LD.

Coming in the other direction, a shared taxi as far as the border from Sabratha costs 3LD and 2LD from Zuara.

Egypt

The Libyan-Egyptian border is 139km east of Tobruk at Amsaad or Al-Burdi and 12km west of Sallum in Egypt. This remote and, in summer, perishingly hot frontier is another busy crossing point, which one traveller described as having a 'Wild West atmosphere... dirty, chaotic and very busy'. Although snacks are available, you should bring your own water. Foreign travellers are often, embarrassingly, shepherded to the front of the queue, although we've never heard of anyone turning down such an offer as a matter of principle. There are few moneychangers in Sallum, but they do gather just on the Egyptian side of the border.

Bus Long-distance buses run from Benghazi to Alexandria (35LD to 45LD) and Cairo (45LD to 55LD). Again, travelling with this many passengers will slow your advance across the border.

Taxi Shared taxis run from the taxi station in Tobruk all the way to the border (5LD). On the other side, shared taxis go to Sallum (E£2) where there are buses on to Marsa Matruh. Occasionally, shared taxis go all the way to Marsa Matruh for around E£15. While some travellers have made it from Derna in Libya to Marsa Matruh in Egypt in one very long day, you'd have to be in a real hurry to want to try it.

Niger

The route between Niger and Libya is only for serious desert travellers and the thousands of immigrants from sub-Saharan Africa making the dangerous journey north in search of work. Every year, trucks lose their way across the desert with their inhabitants condemned to die of thirst (see the boxed text 'A Grim Road to Nowhere' in the Fezzan chapter). The border post is at the incredibly remote shacks of Tumu, 310km south of Al-Qatrun; you may have to complete passport formalities in Al-Qatrun. Trucks run between Sebha and Agadez in Niger, a distance of 1768 arduous desert kilometres. The sandy journey would be madness in summer and at all times you'll need to be fully self-sufficient and aware of the risks involved.

Algeria

The only border crossing with Algeria open to foreign travellers is the one in the extreme south-west of Libya. A track runs from Ghat to the Algerian oasis town of Djanet. Even here, however, independent travellers would be viewed with suspicion, and the only travellers we heard of making the crossing were with tour groups heading to Tamanrasset. In those circumstances, border formalities are generally hassle-free and relatively quick.

Chad

The main Libyan-Chadian border post is at the historically contested town of Uzu (Aouzou in Chad), but is closed to foreign travellers because of mines in the area and ongoing rebel activity on the Chadian side of the border.

Sudan

The Libyan-Sudanese land border is closed to travellers. The remote border post in the extreme south-east of the country is at Al-Aweinat (not to be confused with the town in Fezzan of the same name), 325km south-east of Al-Kufra.

SEA

Since the lifting of the UN air embargo in 1999 and the resumption of international flights into Libya, international ferry services to Libya have been in a state of flux. From the Libyan side, ferry services are operated by the General National Maritime Transport Company (GNMTC; ☎ 021-3331710, 333 3155), Sharia Mohammed Megharief in Tripoli. There is currently talk of a reduction in services. See Getting There & Away in the Tripoli chapter for some scheduled departures. In Malta, try Sea Malta (☎ 356-2599 4213, fax 356-239179), which acts as the agent for GNMTC.

From France and Italy, SNCM (Ferryterranee) was running twice-weekly services to Tunis from Marseilles (return fare for a cabin with bathroom €334, 24 hours, twice weekly) and Genoa (€229, 22 hours, once weekly). If you want to take a four wheel drive vehicle with you, the corresponding fares are €998 and €803. Check out the Web site at **w** www.sncm.fr.

Departure Tax

The departure tax for passengers departing by sea is 10LD.

ORGANISED TOURS

European tour companies also run highly professional tours of Libya and can arrange visas, provided you give them a minimum of six weeks notice. They tend to be more expensive than Libyan companies.

The UK

British Museum Traveller (☎ 020-7436 7575, **w** www.britishmuseumtraveller.co.uk) 46 Bloomsbury St, London WC1B 3QQ, UK

Caravanserai Tours (☎ 020-8855 6373, fax 8855 6370, **e** info@caravanserai-tours.com, **w** www.caravanserai-tours.com) 1–3 Love Lane, Woolwich, London SE186QT, UK
Dragoman (☎ 01728-861133, fax 861127, **w** www.dragoman.co.uk) Camp Green, Debenham, Stowmarket, Suffolk, IP14 6LA, UK
Exodus (☎ 020-8772 3822, fax 8673 0859, **e** sales@exodustravels.co.uk, **w** www.exodustravels.com) 9 Weir Rd, London SW12 0LT, UK
Jasmin (☎ 020-7675 8886, fax 7673 1204, **e** info@jasmin-tours.co.uk) 53–55 Balham Hill, London SW129DR, UK
Prospect Music & Art Tours (☎ 020-7486 5704) 36 Manchester St, London W1M 5PE, UK

Continental Europe

Antichi Splendori Viaggi (☎ 011-8126715, fax 8123542, **e** antichi@aerre.it) Via Vanchliga 22a, 10124 Turin, Italy
Association Zig-Zag (☎ 01-4285 1393, fax 4526 3285, **w** www.zig-zag.tm.fr) 54 Rue de Dunkerque, 75009 Paris, France
Dabuka Expeditions (☎ 06442-962 728, fax 962 785, **w** www.dabuka.de) Gartenstrasse 35, 35619, Braunfels, Germany
Hommes et Montagnes (☎ 04 76 66 14 43, fax 04 76 05 43 20, **w** www.hommes-et-montagnes.fr) 125 Jean Jaurès, BP 223, 38506, Voiron Cedex (Isère), France
Jambo Tours AB Scandinavia (☎ 08-240055) Lastmakorgaton 8, S-111 44, Stockholm, Sweden
Les Voyages (☎ 03 81 81 21 24), 37 Rue Battant, 2500 Besançon, France
Osservando il Mondo (☎/fax 030-3541719) Via Boves 5, 25124 Brescia, Italy
Shiraz Travel Tours (☎ 065-115708, fax 110987, **e** scirins@tin.it, **w** www.shiraztravel.com) Via Tito Omboni, Rome, Italy

Worldwide

The Imaginative Traveller is a worldwide network of tour companies sharing a similar philosophical background (and including Intrepid and Peregrine Adventures). Some offer tours to Libya. For further information, check out the Web site at **w** www.imaginative-traveller.com.

Getting Around

Libya is quite an easy country to get around, especially in this era of group tourism. The choice of which mode of transport to take may, therefore, be one that you don't have to confront. While travelling as part of a tour will limit your freedom, it does mean that you will travel in comfort, you won't waste time waiting for transport to fill and you won't have to make any of the arrangements yourself. The information in this chapter covers both independent and tour group travel because it's likely that visa regulations will change during the life of this book.

There are five functioning airports with regular internal flights on Libyan Arab Airlines, while more airports are likely to reopen as Libya recovers from the strictures of the UN embargo. Buses connect the major cities while shared taxis go just about everywhere, although getting to the smaller mountain villages can be difficult. The country's 47,590km of paved roads are generally in excellent condition. Along the northern coast, a good sealed road runs uninterrupted from the Tunisian border to the frontier with Egypt and, increasingly, long stretches of this road are being converted into dual-carriageways. A paved road also runs from Tripoli to Ghat and from Ajdabiya to Al-Kufra. In the desert of southern Libya, well-worn tracks run across the sand and demand at least two four-wheel drive (4WD) vehicles and an experienced local guide. This is the only way to travel from the south-west of Libya to the remote south-east.

Public transport is usually moderately priced, although you may find it expensive if you're arriving from Egypt. Shared taxis and minibuses (known throughout Libya as micros) often travel the same routes and while micros are invariably cheaper (as little as half the price of a taxi), they take a lot longer to fill. Waiting around for transport to fill can take hours, although once you're on the road there's little messing about. Checkpoints are also a constant feature of travelling in Libya.

AIR

Libya is a vast country and you should consider flying to make the most of your time. Flying is cheap – an economy seat from Tripoli to Benghazi or Sebha costs 28LD one way. First-class tickets cost less than twice an economy seat, but the first-class sections are nothing special, and the longest flight is no more than four hours.

Internal flights within Libya are not, however, without their problems. Most flights are overbooked and the seats are sold out well in advance to tour companies or government officials. As soon as you know your preferred date of travel book a ticket through Libyan Arab Airlines (☎ 021-3616738/42), one of the tour companies or a local travel agency. Even then, the seat you always thought you had booked may suddenly turn out to be nothing more than a position on a waiting list. To avoid this, always get to the airport at least two hours before departure time. This is definitely a potential problem on the popular Tripoli-Sebha route, on which there are only six flights a week. One more potential difficulty is that tickets are often printed in Arabic and well-meaning officials can sometimes write the wrong time on the ticket when they try to give you the details in English. Always double-check your departure time at least a day in advance.

Another problem is flight cancellations. This was a critical issue during the air embargo when spare parts could not be imported. This difficulty remains, but is diminishing and these days the cancellations are more often caused by unfavourable weather conditions such as Saharan sandstorms or the fiercely hot ghibli wind. It is not unusual to see tour operators racing around at the last minute arranging a bus and rearranging the itinerary to take account of new travel times.

If you've flown Libyan Arab Airlines elsewhere, you'll know not to expect five-star comfort or service. Nonetheless, most of the aircraft are perfectly adequate for the short journeys you're likely to be undertaking. Planes in use vary from 80-seat Fokkers to 15 seaters.

At the time of writing, the airports at Tripoli, Benghazi, Sebha, Tobruk and Al-Kufra were open. If you're flying between Tripoli and Benghazi and Tobruk, keep an eye out the window for the ruins of Leptis Magna, which the planes sometimes fly over. There are also airports at Ghat, Ghadames and Ubari although services at Ubari were yet to resume when we visited.

If you're part of a large enough group with limited time and money to burn, you can reach Ghadames or Ghat by chartering a plane. An-Nakhl al-Khafeef, a subsidiary of Libyan Arab Airlines, runs a small number of 15-seater aircraft. A one-way flight from Tripoli to Ghadames costs 3500LD. Trying to book this through Libyan Arab Airlines is like the search for the Holy Grail so make the arrangements through one of the tour companies listed later in this chapter.

BUS

Libya does not have the largest fleet of buses, but there are daily connections between the major cities. Services along the coast are quite frequent. Beyond that, you'd be fortunate to find one travelling further south than Sebha. Most are air-conditioned, although the quality is variable, ranging from cramped buses well past their use-by date to those that are of more recent vintage and very comfortable. The two major companies are the government-owned An-Nakhl as-Seria (Fast Transport Company), and Al-Itihad al-Afriqi (the United Africa Company), which tends to have a slightly newer fleet. In Tripoli and Benghazi, these companies have depots close to the centre of town. Elsewhere, there are an insufficient number of departures to merit a dedicated bus station so bus-company offices are usually a stone's throw from the shared-taxi station.

On some routes (including between Tripoli and Ghadames) it is also possible to travel in an Iveco micro that is more spacious (and often newer) than most micros. The cost is generally the same as for a large bus.

Reservations

Given the fact that bus departures rarely take place more than once a day, they're pretty popular and booking ahead is essential if you want to be certain of getting a seat. This should always be done by visiting the office in person a day in advance at the very least; reservations made by phone have a habit of getting lost. It is also a good idea to get there a couple of hours before the bus is due to leave as it is not unheard of for underbooked services to be cancelled at short notice, at which point you'll need to scamper off to the shared-taxi station.

Costs

Bus travel doesn't come cheap. A bus from Tripoli to Benghazi or Sebha can cost 20LD, only 8LD cheaper than flying, although this is because flying is so cheap rather than buses being hideously expensive.

TAXI & SHARED TAXI

The yellow-and-white shared taxis are alternately called *siara al-arma*, *taksi moshtarak* or *saba'a taksi* (seven seater). This workhorse of the Libyan public transport system can be found anywhere where there is a paved road. Along the coast, you'll rarely have to wait long for a taxi to fill. It is customary simply to turn up at the shared-taxi station (often little more than a glorified parking lot), ask around for the next taxi leaving for where you want to go, pay the driver and then wait for the seats to fill up. Occasionally there is a ticket booth or a man roaming the yard with a ticket book, although he'll normally find you before you track him down; drivers, eager for business and to get on the road, will often help locate him. At taxi stations near international borders (eg, Tobruk and sometimes Ghat), your passport number may be required so keep it handy.

Like shared taxis throughout the Arab world and Africa, Libyan shared taxis make no concessions to comfort and, although they don't cram you in quite as tight as in the African countries to the south, the absence of leg and shoulder room can still make for an uncomfortable journey.

As a general rule, shared-taxi fares are charged at the rate of 2.5LD per 100km or 0.5LD per 20km. This may vary on some routes, especially those without regular services. Overcharging of foreigners is rare and any problems are more likely to arise from misunderstandings over language; few drivers speak anything other than Arabic.

Travel by shared taxi (or bus) is ideal for those long stretches of Libyan countryside with no sights in between (eg, Misrata to Benghazi or Tripoli to Sebha).

Private taxis (black-and-white) are not really an economical way of getting around (eg, a taxi from Sabratha to the Tunisian border costs at least 40LD), but they do enable you to dictate the journey. Make sure that your requirements are clearly spelled out when negotiating your price beforehand.

TRAIN

At the time of writing there were no rail services in Libya, but that is set to change in a big way. There is a railway line under construction from the Tunisian border all the way to the Egyptian frontier, with a branch line connecting Sirt with Sebha – a total distance of more than 3000km. Libya's contribution is unlikely to be finished during the life of this book.

CAR & MOTORCYCLE

If you do have your own vehicle, especially a 4WD, there are few limits on where you can go (the Tibesti region is one exception). Until the Libyan Government decides to relax its visa regulations, you will need to be accompanied by at least one representative of the Libyan tour company who arranged your visa and who remains responsible for you for the duration of your stay.

All road signs are in Arabic so it's a good idea to familiarise yourself with the written Arabic for your destination and other towns en route (see each town's individual listing). At most important nonurban intersections,

Road Distance Chart (km)

	Ajdabiya	Al-Bayda	Al-Khoms	Al-Kufra	Benghazi	Derna	Ghadames	Gharyan	Ghat	Houn	Misrata	Murzuq	Nalut	Sebha	Sirt	Tobruk	Tripoli	Ubari	Zuara	Zueila
Ajdabiya	---																			
Al-Bayda	363	---																		
Al-Khoms	743	1106	---																	
Al-Kufra	905	1268	1648	---																
Benghazi	161	202	904	1066	---															
Derna	513	150	1256	1418	372	---														
Ghadames	1485	1848	731	2390	1646	1998	---													
Gharyan	870	1233	128	1776	1031	1383	615	---												
Ghat	1554	1917	1462	---	1715	2067	1425	1462	---											
Houn	672	1000	521	1542	798	1150	848	887	882	---										
Misrata	649	1012	94	1554	810	1162	825	222	1556	427	---									
Murzuq	1172	1535	893	---	1333	1685	1043	765	527	500	927	---								
Nalut	1138	1501	395	2043	1299	1651	336	288	1661	1034	489	1189	---							
Sebha	1002	1365	723	---	1163	3166	873	595	552	330	757	170	1019	---						
Sirt	400	763	343	1305	561	913	1085	471	1144	262	249	762	738	592	---					
Tobruk	372	292	1115	1277	494	142	1857	1242	1926	1044	1021	1544	1510	1374	772	---				
Tripoli	863	1226	120	1768	1024	1376	611	84	1342	641	214	960	275	790	463	1235	---			
Ubari	1192	1555	913	---	1353	1705	1063	785	362	500	947	165	1209	190	782	1564	980	---		
Zuara	972	1335	229	1877	1335	1485	535	193	1451	750	323	1069	199	899	572	1344	109	1089	---	
Zueila	1202	1565	923	---	1565	1715	1073	795	657	530	957	130	1219	200	792	1574	990	295	1099	---

there are checkpoints where you can confirm you're headed in the right direction.

Libyan roads are as good as you'll find anywhere in North Africa as public infrastructure has been a priority for a government flush with oil money. Nonetheless, some roads that experience heavy traffic (especially along the coast) are in need of maintenance, having occasional potholes and cracks; always be careful when approaching bridges as many entry/exit points have deteriorated to quite a bump on either side of the road.

The good news is that petrol is ridiculously cheap, a fact that has encouraged a high rate of ownership in Libya (close to one car for every seven Libyans). 'Normal' petrol costs 10.5 piastres (0.105LD) per litre, super is 14 piastres a litre and diesel 11 piastres per litre. Perversely, given Libyan relations with the West, when asking for directions to the nearest petrol station, you'll need to ask *'ayna Shell?'*. With regards to finding ancient sites, ask using their name or *al-attar* (the ruins), *al-mathaf* (the museum) or *al-qasr* (the fort or castle).

If you're travelling in the desert, there is no substitute for an experienced local guide (mandatory in some parts) who knows the terrain. A Global Positioning System (GPS) can also be useful for pinpointing exact locations, but they can't tell you the best route to take. A good guide will know that not all sand dunes are the same: Some areas in the south-west of the country are entirely given over to *fish-fash,* an extremely fine sand, which makes for slow going and dramatically increases your fuel consumption. You should also notify someone of your planned route and expected arrival time, and be self-sufficient in water, food and, where you can get it, firewood.

Checkpoints

You'll find checkpoints all over Libya. While they are generally restricted to the roads into each town and major road intersections, their prevalence can slow travel times considerably.

It is rare that a checkpoint will, for foreign travellers, be anything more than a formality, and often a surprisingly pleasant one at that (see the boxed text 'Some Very Libyan Checkpoints'). On most occasions you may be asked for your carnet, passport or, if you're travelling as a part of a group, a copy of your itinerary. No matter how many times you have been waved through a checkpoint, never assume that you will be. Always slow down or stop until you get the wave from your friendly machine-gun-toting soldier.

There are two types of checkpoints. Those manned by the army (green uniforms) are on the lookout for people who haven't com-

Some Very Libyan Checkpoints

At first the rapid-fire questions directed at our driver had us worried. Was our documentation not in order? Had we pointed our camera at the wrong sand dune? It soon became clear that the formalities had long been over and the soldiers, or police, were asking us whether we needed any help, some tea, water or petrol.

Close to Ras Lanuf, we were 'ordered' out of the car and plied with Pepsis and scalding cups of dark tea with camel's milk, all in the space of a very few minutes.

On the remote road to Ghirza, a miscalculation saw our petrol supplies dwindling dangerously low. The soldiers sheltering in a tin shack in the searing heat mustered an impressive degree of enthusiasm in making sure that we had enough petrol to make it to Misrata. Elsewhere, tea, tea and more tea.

It is always worth remembering that, particularly in remote areas, the formidable-looking uniforms are sometimes filled by bored young men merely completing their military service. Chances are, they've probably stopped you because they're in need of company. The constant stopping can be tedious, but if you're in need of a break in the journey, it's a good place to enjoy some unlikely Libyan hospitality.

pleted their military service, while the police (blue uniforms) are more concerned with flushing out illegal immigrants, drivers who have been involved in accidents or stolen cars. Tourists are rarely the target, and there seems to have been a government directive to allow visitors to progress without delay.

Road Rules
Believe it or not, Libya does have road rules. Driving is on the right-hand side of the road, and speed limits, which are rarely enforced, follow a set pattern with gradations depending on the type of road and car. For the record, cars (which applies also to 4WD vehicles) must stay on or below 100km/h on highways, 85km/h on main roads outside towns, 70km/h on small roads outside towns and 50km/h inside towns. The corresponding figures for taxis are 85/70/60/60km/h, while large vehicles (trucks and buses) must adhere to limits of 65/60/50/30km/h. In reality, Libyan drivers generally drive as fast as they think they can get away with. Fines are the official punishment for speeding, but no Libyans we spoke to had heard of anyone getting one, nor did they know how much they amounted to.

Parking restrictions also apply in most cities of any size and these *are* often enforced to the tune of a 30LD fine. The No Parking areas are indicated by signs sporting a black circle with a white cross or red diagonal line. Be especially careful around Green Square in Tripoli as the whole area can be cleared for public events and your car towed away.

Of far more credence than the official road rules are those unwritten rules. Many dual carriageways are punctuated with breaks in the roads where drivers undertake perilous U-turn manoeuvres. If you slow down too much, these drivers take that as permission to cross, but if you approach with a succession of short, quickly consecutive toots, they'll generally wait until you pass. The same applies to traffic entering from a side road.

If someone flashes their lights at you, it is usually a warning of some impending danger up ahead, such as an accident or sheep or camels grazing by the roadside. Camels can be a particular problem and they are at

Gaddafi's Rocket Car
In September 1999 at the Organisation of African Unity summit, Colonel Gaddafi unveiled his (or rather his scientists') latest invention – a prototype of the safest car on earth. The *Saroukh al-Jamahiriya* (Libyan rocket) is, dare we say it, surprisingly stylish and a far cry from the days when the coup leader got around in an old VW Beetle. The sporty lines (the front and rear are shaped like a rocket) and tinted windows are enhanced by a metallic shade of Libyan revolutionary green. Safety features included air bags, an in-built electronic defence system and specially designed collapsible bumper.

Libyan press reports, true to form, described the car as a 'revolutionary' moment in automotive history. A Libyan spokesman assured the sceptics that 'The invention of the safest car in the world is proof that the Libyan revolution is built on the happiness of man' and evidence that despite sanctions, Colonel G has been 'thinking of ways to preserve human life all over the world'. In a none-too-subtle play on words, the car's name was seen as proof that while other countries made rockets designed to kill, Libya designed them 'for humane and peaceful purposes'.

their most dangerous when on both sides of the road – slow to a crawl until you're well past. Camels are also a big danger if you are travelling desert roads at night while, everywhere throughout the country, cars with a single headlight are a common hazard after dark. Sand blown across the road in southern and western Libya is also a problem.

Motorcyclists should be especially careful as Libyan drivers are not on the lookout for two-wheeled transport and rarely take such possibilities into account when overtaking.

There is, nonetheless, a Tripoli Motorcycle Federation (☎ 021-4441274), PO Box 12794 Tripoli, whom you just might want to contact.

Rental
The major international car-rental agencies do not operate in Libya and are unlikely to

do so in the foreseeable future. Local companies can be quite expensive, although it's usually not that much more for a driver.

Car-rental agencies are most likely to be found in the lobbies of upmarket hotels and at Tripoli airport. The cheapest rate that we found (see Getting Around in the Tripoli chapter) were for run-down, nonair-con cars at 50LD per day, which included 300km free per day (0.25LD per extra km). Otherwise, prices hover around 100LD per day, with the first 100km free, for half-decent cars. Some also require a three-day minimum booking. If you only want a car for a day or even a couple of days, you might be better off negotiating a deal with a local taxi driver.

Purchasing & Importing

Purchasing a car in Libya can be a bureaucratic nightmare, and it's hard to imagine a circumstance where it wouldn't be easier to purchase it elsewhere. Every Friday evening in Tripoli, a wildly busy used-car market takes place in the Al-Fallah district of Sharia as-Swani, about 5km south-west of the Parliament building. Even if you're not looking to buy, the atmosphere's fun.

Importing cars for resale or long-term private use involves whole forests of paperwork – contact a Libyan tour company (see Organised Tours later in the chapter) for sources of assistance and advice.

BICYCLE

In this era of group tourism in Libya, it's rare to find cyclists traversing the roads, and indeed cycling is not a passion to which Libyans are generally predisposed. Although the roads are well-surfaced and flat, the speed at which most Libyan traffic moves would make it an adventurous undertaking. Cycling lanes are also unheard of and even on some highways there is little additional space on the road outside the motor-vehicle lanes. Overtaking is also sometimes done on the inside with little forethought for two-wheelers that may be trying to stay out of trouble. If you do decide to cycle, you'll also need to be self-sufficient in spare parts, which, along with replacement bikes, can be hard to come by. Always wear a helmet.

HITCHING

Hitching is never entirely safe in any country, and we don't recommend it. Travellers who decide to hitch should understand that they are taking a small but potentially serious risk. People who do choose to hitch will be safer if they travel in pairs and let someone know where they are planning to go.

That said, there are many places – the Jebel Nafusa, the mountains of Cyrenaica and some of the more remote towns of the Fezzan – where local transport can be irregular to the point of nonexistent. Although we've received no reports of any incidents, and Libya is one of the safest countries in the region to visit, lone women travellers should never hitch on their own.

LOCAL TRANSPORT
To/From the Airport

At the time of writing, no Libyan airports had regular bus or taxi services into the nearest city. You might be lucky to find enough people from your flight heading in the same general direction to convince a taxi driver to take you all for the price of a shared tax (ie, the price of a seat). On most occasions, however, you'll have to pay for the taxi all to yourself. Of course if you are part of a tour group, this is not something that you'll need to worry about.

Micro

There are no large bus services within Libyan towns. White micros crisscross most towns, usually for half the price of a shared taxi on the same route. They usually congregate at the main shared-taxi station and follow roughly set routes, although they sometimes make small detours if demand requires it. There are no timetables and micros usually don't leave the station until full. If the stations aren't convenient, stand on a main street en route to your general direction, hail down a micro and call out your destination as it slows. Tripoli even has a few designated bus shelters where micros stop.

Taxi

Libyan cities generally have plenty of shared taxis and operate under the same system as the micros. While more expensive, shared taxis do fill more quickly and can therefore be better if you're in a hurry and don't want to pay for a private taxi.

Within cities, private taxis are reasonably priced and journeys, other than those to the airport, are unlikely to cost more than 5LD.

ORGANISED TOURS

Libya has some very professionally run tour companies. Unlike European agencies, who can be almost twice as expensive, most Libyan companies are willing to custom-make your itinerary with accommodation in places ranging from youth hostels to five-star hotels. If you go with a good company, everything is organised for you – hotel bookings, airport transfers, transport, visa applications and passport registration, guides for major sites – and included in the price, which can be calculated on a full- or half-board basis. Groups can range in size from two or three people up to as many as you wish. Clearly, economies of scale demand that members of smaller groups will pay more per person.

There are three companies that we strongly recommend:

Azar Libya Travel & Tours Co (☎/fax 025-24821, e Azartours@aol.com) Sharia Jamal Abdul Nasser, Zuara; postal address: PO Box 101/510 Zuara. A good agency with lots of experience and few complaints from travellers.

Robban Tourism Services (☎ 021-4441530, fax 4448065, e robbantours@hotmail.com) Off Sharia as-Sarim, Tripoli; postal address: PO Box 84272 Tripoli. This small company is very professional, has excellent guides, flexible itineraries and good transport. Best of all, its tours always carry a personal touch. The owner, Hussein Founi, should be your first port of call.

Winzrik Tourism Services (☎ 021-3611123/5, fax 3611126, mobile ☎ 091225687, e gher wash@ hotmail.com) Sharia 7 November, Tripoli; postal address: PO Box 12794. This is Libya's largest travel agency with decades of experience. In recent years the company has branched out into hotels and other tourism services and some travellers have contacted us to say that with greater size has come a lack of attention to detail. Check its Web site at w www .winzrik.com.

Other companies that readers and travellers we met have recommended include:

Africa Tours (☎ 021-3350900, fax 3350198, e africatravellyb@hotmail.com) Dhat al-Ahmat Tower 3, Ground floor, Tripoli; postal address: PO Box 91058 Tripoli

Agence Akacus Voyages (☎ 0724-2804) One of the pioneers of desert tourism in Libya's south, this Ghat-based agency is predominantly French-speaking.

AIEL Travel & Tour Services (☎ 061-9092385, fax 9080272) Islamic Call Bldg, Level 7, Benghazi. The owner, Sami al-Ghibani, has a reputation for running an efficient and flexible company.

Al-Fridgha Voyages (☎ 071-631434, fax 630433, e afri.vog@hotmail.com, w www.afrivog.bizland.com) Funduq Kala, Sharia Jamal Abdul Nasser, Sebha

Arkno Tours (☎ 021-4440737, fax 3332618, mobile ☎ 2140262, e jamal@arkno.com, w www.arkno.com); postal address: PO Box 2170 Tripoli

Attair Travel & Tourism Co (☎ 021-4449544, fax 4449531, e attair@attairtours.com, w www.attairtours.com) Sharia al-Khitouni, Tripoli; postal address: PO Box 6165 Tripoli

Bright Focus (☎/fax 061-9091639, 9091467, e nasir@brightfocus.com.ly); postal address: PO Box 17824 Benghazi

Corin Travel & Tourism (☎ 021-3350192, fax 3350070) Dhat al-Ahmet Tower 1, Level 1, Tripoli; postal address: PO Box 91913 Tripoli

El-Meimon Tours (☎ 021-3351602/3, fax 3351605, e elmeimon@hotmail.com) Burj al-Fateh, Level 2 No 36, Tripoli

Germa Travel & Tourism (☎ 021-3341660, fax 4449596) 22 Sharia Jakarta; postal address: PO Box 76118 Tripoli

Oea Tours (☎ 021-3338237, fax 3338369, e oeatours@hotmail.com) Sharia 1st September, Tripoli

Taknes Co (☎ 021-3350526, fax 3350525) Funduq Bab al-Bahar, Tripoli; postal address: PO Box 91218 Tripoli. The owner is the helpful Ali Shebli.

Tripolis Travel & Tourism (☎ 021-4442323, fax 3333998, e allaghi@hotmail.com, w www.tripolistours.com) Sharia Abu Maliana, Tripoli; postal address: PO Box 82825 Tripoli

Wings Travel & Tours (☎ 3331855, fax 3330881) Green Square, Tripoli

Tripoli

طرابلس

TRIPOLI

☎ 021 • pop 1.7 million

And now again the story of Tripoli changes. But whatever the outcome, she will still have her limpid skies, her air like wine, and a climate where it is a sin to acknowledge an ache or a pain, old age or unhappiness.

Mabel Loomis Todd
Tripoli the Mysterious

Tripoli (At-Tarablus in Arabic) is Libya's largest and most cosmopolitan city. Set on one of North Africa's best natural harbours, the city exudes a distinctive Mediterranean charm infused with a decidedly Arab/Islamic flavour. With such a rich mosaic of historical influences, few travellers leave disappointed.

Tripoli has worn many guises throughout history. The ancient Oea of Roman antiquity yielded to an Islamic city fought over by successive North African dynasties. Later, Turkish and Italian influences gave birth to a charming white city of elegant facades, which earned the city the sobriquet of the 'White Bride of the Mediterranean'. Tripoli was the ultimate destination of ancient trans-Saharan caravans and the gateway to the unexplored riches of Africa. In more recent years, Libya's oil wealth has seen it become the destination of many sub-Saharan Africans in search of their own El Dorado.

The disparate civilisations that have occupied the city have all left their mark, from the Roman Arch of Marcus Aurelius and the Turkish mosques of the medina to Italianate villas fronted by palm trees along the waterfront. Every era of Libyan history is also showcased in the Jamahiriya Museum. An undoubted highlight of any visit to Tripoli will be the hours spent wandering through the medina with its meandering souqs and beautiful facades, every one of which is a signpost to history.

Away from the medina, especially to the west of the city in Gargaresh, is an entirely different Tripoli – a modern city well adapted to the demands of the 21st century.

Highlights

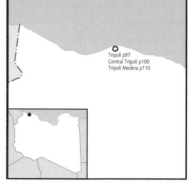

Tripoli p97
Central Tripoli p100
Tripoli Medina p110

- Wander through the enchanting lanes of Tripoli's whitewashed medina.
- Enjoy the splendour of the Ottoman mosques of Gurgi, Draghut and Karamanli and the Roman Arch of Marcus Aurelius.
- Shop to your heart's content in the souqs of the medina.
- Marvel at Libya's history in the exceptional Jamahiriya Museum.
- Search for ghosts in the intriguing Assai al-Hamra (Tripoli Castle).
- Experience the clamour and excitement of the markets in Sharia ar-Rashid.

Therein lies the secret of Tripoli. It is a sophisticated modern city that beats with an ancient heart.

HISTORY

Called Oea in antiquity, Tripoli was founded by the Phoenicians in around 500 BC. It became one of the four Punic settlements of significance (the others being Carthage, Sabratha and Leptis). Tripoli is Libya's only ancient city to have been continuously occupied since that time, although few relics of the early settlements survive.

TRIPOLI

PLACES TO STAY & EAT
7 Funduq Bab al-Bahar
8 Funduq Bab al-Medina
9 Funduq Bab al-Jadid
11 Funduq al-Jawda
12 Funduq Bahr al-Abyad
13 Funduq Atlas
15 Funduq al Wahat;
   Al-Kashaf Theatre
22 Funduq Winzrik

OTHER
1 Shared Taxi & Minibus
   Station

2 Dhat al-Ahmat Tower 5;
   Air Malta; Emirates
3 Dhat al-Ahmat Tower 4;
   Belgian Embassy; Japanese
   Embassy; Lufthansa
4 Dhat al-Ahmat Tower 3;
   Mat'am Dhahabi; Africa
   Tours; Austrian Airlines;
   Swiss Air; Alitalia; Horizons
   Travel
5 Dhat al-Ahmat Tower 2
6 Dhat al-Ahmat Tower 1;
   Corin Travel & Tourism;
   Bank

10 Burj al-Fateh Complex; Al-Ofq
   Internet, UK Embassy,
   Next Century Aviation
   Services; Amanco Travel &
   Tourism Services; El-Meimon
   Tours; Al-Mat'am
   al-Hawar Burj al-Fateh;
   KLM; British Airways;
   Malev-Hungarian Airlines
14 Libyan Arab Airlines
16 General People's Congress
   (Parliament)
17 Mechanics Workshops
18 Robban Tourism Services

19 Jawazzat
20 DHL
21 General People's Committee
   for Tourism
23 Dar al-Founoun (House of Art)
24 New Mosque
   (Under Construction)
25 Algerian Consulate-General
26 Tunisian Embassy
27 Tunisian Consulate-General
28 Tripoli Zoo (Hadikat
   al-Haywan)
29 Emergency Hospital
30 Al-Khadra Hospital

Following the fall of Carthage in 146 BC, Oea came briefly under the jurisdiction of the Nubian kingdom, before becoming a Roman protectorate. Under the Romans, Oea grew very prosperous and, together with Sabratha and Leptis Magna (the other cities of the 'tripolis' that gave Tripoli its name), provided the Roman Empire with grain, wild animals and slaves.

After the golden age of the 2nd century AD Oea fell into decline. When the Vandals overran North Africa in the 5th century, the damage to the city was devastating. The conquest by the Byzantines in AD 533 arrested the decline, but Tripoli nonetheless spent the following centuries in a much reduced state.

The Arab invasion in the 7th century saw a new town, named At-Tarablus, built among the ruins of the old. The city grew and, by the 10th century, the Arab geographer Ibn Hawkal described Tripoli as a wealthy and powerful city with a vast market and a busy port. By AD 1000, Tripoli had become an important centre of intercontinental trade between sub-Saharan Africa and southern Europe, as well as Egypt and the Middle East. It was after the second Arab invasion in 1046 that the old city walls were rebuilt, using Roman remains as foundations. Roman pillars are still in evidence in parts of the medina.

Despite a very temporary Norman occupation, from 1146 to 1158, the Arab town flourished in the 14th and 15th centuries. In 1460 the Tripoli declared itself an independent city-state. During the 16th century the city was occupied in quick succession by the Spanish and the Knights of St John of Malta. The most visible result of their occupation is the work they carried out on the Assai al-Hamra (Tripoli Castle).

The most lasting architectural monuments in the old city were built by the Ottoman Turks, who occupied Tripoli from 1551. In the centuries that followed, they constructed most of the mosques, hammams and souqs visible today, defined the boundaries of the old city and laid out the city's winding lanes. They called the city Tarablus al-Gharb (Tripoli of the West) to distinguish it from the Lebanese city of the same name. By the end of the 17th century, Tripoli was Libya's only city of size and had over 30,000 inhabitants. In 1783, a British resident of the city described Tripoli on arriving by sea:

The whole of the town appears in a semicircle, some time before reaching the harbour's mouth. The extreme whiteness of square flat buildings covered with lime, which in this climate encounters the sun's fiercest rays, is very striking. The baths form clusters of cupolas very large, to the number of eight or ten crowded together in different parts of the town. The mosques have in general a small plantation of Indian figs and date trees growing close to them, which, at a distance, appearing to be so many rich gardens in different parts of the town, give the whole city, in the eyes of an European, an aspect truly novel and pleasing.

From the correspondence of Richard Tully
Narrative of a Ten-year
Residence at Tripoli in Africa

It was after the Italians invaded and conquered Libya that the city burst out of the confines of the city walls. The centre of modern Tripoli used to be farms and gardens. The Italians built colonnaded streets and numerous public buildings.

After WWII many families left the old city to live in the newly vacated Italian apartments and houses. The old city, damaged by bombing during the war, fell into disrepair and remains under threat of neglect to this day.

Notwithstanding the process of political decentralisation, Tripoli remains the political and economic capital of Libya (see the boxed text 'Libya's Shifting Capital' in the Facts about Libya chapter). At last count, all but two of the General People's Committees were relocated to other parts of country, with most going to Sirt (see the boxed text 'Winning Hearts & Minds').

ORIENTATION

Tripoli's most recognisable landmark is the castle, Assai al-Hamra, which sits on the eastern corner of the medina alongside the central Green Square (As-Saha al-Kradrah or Martyrs' Square). Until the 1970s, when around 500m of land was reclaimed, the castle and square were right on the water; a motorway now separates the castle from the waterfront in spite of what most maps may tell you. Green Square was cleared after the revolution as a venue for mass rallies. All the main shopping and business streets radiate out from the square.

East of Green Square are a number of upmarket hotels and the ferry port (almost opposite the Funduq al-Mehari). South-east of the square, in the districts of Garden City and Bin Ashour are many of the embassies; the long-distance Dahra Bus Station is also nearby. The remainder of the transport options are south and west of the medina.

Immediately west of the medina along the waterfront are the five towers known as Dhat al-Ahmat, as well as the Burj al-Fateh complex; these skyscrapers are home to many airline offices, travel agencies and some embassies with plenty of hotels nearby. The modern suburb of Gargaresh, around 4km west of the city centre, hosts the remainder of the embassies, many restaurants, a youth hostel and shopping complexes.

INFORMATION
Tourist Offices
As in most cities in Libya, there is no tourist office in the traditional sense. For all but the most basic tourist information, you are better off contacting one of the many privately run travel agencies around town (see Organised Tours in the Getting Around chapter).

The General People's Committee for Tourism (☎ 3603405, fax 3603400) is near the ferry port on the main road to Janzur.

Jawazzat
The *jawazzat* (passport office; ☎ 3334657), on Maidan al-Falisteen or Palestine Square, is the place to go for visa registration and extensions. It's the five-storey concrete block behind the Sidi Munedir Islamic Cemetery.

At the time of research the procedure involved collecting two forms outside the main building (1LD) and delivering them (and 5LD) to the officers, seated at a small table on the right-hand side of the compound, who will fill in the form and attach the requisite stamps. Take your passport and forms inside the main building and queue at Counter

Winning Hearts & Minds
One apocryphal story highlights the unspoken reluctance of many of Libya's politicians and bureaucrats to follow their leader along the road to Sirt. A former prime minister in the government simply couldn't bring himself to leave behind the sophistication of cosmopolitan Tripoli. Accordingly, whenever someone from Colonel Gaddafi's office, or the Colonel himself called the minister, he pretended that he had been called to Tripoli for a meeting. It wasn't long before the Leader of the Revolution discovered that the minister had never in fact moved to Sirt, nor did he have any intention of doing so, and indeed had been fielding calls from his office overlooking Green Square. Soon after, the building housing the office was razed and a coffee shop built in its place.

Three. To retrieve your passport with a releasing stamp, head to Counter Four, whereupon, as one traveller put it, 'take your passport and be happy'. Ask to be pointed in the right direction as procedures (and prices) often change.

See Visas & Documents in the Facts for the Visitor chapter for details on the registration requirements.

Money
The most easily accessible banks (*masraf*) are in the streets between Green Square and Maidan al-Jezayir (Algeria Square). There is a useful branch in the lobby of Funduq al-Waddan, as well as branches on Sharia ar-Rashid, in the Dhat al-Ahmat complex (Ground floor, Tower 1) and along the main thoroughfare of Gargaresh. Masraf al-Umma and Masraf al-Jamahiriya have the most branches around town.

A small black market operates in the medina's Souq al-Mushir and Souq al-Turk; many jewellery shops throughout the old quarter are also good places to try. Avoid changing money at your hotel (most are reluctant anyway) unless there is a proper bank attached; rates are considerably better in the banks. See Exchange Rates under

TRIPOLI

CENTRAL TRIPOLI

PLACES TO STAY
1 Hotel Under Construction
5 Funduq an-Naher
6 Funduq al-Jebel al-Akhdar
8 Funduq al-Ma'moun
11 Funduq an-Nasr
14 Funduq al-Manar
16 Funduq as-Siyahe
33 Buyut ash-Shabaab;
  Laundry
40 Funduq al-Kebir
59 Funduq as-Safwa
66 Funduq al-Waddan;
  Assalama Car Rental;
  Masraf al-Umma
70 Funduq Qasr Libya;
  Al-Mansura Car Rental

77 Funduq al-Mehari;
  Al-Mehari Car Rental

PLACES TO EAT
13 Al-Mat'am as-Samak
  at-Taazej
17 Cheap Restaurants;
  Patiseries
18 Mat'am as-Safira
20 Cheap Restaurants
23 Pizza Restaurant
24 Hamburger Restaurant
25 Open-Air Teahouse
26 Open-Air Teahouse
35 Hamburger Restaurant
36 Hamburger Restaurant
38 Shwarma Restaurant

42 Mat'am as-Safir
46 Helawiyat 'Abembir Afra
47 Al-Mat'am al-Turkiye
49 Mat'am al-Jedda
50 Mat'am al-Murjan
51 Sonober
53 Hamburger Restaurant
55 Mat'am Thatul Sawari
56 Mat'am al-Masabiyah
67 Gazebe Café; Fountain

OTHER
2 Felatel Stand
3 Bourgeiba Mosque
4 Al-itihad al-Afriqi (United
  Africa Bus Company)
7 Masraf al-Umma

9 An-Numan Photo Shop
10 Shared Taxis to Tarhuna
12 Local Shared-Taxi Station
15 Studio Mukhtar
19 Masraf al-Umma
21 Cinema
22 Anai Travel & Tourism Co
27 Wings Travel & Tours
28 GNMTC (Ferry Tickets)
29 Manara Information
  Technology & Internet;
  Open-Air Teahouse;
  Galleria De Bono
30 Mamer Seriya; Ghadames
  Art Gallery
31 Fergiani's Bookshop
32 Sebha Bookshop

34 Oea Tours
37 Modern World
  Communications
39 Syrianair
41 Echo Net
43 Royal Jordanian Airlines
44 United Africa Internet
45 Mediterranean Travel &
  Tourism Co
48 Cinema
52 Tunis Air
54 Mosque (Former Cathedral);
  Islamic Call Society
57 Main Post Office; Main
  Telephone Office
58 Jamahiriya Computer
  Systems

60 Greek Embassy
61 Algerian Embassy
62 Netherlands Embassy
63 United Nations
  Building
64 National Library
  (People's Palace)
65 Islamic Call Society;
  Africa Centre
68 Italian Embassy
69 Egyptian Embassy
71 San Francisco Church
72 Masraf al-Jamahiriya
73 Dahra Bus Station
74 Grocery Store
75 Ferry Port
76 Mosque

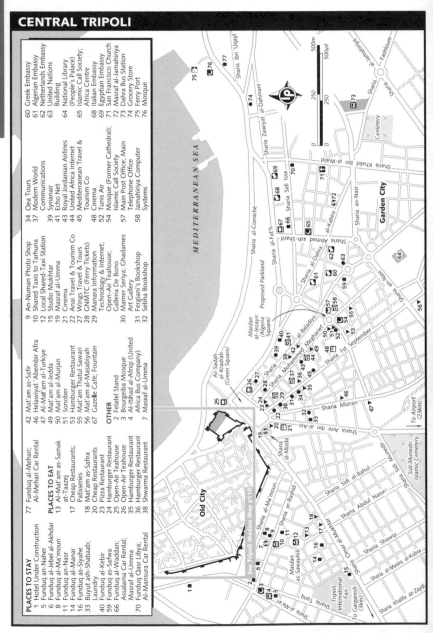

Money in the Facts for the Visitor chapter for more details on exchanging money.

Post & Communications
The main post office is on Maidan al-Jezayir (open 7am to 7pm Saturday to Thursday). There is a reasonably efficient poste restante service; make sure you bring your passport.

The main telephone office is on your left just before you enter the cavernous main hall; early morning is the best time. Inside the main hall there is a useful fax restante service (fax 3331199, 3340040) for a small fee (no more than 1LD) – look for the 'Fax Service' sign in English.

Cybercafes are springing up all over Tripoli and connections are generally fast; most are closed on Friday morning.

Al-Ofq (☎ 3351219, ℮ Al_Ofq@hotmail.com) Burj al-Fateh complex, Level 2, Room 29. One of the few places west of the medina, the sign on the door says 'Internet Service'. Open 9am to 5pm; 3LD per hour.

Echo Net (☎ 3343952, ℮ echonet@hotmail .com) Sharia al-Baladiya in the back of the Funduq al-Kebir building. A professionally run and high-tech place, which is open 10am to midnight; 3LD per hour.

Jamahiriya Computer Systems (☎ 4444496, fax 4448521) Sharia Mohammed Megharief. Signed simply as 'Internet' on the glass entrance door. Open 8.30am to 7pm; 2LD per hour.

Manara Information Technology and Internet (☎/fax 3332518, ℮ taher.elsonni@undp.org) Sharia al-Qahira. Another well-run place with fast connections and free tea and coffee; it's the closest option to Green Square. Open 9am to midnight; 2.5LD per hour.

Modern World Communications (mobile ☎ 091 2130428) Just off Sharia 1st September not far from Green Square, this place is open 9am to 1am; 2LD per hour.

United Africa Internet (☎ 3342143) Sharia Mohammed Megharief. Also good, it's signed as 'Web Development' on the window outside. Open 9am to midnight; 2.25LD per hour.

Travel Agencies
For Tripoli-based tour companies who run tours throughout Libya, see Organised Tours in the Getting Around chapter.

There are a number of travel agencies in Tripoli that specialise in selling domestic

and international air tickets (see Buying International Tickets in Libya under Air in the Getting There & Away chapter).

Amanco Travel & Tourism Services (☎ 335 1187, fax 3351187) Burj al-Fateh complex, Level 2, Room 37

Anai Travel & Tourism Co (☎ 3343585, fax 3343586) Sharia 1st September

Horizons Travel (☎ 3350456, fax 3350457) Dhat al-Ahmat, Ground floor, Tower 3

Mediterranean Travel & Tourism Co (☎ 444 0837, fax 4446966) Sharia 1st September. A professional and helpful agency that sells air tickets, ferry tickets and claims to assist with visa registration and hotel reservations

Next Century Aviation Services (☎ 3351026, fax 3351028) Burj al-Fateh complex, Level 2

Bookshops
Fergiani's Bookshop (☎ 4444873) on Sharia 1st September (postal address: PO Box 132), is open 10am to noon and 5pm to 9pm Saturday to Thursday, 5pm to 9pm Friday. It has an excellent selection of Arabic and English-language books, coffee-table books, fascinating travel literature, modern studies of Libya, a smaller number of books in French and Italian and excellent postcards. This is a good place to pick up your copy of *The Green Book* (5LD).

At the time of research, the friendly Sebha Bookshop (☎ 3340920) on Sharia Mizran was Tripoli's only second-hand bookshop catering to a non-Arabic readership. It's open 8am to 8pm Saturday to Thursday, 2pm to 8pm Friday. The eclectic selection (Italian, English and French) is a bit top-heavy on sciences, but does range from back issues of *Obstetrics and Gynaecology* to DH Lawrence's *Sons and Lovers*.

There are also plans for a second-hand bookshop opposite the Banco di Roma in the medina. The friendly owner, Mukhtar, has an encyclopaedic knowledge of the medina and it should also be a good place to offload the books weighing down your backpack.

Film & Photography
There are some excellent photo shops (they generally open 9am to 1pm and 5pm to 7pm Saturday to Thursday) scattered around

town where you can buy print and slide film, get passport photos taken and have print film developed.

The only place that we could find to get slide film developed (but not mounted) was Mamer Seriya (Express Photo; ☎ 4442241) on Sharia 1st September. It charges 20LD for a roll of 36 slides. It's also the cheapest for developing print film at 1.5LD for the negatives, plus 0.25LD for each 10cm by 15cm print. Look for the Agfa sign about 100m south-east of Green Square.

Also good is Studio Mukhtar (☎ 333 2230) on Sharia Omar al-Mukhtar (postal address: PO Box 82411). The front of the shop is emblazoned with a Konica sign. Also consider An-Numan Photo Shop (mobile ☎ 091 2130750), on Sharia ar-Rashid, which specialises in Fuji products.

Taking photos in Tripoli is generally no problem if you ask permission first and if you're discreet when snapping crowded street scenes. One unmarked police station to be especially careful of is underneath the castle walls on Green Square between the entrance to the museum and Mussolini's balcony.

Laundry

There are laundries throughout Tripoli, although most are in the residential districts away from the centre of town. One centrally located place to get your washing done is the laundry on the small square off Sharia Amr ibn al-Ass, behind the Youth Hostel. Shirts cost 1.5LD.

Hammams

There are at least three hammams (bathhouses) in the old city. Hammam Draghut is next door to the Draghut Mosque and open 7am to 5pm for women on Monday, Wednesday and Thursday and alternate days for men; it sometimes opens for men on Friday. Hammam al-Kebira is open the same hours. Hammam al-Heygha, near the Souq al-Attara, is open Tuesday, Wednesday and Friday for men, the other days for women. Charges are 1LD for a steam bath, 2LD for a massage and 5LD for the full-scrubbing works.

Toilets

There are no public toilets in Tripoli, but you're never too far from a restaurant or mosque, where they're usually happy to point you in the right direction in the event of an emergency; ask for 'al-hammam' or 'mirhab'.

Left Luggage

The best place to leave your luggage if you're leaving town for a few days is with your tour company. Most hotels are also fine, although some will try and charge you.

Medical Services

There are plenty of government hospitals and private clinics around. The best idea is to get a recommendation from your tour company or embassy. Perhaps the best hospital is Naqaz at-Tubi (Medical Centre; ☎ 4263701/15) on Sharia Jamia near Al-Fatah University. Rebuilt in the late 1990s, it's relatively new.

Other decent hospitals include Al-Khadra Hospital (☎ 4900752) on Sharia al-Hadba, Shara Zawya Hospital (☎ 3600501) on Sharia Zawya, and the Emergency Hospital on the second ring road.

Dangers & Annoyances

Few travellers encounter any difficulties in Tripoli and the most arduous task you're likely to encounter is finding your way in a city where most of the street signs are written in Arabic.

One potential hazard is, inevitably, the dangers of crossing the street. Roads where you should exercise particular caution include the one circling Green Square, as well as Sharia Omar al-Mukhtar and Sharia al-Corniche (especially around the Burj al-Fateh and Dhat al-Ahmat tower complexes). Avoid sudden and unpredictable movements and, especially around Green Square, work your way across one lane at a time. If in doubt, ask a local to help out.

As more travellers make their way to Libya, the incidence of petty theft, once unheard of in Libya, is likely to increase, although reports of pickpocketing and other crimes against travellers are still extremely rare. One area where you may want to be careful is the Sharia ar-Rashid area, south-west of Green Square.

JAMAHIRIYA MUSEUM

Tripoli's Jamahiriya Museum houses one of the finest collections of classical art in the Mediterranean and is worth as much time as you can give it. Indeed, some travellers have compared it favourably to the British Museum, although here the antiquities are actually part of Libyan heritage and haven't been plundered from other countries. Built in consultation with Unesco at enormous cost, it is extremely well designed and provides a comprehensive overview of all periods of Libyan history, from the Neolithic period right up to the present day. The 47 galleries follow a chronological order.

If your time is limited, you may want to restrict yourself to the ground floor, which is undoubtedly the most impressive of the five levels. Also of considerable interest are the Islamic rooms (Gallery 20) on the 3rd floor as well as those devoted to Libyan resistance (31) and the revolutionary rule (32–37).

Information

The entrance to the museum (☎ 3330292; admission 3LD, camera/video 5/10LD; open 9am-1pm & 3pm-6pm Tues-Sun) is off the north-west corner of Green Square through a large wooden door. All bags (other than camera bags), must be left at the counter on your left as you enter. The ticket office is a bit further on.

The museum's only drawback is that most of the exhibits are labelled only in Arabic, although there are informative general descriptions in English of the relevant period of history in each room. The details that follow should be sufficient for most travellers, but using a guide (50LD) can make for a rewarding experience. Although this is expensive, if you can get a group together it becomes excellent value for money; depending on how long you spend in the museum, you may be able to get a brief tour of the castle or medina included in the price. If he's not already booked up, try and get the wonderful Dr Mustafa Turjman who works with

the Department of Antiquities (☎ 3333042). The other guides are also good.

The toilets are on the ground floor, although you may have to ask the attendant to unlock them.

Ground Floor (Galleries 1–9)
Entrance Hall (Gallery 1) This gallery provides a stunning overview of the museum's contents. On the right as you enter is an elegant statue of Venus, which was stolen during the colonial era, but finally repatriated to Libya in November 2000. On the wall behind the statue are mosaics from the 2nd century AD showing scenes of gladiatorial contests in the Leptis amphitheatre. On an adjacent wall is an attractive mural of Tripoli's ancient medina and harbour – note how the water comes right up to the gates of the castle. Opposite the statue, on the left as you enter, is an imposing stone mausoleum and some tablets from Ghirza, a Roman-era Libyan community that drew strongly on Roman architectural influence.

The second half of the gallery is overseen by an enormous map of Libya on which buttons light up prehistoric sites; areas of Punic, Greek and Roman dominance; trade and caravan routes; the Islamic conquest; and modern-day museums and archaeological sites. The map is a great way of placing Libyan history in its geographical context.

Just before leaving the gallery, it's impossible to miss the funky green VW Beetle used by Colonel Gaddafi around the time of the 1969 revolution.

The Prehistoric Era (Galleries 2–4)
Gallery 2 contains some 300,000-year-old hand axes that were used for killing animals. The glass cabinet in the centre of the room contains a fossilised tree found in the Libyan Sahara, while there are also examples of rock art and pottery dating from 8000 to 5000 BC.

Gallery 3 shows ceramics cast in the time before wheels were used in pottery, and are hence far less rigid in structure. They date from between 8000 and 3750 years ago.

Gallery 4 is devoted to rock art and shows you what you're missing if you don't make it down to the Jebel Acacus in south-western Libya. Most of the paintings and carvings are superb reproductions of the originals, which remain on the remote mountain walls of the Sahara. Those on display span most of the known periods of Saharan rock art (see the special section 'Rock Art of the Libyan Sahara' in the Fezzan chapter) and include representations of giraffes, chariots, examples of writing and, arguably the highlight, a wedding scene. The photos around the walls show the Acacus landscape. In the central display cabinet is a well-preserved child's skeleton, which was 5400 years old when it was found by Professor Mori in Wadi Tashwinat in 1958.

Libyan Heritage (Gallery 5)

This room showcases Libyan contributions to civilisation not subsumed into Roman, Greek or Punic history. The room is dominated, not surprisingly, by the relics of the Garamantian empire. The centrepiece of the gallery is a royal Garamantian tomb with a stone offering tablet outside the entrance. On the right wall as you enter are displays of pottery found in the tombs, along with other objects showing the largely commercial nature of Garamantes relations with the outside world. There are also artefacts from Zinchecra, the forerunner to Garama (now Germa) as the Garamantian capital.

The south wall contains a number of tomb and temple reliefs from Slonta (south of Al-Bayda). There are also more examples of the stonework of Ghirza, including a wonderful, simple relief carving of a camel and oxen ploughing the earth.

Phoenician (Gallery 6)

As the Phoenician (Punic) cities disappeared under subsequent Roman and Greek settlements, this relatively small gallery is one of the few surviving collections of Libyan-Punic artefacts. Those on display include a water pitcher, a representation of a Punic priest from the 2nd century BC, two stone lions from the ancient city of Oea (Tripoli), tablets of the Punic language (which was read from right to left) and the ancient symbol for Tarnit (the wife of the god, Baal).

Greek (Galleries 7 & 8)

The central display features a model of Cyrene's Temple of Zeus in Sabratha as well as the agora, as they appeared in the 2nd century AD. On the north wall (hard right as you enter) are a number of particularly fine decorative pottery pieces (3rd to 6th century BC), which were not for practical use, but rather sold as souvenirs to pilgrims and tourists outside the Temple of Zeus; tourism is clearly an ancient pursuit. Also in Gallery 7 are imposing statues of Dionysius and Fortuna.

The tiny Gallery 8 off the main room contains a captivating statue of the Three Graces from Cyrene; these comrades of Aphrodite were famous for their beauty and the statues reflect this superbly. On the left as you enter is a faceless Persephone, the wife of Hadis, King of Hades. Facing her is a martial statue of Athena, the God of Wisdom.

Roman (Gallery 9)

This large gallery, which consists of three parts, is the finest in the entire museum. The first room is devoted to Leptis Magna. The row of statues on the right are superb, with those of Artemis and Venus at the right-hand end particularly well crafted. The large mosaic adorning the wall that faces Gallery 7 is a magnificent example of a Roman Four Seasons mosaic with its pastoral scenes. The model representation of Leptis in the central glass case gives an idea of the city's former grandeur. There is a suitably imperious Tiberius in the maroon alcove to the left as you move through the gallery. Above the low ceiling over the stairs is an inauguration tablet from the Leptis amphitheatre with inscriptions in both Latin and Punic – a reminder that Leptis was quite a multicultural city.

In the small transitional room between the two main rooms, the floor is covered with a beautiful mosaic from Roman Oea. The scenes and portrait in the centre of the mosaic are surrounded by a much larger area of geometric designs on which people sat on cushions, leaving the centre free to be admired. On the left are marble busts of the Roman emperors Hadrian, Marcus Aurelius and Lucius Verus with their wives to their left. The display cabinets contain glassware used commonly in the 1st century AD for ash and bone after cremation, suggesting a Roman belief in the afterlife.

The final (eastern) section of Gallery 9 is devoted to Sabratha. There are many highlights in this room, including pillars and squat column bases with carved stone-relief scenes, breathtaking mosaics around the walls (including some comprised of exquisitely small tiles) and one statue (among many) of a beautiful woman washing her cascading curls. There's also a model of Sabratha in the centre of the room. This is a room in which to quietly sit and take it all in. As you leave the room, note the mosaic of Medusa heads above the exit, and the horns once used on dwellings to ward off evil.

First Floor (Galleries 10–14)

The 1st floor marks the transition from the Roman period to the Byzantine and then Islamic eras.

Gallery 10 is a continuation of exhibitions from the Roman period and most of the items date from the 1st to 3rd centuries AD. There is an excellent row of statues depicting, among others, Victoria (the God of Wind) and Apollo. Note also the particularly fine small marble statues of two children. In the glass display cabinets are a collection of delicate bronze items, miniature pottery amphorae and oil lamps. The second half of the gallery, up a few steps, contains some mildly interesting coins and oil lamps; see if you can find the small dice, which suggest that there was more to the lives of the ancients than sculpting.

Gallery 11 is dedicated to the Arch of Septimus Severus at Leptis, including some original panels (see if you can guess which head is a copy) and a forbidding bust (2nd century AD) of the man himself, which was found in the theatre at Leptis.

Galleries 12 and 13 cover the Byzantine period and contain a motley array of glass bottles, photos of mosaics, stone grave covers, an unfinished coffin and some impressive stone windows found in the Green Church in Tarhuna. The latter provide a good example of how a church's exterior must have looked in the 5th to 6th centuries AD.

Second Floor (Galleries 15–19)

These galleries contain some fine examples of Islamic architecture. The best, in Gallery 15, is a vernacular arch, made of mortar and sun-dried brick, its palm roof and stonework highlighting a simplicity of design and construction. Note also the massive green Quran.

Gallery 16 has model displays of sandstone tombs from Ajdabiya and Medinat Sultan, as well as a map of the world as it was understood in 1349.

Gallery 19 is also worth visiting for its excellent model of Assai al-Hamra, wonderful old map of Oea and a painting of the interior of the Karamanli Mosque with its pleasing blue tile work and sombre dark ceiling. Other good exhibits include an evocative old wooden door, a reconstructed interior of a Ghadames house and a Tripolitanian bedroom; this latter room, with its ornate inlaid chair, carpets, cushions and sombre wall-hangings, was reserved for the bride and groom on their wedding night.

Third Floor (Galleries 20–30)

At the top of the stairs, and before entering the galleries, look over the ledge for a fine view of the mosaic from Roman Oea in Gallery 9 on the ground floor.

Most of the 3rd floor dates from the Islamic/Turkish era and the galleries are organised around rural and folklore themes from the period.

Gallery 20 is filled with a diverse range of artefacts, with lovely samovars, silver jewellery and a huge incense container being stand-out features. Off the main room, on either side of the entrance, are two small rooms, one devoted to a Turkish kitchen, the other to weaving. The corridor leading to the next room is home to a glass cabinet that showcases traditional costumes of Ottoman Libya. The mannequins represent, from left to right, a woman from Benghazi, a man from eastern Libya, a Tuareg woman, a Tripoli man, three people in everyday central-Libyan wear, a shepherd, the blue and black robes of Murzuq, a Tuareg, an unknown woman and another Tuareg; there is also a mannequin of a small

Bedouin girl from the east in a glass case nearby.

Galleries 21 to 27 are only mediocre. Gallery 21 is devoted to the Tuareg, with photos on the walls and glass cases containing Tuareg leather items and spears. Gallery 23 has items from southern Libya (basketwork for use in the kitchen, a thatched hut, medicines and more Tuareg leatherwork), while Gallery 26 contains an oil-press used until recently in the Jebel Nafusa, other elements of olive-oil production and a stone relief from Ghirza showing a farming scene. The agricultural theme is continued in Gallery 27, which includes good displays of farming implements and techniques. Beekeeping enthusiasts and devotees of the virtues of palm trees also haven't been forgotten.

The folklore exhibitions (Galleries 28–30) are also patchy, and some of the rooms were almost empty when we visited. Among the dusty exhibits are items used in circumcision rites, some informative posters on Libyan folklore and a few musical instruments.

Fourth Floor
Libyan Resistance (Gallery 31) The
years of resistance to Italian rule make for some sobering viewing, although the exhibits are quite understated: weaponry (note the small toy-like cannon), and the personal belongings of the prominent writer and resistance figure Suleiman al-Baruni (the photo was taken in 1912, a year before he led an ill-fated rebellion in the Jebel Nafusa) and Omar al-Mukhtar (see the boxed text 'The Lion of the Desert' in the Facts about Libya chapter). There is a copy of the famous photo of Omar al-Mukhtar being led to trial, shortly before his execution, in 1931. There is also a chart documenting the exile of Libyan prisoners of war in Italy – 1911 and 1915 were the obvious low points.

Revolutionary Libya (Galleries 32–7)
If you're a connoisseur of images of Colonel Gaddafi, you'll kick yourself if you miss these galleries. After refreshing your memory as to the noble aims of the English translation of the Declaration of the Estab-

lishment of the Authority of the People in 1977, you'll find photos of shouting youths, women soldiers and a child wearing a Colonel Gaddafi T-shirt (Gallery 34).

Gallery 35 depicts Colonel Gaddafi the statesman, the revolutionary leader, the munificent leader of his people. The first panel of photos on your right as you enter include a 1966 photo of the decidedly self-conscious Colonel walking along a London street (second row from the top), one of the first photos taken of Gaddafi after the revolution (next row down), and photos of where he grew up (top row). Other definite highlights include the departure of some very sour-looking British troops in the early 1970s (third panel on the right) and a collection of photos of Colonel Gaddafi smiling with world leaders, many of whom would later scotch his vision of Arab unity.

Gallery 36 lauds Libya's oil industry and the Libyan contribution to modern technology, and Gallery 37 is given over to a long corridor containing the people's written adorations to Colonel Gaddafi – very entertaining if you can read Arabic.

Natural History (Galleries 38–47) It's
galling to find that the least interesting galleries in the museum contain some of the best English-language labels. Gallery 38 is rocks and geology, Gallery 39 showcases animal fossils, while Gallery 40 is home to stuffed desert animals, including the waddan (see Flora & Fauna in the Facts about Libya chapter). Gallery 41 has a strong whiff of the macabre – camel embryos in glass jars and deformed animals. The stuffed animals in the central glass case include a fennec fox, small desert mice and a wolf. The remaining galleries contain insects and butterflies (42), birds and their migratory patterns, though most of them seem to bypass Libya (43–44), fish and the huge skeleton of a sperm whale (45-46) and Libyan plants (47).

ASSAI AL-HAMRA (TRIPOLI CASTLE)
Assai al-Hamra (Tripoli Castle or Red Castle) represented the seat of power in Tripolitania until the 20th century. It has evolved

over the centuries into a citadel containing a labyrinth of courtyards, alleyways and houses. The total area of the castle is about 13,000 sq metres, including the area surrounded by high defensive walls now given over to the museum.

History

Excavations have revealed that the castle was built on the site of the Roman *castrum* (Roman fortified camp; a public bath from the 2nd century AD has been excavated on the site), but the fortress proper was probably not built before the Arab invasion of AD 644. Under the Spaniards and the Knights of St John of Malta in the 16th century, the defences were built up with the addition of defensive towers in the south-west and south-east of the citadel. The Turks occupied the castle in 1551. After extensive works were carried out, the governors used it as their official residence. Plans from the 17th century reveal that the castle was at that time totally surrounded by water. Under the Karamanlis (1711–1835) harems and a large reception room *(selamlik)*, in which official visitors were received, was built. Much of the castle's existing interior dates to this period. The castle was also quite self-contained, with a mint, courthouse, shops, jails and mills. After the Italian conquest the governor used the castle as offices and parts turned into a museum. Most of the buildings inside the castle are now used by the Department of Antiquities and there is also a library.

Information

Entrance to the castle (☎ *3333042, Green Square; admission 3LD, camera/video 5/10LD; open 9am-1pm & 3pm-6pm Tues-Sun)* is off Green Square via the door just to the south of the museum. Allow one to two hours to explore it properly.

Exploring the Castle

Just after entering the castle, look for the attractive tile work on the left. A ramp leads into the heart of the castle, before which, off to the left, are the remains of a small residence with residual pillars and a well. After ascending the ramp, turn left to visit the cells

Tales of the Assai al-Hamra

The genteel decay of the Assai al-Hamra hides the fact that it has been the scene of much intrigue and violence.

When the Ottoman armies of Süleyman the Magnificent, Sultan of Turkey, launched a final assault in 1551 to drive the Christians from Tripoli, the newly reinforced bastions stood up to the fire. However, the defenders of the Knights of St John of Malta proved less resilient – an act of treachery from one of the soldiers, who provided information to the enemy pinpointing the weakest spot in the defences, meant the walls were duly breached. When the governor emerged waving a flag of truce he was unceremoniously clapped in irons, stripped and cast into slavery.

A succession of Turkish leaders *(beys)* were to meet a similar fate. Suleiman Bey withstood a punitive mission from the Ottoman sultan, only to be tricked out of the castle, taken on board one of the sultan's fleet and promptly crucified on the poop deck. The janissaries plotted to overthrow his successor, Sharif Pasha, whereupon he barricaded himself in the castle. He too was tricked out of the castle. He was cut to pieces by those lying in wait for him.

Ramadan Bey, who succeeded him, was persuaded to hand over power by a cunning corsair named Mohammed Saqizli. The wily Saqizli contrived to marry Miryam bint-Fawz, wife of a tribal leader, by poisoning her husband and then inviting her to come to the castle for the marriage. Bringing her wealth with her, she arrived at the castle only to be turned over to the executioner as soon as the wedding ceremony had taken place. Poetic justice prevailed : Mohammed Saqizli died at the hands of his Christian doctor who fittingly dispatched him with a poisoned apple.

From then until the Karamanlis seized power in 1711, a bewildering number of rulers came and went. One died from plague, several were killed and the rest were deposed and exiled; only one managed to die of old age.

of the grim prison. Up a small set of stairs, again to the left, is the old Governor's Quarters, which successive Turkish governors

Palace Intrigue

In 1790 the three Karamanli sons of the governor, or pasha, met in the Governor's study. The youngest of the three, the ambitious Crown Prince Yusuf Karamanli, called the meeting supposedly in order to defuse simmering tensions over succession. He also asked their mother to be present as witness. The meeting progressed well, with the brothers reaching an apparent reconciliation. The Crown Prince asked them to swear their agreement on the Quran and called his servant to bring the holy book. What he brought, in accordance with the plan, was not the Quran but a box concealing a pistol, which he drew and shot dead his two brothers. He later succeeded his father and ruled Libya from 1795 to 1835.

used as a study. Although they now serve a functional purpose (the offices for the administration of the castle), it was here in 1790 that another grisly act of fratricide took place (see the boxed text 'Palace Intrigue').

A door leads off the small courtyard of the Governor's quarters to the Spanish courtyard, which was laid out during the brief occupation by the Spanish (16th century). Around the courtyard, which is delightful in spring when it is adorned with flowers, are a number of stone lions. Stairs descend into a much larger, open courtyard with a lovely fountain as well as some pretty tile work around the perimeter. The exit leads off to the south-east and onto the eastern limb of Souq al-Mushir. The imposing arched stone gateway, which was the original entrance to the castle, but is no longer in use, is on the way back to Green Square from the souq.

MEDINA

Tripoli's whitewashed medina doesn't rival the magnificent old cities of Morocco, either in architecture or atmosphere, but it is still a wonderful place to wander around. The first fortified wall around the medina was built in the 4th century, while further ramparts and reinforcements were added by subsequent occupiers to safeguard the city from seaborne attack. Most of the mosques, public buildings and houses in the medina date from the Turkish period and it was not until the 19th century that the city spread beyond the medina's walls. Many of the exterior walls of houses within the medina also show a strong European influence, with wrought-iron balconies and wooden shutters. During the Italian occupation and the bombing of the city in WWII, the walls and some of the buildings sustained heavy damage. The layout of the city follows the blueprint of the old Arab city and although much modified, its design has changed little.

The original construction materials consisted of earth and lime, covered with whitewash and decorated with colourful ceramics, although these were used sparingly. Marble was also imported from Malta for use in the homes of the wealthy.

Traditionally, the houses of the medina were built around an open internal courtyard. The most striking feature of the residences' exterior are the doors, atop most of which small arches of intricate metalwork with geometric and floral motifs radiate out from the centre. Although primarily ornamental they also served a practical purpose, allowing air and light into the interior without compromising the privacy of the inhabitants. There was often similar decoration on the banisters of internal staircases. In addition to providing some much-needed shade in summer, the roofs that cover some of the thoroughfares also serve the purpose of reinforcing the walls of the adjoining houses.

Most of the 38 mosques in the old city, which once had adjoining hammams and madrassas (Quranic schools), have roofs with small cupolas supported by numerous pillars in the main sanctuary. Many also contain the tombs of their founders or the person to whom the mosque was dedicated. The minarets alternate between the rectangular North African style and octagonal ones built in the Ottoman style. The largest market in Tripoli's medina was Souq al-Turk, but there are many souqs throughout the eastern corner of the medina. The old city also contained synagogues (now converted into mosques) and churches.

Restoration began in the early 1990s and, while still proceeding, many of the buildings remain under threat. In some cases this is due to a lack of collective political will, but another problem is the fact that houses once owned by one man have since been inherited by large numbers of children, and restoration subsequently often gets no further than a dispute over who will pay for the work.

According to the last estimate, about 3500 people still live in the medina, and 65,000 still work within its walls.

Walking Tour

The best way to get a feel for the medina's rich architectural inheritance is on foot. If necessary, you could see all of the areas covered below in a couple of hours.

The best place to start is outside the entrance to the museum. Head south-west along the perimeter of Green Square, past the small **balcony** high on the castle's external wall – it was from here that Mussolini once addressed crowds. The second street leading off the square to the north-west leads into

Souq al-Mushir and the stone archway above its entrance nicely frames the buildings of the souq and the **Ottoman clock tower** (19th century) at the far end. This was once one of the main gates to the old city and it was through the souq that merchants and visitors entered the medina. Directly in front of the clock tower is a small open square with a traditional teahouse (see Magha as-Sa'a under Teahouses in Places to Eat later in this chapter). Resist the temptation for now to linger for a *shay* (tea) and nargileh (water pipe) and take the small lane that runs in behind the tower. If you can't find it, simply follow the clanging of artisans patiently hammering out their wares in the **Souq al-Ghizdir (Copper Souq)**. Their specialties include crescents *(jammour)* that will one day adorn the tops of minarets; until that time many lie here against the lane's walls.

At the end of the copper souq, turn left into a covered lane that leads onto the main **Souq al-Turk**, which almost runs the length of the medina. Built during the Ottoman period and once covered by a roof (as opposed to the

Preserving the Medinas of North Africa

The medinas (old cities) along the North African coast are under threat and Tripoli's is no exception. The medinas once housed close-knit communities and centres of trade with strong connections to the rural hinterland. The growing demands of urbanisation that have seen the cities expand well beyond their original boundaries, along with individual demands for modern facilities like electricity, air-conditioning and reliable plumbing have seen the medinas marginalised, in danger of becoming little more than tourist attractions. Unesco is seeking to redress this decline and a wander around Tripoli's medina shows how desperate funding is needed. Unesco has decided that Tripoli's medina is not one of its priorities, but that the cost must be borne by local landowners and the Libyan Government. Sadly, government help has so far been largely unforthcoming.

The key, according to Unesco, is recognising that modern imperatives must be balanced against a return to traditional ways of living in an integrated strategy. The first step is encouraging people to use traditional housing by providing adequate funding. This requires restoring the traditional houses, but also revitalising the traditional skills and markets that were once the medina's lifeblood. As part of the attempt to reinvigorate communities within medinas, basic community-building exercises, such as building schools and hospitals and providing employment opportunities, must take place. As painful as it is, this may involve demolishing a number of old buildings that are beyond repair. If medinas are to survive, it is not enough that they remain ever-decaying storehouses of ancient ways of living; they must be provided with a modern purpose. In the past their adaptability was their greatest guarantee of survival and so it must be again.

For more information on Unesco, visit the Web site at [w] www.unesco.org/whc. For more information on efforts to restore Tripoli's medina, contact the Project for Tripoli Medina (☎ 3336725, fax 3331069, postal address: PO Box 10332 Tripoli).

TRIPOLI MEDINA

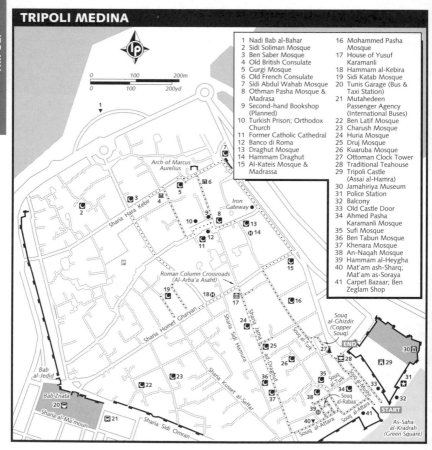

0   100   200m
0   100   200yd

1 Nadi Bab al-Bahar
2 Sidi Soliman Mosque
3 Ben Saber Mosque
4 Old British Consulate
5 Gurgi Mosque
6 Old French Consulate
7 Sidi Abdul Wahab Mosque
8 Othman Pasha Mosque &
   Madrasa
9 Second-hand Bookshop
   (Planned)
10 Turkish Prison; Orthodox
   Church
11 Former Catholic Cathedral
12 Banco di Roma
13 Draghut Mosque
14 Hammam Draghut
15 Al-Kateis Mosque &
   Madrassa

16 Mohammed Pasha
   Mosque
17 House of Yusuf
   Karamanli
18 Hammam al-Kebira
19 Sidi Katab Mosque
20 Tunis Garage (Bus &
   Taxi Station)
21 Mutahedeen
   Passenger Agency
   (International Buses)
22 Ben Latif Mosque
23 Charush Mosque
24 Huria Mosque
25 Druj Mosque
26 Kuaruba Mosque
27 Ottoman Clock Tower
28 Traditional Teahouse
29 Tripoli Castle
   (Assai al-Hamra)
30 Jamahiriya Museum
31 Police Station
32 Balcony
33 Old Castle Door
34 Ahmed Pasha
   Karamanli Mosque
35 Sufi Mosque
36 Ben Tabun Mosque
37 Khenara Mosque
38 An-Naqah Mosque
39 Hammam al-Heygha
40 Mat'am ash-Sharq;
   Mat'am as-Soraya
41 Carpet Bazaar; Ben
   Zeglam Shop

aluminium that now keeps the sun out), this is a place simply to absorb the atmosphere and breathe in the aromas. Although it's worth wandering south-east (left) for a few hundred metres, continue north-west for about 200m where a road leads towards what used to be the waterfront. Along this route you'll pass the unadorned **Al-Kateis Mosque and Madrassa**. About 100m north-west along the medina's perimeter is a magnificent **iron gateway**. A further 150m away is the attractive **Sidi Abdul Wahab Mosque** and one of the last surviving remnants of the **original city wall**. This wall, built by the Muslims as

a protection against the sea-faring Byzantines, used to run all the way to the castle. Mussolini reportedly tried to tear down both the mosque and wall as it appealed to his sense of grandeur that the Roman Arch of Marcus Aurelius could be seen from the port. It was only through the efforts of a brave Italian archaeologist, Salvatore Aurigemma, that the buildings were saved.

Visible from the mosque to the south-west is the **Arch of Marcus Aurelius**. Immediately behind the arch is the **Gurgi Mosque**. Make sure you look at the wonderful old door knockers on the northern door. Return to the narrow lane that runs south-east from above the arch. Not far along is the **Old French Consulate**, which is marked by a cream-coloured arch above a blue door. The lane leads into an open crossroads with superb monuments around its perimeter. Most obvious is the shell of the **Banco di Roma** that wears a tragic elegance with its broken-down wooden shutters. It was built in 1870 as part of an attempt by the Italians to cement their commercial links in Libya. Opposite the Banco di Roma to the east is a small **Roman pillar** built into the wall. Behind this wall is the **Othman Pasha Mosque and Madrassa**, while further along the lane is the **Draghut Mosque** and **hammam**. Returning to the crossroads, the **Turkish Prison**, opposite the Banco di Roma, and was used for detaining Christian prisoners. It was built in 1664 during the reign of Othman Pasha al-Saqizli, a former janissarie credited with being the first ruler to unite Tripolitania and Cyrenaica. Behind its walls is a small **Orthodox church** that still services Tripoli's Orthodox community. A little further to the west, on the opposite side of the square, is the newly renovated **former Catholic Cathedral**.

The lane leading north-west almost opposite the cathedral leads to Sharia Hara Kebir, one of the medina's main thoroughfares; it follows the path of the old decumanus. Just around the corner is the **Old British Consulate**. About 100m south-west is crossroads where a left turn takes you past an attractive row of facades with decrepit wrought-iron balconies, pastel coloured shutters and six doors. A little further on you pass more colourful doors with intricate wrought-iron crowns. Continuing through the next main crossroads, you pass under five consecutive arches into a narrow lane lined with crumbling walls, high ornate doorways and fanciful, human-hand-shaped door knockers. You may be able to see into the internal courtyards if the doors are open. If you take the first right and then left under the blue and white arches, you'll find yourself in some of the quietest lanes of the medina. This is the heart of the old city's residential district. Some of the doors in this area have door knockers in the shape of a lion's head, espe-

cially at the southern end near Sharia Homet Gharyan.

Turn right on this bustling lane and you very shortly come to another crossroads with the street continuing under five sturdy old **stone arches**. Turn right to see some more lovely old doors of peeling pastel shades and some with ceramic tiles above the doors. Returning north-east along Sharia Homet Gharyan, through a minor **market** containing shoe repairers, you pass grocery stores, tailors and **Hammam al-Kebira**. Soon after entering the covered area, you come to the **Roman Column Crossroads** (Al-Arba'a Asaht) and immediately after turning right into Sharia Jama ad-Draghut you find the **House of Yusuf Karamanli** (known in Arabic as Hosn al-Harem or Dar al-Karamanli). The street soon broadens out, marking the transition between the residential and commercial districts of the medina. Some of the buildings in this area had been freshly whitewashed when we visited. The **Druj Mosque** stands on a corner and has an attractive doorway on the northern side, while the street running off to the north-east is lined with pastel doors, shutters and occasional balconies of wrought-iron. About 150m further south-east along Sharia Jama ad-Draghut you pass under seven white arches, just before which on the right are three ornate doorways, one with a tiled arch.

Approximately 50m beyond the arches is a busy crossroads. From the crossroads, some of the old city's most attractive Italianate facades are visible to the south. From the junction, take the walkway leading to the north-east that takes you into **Souq al-Attara**. This is one of the liveliest thoroughfares of the medina with an **impromptu souq** home to a crowded mix of shops and temporary stalls set up by traders without a licence; these stalls evaporate quickly as soon as a policeman is spotted. Off the north-eastern side of this branch of the Souq al-Attara is the covered **Souq al-Rabaa**, which has vaulted ceilings. At the western end of the impromptu souq, a left turn leads to the **An-Naqah Mosque**, which is said to be 1200 years old, but most of which dates from the 17th century. It is named after the first mosque in the medina, which was built where the Prophet Mohammed's camel stopped and where the Prophet prayed. The exterior and much of the interior is simple and largely unadorned, but the main prayer hall does have lovely white arches supporting the low roof. Almost opposite is a small **Sufi Mosque** with a squat white minaret with green lines.

Returning to the south-west, **Souq al-Attara** has some of the best souqs in the country, with an old khan or caravanserai now given over to a jewellery bazaar, busy thoroughfares lined with whitewashed buildings and the small **carpet bazaar**, which is reached via an elevated, covered walkway. Emerging on Souq al-Mushir, turn right under the arch and then hard left to the street that runs along the castle's western wall. The original **castle door** is under the trees on the right, while the left side of the road is given over to jewellery shops. This road soon leads back to the square with the Ottoman clock tower and the traditional teahouse – the perfect place to rest those weary legs.

Arch of Marcus Aurelius

This last intact remnant of the ancient Roman city of Oea was completed in AD 163–64. It stood at the crossroads of the two great Roman roads of the city – the cardo (running north to south) and decumanus (east to west). It therefore stood at the city's most important junction as well as providing an entrance to the city from the harbour. The fact that Oea had a triumphal arch (Leptis had five, while Sabratha had none) was a reflection of Oea's importance in the Roman Tripolis. Above the eastern arch are carvings of Apollo and Minerva, the mythical protectors of Oea in ancient times. The facades of the pillars facing to and away from the port contain niches that once hosted statues of Marcus Aurelius and Lucius Verus, above which are weather-worn portraits in relief. One reason for the preservation of the arch is that an ancient prophecy foretold terrible punishments for anyone who removed a stone. On the raised level to the right, behind the arch, are the remains of the pediment of the Temple of Taki (god of fortune), which dates from AD 183–85. On the tablets are the figures of Apollo, Taki and Minerva as well as some Roman inscriptions. There is no entrance fee.

Ahmed Pasha Karamanli Mosque

The largest mosque in the medina and with a fine octagonal minaret, the richly decorated Karamanli Mosque was opened in the 1730s. The five doorways leading into the prayer hall have some superbly crafted floral decorations carved into the wood. These motifs include flower pots, cypress trees and small flowers, and are thought to symbolise growth and progress. The prayer hall is covered by almost 30 domes and the floral theme is continued in the colourful ceilings of the balconies, which surround the prayer hall on three sides. These are considered some of the finest examples of woodwork in Libya. Experts believe that the carvings, colours and use of arches suggest a high degree of Moroccan and Andalusian influence. The tombs of Ahmed Pasha and his family are in one of the rooms off the prayer hall.

Gurgi Mosque

The Gurgi Mosque, just west of the Arch of Marcus Aurelius, was built in the 19th century and was the last mosque built in Tripoli under the Turks. Although quite small, its interior is one of the most beautiful in the city. The main prayer hall contains imported marble pillars from Italy, ceramic tile work from Tunisia and intricate stone carvings from Morocco. The large, covered platform was reserved for VIPs. The mihrab (niche facing Mecca) and the domes above the main room are adorned with extremely beautiful stone lattice carvings with floral motifs; the dome above the mihrab is particularly fine. There are 16 domes in all. The tomb of Mustapha Gurgi (a Tripoli naval captain) and his family are in an antechamber at the back, to the right of the minbar (pulpit).

Othman Pasha Mosque & Madrassa
Immediately east of the Banco di Roma, this mosque and madrassa was built by Othman Pasha (who ruled Libya for 25 years) is one of the oldest Turkish sites in Tripoli. It is set around a delightful courtyard with marble pillars from Carrara in Italy and topped with local limestone. The portico is surrounded by wooden doors underneath stone arches, and immediately left after coming in the main entrance is the stone ablutions fountain with arabesque decorations. Out the back are the tombs of the mosque's builders as well as a small garden. The Roman-era pool was used for washing the boards on which verses of the Quran were written – some are still lying up against the walls. It's a tranquil place with unusual cupolas on the domes, and it's renowned for, unusually, having three domes, one each for the graveyard, mosque and main entrance. The school has been in use for over 350 years.

Draghut Mosque
This 16th-century mosque, the entrance of which is opposite the Othman Pasha Mosque and Madrassa, bears the name of an infamous corsair admiral and governor of Tripoli. Its elegant pillars and arches (there are 15 in the main prayer hall alone with many more in adjoining rooms) are quite stunning. The distinctive, brightly coloured mihrab, though not as finely wrought as the one in Gurgi Mosque, is attractive nonetheless, as are the green-and-white calligraphic and arabesque relief inscriptions used sparingly against a white background.

Old British Consulate
This building, west of the Gurgi Mosque on Sharia Hara Kabir, was first constructed in 1744 as a residence for Ahmed Pasha (the founder of the Karamanli dynasty) during the final phase of his reign (r. 1711–45). From the second half of the 18th century until 1940, it was the office of the British consul. In addition to diplomatic representation, the consul's representatives used their position to launch expeditions into the Sahara with an eye on lucrative trade routes. On a plaque outside the entrance, this history is, not without some justification, viewed with unconcealed anger. It claims that 'the so-called European geographical and scientific expeditions to Africa, which were in essence and as a matter of fact intended to be colonial ones to occupy and colonise vital and strategic parts of Africa, embarked from this same building'. The consulate also provided a place of refuge for the expatriate community during various invasions.

The entrance is through a large wooden door under an archway that leads to a large courtyard paved with marble. The courtyard is surrounded on all sides by a beautiful two-storey building with elegant Moorish archways fronting the verandahs, behind which are the rooms that once included consular offices as well as kitchens, servants quarters and bedrooms. It will have a wonderful air of tranquillity once the hammers of restoration fall silent. The building houses a general scientific library and there is talk of extending the building so that it can be used for artistic exhibitions.

When the restorations and extensions are completed, expect to pay 3LD to gain entry.

Old French Consulate
The Old French Consulate, not far south of the Arch of Marcus Aurelius, dates from 1630 and was being extensively restored when we were there. The consulate is set around a compact, high-walled courtyard,

which contained offices, a prison and wells. There is some fine tile work around the perimeter and the wooden doors on the 1st floor have some interesting carvings, including a crescent and a Star of David. Entry is likely to cost 3LD when the work is finished.

House of Yusuf Karamanli

Just south of the Roman Column Crossroads, the private residence of Yusuf Karamanli *(Hosn al-Harem or Dar al-Karamanli; admission 3LD, camera/video 5/10LD; open 9am-noon & 3pm-6pm Tues-Sun)* dates from the beginning of the 19th century and is now a museum of sorts. The courtyard is surrounded by balconies. On the 1st floor were the private living quarters, some of which now contain furniture, musical instruments and costumes from the 19th century. From the roof there are fine views over the medina.

SAN FRANCISCO CHURCH

This Catholic church *(☎ 3331863, off Sharia Khalid ibn al-Walid; open daylight hrs)* was built in the 1930s and offers services primarily for Libya's expat community. The sanctuary is quite simple, with a towering mural behind the altar. On the walls around the 1st-floor balcony are murals of the Twelve Stations of the Cross.

Mass is conducted in English at 10.30am and 4.30pm and in Italian at 6pm on Friday, in French at 6pm on Saturday, in English at 10am and noon, and in Italian at 8.30am and 6pm on Sunday.

AROUND MAIDAN AL-JEZAYIR

The austere structure overlooking the square is the **former cathedral**, built as a Catholic cathedral in the neo-Romanesque style by the Italians in 1928. It has some fine buttresses on either side and is quite imposing, as is the towering steeple (now minaret). On 29 November 1970 in the days after the revolution, it was converted into a mosque. Immediately east of the cathedral, the continuation of Sharia Mohammed Megharief leads to the domed **National Library**, which is very photogenic just before sunset. Built in the 1930s, it was the Royal Palace

under the monarchy and the People's Palace immediately after the revolution.

ART GALLERIES

There are no art galleries containing permanent exhibitions in Tripoli, although **Dar al-Founoun** *(House of Art; ☎ 3604477, fax 3604478, Sharia 7th November)* stages reasonably regular shows. Contact Hussein Founi of Robban Tourism Services (☎ 444 1530, fax 4448065, **e** robbantours@hotmail.com; off Sharia as-Sarim) to see if anything is happening while you're in town.

TRIPOLI WATER PARK

Just north of Tripoli Zoo *(Hadikat al-Haywan; adults/children 1/3LD; open 10am-5pm Wed-Sun)*, in the 200-hectare An-Nasr Forest, is the site for the proposed Tripoli Water Park. Facilities are expected to include water slides, a dry ride for those who wish to remain fully clothed, an artificial wave machine and a children's water playground. It's unlikely to be completed for a while. To get there, take a shared taxi to Abu Salim, from where it is a short walk.

SWIMMING

Most of the beaches around Tripoli are neither tranquil nor particularly clean. If you can wait, there are better beaches between Sabratha and the Tunisian border, along the coast near Al-Khoms and in Cyrenaica in north-eastern Libya. If you can't wait, there is a small beach less than a kilometre west of the Dhat al-Ahmat towers – the entrance is a little way south of the three waterfront hotels on Sharia al-Corniche.

PLACES TO STAY

For a city of its size, Tripoli does not have a huge number of hotels from which to choose and, particularly in the mid-range and top-end categories, many are booked out by the increasing number of tour groups passing through. If you're not part of a tour, making a reservation, either through the hotel directly or through one of the tour companies (see Organised Tours in the Getting Around chapter), can be a good idea, at least for the first couple of nights.

All prices for mid-range and top-end hotels include a private bathroom and breakfast unless otherwise stated.

PLACES TO STAY – BUDGET
Buyut ash-Shabaab
(Youth Hostels)
Both of Tripoli's youth hostels sometimes require you to vacate the rooms between 10am and 2pm.

Buyut ash-Shabaab (Central Youth Hostel; ☎ 4445171, fax 3330118, Sharia Amr ibn al-Ass) Dorm bed with/without HI card 4/6LD. The location is ideal and the shared bathrooms are fine, but otherwise it's a pretty basic place. There's a cheap restaurant on the 2nd floor doing simple spaghetti dishes for 1.5LD.

Buyut ash-Shabaab (Gargaresh Youth Hostel; ☎ 4776694, 4474755, off Sharia Gargaresh) Dorm bed with/without HI card 3/5LD. This well-run hostel, located 5km south of the town centre in the lively district of Gargaresh, is marginally better than its more central counterpart, although it's a long way from Tripoli's sights.

Hotels
There are few really appealing budget choices in Tripoli.

Funduq Atlas (☎ 3336816, Sharia Omar al-Mukhtar) Singles with shared bathroom 10LD, singles/doubles/triples with private bathroom 12/15/20LD. The friendly Funduq Atlas has basic, but perfectly habitable, rooms. Some bathrooms are better than others so ask to see a few rooms; the hot water is generally reliable. The location, on the busy Sharia Omar al-Mukhtar and a fair walk to Green Square, isn't brilliant, but is decent value.

Funduq Bahr al-Abyad (☎ 3616711/4, fax 3616710, off Sharia Omar al-Mukhtar) Singles/doubles 10/15LD. It's easier to list the things wrong with this hotel than its good points; it's not the friendliest place in town, the grand lobby ensures the rooms will disappoint, the lifts are so ramshackle they could break down any day and getting hot water can be problematic. For Tripoli, however, its simple rooms with private

bathroom are not bad budget value and certainly preferable to many elsewhere.

The main gathering of cheap hotels is around Sharia ar-Rashid and Maidan as-Sawayhli. Most are noisy and rooms are generally of a very poor standard and the area can be a little seedy. Few Western travellers stay here. The following are among the better options in this area.

Funduq as-Siyahe (☎ 4448372, Sharia al-Jamila) Singles/doubles 10/16LD. This is one exception to the rule and is far and away the best (and cleanest) budget choice in the area. The rooms (all with very clean shared bathroom) are tidy and simple. There is little English spoken, although the staff make up for this in general goodwill. If the lift isn't working, it's quite a climb if your room is on the 5th floor. You can, however, walk to Green Square with much less effort.

Funduq al-Manar (Sharia al-Kameet) Singles/doubles 10/15LD. Around the corner from the Funduq as-Siyahe, this place is pretty bleak and unappealing, with shared bathrooms.

Funduq an-Nasr (☎ 3336479, Maidan as-Sawayhli) Singles/doubles 10/16LD. A favourite for furtive rendezvous and for once you may be glad of the street noise to drown out the activities of your neighbours. Convenience for the bus and shared-taxi stations is the only virtue as the rooms are pretty grotty. Bathrooms are shared.

Funduq al-Jebel al-Akhdar (☎ 3336603, Tunis Garage) Singles/doubles 10/15LD. This wins the prize for the noisiest of the lot, hard-up against Tunis Garage with all of its grimy, diesel-fuelled ambience – leave every standard you possess at the door and resign yourself to a fitful night's sleep. Bathrooms are shared.

Funduq al-Ma'moun (☎ 3333372, Sharia al-Ma'moun) Singles with shared bathroom 15LD, doubles with private bathroom 30LD. Also handy for transport, the rooms here are uninspiring and overpriced.

PLACES TO STAY – MID-RANGE
Funduq Bab al-Jadid (☎ 3350670, Sharia al-Corniche) Singles/doubles 25/35LD, suites 75-100LD. Newly opened in 2001,

the Bab al-Jadid is excellent value and will be even more so once the sea-facing rooms have been completed. Staff are eager to please and the rooms are spacious, spotless and well appointed. The only drawback is the lack of air-con in most rooms.

Funduq Bab al-Medina (☎ *3350650, fax 3350675, Sharia al-Corniche, postal address: PO Box 10619)* Singles/doubles 30/40LD, suites 55-65LD. Immediately next to Funduq Bab al-Jadid, this place is not bad, but that's about it. The rooms with sea views are better but the absence of air-con can be punishing in summer.

Funduq al-Jawda (☎ *6604777, Sharia al-Corniche)* Singles/doubles from 20/30LD, suites 40LD. The cheapest rooms can be a bit cell-like although the north-facing ones are better. The suites (with two bathrooms, a sitting area and balcony) are comfy, though far from palatial, and some are quite run-down; Room 508 has nice views.

Funduq Qasr Libya (☎ *3331180, fax 3336688, Sharia Sidi Issa, postal address: PO Box 727)* Singles/doubles from 20/30LD, suites 45LD. This rambling place in the Dahra district is big, busy and has seen better days; it definitely pays to look at as many rooms as possible. The management is friendly and most of the jaded rooms (all with air-con) are clean and reasonable value. However, hot water can take an age to arrive and sometimes doesn't. The suites are overpriced.

Funduq al-Waddan (☎ *3330041/5, fax 4445601, Sharia Sidi Issa, postal address: PO Box 2309)* Singles/doubles 38/53LD, suites 100LD. It's certainly not the five-star hotel it claims to be, but is nonetheless comfortable and still good value in the upper mid-range bracket. There's a restaurant, car-rental agency and a branch of the Umma Bank in the lobby.

Funduq al-Wahat (☎ *3612021, fax 3602041, Sharia Omar al-Mukhtar, postal address: PO Box 10799)* Singles/doubles without breakfast from 35/45LD, suites 90/100LD. While you can probably find better value elsewhere, the rooms here are still decent value.

PLACES TO STAY – TOP END

Tripoli's top-end hotels are generally just a touch below the standard of five-star hotels in other countries, but they're also cheaper and very comfortable. Most of the lobbies have an airport-style ambience with their baggage X-ray machines at the main entrance. Most are also a fair walk from the centre of town.

Funduq Bab al-Bahar (☎ *3350676, fax 3350711, Sharia al-Corniche)* Singles/doubles from 45/60LD, suites 120/130LD. The best value rooms are the 'Special Rooms' (55/70LD), which are a touch nicer and better maintained than the standard rooms. All rooms come with satellite TV and a balcony overlooking either the Mediterranean or south towards the city. The hotel has a gift shop, coffee shop, mediocre restaurant, barber and travel agency. The 24-hour room service is expensive, but the cost of the laundry is surprisingly reasonable. The swimming pool was empty when we visited.

Funduq Winzrik (☎ *3343947, fax 3342871, Sharia ash-Shatt, postal address: PO Box 12794)* Singles/doubles 45/55LD, suites 100LD. This new hotel run by the tour company of the same name has already generated a popular following, especially among business travellers. The rooms (which include a minibar) are very comfortable and facilities include an Internet and photocopy office, car-rental agency and a good restaurant.

Funduq an-Naher (☎ *3334645, fax 4444690, Sharia Tariq)* Singles 44-70LD, doubles 70-85LD. This would be one of the best choices in the lower top-end range were it not in the noisy heart of the Sharia ar-Rashid district. It's handy for the bus station, but if you can afford to stay here then you can probably afford a taxi anyway. All rooms are good, but the larger ones with balcony are semiluxurious and come with air-con, minibar, phone and satellite TV.

Funduq al-Kebir (☎ *4445940/58, fax 3606781, Sharia al-Fat'h, postal address: PO Box 275)* Singles/doubles 58/68LD, suites 105-135LD. One of Tripoli's top hotels and very close to Green Square, Funduq al-Kebir has very comfortable if unspectacular rooms. The views from the top floors can be superb. It's a favourite of people on government business and there's the usual flash restaurant and coffee shop.

Funduq as-Safwa (☎ 4443257, fax 4449062, Sharia Mohammed Megharief) Suites 120LD. This suites-only hotel is in a good location and its large, semiluxurious rooms are good value for those with plenty of cash. There's a very good restaurant downstairs.

Funduq al-Mehari (☎ 3334091/6, fax 4449502, Sharia al-Fat'h, postal address: PO Box 84278) Singles/doubles from 65/75LD, suites 120LD. Rooms at Tripoli's most prestigious hotel have satellite TV and come with most of the luxury bells and whistles. It certainly does have a touch of class and great views from the upper floors. The lobby is given over to high-quality jewellery, suit and handicrafts shops with prices to match. There's also an expensive car rental agency, two restaurants and a coffee shop.

The city authorities, keen to cash in on the rapidly expanding tourist dollar, have begun construction of new five-star hotel complexes. These include what may be Tripoli's most exclusive hotel immediately west of the medina. Further afield, the Tripoli National Resort and New City, 7 to 8km east of the city centre, is an ambitious 700-hectare development comprising a Business City (supermarket, souqs, duty-free shops, banks, Internet clubs), a Science City (botanical garden, planetarium), an amusement park, residential housing, exhibition and Islamic cultural centres, cinemas, a modern-art museum, a sports stadium, ice rink, equestrian centre, 10 restaurants and three- to five-star hotels. All power to their arm!

PLACES TO EAT

Libya's reputation among travellers as something of a culinary wasteland clearly didn't start in Tripoli.

Budget Dining

There are loads of **fast-food restaurants** and **snack bars** all over Tripoli. Apart from price, the advantage of these places is that they are invariably open in the afternoon when most other restaurants are closed. (The hours are from 11am to 11pm.) Standard fare is shwarma (grilled chicken kebab; 1LD to 2LD), hamburgers (1LD to 1.5LD) and pizzas (1/5LD for small/large).

The greatest concentration is along Sharia al-Baladiya, Sharia 1st September and the narrow Sharia al-Mizda off the south-western corner of Green Square. The perimeter of the Tunis Garage off Sharia ar-Rashid is the place to go if you're craving a felafel sandwich (0.5LD), although the quality is variable. One part of town where you may struggle to find something is west of the medina around the Dhat al-Ahmat and Burj al-Fateh complexes. West of town in Gargaresh, most of the restaurants, even some of the more expensive ones, do cheap kebabs on the street outside.

Mat'am as-Safira (☎ 3339272) Mains 0.75-6.5LD, sandwiches & hamburgers 0.75-2LD. Open 11am-midnight daily. Probably the pick of the cheap restaurants around Maidan as-Sawayhli, this cheap and cheerful place serves 'Kentucky Fried Chicken' with potatoes.

Restaurants

Eating out at sit-down restaurants in Tripoli can be expensive, but there are a few that won't break the budget. All are open noon to 3.30pm and 6.30pm to 10.30pm Saturday to Thursday, and 6.30pm to 10.30pm Friday unless stated otherwise.

Mid-Range Meals in this range usually cost between 10LD and 15LD.

Mat'am Thatul Sawari (☎ 3333728, Sharia Mohammed Megharief) Meals 13LD, soups 4LD. This friendly restaurant, which has no pretensions to luxury, serves a range of soups as well as the usual banquet meals with tasty, well-cooked kebabs with peppers and onion. Its card claims enigmatically to cater 'for all public and private bodies'.

Mat'am al-Jedda (☎ 3336667, Sharia Mohammed Megharief) Meals 10-13LD. Also excellent value, the Al-Jedda is handy for Green Square and does meals that include a choice of spaghetti, beef steak, grilled chicken or grilled fish as well as buffet salads. The service is attentive without being overbearing.

Mat'am Dhahabi (Golden Restaurant; ☎ 3350069, fax 3350072, Dhat al-Ahmat, Tower 3, Level 3) Mains 10-15LD. The menu is mostly a la carte and includes Swiss Veal Steak and *shish tawouq* (grilled chicken). There are good views over the waterfront. It also does takeaway.

Al-Mat'am al-Turkiye (mobile ☎ 091 2138240, Sharia Mizran) Meals 10LD. It does the usual Turkish kebabs and salads as well as excellent Turkish pizzas *(pides)*.

Mat'am ash-Sharq (☎ 4441427, Souq al-Attara, Medina) Meals from 10LD. Located above one of the liveliest thoroughfares in the medina, this bright and busy place has basic decor, but excellent food. Its speciality is the delicious *rishda* (noodles with chickpeas and onions – see Food in the Facts for the Visitor chapter; 10LD). It is also known for its *osban* (sheep's stomach filled with meat, rice and herbs).

Mat'am as-Soraya (☎ 4441459, Souq al-Attara) Meals from 10LD. Just a few doors to the north on the same lane, Mat'am as-Soraya is almost identical in terms of food, but has a marginally nicer ambience; try and get the balcony table (for two) overlooking the market; look for the tiled staircase. It doesn't always open for lunch.

Top-End For a small step up in price, there are some fine restaurants from which to choose.

Mat'am al-Masabiyah (☎ 3337815, Sharia al-Fateh) Meals 15-25LD. Open 12.30pm-4pm & 6pm-10pm Sat-Thur, 6pm-10pm Fri. Particularly popular with well-to-do locals on Wednesday night, the service and food here are good and the food is tasty. The mixed grill is a highlight and for drinks you can choose from the *masabiyah jamaica* (see Drinks in the Facts for the Visitor chapter) or *carcedy*, a strong Sudanese drink made from leaves and served hot (2LD). It also does pastas of varying quality (3LD to 10LD) and for dessert, don't miss the *mihallabia* (rice with milk), which goes for 2LD.

Mat'am as-Safir (☎ 4447064, Sharia al-Baladiya) Meals 25LD. In one of Tripoli's embassy districts and close to Green Square, this place is also the place of choice for many middle-class Libyans; look for the red-tiled awnings opposite the back of Funduq al-Kebir. The dining room is reminiscent of an ancient hammam and has a pleasant atmosphere in the evenings. Don't neglect to try the *tajeen* (spiced lamb).

Al-Makulaat al-Lubnaniya (☎ 4776978, Sharia al-Gargaresh) Meals 15LD. Open noon-4pm & 6.30pm-11pm Sat-Thur, 6.30pm-11pm Fri. This restaurant is popular with expats and is the place to come if you crave good-quality Lebanese food. It's on the south side of the road, 4km from the centre, just along from the second mosque as you're coming from Tripoli. The lively Sharia al-Gargaresh is a fun place to wander after your evening meal.

Al-Mat'am al-Hawar Burj al-Fateh (☎ 3351212, Burj al-Fateh complex, Level 26) Meals 35-50LD. Open 12.30pm-3pm & 7pm-11pm Sat-Thur, 7pm-11pm Fri. Tripoli's most exclusive restaurant, the 'Great Revolving Restaurant' doesn't revolve very often these days, but it still affords spectacular panoramic views over Tripoli and is a great place for a splurge. This is the place to come if you have your heart set on grilled prawns (40LD) or pepper steak (40LD). Seafood entrees start at 15LD. The service is in keeping with the luxury surrounds. Reservations are strongly recommended. Take lift No 6 to the 26th floor of the Burj al-Fateh complex.

Fish Restaurants High-quality fish dishes are an undoubted highlight of eating out in Tripoli.

Mat'am al-Murjan (☎ 3336507, fax 4446635, Maidan al-Jezayir) Meals 25LD. Highly recommended, Mat'am al-Murjan, directly opposite the main post office on Maidan al-Jezayir, has pleasant decor, attentive service and great food. You can choose from up to 20 self-service salads (the salad buffet costs 6.5LD), a mixed plate of shrimps, fish and calamari (22-24LD) or a range of local and North African fish dishes.

Al-Mat'am as-Samak at-Taazej (☎ 444 3683, Sharia al-Kameet) Meals from 16LD. This place is great value, and the huge and varied servings are presented in the squeaky-clean dining room by the ever-obliging waiters. It's something of a haven from the clamour outside, close as it is to Maidan as-Sawayhli, which is either dodgy or delightfully seedy, depending on your perspective; we prefer the latter.

Nadi Bab al-Bahar (☎ 3354242, Sharia al-Corniche) Meals 20LD. Open 6.30pm-11pm daily. Although right on the waterfront not far from the fish market, this place, sadly, has no sea view. Still the fish dishes are really good. Like other fish restaurants, an inability to speak Arabic is no impediment – simply point to your choice in the glass cabinet. The selection includes swordfish most nights.

Local connoisseurs of excellent fish dishes assure us that the best seafood restaurants are in Gargaresh to the west of the city. Premier among these, and certainly living up to their admirers' claims are *Mat'am As-Sayadd* (☎ 4774522) and *Mat'am Ash-Shi-raa'* (☎ 4775123), both of which are located in the Azhni Hat ash-Shatti shopping centre on the north side of the road. Another really excellent place is *Mat'am Dandeshi* (☎ 4773986, Sharia al-Gargaresh), which is along the main road on the left as you come from Tripoli. At each of these three places, expect to pay 20LD to 25LD for a meal and to leave well satisfied.

Patisseries

To round off your meal or simply for a snack, it's hard to go past Tripoli's wonderful patisseries. You're most likely to find them south-east of Green Square, especially along Sharia Mizran and close to Maidan al-Jezayir. Most are open 11am to 8pm Saturday to Thursday and 2pm to 8pm Friday.

Sonober (mobile ☎ 091 22113036, Maidan al-Jezayir). Cakes by the piece/complete from 1-2LD/15LD. This super-clean place has one of the widest selections and thus presents you with some of the more difficult (and pleasurable) decisions you'll have to make in Tripoli. Hedgehogs are very

nice, and the shop can bake cakes for special occasions.

Helawiyat 'Abembir Afra (☎ 3332234, Sharia Mizran) Coconut/almond cookies 10/7LD per kilo, pieces of cake 1.3LD, baklawa 5LD per kilo. This patisserie is smaller, but nonetheless excellent. The sickly sweet and utterly delicious baklawa is a bargain.

Teahouses

One place where the city does fall behind other Arab cities is in the field of atmospheric teahouses and you won't find the Cairo or Damascus tradition of whiling away an evening in smoke-filled rooms over games of *tawle* (backgammon).

There are, however, a number of pleasant *outdoor tea gardens*, which are good places to watch the world go by, smoke nargileh (1LD) and drink tea (0.5LD). The better ones are the *Gazelle Cafe* on Sharia al-Fat'h, next to a 1920s-era fountain; a *tea garden* by the small lake next to the entrance to the Jamahiriya Museum; and a *tea garden* in the open area next to where Sharia al-Baladiya meets Green Square. Also not bad, although more for the setting than the ambience, are the *tables* under the arches on Maidan al-Jezayir and the elegant *Galleria De Bono*, off Sharia 1st September.

Magha As-Sa'a (Clock Tower Teahouse), one traditional teahouse that bucks the trend, is opposite the Ottoman clock tower in the medina. You can sit outside, but make sure you check out the ground-floor room with its eclectic and distinctly musical themes – an old electric guitar, an archaic duke-box and gramophone. There are good views over the square from upstairs. Not surprisingly, this place has become a favourite of tour groups, but enough locals also turn up for it to feel authentic.

ENTERTAINMENT

Tripoli is the sort of place where you can linger over your evening meal or get an early night, safe in the knowledge that you're not missing out on much. The city's streets are quite lively around sunset, after the afternoon siesta.

There are plenty of cinemas (1LD) scattered around town, although most of the movies shown are either Egyptian, Indian or Western movies dubbed into Arabic. Beyond the usual infatuation with Jackie Chan, the fact that one Tripoli cinema was still showing *Titanic* in April 2001 should give you some idea as to what's on offer.

There are also seven or eight theatre groups in Tripoli, although their performances are poorly advertised. Most such events take place in the *Al-Kashaf Theatre* *(Sharia Omar al-Mukhtar; tickets 3-4LD)*. There's also a small *Children's Theatre* tucked in behind the carpet sellers, just off Souq al-Attara. Hussein Founi of Robban Tourism Services (see Art Galleries earlier in this chapter) is a good person to contact to see if anything of interest is in the offing.

Otherwise, bring a good book.

SPECTATOR SPORTS

The *Sports City (Al-Medina ar-Riyaddiyat)*, 5km south-west of the Parliament building and not far off the road to Sabratha, is home to most of Tripoli's sporting activities. This is the headquarters of Libya's premier football club, Al-Ahly, and there's usually at least one weekly match (3LD), except in summer. During the qualifying rounds of the African Nations Cup, where Libya plays against other African countries in both home and away matches, you might also see an international match. The stadiums are rarely packed so simply turn up. The Sports City is also home to occasional games of basketball, handball, volleyball and table tennis.

SHOPPING

Tripoli is the best place in Libya to shop, and the souqs of the medina are definitely the most atmospheric place to pick up a gift for people back home.

Medina

There are a smattering of handicraft stores around the south-east corner of the medina, close to the eastern end of Souq al-Turk, many of which specialise in tourist kitsch. *Ben Zeglam Shop (☎ 4443168, Carpet Bazaar)* Open 11am-1.30pm & 6pm-8.30pm

Sat-Thur. This is one shop that stands out in terms of quality, price and range for Libyan (mostly Berber) items such as pottery, Tuareg jewellery, knives and boxes, flat-weave kilim cushions and larger rugs.

The other carpet shops in the vicinity specialise in the heavy-weave Berber rugs that have animal motifs.

There's a wonderfully atmospheric market along a tributary branch of the Souq al-Attara (see Walking Tour under Medina earlier in this chapter). This is the place to go if you've always craved a Colonel Gaddafi watch (from 15LD) although you can also pick up cheap clothing and perfumes. Running west off the northern end of the lane is the relatively tranquil Souq al-Rabaa, where they sell a good range of *galabiyyas* (men's robes), including ones ideal for that three-year-old back home.

The medina is also awash with shops selling jewellery (especially gold) aimed primarily at the local market; prices are rarely inflated for tourists. Souq al-Turk and the lanes in the far east of the medina are the best areas to start looking.

East of Green Square

Ghadames Art Gallery (☎ 3336666, 50/52 Sharia 1st September, postal address: PO Box 2895) Open 10am-noon & 5pm-9pm Sat-Thur, 5pm-9pm Fri. Not far from Green Square, the Ghadames Art Gallery is run by the avuncular Mustafa Gayim who sells old paintings and sketches of Tripoli and Libya starting at 20LD.

Sharia 1st September is also a surprisingly good place to pick up good quality men's suits in a range of fabric blends, including polyester wool mix and 100% wool. Prices start at around 250LD; ridiculously cheap compared to back home. There are also loads of women's shoe shops on the same street.

Sharia ar-Rashid

The basic rule for the markets along Sharia ar-Rashid is that if it isn't nailed down then it's probably for sale. Items on offer range from cameras to cheap cigarettes, Juventus shirts to galabiyyas, while the eastern end has some pretty distressing scenes of macaws, cats and the occasional baby gazelle for sale. Around the chaotic Tunis Garage at the western end are spare parts for cars, televisions, and African folk medicines sold by colourfully attired women from sub-Saharan Africa. It's worth wandering around here at least once, particularly in the evening when it can throng with people, although keep a close eye on your valuables.

If you absolutely must have that Mohammed Hassan or Umm Kolthum cassette, there are shops along Sharia ar-Rashid.

Upmarket Shops

Worlds away are the exclusive shopping centres of Gargaresh and the lobby of the Burj al-Fateh building where the latest sound systems, designer labels and household items come at a price not dissimilar from what you'd pay back home.

GETTING THERE & AWAY

There were, at the time of research, well-developed plans to relocate all long-distance bus and shared taxi stations outside the city in order to ease congestion. For destinations to the east, the new terminal will be in Tajura. For the west, it will be in Al-Ghaeran, 11km west of the medina on the main road to Janzur. Those heading south should head to Bowabed ad-Djebbs, near the checkpoint 8km south-west of the Parliament building on the road to Al-Aziziyah. No-one seemed to know exactly when these would become operational, nor whether destinations to the south-west – Ghadames and the towns of the Jebel Nafusa – would leave from the southern or western station.

Air

Tripoli airport is a 1970s era building on a grand scale, though in subsequent years has come to resemble a huge warehouse. Don't be put off by the bewildering slogan that claims 'In need, freedom is latent'. Somewhat more helpfully, the arrivals hall has a bank where you can change money (although it isn't always manned if your plane arrives at 3am) and a car rental agency. Most of the airlines maintain offices here. The telephone area code is 022.

The check-in counters for departing passengers are facing you on the left as you enter the building. After checking in, you must pay your departure tax (6LD) at the counter next to the left-luggage office before you will be allowed to proceed through immigration. There is a decent cafe (and an Internet cafe that is occasionally open) up the escalator where you can wait before passing the strict security checks and entering the departure lounge.

For arriving passengers, there are usually taxis waiting outside in the event that your tour representative hasn't turned up.

International Most airlines that fly to Libya have offices in Tripoli. They include:

Air Malta (☎ 3350578, fax 3350580) Dhat al-Ahmat, Tower 5, Level 1
Alitalia (☎ 3350296, airport ☎ 022-3619591) Dhat al-Ahmat, Tower 3, Mezzanine (Level 1)
Austrian Airlines (☎ 3350241, airport ☎ 022-3618102, fax 3350244) Dhat al-Ahmat, Tower 3, Level 6
British Airways (☎ 3351277, fax 3351283, airport ☎ 022-3605332, airport fax 3605313) Burj al Fateh, Level 19, Room 191
Emirates (☎ 3350597) Dhat al-Ahmat, Tower 5, Level 5
KLM-Royal Dutch Airlines (☎ 3350018, fax 3350020) Burj al-Fateh, Level 19, Room 194
Lufthansa Airlines (☎ 3350375, fax 3350378, airport ☎ 022-3619516) Dhat al-Ahmat, Tower 4, Level 12, postal address: PO Box 91518 Tripoli
Libyan Arab Airlines (☎ 3616738/42, 3337 500, airport ☎ 022-3605041) Sharia Omar al-Mukhtar
Malev-Hungarian Airlines (☎ 3351254, fax 3351255, e szelle.kalman@malev.hu) Burj al-Fateh, Level 2; the staff are particularly helpful
Royal Jordanian (☎ 4441565) Sharia Mohammed Megharief
Swissair (☎ 3350022, fax 3350054) Dhat al-Ahmat, Tower 3, Level 4
Syrianair (☎ 4446716, fax 3336648) North of Sharia al-Baladiya
Tunis Air (☎ 3336303) Off Algeria Square
Turkish Airlines (☎ 3351252/3, fax 3351351) Sharia Mohammed Megharief

Domestic As Libya emerges from the sanctions imposed upon it by the United Nations, there is likely to be an increase in the destinations within Libya as well as in the frequency of flights on existing routes. At the time of research, Libyan Arab Airlines was flying from Tripoli to Benghazi (28/56LD for one-way economy/1st class, four times daily), Sebha (28/56LD, daily except Sunday), Tobruk (44/88LD, three times weekly), and Al-Kufra (51/102LD, weekly).

Bus

There are two main departures for long distances buses – the area around Tunis Garage (Al-Itihad al-Afriqi or United Africa Bus Company) at the western end of Sharia ar-Rashid, and the Dahra Bus Station or Mahattat Hafilat Dahra (An-Nakhl as-Seria or Fast Transport Company).

International Most international services connect Tripoli with other cities in North Africa and the Middle East. Al-Itihad al-Afriqi (☎ 3342532) on Sharia al-Ma'ari is the best choice for international departures. Most of the larger buses are good. Destinations include: Tunis (45LD), Jerba (30LD),

Algiers (110LD) and Cairo (85LD, 36 hours). If demand isn't great, they'll direct you to the shared taxis, which leave more frequently from Tunis Garage. The bus office is just around the corner from Bourgeiba Mosque. Book at least two days in advance.

Other companies have shopfronts around the perimeter of Tunis Garage, although the quality can be as unpredictable as their destinations are ambitious. Mutahedeen Passenger Agency (☎ 4443517), on the northeast side of the square, sells tickets to Damascus (150LD), Beirut or Aleppo (160LD), Baghdad (170LD), Amman (130LD) and, for those intent on circumnavigating the Mediterranean as quickly as possible, İstanbul (230LD) – you'd have to be mad.

Domestic If you want to avoid the madness and uncertainty of the Tunis Garage, Al-Itihad al-Afriqi also has daily buses to cities within Libya. Departure times change frequently so please check when booking your ticket.

The usually cheaper An-Nakhl as-Seria operates from the Dahra Bus Station (Mahattat Hafilat Dahra). The ticket office is at the back of the terminal. For destinations within Libya, it is essential to book tickets in advance. See the table 'Domestic Buses from Tripoli' for information.

Car

One of the cheapest agencies is Assalama Car Rental (☎ 3344169, airport ☎ 3618947, airport fax 4449526) in the lobby of Funduq al-Waddan on Sharia Sidi Issa, with another office at the airport. Prices for a pretty rundown sedan start at 50LD per day, which includes 300 free kilometres per day (0.25LD per extra kilometre). Prices elsewhere are much more expensive. You could try Al-Mehari Car Rental (☎ 3333753, fax 3342871, e tajori@hotmail.com) on Funduq al-Mehari, which charges 90LD per day with 100 free kilometres (0.25LD for each additional kilometre); a minimum booking of three days is required. Another reasonable option is Al-Mansura (☎ 3331180, fax 3336688) on Funduq Qasr Libya, which

Domestic Buses from Tripoli

Al-Itihad al-Afriqi Buses

destination	price (LD)	departure times	duration (hrs)
Al-Kufra	45	variable	32
Benghazi	20	8am, 4pm	12
Ghadames	15–20	4pm	8
Nalut	12–15	4pm	5
Sebha	15–20	6am	12
Sirt	15	8am, 4pm	5

Al-Nakhl as-Seria Buses

destination	price (LD)	departure times	duration (hrs)
Al-Khoms	1.5	7am	1½
Benghazi	13.5	7am, 10am	12
Ghadames	8	7am	8
Gharyan	3	1pm, 5am	2
Jadu	4	1pm	1½
Sebha	13	5am	12
Sirt	6	7am, 10am	5
Nalut	6	7am, 1pm	5
Yefren	3.5	2pm	1¼

charges 100LD per day including 100 free kilometres.

Shared Taxi & Micro

Most long-distance shared taxis and micros (minibuses) leave from Tunis Garage at the western end of Sharia ar-Rashid, at least until the stations are moved to the city's outskirts. There are reasonably regular shared-taxi departures for Gharyan (2.5LD), Al-Khoms (for Leptis; 2.5LD), Nalut (10LD), Misrata (6LD) and Zliten (3LD). Taxis undertaking long-haul journeys fill up much faster early in the morning or in the late afternoon. These include Benghazi (25LD), Sirt (15LD), Ghadames (17LD) and Sebha (25LD). Micros are cheaper, but can take an age to fill.

You might also find the occasional shared taxi to Sabratha (2LD) here, but they leave more frequently from the local shared taxi and micro station along Sharia al-Corniche.

There are also surprisingly regular shared taxis to Tunis (50LD) from Tunis Garage.

For destinations closer to Tripoli, shared taxis leave from the other stations along Sharia ar-Rashid, near Maidan as-Sawayhli.

Sea

Ferries depart from the terminal east of the centre and near Funduq al-Mehari. Since the embargo was lifted, ferry services have been unpredictable. To check timetables (and buy tickets), go to the office of the General National Maritime Transport Company (GNMTC; ☎ 3331710, 3333155), on Sharia Mohammed Megharief. It's open 9.30am to 1.30pm Saturday to Thursday, and is a small block east of Green Square – look for the ship sign above the footpath between two blue signs with white Arabic writing. Departures at the time of research included: Tangiers (Morocco; 186/350 one-way/return, two to three per month, two to three days duration); Valletta (Malta; 115LD return only, every second day, 14 hours); and Izmir (Turkey, 285LD return only, intermittent departures only, four to five days via Benghazi). Mediterranean Travel & Tourism Co (see Travel Agencies under Information earlier in this chapter) also sells tickets.

GETTING AROUND
To/From the Airport

Tripoli international airport is located around 25km south of the city, and there are no regular buses or shared taxis in either direction. You might occasionally find one (2LD to 2.5LD) in the local bus station along Sharia al-Corniche, west of the medina, but this is unlikely and it may not fill up in time. A private taxi costs 15LD, but if you're leaving after midnight, the drivers will ask for 20LD.

Car & Motorcycle

Tripoli has a difficult system of one-way streets in the area west of the medina. If you're heading to Dhat al-Ahmat (or the hotels nearby) from Green Square, take Sharia Omar al-Mukhtar to near the Funduq Bahr al-Abyad. One option is to turn right on Sharia al-Corniche and undertake a perilous manoeuvre across three lanes of traffic to the gap in the dual carriageway – probably best left to local taxi drivers. An easier (though longer) way is to continue back along Sharia al-Corniche to the large roundabout under the medina and do a U-turn.

If you want to get to Green Square from Dhat al-Ahmat, there is no direct access from Sharia al-Corniche. After passing between the fish market and the Arch of Marcus Aurelius, take the small street that runs southeast leading behind the castle.

Shared Taxi & Micro

Yellow-and-white shared taxis to destinations within a 7km to 8km radius of Green Square (ie, most of the places you're likely to visit) cost 0.5LD; micros cost 0.25LD. The easiest way to catch one is to go to the local micro/taxi stations on Sharia al-Corniche (west of the medina) and Maidan as Sawayhli. Alternatively, simply stand by a road heading in your direction and shout out your destination when one slows down; some streets have bus stops. For Gargaresh (0.5LD), head to Maidan as-Sawayhli or the station on Sharia al-Corniche.

Private Taxi

Black-and-white private taxis are everywhere in Tripoli and a trip usually costs

5LD, although it may be a touch more for outlying suburbs.

Around Tripoli

JANZUR جنزور
☎ 021

The small town of Janzur, 13km west of Tripoli, is in danger of being swallowed up by Tripoli's relentless sprawl. While there is little of interest, the 200-year-old **Sidi Amara Mosque** and **museum** are worth a look if you're passing through. Housed in one of 18 underground tombs found in the area in 1958, the museum contains some good frescoes including one that takes the form of a river from earthly life to the afterlife. This stretch of coast is famous for its orange groves and in winter the main highway between Tripoli and Sabrata is lined with impromptu stalls selling the produce.

Janzur is something of a summer resort and has a decent beach.

Qaryat Janzur as-Siyahe (Janzur Tourist Village; ☎ *4890421, postal address: PO Box 76791 Janzur)* Singles/doubles 25/35LD, villas 50LD. Tastefully designed, this is one of Libya's better tourist complexes, but you'll have to book up to three months in advance to get a room in summer. Janzur is best suited to a day trip; shared taxis and micros pass through the southern outskirts en route from Tripoli to Sabratha.

TAJURA تـاجوراء
☎ 026 or ☎ 021

The small town of Tajura, 14km east of the capital, is a summer resort for Tripoli residents who don't want to stray too far from home. The settlement goes back to medieval times, and it was a refuge for the elites of Tripoli who fled during the brief Spanish occupation in the 16th century. Its main attraction is the large **Murad Agha Mosque**, which dates from the middle of the 16th century. It is very plain from the outside and features a large square minaret. Inside it has a large arcaded prayer hall with 48 columns, which were brought from Leptis Magna.

Tajura is home to two tourist villages, although again you'll need to book three months ahead of season.

Qaryat Tajura as-Siyahe (Tajura Tourist Village; ☎ *3696060)* Doubles 15/18LD in winter/summer. About 5km east of Tajura on the main highway, this sprawling place is the older of the two and a little run-down, but it does front the slightly nicer beach.

Qaryat Sidi al-Andalous (Sidi Andalusia Tourist Village; ☎ *3690034)* Doubles 15/25LD in winter/summer. This place is just 1km east of Tajura and is a little better maintained. Prices don't include breakfast.

SOUTH OF TRIPOLI

The coastal plain stretches south of Tripoli for almost 75km with olive groves the only bump in the landscape. Not far before the plain runs hard into the escarpment of the Jebel Nafusah, 43km south of Tripoli, is the town of **Al-Aziziyah (L'Aziziyah)**. It's a reasonable place to stock up on snacks, with well-stocked fruit and grocery stores the length of the main street. There's a post office and a bank (Masraf al-Jamahiriya). Don't linger in summer – L'Aziziyah has recorded one of the hottest temperatures in the world (57°C).

Coastal Tripolitania

The ancient Roman province of Tripolitania in the north-west is home to some of the best-preserved Roman cities anywhere in the Mediterranean; many consider Leptis Magna and Sabratha to be Libya's premier attractions. Along with Oea (now buried beneath Tripoli's medina) these cities gave the province its name – Tripolitania was 'the land of three cities'. The wealth of the area was based on expansive olive and cereal cultivation as well as trade in ivory and wild animals.

Modern Tripolitanians still look outwards, towards the Mediterranean, and like their Roman forebears they still keep one wary eye firmly fixed on the harsh desert to the south.

Coastal Tripolitania is Libya at its most diverse and the place where travellers usually spend most of their time.

West of Tripoli

SABRATHA
صبراتة
☎ 024

The ruins of the ancient Roman city of Sabratha, around 80km west of Tripoli, are among the highlights of any visit to Libya. While never as remarkable as Leptis, Sabratha does boast one of the finest theatres of antiquity and receives fewer visitors, making it more pleasurable to wander around.

The modern town of Sabratha has grown considerably in recent years and is home to banks, a post office and a decent number of hotels – a good place to get away from Tripoli's bustle. Alternatively, it's an easy day trip from Tripoli.

History
The origin of the name of Sabratha has been lost to time, although it is thought to possibly have been a derivation of a Libyan-Berber word meaning 'grain market'. There was a periodic (possibly nomadic) settlement here in the 5th century BC, but it wasn't until

the next century that a permanent settlement was established; Punic settlers from the neighbouring stronghold of Carthage chose the site because of its safe harbour. The Punic city consisted of narrow, winding streets with most houses facing the north-west to take full advantage of the seaborne winds. Its Punic character was diluted somewhat by the arrival of Greek (Hellenistic) settlers who began to influence the city's architecture in the 2nd century BC. At this time, Sabratha was renowned as a wealthy city and important regional centre covering at least four hectares.

A violent earthquake shook the city in the 1st century AD. In the subsequent rebuilding phase (using soft, local sandstone coated with lime and, later, imported marble), the city's architects began to turn towards Rome for inspiration, resulting in the

COASTAL TRIPOLITANIA

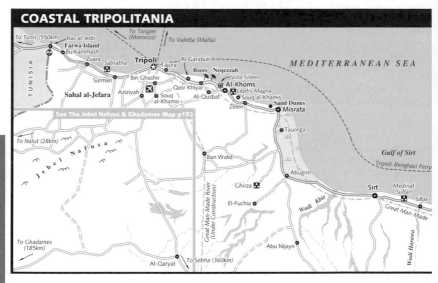

Roman character so strongly evident today. The forum was rebuilt, along with the Temple of Liber Pater, the Judicial Basilica and the Temple of Isis.

By the end of the 1st century AD, the last vestiges of Punic influence began to die out under the inexorable weight of Romanisation. Like the other cities of the Tripolis, Sabratha's heyday was during the reigns of the four Roman emperors Antoninus Pius (AD 138–61), Marcus Aurelius Antoninus (AD 161–80), Lucius Aelius Aurelius Commodus (AD 180–92) and Septimus Severus (AD 193–211). Although it never competed in terms of significance and grandeur with Leptis Magna, it grew significantly in size and status, and was given the coveted title of colony *(colonia)* in the 2nd century AD. Under Marcus Aurelius and Commodus, the extravagant, monumental heart of Sabratha extended further south at the expense of formerly Punic structures; under Commodus, the theatre was built. The city's wealth depended on the maritime trade in animals and ivory from Africa while it had to defend against invasion from Saharan tribes.

The city's decline began in the 3rd century AD, first with the decline of Rome's economy and later sealed by massive earthquakes (especially in AD 365) in which the soft sandstone structures crumbled. With the tide of Christianity sweeping the region, none of the ancient temples were rebuilt and a smaller city, a shadow of its former self, grew up over the ruins. In AD 533, the Byzantine general Belisarius launched a campaign to retake Africa, shortly after which Sabratha fell. When the Byzantines rebuilt the city walls, they enclosed only the western port and central area (an area of 18 hectares although some local experts claim nine hectares), leaving the Roman parts of the city further to the east exposed and abandoned. Many of the ancient monuments were used as homes for squatters. The city survived for at least a century after the Islamic arrival in the 7th century AD. But after then it was abandoned, left to the sands and Mediterranean winds, until it was rediscovered by Italian archaeologists in the early years of the 20th century.

Orientation

The ancient city occupies the prime coastal position, strung out along the water's edge, while the modern town extends from the southern edge of the ruins to the Tripoli-

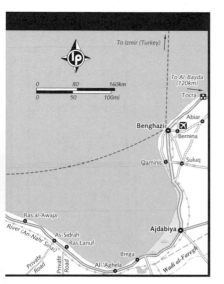

COASTAL TRIPOLITANIA

daily), but there often aren't enough to go around so you should be able to wander around alone if you wish. Recommended guides include Dr Mustapha Turjman and Bashir, who speaks French and English. Outside the entrance are a couple of stalls selling snacks, water and postcards; a restaurant is 50m to the east. There is a public toilet inside the site, in front of the Roman Museum; the women's section is around the back.

Roman Museum From the site entrance, the road arcs to the north-west. About 150m down the road is the Roman Museum *(admission 3LD, camera/video 5/10LD; open 8am-6pm Tues-Sun)*, which is set back from the path and well worth a visit. The statues in the main courtyard include a winged Victoria writing on a shield and flanked by two barbarian prisoners begging for mercy.

The museum is divided into three sections. The **western wing** contains underground objects found in the tombs of Sabratha. The **central** or **southern wing** contains some wonderful mosaics from the Basilica of Justinian. The mosaic from the central nave is on the floor and shows a scene of considerable abundance, including a vibrantly coloured peacock. The mosaics from the basilica's two aisles are on the wall. The columns and bases are copies of the originals that remain in the basilica.

The **eastern wing** also contains some superb mosaics and frescoes from a private house whose ornate decoration highlights the one-time wealth of Sabratha and its inhabitants. There are also some statues from the former Temple of Zeus that was at the western end of the forum. In the fourth room is a mosaic of the Three Graces and a stunning one of Oceanus lifted from the centre of the baths that bear his name. In the final room, there is a mosaic of nymphs grooming the mythical winged horse Pegasus.

Punic Museum Around 50m west of the Roman Museum is the Punic Museum *(admission 3LD, camera/video 5/10LD; open 8am-6pm Tues-Sun)*, which is probably not worth the effort unless you have an expert's interest in the city's earliest history. Exhibits

Zuara highway. The highway, which runs along the coast to the west of town, turns inland and doubles as the town's main street, Tariq as-Sahli. Along the main street, which runs north-south, are some banks and cheap hotels. The highway again turns east, just after which another road runs north towards the coast – a junction is marked with an abandoned church and a stone arch. This road runs for about 2km, directly into the car park and entrance to the old city.

Ancient City

Some of Sabratha's monuments are faithful modern reconstructions of the Roman originals; the most stunning example is the theatre. The remainder are in varying stages of decay, with most retaining the skeleton structure or mosaic or marble fragments of the original buildings. These are more than sufficient to provide a glimpse of the original layout and function of the structure. Of these, the monuments in the centre of ancient Sabratha, as well as the Seaward Baths and Temple of Isis, are the most intact.

Officially, guides (50LD) are compulsory for entrance to the site (☎ 622214; admission 3LD, camera/video 5/10LD; open 8am-6pm

COASTAL TRIPOLITANIA

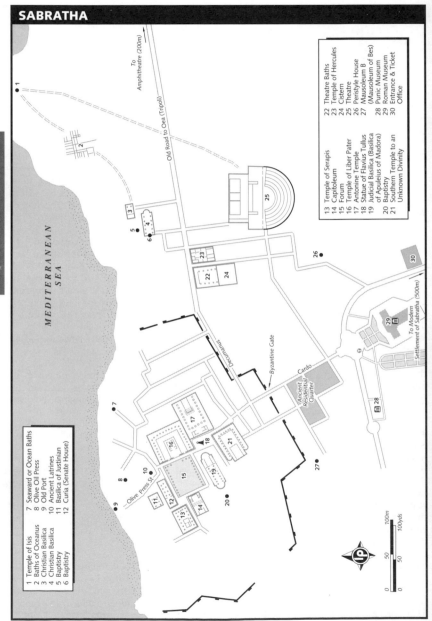

SABRATHA

MEDITERRANEAN SEA

To Amphitheatre (200m)

Old Road to Oea (Tripoli)

Decumanus

Byzantine Gate

Cardo

Ancient Residential Quarter

Olive Press St.

To Modern Settlement of Sabratha (500m)

1 Temple of Isis
2 Baths of Oceanus
3 Christian Basilica
4 Christian Basilica
5 Baptistry
6 Baptistry
7 Seaward or Ocean Baths
8 Olive Oil Press
9 Old Port
10 Ancient Latrines
11 Basilica of Justinian
12 Curia (Senate House)

13 Temple of Serapis
14 Capitoleum
15 Forum
16 Temple of Liber Pater
17 Antonine Temple
18 Statue of Flavius Tullus
19 Judicial Basilica (Basilica of Apuleius of Madora)
20 Baptistry
21 Southern Temple to an Unknown Divinity

22 Theatre Baths
23 Temple of Hercules
24 Cistern
25 Theatre
26 Peristyle House
27 Mausoleum B (Mausoleum of Bes)
28 Punic Museum
29 Roman Museum
30 Entrance & Ticket Office

0   50   100m
0   50   100yds

Sabratha was once a Roman centre for trade in African animals and ivory and its former wealth is still evident in its ruins: the Puno-Hellenistic Mausoleum of Bes (top left); one of the theatre's classical statues (top right); and the bas-relief on the pulpitum below the stage in the theatre (bottom).

Excavated remains of Roman tombs constructed near the ancient port city of Tocra

Tobruk (Commonwealth) War Cemetery, maintained in honour of Allied forces who died in WWII

include underground ceramic objects and fragments from Mausoleum B (Mausoleum of Bes), representations of lions, male figures and the physically repugnant deity of the Egyptian god Bes in all his glory.

South-Western Quarters The path that leads north towards the sea from the Roman Museum is the old Roman **Cardo**, the main north-south thoroughfare in Roman times that led into the heart of the city. One of Sabratha's old **residential quarters** is off to the left where some houses contain cisterns and pottery remnants.

Mausoleum B (Mausoleum of Bes), nearly 100m north-west of the Cardo, has been completely reconstructed by archaeologists. Punic in origin, the mausoleum is nearly 24m tall and stands on the site of an underground funerary chamber dating from the 2nd century BC. It has a triangular base, concave facades and a small pyramidal structure on the summit. The motifs (originals of which are in the Punic Museum) show Bes and Hercules, who are thought to have been the protectors of the tomb, as well as lions. The mausoleum was dismantled by the Byzantines, who used the materials to build their wall around the city.

Byzantine Wall In the 6th century, the Byzantines, mindful of the dangers of attack by Berbers, built the wall to encircle and protect the city. The **Byzantine Gate** was once flanked by small towers and marked an important point where access to the central commercial, administrative and religious districts could be controlled. The wall is at its most intact around the gate.

Southern Temple to an Unknown Divinity The first major building on the left after you pass through the Byzantine Gate is a Roman temple built to an unknown deity; it's also known as the South Forum Temple. Much of the large rectangular courtyard still bears the original marble floor. It dates from the 2nd century AD, the great period of Roman monument building when cipolin columns and a portico once surrounded the courtyard. Apart from the marble floor, the

capitals and pediment fragments are the only remaining original items.

Antonine Temple This elevated temple is believed to have been dedicated to the Roman emperor Antoninus Pius although some archaeologists believe that Marcus Aurelius was the real inspiration. It once had a small porticoed courtyard. A modern staircase allows you to climb to the top without damaging the crumbling gradations on either side. The views from the top are superb, showcasing Sabratha's prime coastal location and overlooking the adjacent public buildings that stood at the monumental heart of Roman Sabratha. Immediately outside the temple is a fine fountain and headless **Statue of Flavius Tullus** in commemoration of this fine 2nd- century citizen who commissioned an aqueduct to bring water to Sabratha.

Judicial Basilica Also known as the Basilica of Apuleius of Madora (see the boxed text 'The Defence of Apuleius') or House of Justice, this building was originally built in the 1st century AD, although most of what remains (marble columns and some excellent paving fragments) dates from around AD 450 – enough to give an idea of the basilica's structure. Between these dates, the building changed function as Sabratha made the transition from a Roman city to a Byzantine city. Its early manifestation was broadly equivalent to a court and consisted of a large hall measuring 50m by 25m and surrounded by a portico. A large room next to the southern entrance was once the tribunal used by the magistrates of the day. In the 5th century the building was converted into a Byzantine basilica in which the main sanctuary was divided into a nave and aisles.

Forum Like all great Roman forums, Sabratha's formed the centrepiece of the ancient city and served as a market and public meeting place where the news (and gossip) of the city was disseminated. Most of what remains dates from restoration work in the 4th century AD; this work probably restored damage caused by the earthquake in AD 365. The original structure was built in the

The Defence of Apuleius

In AD 158, a sensational trial rocked Sabratha from its decadent slumber with all the scandal of a modern soap opera. Apuleius was a renowned philosopher who travelled throughout the colonies expounding his theories in Latin and Greek to great acclaim. One of Apuleius' speaking tours took him to Sabratha, where he married Pudentilla, a rich widow many years his senior. The citizens of Sabratha were outraged and the city descended into an unseemly round of scandal mongering. One family, which stood to lose out on the widow's massive inheritance, formally brought a charge against Apuleius. The accusation? Using his magic powers to win over the widow (there is no record of whether she was given a say). The trial of the decade was presided over by the Roman proconsul Claudio Massimo in the Judicial Basilica. In a captivating oration that lasted three (some say four) days, Apuleius won his freedom. As other celebrities through the ages have discovered, the publicity only enhanced his reputation.

1st century BC or 1st century AD. Before the Antonine Period (AD 138–61), the forum was only accessible via a single entrance. Over time, the shops and offices became more grand and more permanent, and a portico was built with grey columns of Egyptian granite. Some of these remain.

Capitoleum The Capitoleum, also known as the Temple of Jupiter or Zeus, was the principal temple of the city and dedicated to Jupiter, Juno and Minerva. The huge bust of Jupiter in the Roman Museum was found here, as were a rich storehouse of statues. The Capitoleum was first built in the 1st century AD and then reconstructed in marble the next century. Overlooking the forum as it did, its platform was the soapbox of choice for the great orators of the era. The original adornments of the platform are either gone or are now in the Roman Museum.

Curia On the northern side of the forum is the Curia, or Senate House, marked by a restored archway at the entrance. The Curia was the meeting place of the city's magistrates and senators and consisted of a four-sided courtyard covered with a mosaic. The wide steps around the perimeter were used for portable seats upon which the great senatorial backsides could sit. It was one of the few major buildings rebuilt after the earthquake of AD 365; a portico was added during the reconstruction. Its grey-granite columns are a feature. There were three entrances to the forum from the Curia and the niches in the perimeter were adorned with statues.

Temple of Liber Pater East of the Curia is the Temple of Liber Pater (or Temple of Dionysius), which was never rebuilt after the AD 365 earthquake. It is marked by five columns (four tall and one shorter) in light sandstone on a high podium overlooking the monument heart of ancient Sabratha. It was flanked on three sides by a double colonnade of sandstone columns. Dedicated to one of the most revered gods of Roman Africa and second only in importance to the Capitoleum in the hierarchy of temples in Roman Sabratha, this temple sat atop an elevated platform that was reached via a wide staircase. It was constructed in the 2nd century AD on the site of an earlier temple. Only the column bases and two of the columns are original.

Temple of Serapis Immediately east of the Curia, this temple is dedicated to Serapis, a healer and miracle worker. The cult of Serapis, which originally came from Memphis in Egypt, was often associated in Sabratha with that of Isis. It is thought to be one of the oldest temples in the city, although its date of construction is not known. Some of the columns of the portico are still present in a combination of grey marble and limestone.

Basilica of Justinian This was one of the finest churches of Byzantine Sabratha. Built in the 6th century AD, its main nave and aisles were adorned with breathtaking mosaics that now reside in the central wing of the Roman Museum. Many features date from an earlier period, as construction materials were taken and reused from other parts of the city, for example, the magnificent, square-sided column on the apse with intricate acanthus motifs (2nd century AD). The mosaics in the museum make it easy to imagine the grandeur of this church, which also had three naves, a pulpit and an altar (the foundations of each remain clearly visible). The pulpit originally formed a part of the cornice on the Capitoleum.

North-Western Quarter The buildings around the Basilica of Justinian, overlooking the Mediterranean, are some of the oldest in Sabratha, many dating from the 1st century AD when the city was still primarily Punic in character. This was the site of the main **port**, the launching pad of Sabratha's wealth. This was also a residential area. The ruins of an old **olive oil press** are nearby as are, back towards the Temple of Liber Pater, the public **latrines** that doubled as a meeting place (it's a pity their existence doesn't spur on the modern Libyan authorities to provide similar amenities in their cities).

Don't miss the **Seaward** or **Ocean Baths**, which are superbly located looking east along the coast. One of many such complexes in Sabratha, the baths are famous for their lovely mosaics overlooking the water and for the hexagonal latrine, which is paved and lined with fine marble.

Theatre Quarter About 150m south-east of the baths is the **Decumanus**, the main east-west thoroughfare of the Roman city. Flanked by part of the old Byzantine Wall, it runs past the **Temple of Hercules**, behind which is a large **cistern** used for storing water for the **Theatre Baths**, which are immediately opposite, across a small lane. These baths enabled the patrons of the arts to unwind before or after a performance and contain some mosaic fragments on the floors.

North-west of these buildings are two **Christian basilicas** dating from the 4th to 5th century AD. They once formed part of a large religious complex under the Byzantines. A little further north-east are the **Baths of Oceanus**. The decoration of these public baths was extraordinarily lavish,

with marble on every surface. You can see the *tepidarium* (warm room). The mosaic that is missing the central fragment once bore the head of the god Oceanus, but he now rests in the Roman Museum.

Temple of Isis The superb Temple of Isis, north-east of the Baths of Oceanus, is arguably the finest of Sabratha's temples. Built in the 1st century AD, it faces onto the Mediterranean in keeping with its dedication to the Egyptian goddess Isis, who was seen here as a protector of sailors. Every spring, a great feast was held to celebrate the start of the sailing season. The colonnaded courtyard has a row of eight Corinthian columns. Look beyond the temple to the north and you can see part of the temple foundations that have been eroded by the sea; beyond that are parts of the city lost to the waves during the earthquake.

Amphitheatre If you're not too tired, it's worth wandering out to the amphitheatre, which is east of the main old city along the old road to Oea (Tripoli). Built in the 2nd century on the site of a converted quarry, it was known a century later as a place where Christians were fed to the lions. The amphitheatre, built of limestone blocks, could once seat 10,000 spectators. The arena, which measures 65m by 50m, is bisected by two deep underground tunnels that were used for storing sets and equipment as well as providing easy access to the arena for

They Called it Sport

The entertainment on offer in Roman amphitheatres was not for the faint-hearted. A typical program consisted of people hunting rabbits and small rodents in the arena in the morning, followed by shackled criminals being left to the mercies of the lions. At least the Christians, who followed the criminals, were allowed into the arena free of shackles, although few escaped. All of this operated as the prematch entertainment for the main event – the epic contests of the gladiators.

COASTAL TRIPOLITANIA

performers. The tunnels were once covered with a wooden roof.

Theatre The outstanding theatre, south of the basilicas, is the jewel in Sabratha's crown. It was rebuilt by the Italian archaeologists Giacomo Guidi (who sadly didn't live to see the masterful results of his work) and Giacomo Caputo in the 1920s. The original theatre was begun in AD 190 under the reign of Commodus although some historians claim it was completed by Septimus Severus the following decade. It was still used into the 4th century until it was destroyed by the earthquake of AD 365. The reconstruction is largely faithful to its original form, although the blocks used by the Italians were only half the original size. With an auditorium measuring close to 95m in diameter, it was once the largest theatre in Africa.

The facade behind the stage is one of the most exceptional in the Roman world. The three tiers consists of alcoves and 108 fluted Corinthian columns that rise over 20m above the stage. There are some exquisite floral carvings atop the columns as well as carvings of divinities. The stage, 43m long and nearly 9m wide, overlooks the orchestra area that was paved with marble slabs. The front of the elevated stage is simply magnificent, and three large concave niches are the highlight. The central curved panel shows personifications of Rome and Sabratha, flanked by military figures and scenes of sacrifice. The left panel (facing the stage) depicts the nine Muses while the one on the right shows the Three Graces and the Judgement of Paris. Set back into the wall are four rectangular facades between the concave niches, which show comedy scenes as well as dancing and a few assorted divinities (including Mercury) and the Greek mythological hero Hercules.

The balustrade at either end of the orchestra area marks the seats reserved for VIPs, who were kept suitably separated from the riff-raff. The seats climb sharply skywards and once had room for 5000 people; even today it can seat 1500. Underneath the seats were three concentric semicircular passageways that were known as promenades, parts

of which were lined with shops. Only two of these promenades have been rebuilt.

Peristyle House On your way back to the exit, it's worth visiting this private residence that has good views back towards the theatre. It has a mosaic representing a labyrinth, a few columns and underground rooms that were used in summer.

Places to Stay & Eat

Buyut ash-Shabaab (☎ 622821) Dorm beds for HI members/nonmembers 3/5LD, camping 5LD. Around 600m east of the entrance to the ancient city, this hostel is basic, clean and well run; you can also pitch a tent in the grounds.

Along the main street (highway), within walking distance to both the shared-taxi station and ancient Sabratha, are a number of cheap hotels. They're not particularly appealing although they're marginally better than their Tripoli equivalents. *Funduq ash-Shatti* and *Funduq Nuzel Sabratha al-Medina* along Tariq as-Sahli are typical examples and charge 10LD per person.

Funduq Sabratha as-Siyahe (☎ 091 2114086) Singles/doubles 10/15LD. Just 200m south of the entrance to the ancient city, this friendly place has simple but clean rooms with bath – most come with a balcony. The owner has plans for a restaurant, while what looked like a swish new hotel was nearing completion next door.

Funduq al-Asil (☎ 620959) Singles/doubles 20/40LD. At the time of research, this was Sabratha's newest and best hotel. It's on the western side of town, around 400m south of the coastal highway to Zuara. The rooms are tidy and spacious, and come with bath. Some at the back of the building have a distant view of the ancient theatre. There's a *restaurant* (mains from 8LD to 30LD), coffee shop and pool table.

Apart from the cheap restaurants along Tariq as-Sahli, the only restaurant of note is *Mat'am al-Bawady* on the highway on the western side of town. The food is good and, at 12LD for a three-course meal, excellent value. *Arous al-Bahr*, the cafe in the car park of the ancient site, is expensive.

Getting There & Away

The shared-taxi station is in a car park at the southern end of Tariq as-Sahli, just before it turns east. Shared taxis run regularly to Tripoli (2LD, 1½ hours) and Zuara (1LD, 30 minutes). To get to Gharyan, and other destinations to the south, you'll probably have to go to Tripoli, although you may find something in Janzur. For Ghadames and the towns of the Jebel Nafusa, you'll have to change in Zuara. There are also irregular shared taxis to the Tunisian border (3LD, 1½ hours).

ZUARA   زوارة

☎ 025 • pop 45,000

Zuara, 60km east of the Libyan-Tunisian border at Ras al-Jedir and 109km west of Tripoli, is a lively Berber town with excellent white-sand beaches. In August, Zuara's **Awussu festival** takes place. If you're within striking distance, joining the locals for sailing, swimming races and folk dancing is definitely the thing to do in Libya's wilting heat.

Like many towns along Libya's northwest coast, most of Zuara is located between the shores of the Mediterranean and the highway. The banks, post office and *jawazzat* (passport office) are east of the main square (known locally as the piazza). Along Sharia Jamal Abdul Nasser are some good travel agencies that do Libya-wide tours and excursions to the Jebel Nafusa. They include: Azar Libya Travel & Tours Co (☎/fax 24821, ⓔ Azartours@aol.com); Shati Zuara Libyan Tourism Services Co (☎/fax 24606, ⓔ shati_zuara@yahoo.com); and Zuara Travel & Tourism (☎ 24670, fax 24669).

Zuara's accommodation options are fairly limited, especially as the *buyut ash-shabaab* (youth hostel), east of the main square in town, was closed for renovations at the time of research.

The only other cheapie is *Al-Ka'shaef*, a basic hostel opposite the main square with beds for 5LD to 10LD. *Funduq as-Salama* (☎22295), next to the petrol station on the main highway at the eastern edge of town, has reasonable singles/doubles with private bathroom for 20/35LD; there is also a *restaurant*. A new hotel is also under construction right on the beach. There are

plenty of *snack bars* around the centre of town.

The shared taxi station is east of the post office, with departures for Ras al-Jedir (2LD, 45 minutes), Sabratha (1LD, 30 minutes) and Tripoli (2.5LD, two hours). There are less-frequent departures to the Jebel Nafusa as well as Nalut (around 5LD, 2½ hours) and Ghadames (about 14LD, seven hours).

ZUARA TO RAS AL-JEDIR

In all likelihood, the most you'll see of this area is out of a shared taxi or tour bus window as it hurtles to or from the Tunisian border. If you have the time, the beaches along this stretch of coast are some of Libya's best.

Bu Kammash, home to a petrochemical plant, is the gateway to **Farwa Island**, which has a clean white-sand beach on the northern side of the island. The rest of the 471-hectare island is covered with almost 4000 palm trees, a few sand dunes and tiny villages. Farwa is separated from the mainland by a 3km-wide lagoon, although a large sand bar at the eastern end almost connects the two. Small ferries cross between Bu Kammash and Farwa (0.5LD) on an intermittent basis. At its widest point, the island is only 1.1km wide. A tourist resort is planned.

East of Tripoli

TAJURA TO AL-KHOMS

If you're heading east along the coast from Tripoli, you pass through the small resort town of (see Tajura under Around Tripoli in the Tripoli chapter), 14km east of the capital. Approximately 75km east of Tajura, you pass through the unattractive town of **Qasr Khiyar**, which is lined with mechanics shops and an occasional grocery store. The post office is halfway through the town on the northern side of the road, while there's a petrol station a bit further on.

Around 90km east from Tajura is the pleasant **Bsees beach** with white sand. A 12-hectare tourist resort with a hotel, golf course and horse-racing track is planned. The main highway in this area is dotted with makeshift stalls selling honey, olive oil and date juice.

There's another beach at **Neqezzah**, 101km east of Tajura and around 20km west of Al-Khoms. This lovely beach is popular with students from the nearby college and the place throngs with people on Thursday afternoon and Friday. It's 4.2km off the main highway (the turn-off is a dip in the road, immediately west of three telecommunications masts). On the road down to the beach is *Funduq an-Neqezzah* (☎ *031-626691/2)*, which has spacious twins/chalets/suites with air-con, TV and phone for 30/40/50LD; prices include breakfast.

AL-KHOMS   الخمس
☎ 031 • pop 120,000

Al-Khoms, 120km east of Tripoli, is a pleasant town and, as the closest town to Leptis Magna, makes a good base for exploring the ruins. There are also some good beaches in the area so it's a great place to relax for a few days.

There's not much to see in the town itself, although the Mosque of Ali Pasha in the centre of town is attractive, with a large conical dome in distinctive cream tones and a fine minaret adorned with vertical and horizontal lines.

Orientation & Information
Most of the action in Al-Khoms takes place along or just off the main street, Sharia al-Khoms, which runs north-east into town from the main highway before turning east at the main roundabout, marked by a small mosque. From here, Sharia al-Khoms continues east through the centre of town to Leptis Magna, around 3km away.

There is an Internet cafe (☎ 628798) on Sharia al-Khoms, around 400m south-east of the roundabout, which is open 10am to midnight Saturday to Thursday. It charges 3LD per hour. The jawazzat (☎ 621375) is 250m west of the Mosque of Ali Pasha, while the post office is next to the mosque on Sharia al-Jamahiriya.

Places to Stay & Eat
Buyut ash-Shabaab (☎ *621880)* Dorm beds for HI members/nonmembers 3/5LD. In a quiet area 2km west of the town centre, this is a basic but friendly hostel. It's quite a walk to Leptis (more than 5km).

Al-Rua al-Bahr *(Sharia al-Jamahiriya)* Dorm beds 4LD. This basic little hostel is central but is often full of immigrant workers; tourists are a rarity. Female travellers

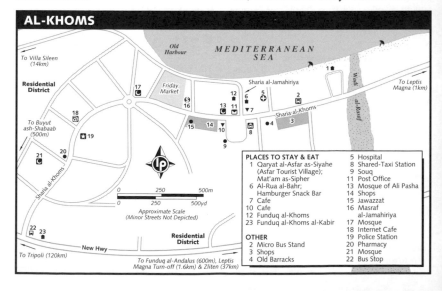

AL-KHOMS

Old Harbour

MEDITERRANEAN SEA

To Villa Sileen (14km)

Residential District

To Buyut ash-Shabaab (500m)

To Tripoli (120km)

Sharia al-Jamahiriya

To Leptis Magna (1km)

Wadi al-Rasuf

Friday Market

Sharia al-Khoms

Sharia al-Khoms

New Hwy

Residential District

To Funduq al-Andalus (600m), Leptis Magna Turn-off (1.6km) & Zliten (37km)

0   250   500m
0   250   500yd
Approximate Scale (Minor Streets Not Depicted)

PLACES TO STAY & EAT
1 Qaryat al-Asfar as-Siyahe (Asfar Tourist Village); Mat'am as-Sipher
6 Al-Rua al-Bahr; Hamburger Snack Bar
7 Cafe
10 Cafe
12 Funduq al-Khoms
23 Funduq al-Khoms al-Kabir

OTHER
2 Micro Bus Stand
3 Shops
4 Old Barracks
5 Hospital
8 Shared-Taxi Station
9 Souq
11 Post Office
13 Mosque of Ali Pasha
14 Shops
15 Jawazzat
16 Masraf al-Jamahiriya
17 Mosque
18 Internet Cafe
19 Police Station
20 Pharmacy
21 Mosque
22 Bus Stop

COASTAL TRIPOLITANIA

will certainly feel uncomfortable. To find it, look for the two green doors (the entrance) next to an enormous hamburger suspended above the footpath.

Funduq al-Khoms (☎ *621140, fax 620 420, Sharia al-Jamahiriya, postal address: PO Box 41303*) Singles/doubles/triples 20/30/45LD. This hotel is owned by one of Libya's most famous musicians, Mohammed Hassan. The rooms are run-down and some have a hospital-ward ambience but they are spacious and have bath, air-con and TV. From some rooms with east-facing balconies, you may be able to see Leptis Magna in the distance. Discounts are available for people staying longer than a couple of days. Prices includes breakfast.

Funduq al-Khoms al-Kabir (☎ *623333, main highway*) Twins/suites 20/40LD. Once Al-Khoms' finest hotel, this place is similarly run-down to Funduq Al-Khoms, although it was undergoing renovations when we visited. The renovations clearly started with the suite, which is excellent value. The other rooms are soulless; the rooms at the back are quieter. Rooms come with bath and air-con. This place is on the junction of Sharia al-Khoms and the main highway. There is a depressing restaurant, a light and airy coffee shop, a billiard table and a tea shop next door.

Funduq al-Andalus (☎ *626667, main highway*) Singles with shared bath 20LD, twins/doubles with bath 30/40LD. The rooms are clean, spacious and come with air-con and TV. Those at the back of the building are quieter. The lobby is a study in kitsch, complete with a fountain. The hotel is 2.5km east of the Sharia al-Khoms turn-off into town and 1km west of the Leptis turn-off. There is a ***restaurant*** (meals 13LD to 30LD).

Qaryat al-Asfar as-Siyahe (*Asfar Tourist Village;* ☎ *628737, fax 629743,* e *asfar_A@ hotmail.com*) Singles/doubles 35/50LD. West of the town centre and less than 2km from Leptis Magna, this is an ideal location for one of Libya's better tourist villages. Even better, it bucks the trend and reserves a quota of rooms for foreign tourists. The suites are tidy, compact and come with a bath, fridge and air-con. The beach is also pretty

good and the staff can arrange snorkelling and diving. The five-hectare site includes a travel agency, games room, tennis courts, on-site bakery, laundry and minisupermarket. In summer, reservations (with cash payment) should be made one to two months ahead (three to four months for Libyans).

Mat'am as-Sipher at the Asfar Tourist Village does reasonable chicken for 17LD, camel kebab or fish for 25LD, or crayfish for 50LD; although expensive, it's probably the best sit-down meal in Al-Khoms.

Otherwise, Al-Khoms is crying out for decent restaurants. There are **snack bars** selling hamburgers, sandwiches and pizzas along Sharia al-Khoms and a small place along Sharia al-Jamahiriya.

Getting There & Away

Al-Khoms is well served by regular shared taxis to/from Tripoli (3LD, 1½ hours) and there are also regular departures to Zliten (1LD, 30 minutes) and Misrata (2LD, one hour). The shared-taxi station is just to the east of the Mosque of Ali Pasha on the opposite side of the road, while cheaper (and less frequent) micros congregate about 100m further east on the northern side of the road. There used to be a bus from Al-Khoms to Benghazi (12LD, 10½ hours), which may start up again in the not-too-distant future. Plenty of shared taxis and micros run past in either direction along the main highway.

Getting to Leptis is easy. Shared taxis (0.5LD) and micros (0.25LD) shuttle between the town and site entrance quite often and you can flag them down at any point along Sharia al-Khoms. Alternatively, it's a leisurely 2.5km walk from the centre of town and some readers have also reported walking along the beach.

VILLA SILEEN   فيلا سيلين

This gracious Byzantine villa is a testament to the fact that wealthy people from this era really knew how to live. When its restoration work has been completed, it will be one of the highlights of Libya's coastline.

Villa Sileen is not yet officially open to the public and the (thankfully) painstaking restoration means that it will be some time before it is. In the meantime, you'll need a permit (3LD). First you'll need to visit the **Department of Archaeology office** *(open 9am-5pm daily)* opposite the main gate to the car park at Leptis Magna (see Leptis Magna later). Permission is usually granted but you'll have more chance of success if you go with a local guide or tour company. No photos are permitted at the site.

In its day, this magnificent former home must have been a prime stretch of real estate and no money was spared in its construction. The floor of every room (and much of the outdoor garden area) is covered with exquisite mosaic tiles. Many mosaics carry a central representation of a human figure or head in tiny, intricate pieces to stunning effect. These in turn are frequently encircled by repeated geometric designs of larger tiles. Most of the walls are adorned with faded frescoes of ochre-coloured human figures and pastoral scenes. The house faces onto the sea and its modern-day seclusion only adds to the beauty.

There is a small garden that looks out over the Mediterranean and is bounded on three sides by the wings of the compact villa. The courtyard has some superb mosaics depicting Nilotic scenes. The western wing has mosaics in varying stages of restoration, including a particularly fine representation of the Leptis hippodrome.

The eastern wing is topped with a number of sand-coloured domes. Inside are the former baths, complete with swimming pools and hot tubs. The frescoes in these rooms are magnificent and are dominated by bath scenes. Some of the walls are made of marble. There are some brilliantly coloured mosaic pieces on the upper architraves in some rooms consisting of tiny bits of tile. The main domed room has fine stonework atop the pillars, with dazzling mosaics of fighting scenes above some of the attractive sandstone alcoves and a wonderful mosaic showing the head of an unidentified man surrounded by sea creatures and birds (swans, crabs etc) in the centre of the floor. Throughout this section of the building are traces of pottery pipes.

Getting There & Away

Villa Sileen is impossible to reach without your own transport, so it's worth hiring a taxi (at least 25LD return, including waiting time) or going as part of a group.

If you're coming from Al-Khoms, take the road running north-west off the main roundabout in Al-Khoms for about 250m. Turn right at the T-junction and then left along the coast road. Around 8.5km from Al-Khoms, there is a turn-off to the north marked by a white wooden sign with faded Arabic letters. If you're not sure, ask for the *Tariq Nahr Sinai* (Great Man-Made River Road), as the road is shadowed by the mounds of the river's construction. Follow this semi-asphalted road for 2.4km, at which point a small track leads off to the right. The track twists and turns through fields and passes farmhouses and some minor tracks that branch off in either direction. After 1.2km, you come to a T-junction; the right road leads right to the gate of Villa Sileen after 1.6km. This stretch of road is in an awful condition and the deeply rutted surface requires slow, careful going. The sandstone domes of the villa should be visible about a kilometre or so before you reach the gate.

An Italian tour company has reportedly bought land nearby, with a view to building a luxury hotel. While this threatens the blissful isolation of Villa Sileen, at least it may lead to an improvement in the road.

LEPTIS MAGNA ليبدة

Leptis Magna is one of the finest Roman cities in the Mediterranean and one of the few sites where one can vividly picture a living city. Unlike Sabratha, which was built of soft sandstone, Leptis was constructed of sturdy limestone that left it more resistant to earthquakes and the ravages of time. Leptis was a showcase of Roman town planning, with streets following an ordered pattern. Above all, it is a testament to extravagance with abundant examples of lavish decoration, grand buildings of monumental stature, indulgent bath complexes and forums for entertainment at the centre of public life. It must have been a great place to live.

Septimus Severus – the Grim African

Lucius Septimus Severus was born in Leptis Magna in AD 145 and spent his formative years in a city that was already one of Rome's great centres. He quickly progressed through military ranks and was declared the governor of a far-off province. After the assassinations of the Roman emperors Commodus (at the end of AD 192) and Pentinax (three months later in AD 193), Septimus Severus was proclaimed emperor by his troops. Emboldened by the fierce devotion of his army, he marched on Rome where he swept all before him to assume full imperial powers in AD 193. A military man first and foremost, he waged a ruthless campaign to extend the boundaries of Rome's empire. By this stage known as 'the grim African', the feared emperor won a further victory over the Parthians in AD 202–03, temporarily dispelled all challenges to his power, and ushered in an era of relative peace.

It was in this period that he returned to his native city with a grand vision of turning Leptis into a centre to rival imperial Rome. He built a new forum (and thus shifted the centre of the city), basllica, the Great Colonnaded Street and greatly expanded the port. His fellow citizens did their part by hastily constructing their own monument to their emperor – the exquisite triumphal arch that bears his name. By AD 207, Rome was once again at war with its neighbours and in 211 Septimus Severus was killed in battle in England.

Leptis Magna (☎ *031-624256, 627641; admission 3LD, guides 50LD, camera/video 5/10LD)* is open 8am to 6pm daily, although you can usually stay inside until around 7.30pm. The car-park gates close at 6pm, so if you want to keep wandering around the city after then, park your vehicle outside the gates. The entrance for foreign visitors is through car park No 1; the open area of the car park has book stalls, a place selling drinks and snacks and a post and telephone office. Libyans enter from car park No 2, a five-minute walk east. Leptis rewards a couple of visits.

It is compulsory to visit Leptis with a guide (50LD). There are usually plenty waiting at the entrance and the better ones are well worth the money. Guides we recommend (ask for them at the ticket office) include Dr Mustapha Turjman, Mahmud at-Taib, Khalifa Wada, Miftah, Mr Darnaoti (who speaks English and Italian) and Hajj Omar (Italian). French- and German-speaking guides can also be arranged. If you're trying to save money, there are usually plenty of large groups visiting the site that may be happy to let you tag along.

History
The first city on the site of what we now know as Leptis Magna is believed to date from the 7th century BC. It began as a peri-

pheral trading port populated by Phoenicians fleeing from conflict in Tyre (present-day Lebanon) as well as Punic settlers from Carthage (to the west, in Tunisia). Little remains from this city, which lasted for up to 500 years, but it was a modest settlement with none of the ordered urban design of the Roman era.

When Carthage fell in 146 BC, Leptis nominally came under the wing of the Numidian kingdom. The shift towards the Roman sphere of influence began in 111 BC, when the city's inhabitants concluded a treaty of alliance and friendship with Rome and large numbers of Roman settlers began to arrive.

Under the emperor Augustus (r. 27 BC–AD 14) Leptis' status as an eminent city began to take shape. The city minted its own coins, the town was laid out in the Roman style and then adorned with monuments of grandeur. It soon became one of the leading ports in Africa, an entrepot for the trade in exotic animals. It also fell under the spell of a wealthy Roman elite with grand visions and money to burn. One local aristocrat, Annobal Tapapius Rufus, was responsible for the construction of the market (8 BC) and theatre (AD 2), giving Leptis the essential touchstones of a Roman city of significance. The grand, monumental city of Leptis began to become a reality.

Imperial Plunder

One of the reasons why Leptis is such a joy to visit is the faithful restoration work of devoted archaeologists, particularly Italian and Libyan archaeologists. Sadly, it was not always the case. From AD 1686 to AD 1708, the French consul to Tripoli, Claude Le Maire, used his post to plunder the wealth of ancient Leptis on behalf of his country. He dug out and exported to France an astonishing amount of marble monuments, especially columns. With complete disregard for local heritage, many columns were excavated and laid out along the shore, only to be abandoned as too heavy. Those hundreds of items that made it to France were often dismantled and used in building the monuments of imperial France, most notably the chateau of Versailles and the church of St Germain des-Pres. The hardest-hit buildings of Leptis were the Severan Forum, the Great Colonnaded Street and the Hadrianic Baths.

After backing the wrong side in one of Rome's internecine spats, Leptis momentarily lost its status as a friendly city and ally of Rome and was punished for good measure by an annual tax of between one and three million litres of olive oil. The city's stability was further threatened by the constant threat of invasion by the hostile tribes of the interior. In AD 69 the city was overrun by the Garamantes people of the Sahara who had been called in to assist Oea in its dispute with Leptis.

Despite these difficulties, Leptis emerged as a prosperous city that owed its wealth to agriculture (especially olives) and trade from caravans and seagoing trade, particularly in exporting live animals to Rome. Successive Roman emperors continued to decorate the city with exceptionally rich public buildings. In the time of Hadrian (AD 117–38) the city secured a lasting water supply via aqueducts, which in turn enabled the construction of arguably Leptis' greatest indulgence – the Hadrianic Baths. In the 2nd century AD, marble began to adorn the city's buildings, embellishing the already superbly rendered limestone

facades, and the city began to grow in size, extending westwards along the coast. But, under the reign of Septimus Severus, Leptis came into its own and has forever since been associated with the dynasty of its favourite son.

Between AD 294 and AD 305, the reforms carried out by the emperor Diocletian saw Leptis become the capital of the new autonomous province of Tripolitania. By then, though, the glory days of Leptis had passed. Earthquakes (especially in AD 365), a catastrophic flood and Rome's general decline took their toll, ushering in two centuries of neglect. By the 6th century AD, the city was in Byzantine hands and the emperor Justinian I built a wall around the city, parts of which survive to this day. There is some evidence that the city survived the Arab invasion of the 7th century AD and was occupied until the 10th century AD, after which it slowly disappeared under the sands.

Leptis Museum

The Leptis Museum (admission 3LD, camera/video 5/10LD; open 8am-6pm Tues-Sun) is very well organised, with labels in both English and Arabic, and informative posters in each room detailing the history of the relevant period. To see the museum properly, be sure to allow a minimum of two hours.

The rooms on the ground floor run in an anticlockwise direction.

Room 1 deals with Libya's prehistory, and has examples of petrified trees from the Libyan desert, an evocative model-map reconstruction of Leptis and stone carvings from the Jebel Acacus. **Room 2** is devoted to the Punic/Phoenician era and includes pottery pieces from the 5th and 6th centuries BC, which were found in the Punic necropolis under the theatre. **Room 3** is also dominated by Punic pottery. The representation of the goddess Tarnit is of special interest, as are the descriptions of Punic town planning and a dedicatory slab from the market place.

[continued on page 146]

LEPTIS MAGNA

At the height of its prosperity Leptis (originally spelled Lepcis and often known locally in Arabic as Lebdah) was the largest and greatest Roman city in Africa. Today its ruins are wonderfully well preserved, and excellent restoration work continues. Leptis wears its age so well in part because, unlike elsewhere, no modern city was built on or immediately adjacent to the site.

Arch of Septimus Severus

This is one of Leptis' signature monuments and a grand introduction to the architectural excesses of the city. It was built in AD 203 to commemorate the emperor and his family, and to mark his visit to his native city. The core of the structure was built of limestone, unusual for the time, and covered with a marble exterior. What you see today has been faithfully reconstructed by archaeologists to stunning effect. Their work is still in progress.

The arch consists of four imposing pillars supporting a domed roof. Each of the four vertical panels on the pillars' exterior was flanked by two Corinthian columns, in between which were carved adornments in relief depicting the great virtues and successes of the Severan era. At the intersection of the dome and pillars are eagles with their wings spread – one of the key symbols of imperial Rome. Above the columns are two panels of fine detail showing triumphal processions, sacrificial scenes and Septimus Severus holding the hand of his son Caracalla. The interior of the pillars show historical scenes of military campaigns, religious ceremonies and the emperor's family.

Hadrianic Baths

The arrival of water and marble in Leptis early in the 2nd century AD prompted the emperor Hadrian to commission the superb baths bearing his name, which became one of the social hubs of the city. The baths were opened in AD 137 (some archaeologists put this date at AD 126–27). In keeping with the well-established Roman tradition, the baths lay along a north-south axis and the symmetry of the buildings was a key requirement.

Entrance to the baths is from the *palaestra* (sports ground). The entrance hall, or *natatio*, contains an open-air swimming pool that was surrounded by columns on three sides and paved with marble and mosaics. Off the natatio was the grandest room of the baths complex and one of the most splendid in Leptis – the *frigidarium* (cold room). Eight massive cipolin columns nearly nine metres high supported the vaulted roof and the chamber measured an impressive 30m by 15m. The floor was paved with marble and the roof adorned with brilliant blue-and-turquoise mosaics. There were pools at either end and the niches around the walls once held over 40 statues, some of which are in the museums in Leptis and Tripoli.

The *tepidarium* (warm room) lies immediately south of the frigidarium. It originally consisted of one central pool, lined on two sides by columns, and two other pools were later added. The rooms of the *calidarium* (hot room) surround the tepidarium. They faced south, as the theory of bath design at the time demanded, and may have had large glass windows on the southern side. The room had a barrel-vaulted roof of wonderful domes

LEPTIS MAGNA

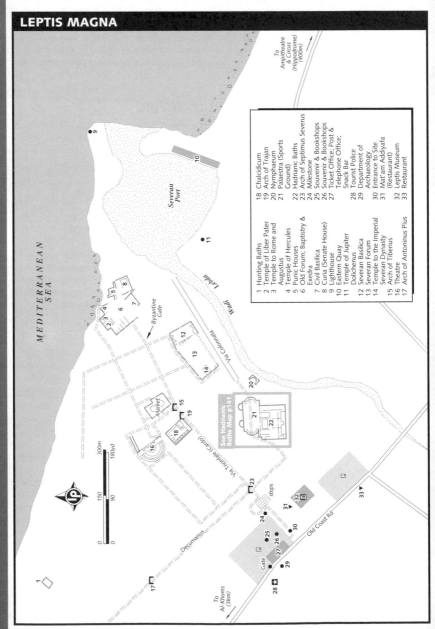

1 Hunting Baths
2 Temple of Liber Pater
3 Temple to Rome and Augustus
4 Temple of Hercules
5 Punic Houses
6 Old Forum; Baptistry & Exedra
7 Civil Basilica
8 Curia (Senate House)
9 Lighthouse
10 Eastern Quay
11 Temple of Jupiter Dolichenus
12 Severan Basilica
13 Severan Forum
14 Temple to the Imperial Severan Dynasty
15 Arch of Tiberius
16 Theatre
17 Arch of Antoninus Plus

18 Chalcidicum
19 Arch of Trajan
20 Nymphaeum
21 Palaestra (Sports Ground)
22 Hadrianic Baths
23 Arch of Septimius Severus
24 Milestone
25 Souvenir & Bookshops
26 Souvenir & Bookshops
27 Ticket Office; Post & Telephone Office; Snack Bar
28 Tourist Police
29 Department of Archaeology
30 Entrance to Site
31 Mat'am Addiyafa (Restaurant)
32 Leptis Museum
33 Restaurant

MEDITERRANEAN SEA

Severan Port

Wadi Lebda

Byzantine Gate

Via Colonnata

Via Trionfale (Cardo)

Market

Decumanus

Old Coast Rd

Gate

steps

See Hadrianic Baths Map p141

To Amphitheatre & Circus (Hippodrome) (400m)

To Al-Khoms (3km)

300m
180yd

0 150 300m
0 90 180yd

HADRIANIC BATHS

1 Palaestra
  (Sports Ground)
2 Natatio (Entrance Hall)
  & Swimming Pool
3 Meeting Room
4 Forica (Latrine)
5 Gymnasium
6 Cryptae
  (Promenade
  Corridors)
7 Frigidarium
  (Cold Room)
8 Apodyteria
  (Changing Room)
9 Laconica
  (Sweat Baths)
10 Tepidarium
  (Warm Room)
11 Laconica
  (Sweat Baths)
12 Apodyteria
  (Changing Room)
13 Basins
14 Calidarium
  (Hot Room)
15 Basins
16 Basins

with five of the *laconica* (sweat baths) added during the time of Commodus. Outside the southern walls were furnaces used for heating the water. On the eastern and western sides of the buildings were *cryptae* (promenade corridors); many of the smaller rooms you'll see were the *apodyteria* (changing rooms). The best preserved of the *forica* (latrines) are on the north-eastern side of the complex – the marble seats must have been pretty cold in winter.

Nymphaeum

East of the palaestra and Hadrianic Baths is an open square overlooked by the Nymphaeum, or Temple of Nymphs. Its superb facade of red-granite and cipolin columns is reminiscent of the facade of Roman theatres and its niches were once filled with marble statues. The monumental fountain was added during the reign of Septimus Severus.

Great Colonnaded Street

The square in front of the Nymphaeum represented the start of a monumental road leading down to the port. Lined with porticos and shops, this thoroughfare was more than 20m wide (plus an extra 20m if you include the porticos, which were reserved for pedestrians) and around 400m long.

Connecting the baths and new Severan Forum with the waterfront, it became one of the most important roads in Leptis during the Severan era.

Severan Forum

Septimus Severus' audacious transformation of Leptis involved reconfiguring the heart of the city – moving it away from the old forum to the new one that bore his name. The open-air Severan Forum measured 100m by 60m and its floor was covered with marble. Ancient remnants of former glories are still strewn around the courtyard. It's easy to picture the forum in its heyday.

In the great tradition of Roman city squares, Septimus Severus' forum was once surrounded by colonnaded porticoes. The columns of cipolin marble rose to arches. On the facades between the arches were Gorgon heads, over 70 of which have been found. Most were symbolic representations of the Roman goddess Victory and included some superb Medusa images as well as a few sea nymphs (look particularly for the heart-shaped eyes, necklaces of serpents and eyebrows of fish fins). Unusually, the arches were of limestone while the heads were carved from marble. In front of the remaining carved heads are vertical panels with dedicatory inscriptions that served as plinths for statues.

Along the shorter, south-western side of the forum was a temple to the imperial Severan dynasty. Roman emperors were deified and their subjects, while believing in their divine status, also undoubtedly saw great political benefits in treating their leaders as gods. Only the staircase, platform and underground storage room remain. Some of the red-granite columns around the forum once belonged to the temple.

Basilica

The Severan Basilica, 92m long and 40m wide, ran along the north-eastern side of the Severan Forum. The basilica, originally a judicial basilica rather than a church, contained two apses at either end, a nave, aisles divided by red-granite columns and possibly a wooden roof. It was started by Septimus Severus and completed by his son Caracalla in AD 216 (read the dedicatory inscription on one of the panels of the nave). The relative austerity of the main hall stands in marked contrast to the extravagantly sculpted pillars at either end, many of which honour Liber Pater (Dionysius) and Hercules. In the 6th century AD, Justinian converted the basilica into a Christian church, with the altar in the south-eastern apse. From the top of the stairs off the north-western corner are good views of the remainder of the ancient city.

Byzantine Gate

North-west of the basilica, a track leads to the Via Trionfale (the Cardo) and the Byzantine Gate. Note the phallic reliefs to the right of the gate – one of many at junctions around the city – which suggest the existence of prostitutes in the ancient city.

Old Forum

The old forum of Leptis Magna was the centre of the first settlement on the site (from the 7th century BC) and the early Roman era. The barely excavated remains of Punic houses are off to the north-east. This square was allowed to fall into neglect after the shift of the city centre to the south, so little remains. Nonetheless, as the monumental heart of the building projects by the emperor Augustus, it remains an important signpost to life in the ancient city. Paved in AD 2, it was surrounded by colonnaded porticos on three sides.

On the left, as you enter the forum if coming from the Byzantine Gate, were three temples. The Temple of Liber Pater dates from the 2nd century AD, but the high podium is all that remains. The Temple to Rome & Augustus (AD 14–19) was built of limestone and may also have been used as a platform for speakers addressing crowds in the square. Next to nothing remains of the Temple of Hercules. On the right as you enter the square, the grey-granite columns mark the site of the Civil Basilica, which was built in the 1st century AD and then rebuilt in the 4th century. It was later converted into a Byzantine church of which the apse, aisles, narthex and seriously eroded columns are discernible. The Curia, or Senate House (2nd century AD), was nearby. In the centre of the forum is a small baptistry in the shape of a cross, as well as a particularly unreligious exedra that local guides like to call the casino.

Port

The port was another key element of Septimus Severus' vision. The lighthouse, of which only the foundation remains, was once more than 35m high. Some historians believe that it was not that different from the more famous Pharos of Alexandria. The best-preserved sections of the port are the eastern quay with warehouses, the ruins of a watchtower and some of the loading docks. Look also for the imposing staircase of the Temple of Jupiter Dolichenus. Jupiter Dolichenus was a little-known Syrian deity at the time of Septimus Severus. It is believed that the appearance of a temple in his name at Leptis Magna was attributable to the fact that Septimus' wife was Syrian.

Don't be fooled by the lack of water. The reason the buildings of the eastern quay are still relatively intact is that the port was hardly used. Soon after its construction, the harbour silted up and is now covered by vegetation.

Market

As you are returning from the port through the forum, head south-west, past the Temple of Serapis, to the market. This is one of the most unusual and attractive of the Leptis monuments, with two reconstructed octagonal halls (approximately 20m in diameter) where stalls were set up to sell the bounty of Leptis farmers and merchants. The northern hall is believed to have been the section for fabrics; next to it is a copy of a stone measuring tablet from the 3rd century AD. The top length equates to a Roman (or Punic) arm (51.5cm), the middle was a Roman (or Alexandrine) foot (29.5cm), while the bottom length was known as the Greek (or Ptolemaic) arm (52.5cm). The other hall was reserved for trading in fruit and vegetables. There were more stalls in the colonnaded portico that surrounded the perimeter.

The market was built in 9–8 BC and rebuilt during the reign of Septimus Severus; some columns with marble capitals date from this latter period. Of the richly decorated facades, the best that remains is of two ships (in celebration of the seafaring merchants of Leptis). Look also for the stone benches with deep lines gouged by ropes.

Monumental Arches

Just outside the southern corner of the market, on the Via Trionfale, is the Arch of Tiberius (1st century AD). A short distance south-west is the Arch of Trajan (AD 109–10), possibly commemorating the accession of Leptis to the status of a colony within the Roman Empire. Both arches are of limestone.

Chalcidicum

This monumental porch is in the block immediately west of the Arch of Trajan. Built in the early part of the 1st century AD under Augustus, its colonnaded portico was reached via steps from the Via Trionfale. It contained a small temple, honouring Augustus and Venus, of which statue bases remain. There are also some cipolin columns and Corinthian capitals from the 2nd century AD. Look for the elephant base in the eastern corner (fronting onto the arch).

Theatre

Leptis' theatre is one of the oldest stone theatres anywhere in the Roman world and is the second-largest surviving theatre in Africa (after Sabratha). It was begun in AD 1–2 and was built on the site of a 3rd- to 5th-century BC Punic necropolis. The most striking feature of the theatre is the stage with its facade of three semicircular recesses surrounded by three-tiered fluted columns dating from the era of Antoninus Pius (AD 138–61). The stage was adorned with hundreds of statues and sculptures that included portraits of emperors, gods and wealthy private citizens. Two remain – Liber Pater (decorated with grapes and leaves) and Hercules (his head is covered with a lion skin).

The VIP seats just above the orchestra were separated from the paying customers by a solid stone bannister that was added in AD 90, while the lower seats were actually carved out of the existing rock at the time of construction. Atop the upper stalls of the *cavea* (seating area) were some small temples and a colonnade of cipolin columns.

Hunting Baths

If you head north-west from the Arch of Septimus Severus, you pass under the Oea Gate, or Arch of Antoninus Pius (2nd century AD). You eventually come to the superb Hunting Baths, recognisable by their consecutive, barrel-domed roofs in light sandstone. These baths never rivalled the Hadrianic

The extravagence and monumental scale of Leptis Magna testifies to its former role as the Roman capital of Africa: the magnificent theatre (top) and one of its Dioscuri (middle right); a lavishly carved column in the Severan Basilica (middle left); and the expansive Severan Forum (bottom).

Leptis Magna's extraordinary state of preservation is partly due to the limestone used in much of its fine masonry: the Hadrianic Baths (top left); the Severan Arch (top right); the northern perimeter of the Severan Forum (bottom left); and the apse of the Severan Basilica (bottom right).

Baths, but the frescoes and mosaics throughout the building are superb. The frigidarium contains the fresco that gave the baths their name – showing hunters and animals in the Leptis amphitheatre. There are also some fine frescoes in the adjoining vaults. On the walls of the bath is an exceptional Nilotic fresco. Watch out for the good marble panelling. The baths, constructed in the 2nd century AD, were used for almost three centuries.

Amphitheatre

The evocative amphitheatre once held 16,000 people and was hollowed out of a hill 1km east of the port in the 1st century AD. The upper stalls may have once been encircled by a colonnaded portico. You can either reach the amphitheatre on foot from the port or by road (go east from the car park and then take a turn-off to the north – a total of about 2km). See the boxed text 'They Called it Sport' in the Coastal Tripolitania chapter for details on the sorts of contests that took place here.

Circus

The circus is reached via a side passage on the western side of the amphitheatre. Dating from AD 162 during the reign of Marcus Aurelius Antoninus, it was home to chariot races attended by up to 25,000 people. The long side of the track ran for 450m while the short sides were only 100m in length. As such, it was one of the largest known circuses outside Rome. These days, it consists of not much more than low-lying foundations. Acrobatic performances were sometimes used in the central area to keep the crowd entertained in between races, as depicted in the mosaics of Villa Sileen. A normal race program included numerous races of seven laps, each run in an anticlockwise direction.

[continued from page 138]

Room 4 is the chamber of Roman triumphal arches, including an imposing two-level relief from inside the Arch of Septimus Severus depicting Septimus and his wife; between them is the head of Hercules draped with a lion's head. **Room 5** has another statue of Hercules draped as a lion, some Roman pillars, dedicatory inscription tablets and, on the northern wall, the symbol of Aesculapius, the god of healing, whose symbol is used by modern medical practitioners. Many of these items were found in the Temple of Jupiter Dolichenus in the port (see under Port in the special section 'Leptis Magna' earlier in this chapter). **Room 6** is given over to busts, including a particularly fine one of Neptune.

Room 7 is one of the museum's most impressive rooms, with superbly sculpted marble statues dating from the Severan age. Clockwise from the left, the statues represent an athlete, an elegant marble woman of Leptis Magna, a young Marcus Aurelius Antoninus, Serapis in the form of Aesculapius, a partial black-stone Serapis, Isis and a Leptis woman from the first half of the 3rd century AD. Note especially the exceptional skill used in sculpting the folds in clothes. The glass cabinet on the right as you enter contains the many faces of the goddess Isis.

Room 8 contains excavations from the Hadrianic Baths, including the huge hand of Septimus Severus and an incredibly skilful marble representation of a seated (and now headless) Mars. There is also a modern painting of the frigidarium. **Room 9** is dedicated to the Nymphaeum and port, and includes a possible (unlabelled) statue of Isis (note the tail of the cornucopia). **Room 10** is another fine room, this time with the theatre as its theme. Items to look out for include representations of Mercury and Venus and a huge dedicatory inscription tablet in Roman and Punic – both languages were used until the 2nd century AD. Note also the statue of a woman with a portly child holding poppies, thought to be a representation of the family of the Roman emperor Hadrian. There is also a model reconstruction of the amphitheatre.

Room 11 showcases the Severan Forum and Old Forum with Medusa and Gorgon heads high on the wall, two column bases from the temple to the Severan dynasty in the Severan Forum. **Room 12** is a ghostly room of headless and handless statues (body parts were often carved separately to increase the statues' resale value). There are also Latin inscriptions commemorating the reconstruction of the market porticos and five portrait busts found in the market. **Room 13** also has an interesting collection of busts representing the diverse faces of Leptis, a pompous statue of a magistrate and an attractive marble panel inscription to a 2nd-century governor of Africa.

A circular staircase leads to the 1st floor, where the rooms are arranged in a clockwise pattern. **Room 14** showcases the ancient trade activity of Leptis and includes the original measuring tablet used in the market. **Room 15** is devoted to the coins of the Misrata Treasure (see the boxed text 'The Misrata Treasure' later in this chapter). **Room 16** fronts onto the open staircase and contains items of everyday Roman life. **Room 17** houses funerary objects, a small statue of a sleeping, winged Eros and ornate urns (alabaster for the wealthy) used to store ashes after cremation. Note also the poignant pottery coffin of a child in one of the glass cases. **Room 18** has more funerary urns and small coffins, as well as a two-faced Janus (Roman god of doorways, passages and bridges) relief and big stone reliefs from the fortified farms of Ghirza. **Room 19** has similar reliefs, this time from Qasr Gilda.

Room 20 marks the transition to the Byzantine period with a dusty but attractive mosaic from a church 60km south of Leptis, as well as tablet reliefs from the four churches that were in Leptis during the Christian era. **Room 21** covers the Islamic period and has beautiful pottery bowls and unimaginative models of a mosque, madrassa (school), mihrab (niche in a mosque) and minbar (pulpit in a mosque). **Room 22** commemorates Libyan resistance to Italian rule with weapons and a woodcarving of the battle of Al-Mergeb. **Room 23**, near the staircase, is given over to a reconstruction of a traditional

Bedouin tent (note the separation of men and women), with dolls showing traditional outfits. **Room 24** has gifts given to Colonel Gaddafi. Highlights of this quirky collection include a map of an undivided Palestine, a huge book made of palm trunk lauding the colonel, and a document of homage written in blood by an Iraqi traveller. **Room 25** has some anticlimactic photos of the Great Man-Made River (GMR; An-Nahr Sinai) and a model of Al-Khoms university. The stairs lead back down to the exit, past the towering painting of Colonel Gaddafi being adored by the masses in the central skylight area.

Places to Stay & Eat

Most people choose Al-Khoms or Zliten as a base for exploring Leptis. It is possible to *camp (5LD)* in car park No 1 under the pine and eucalyptus trees – it's quiet at night and guarded by police from the station opposite.

Between the ticket office and the museum is *Mat'am Addiyafa (☎ 031-621210, open noon-3pm daily)*, which has a pleasant atmosphere. The set lunch is good value for 15LD. There is also a *restaurant* almost opposite the car park entrance where meals cost around 12LD.

Getting There & Away

Shared taxis, micros and buses run regularly along the coastal highway between Tripoli and the towns of the coast (Misrata and Zliten). The turn-off to Leptis Magna is 3.5km east of the main turn-off into Al-Khoms and is marked by a yellow sign with a small painting of the ruins. Ask the driver to be let out at 'Lebdah'. From here, it's about a 15-minute walk north and then west.

If you're coming from Al-Khoms, shared taxis (0.5LD) and micros (0.25LD) shuttle between the town and site entrance quite often and you can flag them down at any point along Sharia al-Khoms. It's 2.5km east of the town centre.

Shared taxis (0.5LD) and micros (0.25LD) run from outside the main entrance of Leptis Magna to the centre of Al-Khoms at reasonably regular intervals. For destinations further afield, you'll need to change transport in Al-Khoms, or walk (or

hitch) from the entrance to Leptis to the main highway where shared taxis and buses regularly pass by.

ZLITEN زليطن
☎ 0571 • pop 130,000

You know you've reached Zliten, 34km east of Al-Khoms, when you find yourself driving between a proliferation of palm trees. The largely unattractive town sprawls along the coast. It has a good hotel and its mosque and tomb are definitely worth the detour. The city's main industry centres on its large fishing port.

Until recently, Zliten's museum was worth a visit for its frescoes from Villa Dar Buc Ammara, a ruined villa nearby. Sadly, the building in which it was housed has been demolished and the exhibits are gathering dust in storage while awaiting a new home. The new location is expected to be in the old part of Zliten, near the post office. In the streets of the old town, most of the houses are derelict and earmarked for destruction but the occasional door has traces of the town's former elegance.

Orientation & Information

The centre of town is 1km north of the highway; if you're coming from Tripoli, the turn-off branches off to the right and then doubles back over the highway. The easiest

---

The Best *Tarbuni* in Libya

Zliten, one of the largest coastal oases in Tripolitania, has a proliferation of date palms that yield what is considered to be the best *tarbuni* (date juice) in Libya. Zliten's dates are particularly moist and the juice is often spread on bread for breakfast. Better still, tarbuni enlivens the dish of *As-Sida*, which is made with flour, boiled with salt, and eaten with olive oil and date juice. While you may find Libyans eating As-Sida at other times, the dish is usually reserved to commemorate the birth of the Prophet Mohammed and is also the celebratory dish of choice for Tripolitanians whenever a child is born into the family. Aside from anything else, it's delicious.

landmark in town for getting your bearings is the large roundabout that is invariably surrounded by migrant workers waiting listlessly in the sun for work. The street running north-west from the roundabout, Sharia al-Jamahiriya, leads to the town's only hotel, while the mausoleum and mosque are just east of the roundabout.

At the time of research, none of the banks in town was willing to change money. The post office is north-east of Funduq Zliten; look for the telecom mast.

Mausoleum & Mosque of Sidi Abdusalam

This is one of the finest modern Islamic buildings in Libya and was reportedly decorated by the same artisans who worked on the Hassan II Mosque in Casablanca. Its distinctive green dome is surrounded by a multitude of minarets and smaller domes. The external panels of the facade contain some superb ceramics with floral and arabesque motifs. The tiled pillars are most attractive, particularly the unusual small, tiled pillars around the minaret's balconies. There is some fine Arabic calligraphy in sandstone on top of the outer pillars of the building saying 'Al-Mulk-'illah' (Everything to God).

Non-Muslims are not permitted inside the mausoleum's inner sanctum but the gilded tomb is clearly visible from the door, as are the marvellous stucco ceilings. Please be especially discreet during prayer time. The tomb belongs to the pious Sidi Abdusalam, who died in Zliten in the 16th century AD. There is also a madrassa on the site.

The sea of minarets can be seen from many spots around town; it's just east of the main roundabout.

Places to Stay & Eat

Funduq Zliten (☎ 620121, fax 620120, Sharia al-Jamahiriya) Singles/doubles/suites 30/40/70LD. It may be the only hotel in town but thankfully Funduq Zliten is one of the best-value hotels in the country. While not luxurious, it has a real touch of class. All rooms come with a bath, TV, phone and balcony, while the suites have all the requisite

luxury bells and whistles, including a king-sized bed and a video; prices include breakfast. The staff are friendly and the reasonably priced *restaurant* has a pleasant ambience. Meals cost from 18LD and the restaurant is open 12.30pm to 3pm and 7pm to 10pm daily.

There is a handful of *cheap eateries* close to the post office and between the highway and main roundabout.

Getting There & Away

Buses travelling between towns to the east and west of Zliten generally don't come into the town centre. Shared taxis connect Zliten with Misrata (1.5LD, 45 minutes), Al-Khoms (or the Leptis Magna turn-off; 1LD, 30 minutes) and occasionally Tripoli (4LD, two hours) and the best place to pick them up is around the main roundabout. Micros cost 50% less but you could walk the distance in the time it takes for some of them to fill.

AROUND ZLITEN

The area around Zliten is renowned for its **marabout tombs** *(turba)*, also known as *zawiyas*, which attract a steady stream of pilgrims. A visit to the holy tombs is said to bestow a greater fertility upon pilgrims; many women come here to ask for help in having a child. Local taxi drivers know where to find the tombs. There is also a good **beach** at Souq al-Khamis.

MISRATA   مصراتة
☎ 051 • pop 170,000

Misrata is Libya's third-largest city and has a different feel to most others, with its well-ordered streets and, remarkably for Libya, 'no smoking' signs in many buildings. There is little to see in town, but as the last major town before the long trek east to Sirt and Benghazi, it makes a decent overnight stop.

In ancient times, Misrata was an important port for the trade in goods and people from the Sahara. Its carpet industry is one of the longest standing in Libya. Two Arab families, the Muntasir and the Adgham, dominated the city's life and led the local tribes in their disputes with the Turkish overlords. Misrata has always been something of an administrative centre and was considered the second city in Turkish Tripolitania. Under the Italians it was again a centre for settlement and administration – a time when the relatively structured layout of the streets was completed. Its modern wealth is due in part to the steel mill that has been built near the town.

Orientation
The centre of town and the main square (Maidan an-Nasser) are around the intersection of Sharia Abdul Rahman Azem (which runs all the way from the highway to the centre of town, north-south all the way) and Sharia Ramadan Asswayhli (which runs east-west through town).

Information
The main post office is 500m north of Maidan an-Nasser on Sharia Ramadan Asswayhli.

The most central place to surf the Internet is Al-Gleb Internet (☎ 628384, [e] leg leb@hotmail.com), Sharia Abdul Rahman Azem. It's 50m east of the intersection with Sharia Ramadan Asswayhli. Open 10am to 11pm Saturday to Thursday and 2pm to 11pm Friday, Al-Gleb charges 3LD per hour. There's also an Internet service in the lobby of Funduq Quz at-Teek on Sharia Dar al-Ry. It's open 10am to midnight Saturday to Thursday and 2pm to midnight Friday, and also charges 3LD per hour.

Although you can negotiate a price for day trips to Ghirza with a local taxi driver or through your hotel, there are a couple of travel agencies that can arrange them; the cost is up to 100LD. Both are easy to find, just off the main square. The nationwide Winzrik Tourism Services (☎/fax 631941) has an office in Misrata (postal address: PO Box 209, Misrata), as does Al-Jamahiriya Travel Agency (☎ 610291, fax 610339). Both are close to Maidan an-Nasser.

Things to See
The town's **souq**, in the lanes off Maidan an-Nasser, has a thrice-weekly market for local clothing and carpets. The only other

The Misrata Treasure
An underground chamber not far from Misrata fooled treasure-seekers for centuries. But in 1981 more than 100,000 coins of unknown origin were discovered there by archaeologists doing routine excavations. The coins, dating from AD 294–333, are thought to have been the property of a garrison rather than a private individual, so immense was the haul. Some of the coins are in the Misrata museum, although the largest collection is on display in Room 15 of Leptis Museum at Leptis Magna.

sight of note is the **Burj al-Golztik** (Tower of Dunes), west of the town centre. This sky-piercing, space-age tower is a monument to the Libyan resistance. Beneath the tower is a small **museum** (*open 9am-1pm & 3pm-6pm Tues-Sun*) containing some pottery artefacts of minor interest, photos of prehistoric Saharan rock art and parts of the Misrata Treasure.

Places to Stay
Buyut ash-Shabaab (☎ *624880*) Dorm beds for HI members/nonmembers 3/5LD. Not up to the standard of other youth hostels in Libya, this place seems to be rarely cleaned.

Funduq As-Siyahe (☎ *619777, Sharia Ramadan Asswayhli*) Singles with shower 20LD, doubles with shower & toilet 25LD. This grand old hotel is a friendly place very close to Maidan an-Nasser. The clean rooms have high ceilings, a touch of old-world charm and many overlook the pleasant courtyard; prices include breakfast. The *restaurant* serves salad or soup for 2.5LD while main dishes start from 8.5LD.

Funduq Safirous (☎ *629620, Sharia Ramadan Asswayhli*) Singles/doubles/triples with shared bath 15/25/40LD, doubles with bath 30LD. Funduq Safirous is in a similarly good location, a couple of hundred metres south of the main square but set back behind a shady open square. It also wins the prize for the cleanest bathrooms (shared and private) in Misrata. All prices include breakfast and there's a *restaurant* (meals 10LD).

Funduq al-Kabir (☎ 620178/9, fax 620180, Sharia Sana Mahidly, postal address: PO Box 30, Misrata) Singles/doubles from 40/50LD, singles/doubles with kitchen 55/65LD, studios for 3/4 people 70/80LD, flats with kitchen for 4/5 people 100/110LD. This professionally run, top-end hotel is excellent value. It's central, but on a quiet street, and the spacious rooms all come with air-con. The huge, three-room flats with a kitchen are great value for groups. There's a good *restaurant* where the soups and salads cost from 3.5LD to 5LD and mains from 8LD to 15LD (for fish dishes).

Funduq Quz at-Teek (☎ 613333, fax 610500, Sharia Dar al-Ry, postal address: PO Box 17352, Misrata) Twins/studios/villas/suites 45/50/70/90LD. If you wake up and suddenly think you're in Tobruk at the Funduq al-Masira, that's hardly surprising – the hotel is identical even down to the tapestries on the wall of the lobby. Right next to Burj al-Golztik, about 2km west of the city centre, this top-end place is also reasonable value. There's an Internet office in the lobby.

Places to Eat

There are a couple of good *patisseries* on Sharia Ramadan Asswayhli, about 400m south of Maidan an-Nasser; look for the sign brandishing a chef. Almost next door is a simple, unnamed *restaurant* doing hearty servings of half a barbecued chicken *(djeaj mahama)* with soup and beans (10LD, including drinks).

Misrata's contribution to cafe culture comes in the form of a swish, semicircular and glass-walled *coffee shop* overlooking the main intersection on the western side. About 100m to the west, just off Sharia Abdul Rahman Azem, is a small *pizza restaurant* that serves, not surprisingly, pizzas for 4LD to 8LD and hamburgers from 1LD.

Getting There & Away

There are regular shared taxis and micros from Misrata to Tripoli (5LD, 2½ hours), Al-Khoms (2LD, one hour), Zliten (1.5LD, 45 minutes) and Sirt (6LD, three hours). You might also find an early morning shared taxi or bus heading for Benghazi

(10.75LD to 15LD, nine hours). The transport area is adjacent to the main square.

AROUND MISRATA

About 17km west of Misrata (31km east of Zliten) are what are believed to be some of the largest **coastal sand dunes** in the world. If you've spent any time in the sand seas of southern Libya, you may wonder what all the fuss is about. Nonetheless if these are the only dunes you're likely to see in Libya, they're worth a small detour. They are 5km north of the highway via a good road. If you can't find them, ask for *'tanaret zray'* (the nearby tuna factory), which is the name by which locals know the dunes. You should be able to convince a Misrata taxi driver to take you there and back for 12LD.

TAUORGA   تاورغاء

Tauorga, 53km south of Misrata by road, has the unusual distinction of being the only town on the Libyan coast, with most of its inhabitants as dark skinned as sub-Saharan Africans. Some locals claim to be the descendants of freed slaves. Others argue that they are related to Libya's original indigenous inhabitants.

Tauorga is renowned for its palm-woven products, including bags, baskets and mats. Many of these items are offered for sale from roadside stalls along the main highway, opposite the turn-off to Tauorga (41km south of Misrata). Here you'll also find the colourful pottery of Gharyan on sale.

After passing the turn-offs to Tauorga, you start crossing the Sahel as-Sirt (Sirt Plain), a flat, scrubby and featureless expanse of nothingness that stretches all the way to Ajdabiya. Strangely, given government efforts to promote Sirt as a city of national prominence, the road after Tauorga can be quite uneven. The politicians and heads of state probably fly to Sirt.

GHIRZA   غرزة

The monuments of remote Ghirza are among the most important indigenous contributions to Libyan civilisation. These 3rd century AD public buildings include temples to an unknown Libyan divinity and tombs (3rd to 5th century AD) as well as a series of fortified farms. If you're unable to make it all the way out here, there are examples of Ghirza's stonework in both Tripoli's Jamahiriya Museum and the museum at Leptis Magna.

Ghirza is believed to have been a 3rd-century settlement on the southern fringes of Roman Tripolitania. It was built by Romanised Libyans and the architecture was heavily influenced by the Roman style of the day. When Arab travellers passed through the area in the 11th century AD, the temples were still in use.

At the far (southern) end of the site are the three **tombs** that are the highlight of Ghirza's remains. There are distinctive, sandstone pillars encircling these elevated, squat mausoleums, each adorned with relief carvings of scenes from everyday life, including evidence of harvests – now difficult to imagine in such a barren landscape. The central tomb has some detailed animal and flower motifs around the facade, while the northernmost tomb features particularly fine stonework atop some of the pillars, and a Roman eagle above the door with Latin inscriptions.

Getting There & Away

It's a hard slog to get to Ghirza and you'll need your own vehicle. There is no public transport to the site; we picked up one local who had been waiting patiently at the checkpoint for hours. The best option is a long (six hour) day trip from Misrata. Try one of the travel agencies in Misrata (at least 100LD) or you might be able to negotiate a cheaper price with an adventurous local taxi driver. It can get fiercely hot in summer, so bring plenty of water with you.

If you have your own vehicle, take the main highway from Misrata towards Sirt. After 82km, take the turn-off for As-Sadaada to the south. After 18km, you reach another road junction with a checkpoint. Ghirza is off to the east, 91.2km away, along a partially asphalted road. The road is shadowed for almost the entire distance by the Great Man-Made River. At a fork in the road 79.7km after the checkpoint, turn right (there is a sign to Ghirza in Arabic). The ruins are a further 11.5km and reached

through the bleak modern village of Ghirza; take the stony tracks leading out from the eastern end of the village.

SIRT سرت

☎ 054 • pop 70,000

Sirt is a custom-built city waiting impatiently for the day when it can be declared the capital of the United States of Africa. Colonel Gaddafi was born, and spent part of his childhood, around Sirt, the city that forms a central pillar of his ambitious scheme for an economic and political community of African states. Built on the site of the ancient city of Euphranta, Sirt was later an important land communication point with the south and an embarkation point for many caravans. Under the Italians it was an administrative centre and since the revolution it has become a rapidly growing city.

Sadly, this supposed showpiece of the revolution is a city without soul, a lifeless place of few charms. It's a friendly enough town but the only reason for travellers to spend any time here is to break up the long journey between Benghazi and Tripoli. If you need to stay overnight, there is decent accommodation and at least one good restaurant.

Orientation & Information

Sirt is a city without a definable centre. The nondescript main thoroughfare, Sharia al-Jamahiriya, sweeps from the south-eastern entrance to the town (the large roundabout on the main highway) to the western perimeter. About 3km from the highway, at the point where Sharia al-Jamahiriya turns west, are most of the facilities you'll need – the main post office, pharmacy and a good grocery store underneath the town's best restaurant. Also on this bend is a bank, Masraf al-Jamahiriya. The main road then continues for over 10km west, passing a couple of hotels and plenty of unexciting grocery stores, furniture shops and mechanics workshops. The coastal corniche is similarly windswept and unattractive.

Things to See

Not a lot really. If you're an aficionado of **revolutionary murals**, the posters of Colonel

Gaddafi may just qualify as Sirt's only tourist attraction. There are some particularly fine examples of the genre. Without any apparent attempt at irony, one proudly proclaims in Arabic that 'The best thing about Sirt is that it is in the centre of Libya'. Most of the billboards laud African unity and the Great Man-Made River. The greatest number are along Sharia al-Jamahiriya at the south-eastern end of town. Even better is the one at the checkpoint 20km east of Sirt on the highway to Benghazi: The mural depicts Ronald Reagan in a coffin with Margaret Thatcher, in the form of a mosquito, fluttering around him.

Sirt is the headquarters for the **General People's Congress (GPC)**. The modern, sprawling parliamentary complex runs along the western side of Sharia al-Jamahiriya, just after the south-eastern entrance to town. Casual visitors are not welcome.

Places to Stay

Sirt arises from its customary slumber whenever parliament sits (usually close to the end of the year) or the city hosts one of its pan-African conferences. Sirt is also home to large celebrations commemorating the 1 September revolution. Finding a bed at these times is near impossible.

Buyut ash-Shabaab (☎ 61825, Off Sharia al-Corniche) Dorm beds for HI members/nonmembers 3/5LD. The youth hostel is a friendly, down-to-earth place without pretensions to luxury; it's often full if you arrive late in the day. Staff can arrange simple meals from 1LD. It's a small block north of the corniche, opposite a college and next to the Red Crescent building.

Funduq Bab al-Medina (☎ 60906, fax 60908, Sharia al-Jamahiriya) Singles/twins/doubles 20/30/35LD. Sirt's only privately run hotel has a run-down air but the rooms, with bath, aren't bad value; prices include breakfast. The hotel is opposite two enormous satellite dishes, 2km west of the town centre.

Funduq Medina (☎ 60160, fax 67407, Off Sharia al-Jamahiriya) Singles/doubles/triples 35/40/60LD. While not the best choice in this price range, the rooms,

with bath, are reasonable; prices include breakfast. This place is in a good location, not far from the shared-taxi station. But eat at the nearby restaurant, as lunch and dinner here cost an exorbitant 25LD.

Funduq al-Mehari (☎ 60100/4, fax 61310, Sharia al-Jamahiriya) Singles/doubles 35/45LD. Funduq al-Mehari is a bit out on a limb, just north of the road almost 6km west of the post office, but the rooms are comfortable, spacious, spotless and pretty good value; prices include breakfast. If the showers are an indication of the achievements of the Great Man-Made River, then it is (literally) a roaring success. Avoid the restaurant if you can as it's soulless and expensive (35LD for a full meal).

Funduq Qasr Mutamarat (☎ 60165, fax 63530, North of GPC) Singles/doubles/suites 45/80/120LD. This is Sirt's showpiece hotel with spacious rooms bordering on the luxurious. This favourite of government officials has replica Great Man-Made River pipes at the gate and a health and sports centre. The manager promised that we'd be blown away by the presidential suite for visiting heads of state, but wouldn't show us inside nor give us the price; it's clearly not for the likes of us. The hotel is just south of the parliament buildings, about 300m west of Sharia al-Jamahiriya

Places to Eat

There are *grocery stores* for self-caterers and plenty of places doing hamburgers and grilled chicken along Sharia al-Jamahiriya in the blocks west of the post office.

Mat'am az-Zuhur (☎ 68700, Sharia al-Jamahiriya) Meals 11LD. Open 12.30pm-2.30pm & 6.30pm-10pm Sat-Thur, 6.30pm-10pm Fri. This is a great choice. The kindly sheikh from Syria and his staff prepare a bountiful platter of dips, salad, flat bread, soup, mixed-grill kebabs, rice, tea and soft drink for 11LD per person – exceptional value. The pleasant dining area overlooks the main street.

Downstairs from the restaurant is a well-stocked *grocery store* selling pharmaceutical items, toilet paper, deli foods, Pringles and Ferrero Rocher chocolates.

Getting There & Away

The main shared-taxi station is just north of the post office. At 592km to Sebha, 561km to Benghazi and 463km to Tripoli, it's a long ride to anywhere; make sure you get an early start. Buses of An-Nakhl as-Seria and Al-Itihad al-'Arabi companies also pass through here en route to Benghazi (7.25-15LD, seven hours) or Tripoli (10-15LD, five hours).

There are no regular passenger air services to Sirt; expect that to change when the new airport is completed.

GREAT MAN-MADE RIVER (AN-NAHR SINAI)

النهر الصناعي العظيم

Although you may see the mounds, pumping stations and construction work of the Great Man-Made River throughout Libya, the reservoir 17km east of Sirt offers an opportunity to take a closer look, if only for the symbolism attached to Colonel Gaddafi's grand vision. The gravel track leading south off the highway leads to the reservoir 2.2km away; you'll be escorted to the dam's edge by a friendly, machine-gun-toting soldier.

The large reservoir is filled with water pumped from wells via underground pipes, some of which are visible beneath the iron grille on the viewing platform. Note the map showing the various stages of the GMR project. Unfortunately, there are (strangely unforeseen) problems with evaporation and there are plans for a new reservoir covered with a plastic dome to the east. For more information see the boxed text 'The Great Man-Made River Project' in the Facts about Libya chapter.

MEDINAT SULTAN

مدينة سلطان

Medinat Sultan, 50km east of Sirt, was an important Fatimid site but is now dusty and derelict. The excavations include the rubble of the old mosque, a couple of kilometres inside the main gate, but you'd require lots of imagination to make any sense of it. Of greater interest are the two **Philaeni brothers**, cast in bronze and enviably muscular, lying in a walled compound just inside the gate. The hollow statues once stood more than 5m tall atop the arch demarcating

Tripolitania from Cyrenaica (200km to the east).

Across the other side of the dirt track which runs through the site, on an open patch of ground 50m north, are some scattered **stone reliefs**. These once adorned the facade of the arch with carved scenes of Italian soldiers. The closest one to the gate shows Mussolini (second from left) being saluted by his soldiers. The dusty and unlabelled museum on the site is not worth any of your time.

The entrance to the site is through a pair of green iron gates on the northern side of the highway. There are no regular opening times although it's usually open from around 9am until just before sunset daily; there's an on-site caretaker, so simply bang on the gate.

The Division of Libya

The Greeks and Romans divided Libya between themselves in a manner that has become the stuff of legend. In the mid-4th century BC, the Greeks and Romans decided that Greek runners should set out from Cyrene in eastern Libya and Roman runners from Carthage (Tunisia; other accounts suggest a more realistic point: Leptis Magna). Where they met, the border was to be drawn.

When the runners met at Ras Lanuf, the Greeks accused the Roman runners, the Philaeni brothers, of cheating. They were offered the choice of either being buried alive or allowing the unsporting Greeks to progress. They chose martyrdom. This myth of the martyrs to the Roman cause was resurrected in the 1930s by Mussolini whose soldiers built an enormous arch over the road, the Arco Philaeni, with one brother facing eastwards towards Cyrenaica, the other facing westwards in the direction of Tripolitania. When Colonel Gaddafi and his revolutionary government came to power in 1969, they saw the arch as a symbol of the fractured nation they were trying to unite and, in 1973, tore it down. Since then, the two brothers, whose only crime was to be too fast, have lain forgotten in the overgrown compound of Medinat Sultan.

MEDINAT SULTAN TO AJDABIYYA

The coastline from Sirt to Ajdabiyya runs past a large area of salt flats. The small towns along the way have little or nothing of interest. The gulf region, known as Al-Khalij and now an administrative province in its own right, is the heart of Libya's most prolific oil-producing areas. These towns along the dip in the gulf – including **As-Sidra**, **Ras Lanuf** and **Brega** – are little more than adjuncts to overgrown oil terminals. Casual visitors are not welcome.

Just 19.2km east of the main turn-off to Ras Lanuf and 197km west of Ajdabiya is the old border between Tripolitania and Cyrenaica. The only evidence of this historically significant spot (see the boxed text 'The Division of Libya' earlier in this chap-ter) is a flattened area of around five sq metres on either side of the road. If you look closely, you can just see the foundation outline of the Arco Philaeni.

One town of particularly grim notoriety is **Al-'Aghela**, 87.4km east of Ras Lanuf. A concentration camp was based to the south of here during the Italian occupation. Thousands of Bedouin died there with over 10,000 people crowded in at any one time. A famous Libyan poem of lament by Rafiq speaks powerfully for a generation of Libyans: 'I have no illnesses but the illness of the concentration camp of Al-'Aghela'.

Note that the town of Al-'Aghela is actually part of Cyrenaica, but we have included it here for ease of navigation – the Colonel would be proud of us for disregarding the border between the two ancient provinces.

Cyrenaica

Cyrenaica, in the eastern part of Libya, is a land of verdant mountains, stunning Mediterranean coastline and superbly preserved ancient Greek cities.

The Jebel Akhdar (Green Mountains) are the highest mountains in northern Libya. Living up to their name, they are as fertile as Libya gets – a refreshing change if you have spent any time in the desert. In the area around Ras al-Hillal, the northern ridges plunge down towards the Mediterranean to spectacular effect.

Geography aside, the main reason for visiting Cyrenaica is to see the wonderful ancient Greek cities. Five sites comprise the old Pentapolis (Five Cities) – Apollonia, Barce, Cyrene, Tocra and Tolmeita. The most glorious is Cyrene, followed by Apollonia, nearby on the coast. The Byzantine Empire also left its mark in Cyrenaica, most visibly in the splendid mosaics of Qasr Libya, Apollonia and Tolmeita.

Through the centuries, Cyrenaica has been the heartland of Libyan resistance to foreign rule, a heritage of which its people are proud. Remains of the historical battles that finally won Libya its independence are scattered across the region, reminders of Libya's path from colonialism to independence. The soil of Cyrenaica gave rise first to the Sanusi Movement and the Jebel Akhdar saw Omar al-Mukhtar's epic guerilla campaign against the Italians. Later, Cyrenaica became one of the most fiercely contested theatres of WWII with Tobruk, in the far east, becoming a byword for the tragedy of war.

Cyrenaica is considered by many to be the meeting place of the Middle East and North Africa. A largely distinct entity under Greek rule, Cyrenaica was centuries later too far away for the Islamic dynasties of the Maghreb (or North Africa) and the region was ruled from Egypt. When the rebellious Cyrenaicans refused to yield to Egyptian rule, hundreds of thousands of families belonging to the Bani Salim tribe from Arabia were transported to Cyrenaica. Their

descendants remain here to this day, giving rise to the claim that Cyrenaica is, linguistically and culturally, the most Arab region in the world outside of the Arabian Peninsula.

This distinctiveness from the rest of Libya is reflected in Cyrenaica's different cuisines, guttural dialects and a tradition of religious and tribal conservatism. Today it is a land known for hospitality and for poetry. Eastern Libya's history of resistance also demanded that women play a greater public role than elsewhere in the country.

Although the town of Al-'Aghela is inside Cyrenaica, we have included it in the Tripolitania chapter for ease of navigation.

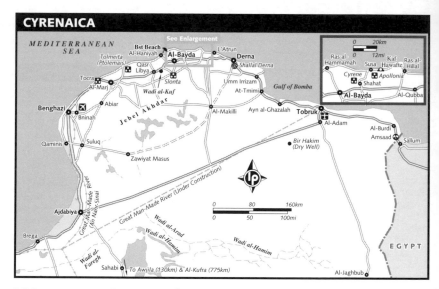

Western Cyrenaica

BENGHAZI
بنغازى

☎ 061 • pop 804,000

Benghazi is Libya's second city and the principal city of eastern Libya. It lacks the obvious Mediterranean charm of Tripoli, while any traces of Benghazi's antiquity are buried beneath a modern commercial centre and port of largely post-WWII construction.

Nonetheless, if you know where to look Benghazi is worth exploring. It can also make a good base for touring the Jebel Akhdar, as well as the Greek cities of Tocra, Tolmeita and (at a stretch) Cyrene and Apollonia. The climate is also one of the more pleasant in Libya; even in summer, you've a good chance of catching a sea breeze. Benghazi is at its best around sunset and early evening, when the streets are often alive with people and the city lights provide the perfect backdrop to the waters of Benghazi's double harbour. Some readers say they think the Benghazi locals are among the friendliest in Libya.

If you've been drinking tap water elsewhere in Libya, you may want to join the locals and refrain in Benghazi, where the

water can be very salty. Bottled water is easily available.

History

Founded by Greek settlers from Cyrene, the original settlement (just south of modern Benghazi) was called Eusperides and first mentioned in historical records in the 6th century BC. It is thought to be the site of the legendary garden of Hesperides, from the Greek myth of the golden apples. By 249 BC, Benghazi was called Berenice, named after a Cyrenaican princess and wife of Ptolemy III of Egypt. The city that bore her name is on the site of modern Benghazi.

The city became part of the Roman Empire, but suffered enormous damage during the Vandal invasion in the 5th century AD and, after a brief period of repair by the Byzantines, fell into obscurity. After the Arab invasion, Benghazi was again neglected in favour of other cities of more strategic importance, such as Ajdabiya. It was only in the 15th century AD that Benghazi was rediscovered by Tripolitanian merchants, taking the city into a new and prosperous phase. Benghazi is named after Ibn Ghazi (also Bani Ghazi), a local holy man, renowned in the 15th century AD for his good deeds

The Turks took Benghazi in 1578, but their attempts to make it a centre for tax collection drove traders to other towns. Benghazi recovered its fortunes during the mid-19th century, but this was not to last. In 1911 the Italians laid siege to the city from the sea. It subsequently became an Italian fortress in the face of fierce resistance by the surrounding tribes. Nonetheless, pockets of Arab culture remained, as the Danish traveller Knud Holmboe wrote in 1930:

Benghazi's Medina is nearly as large as that of Tripoli – one square, whitewashed house after another, and in every street small Arab cafes where for a halfpenny you can get coffee and hookah. The market was closing. The tradesmen had fastened their booths with shutters; the camels from the country stood with their loads on their backs ready to leave; only the cafes were open, and the monotonous Arab gramophone music sounded from them all.

Knud Holmboe, *Desert Encounter*

With the resistance finally subdued by the Italians in the 1930s, Benghazi virtually became an Italian city.

During WWII the city constantly changed hands and came under bombardment from the Allies and the Axis powers. More than 1000 bombs rained down upon the city and by the time the war ended there was very little left.

After independence, the development of the city began again and the harbour was enlarged to accommodate more commercial shipping. Most of the oldest structures still standing in Benghazi date from this period.

Benghazi was bombarded by the missiles of the US Sixth Fleet in April 1986, causing considerable damage and killing as many as 30 people.

Orientation

The older part of the city stretches out from the northern shores of the harbour and covers an area roughly bounded by Sharias Ahmed Rafiq al Mahdawi, 23 July and Al-Jezayir. In this quarter are most of the hotels, restaurants, the *jawazzat* (passport

The Cyrenaica of Herodotus

The earliest historical mention of Cyrenaica comes from Greek historian Herodotus, the so-called Father of History. Writing almost 2500 years ago, he records an encounter with some travellers who had passed through the region. 'Being asked if there was anything more they could tell him about the uninhabited parts of Libya, these declared that a group of wild young fellows, sons of chieftains in their country, had on coming to manhood planned among themselves all sorts of extravagant adventures, one of which was to draw lots for five of their number to explore the Libyan desert and try to penetrate further than had ever been done before' (*The Histories*, Book 2:32). These young men from Cyrene succeeded in their aim of crossing the desert and returned to tell a suitably fantastical tale of attacks by tribes of little people and visiting a land inhabited by wizards. The people of these ancient legends are quite similar to modern Cyrenaicans, who are known as survivors and hardy folk and who have a great tradition of storytelling.

office) and banking facilities. The heart of the 'medina' is the Italianate Freedom Square; to the north-east is the covered Souq al-Jreed, which winds into Al-Funduq Market – home to bus and shared-taxi stations.

Benghazi's two harbours divide the northern sections of the city from the road south to the suburb of Qar Yunis, in which there are newer houses, a university and tourist village. A bridge connects the two areas. The *buyut ash-shabaab* (youth hostel) and sports facilities are at the eastern end of 23 July Lake.

Information

The jawazzat (☎ 9098765) is on Sharia al-Corniche, at the western end of Benghazi harbour.

Post & Communications The main post office is on Sharia Omar al-Mukhtar, about 300m north of the harbour on the south-eastern side of the road. It's run-down and at times seemingly abandoned by its staff.

CYRENAICA

BENGHAZI

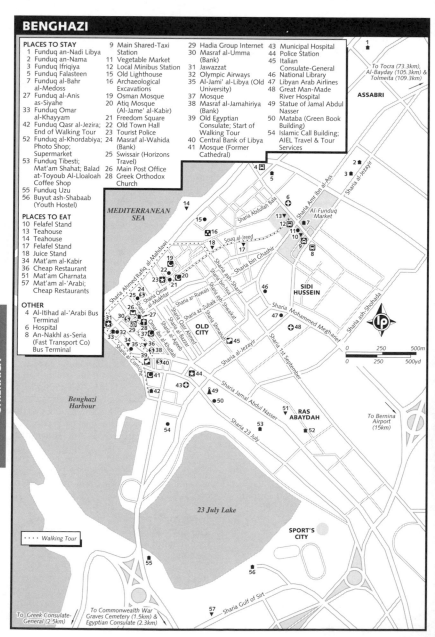

PLACES TO STAY
1 Funduq an-Nadi Libya
2 Funduq an-Nama
3 Funduq Ifriqiya
5 Funduq Falasteen
7 Funduq al-Bahr al-Medoss
27 Funduq al-Anis as-Siyahe
33 Funduq Omar al-Khayyam
42 Funduq Qasr al-Jezira; End of Walking Tour
52 Funduq al-Khordabiya; Photo Shop; Supermarket
53 Funduq Tibesti; Mat'am Shahat; Balad at-Toyoub Al-Lloaloah Coffee Shop
55 Funduq Uzu
56 Buyut ash-Shabaab (Youth Hostel)

PLACES TO EAT
10 Felafel Stand
13 Teahouse
14 Teahouse
17 Felafel Stand
18 Juice Stand
34 Mat'am al-Kabir
36 Cheap Restaurant
51 Mat'am Gharnata
57 Mat'am al-'Arabi; Cheap Restaurants

OTHER
4 Al-Itihad al-'Arabi Bus Terminal
6 Hospital
8 An-Nakhl as-Seria (Fast Transport Co) Bus Terminal

9 Main Shared-Taxi Station
11 Vegetable Market
12 Local Minibus Station
15 Old Lighthouse
16 Archaeological Excavations
19 Osman Mosque
20 Atiq Mosque (Al-Jame' al-Kabir)
21 Freedom Square
22 Old Town Hall
23 Tourist Police
24 Masraf al-Wahida (Bank)
25 Swissair (Horizons Travel)
26 Main Post Office
28 Greek Orthodox Church

29 Hadia Group Internet
30 Masraf al-Umma (Bank)
31 Jawazzat
32 Olympic Airways
35 Al-Jami' al-Libya (Old University)
37 Mosque
38 Masraf al-Jamahiriya (Bank)
39 Old Egyptian Consulate; Start of Walking Tour
40 Central Bank of Libya
41 Mosque (Former Cathedral)

43 Municipal Hospital
44 Police Station
45 Italian Consulate-General
46 National Library
47 Libyan Arab Airlines
48 Great Man-Made River Hospital
49 Statue of Jamal Abdul Nasser
50 Mataba (Green Book Building)
54 Islamic Call Building; AIEL Travel & Tour Services

To Tocra (73.3km), Al-Bayday (105.3km) & Tolmeita (109.3km)

ASSABRI

MEDITERRANEAN SEA

Al-Funduq Market

SIDI HUSSEIN

OLD CITY

Souq al-Jreed

Benghazi Harbour

RAS ABAYDAH

To Bernina Airport (15km)

0   250   500m
0   250   500yd

23 July Lake

SPORT'S CITY

Walking Tour

To Greek Consulate-General (2.5km)

To Commonwealth War Graves Cemetery (1.5km) & Egyptian Consulate (2.3km)

Sharia Gulf of Sirt

CYRENAICA

The international telephone office is at the top of the southern entrance stairs; look for the 'International Communication' sign. In contrast to the main post-office hall, there is usually someone behind the counter.

Most telephone numbers in Benghazi have been converted to the digital system and have seven-digit numbers. Unfortunately the conversion has not been uniform and some analogue (five-digit) numbers remained at the time of research. This may change in the foreseeable future so if you experience difficulty in getting through on a five-digit number, add the prefix '90'.

The most central cybercafe is Hadia Group Internet (☎ 9080376, e info@hadiagroup .com), behind the main post office. It's from 10am to midnight daily (3LD per hour).

Money There are plenty of banks in the central area, including Masraf al-Umma and Masraf al-Wahida along Sharia Omar al-Mukhtar and the Masraf al-Jamahiriya on Sharia Jamal Abdul Nasser. There are also money-changing facilities at Funduqs Tibesti and Uzu (see Places to Stay).

The black market is more openly advertised here than anywhere else in Libya. Between Freedom Square and the southern entrance to Souq al-Jreed, individual money-changers openly approach tourists to offer wads of dinars in exchange for dollars.

Travel Agencies Benghazi's two best tour companies are AIEL Travel & Tour Services (☎ 9092385, fax 9080272), Level 7, Islamic Call Building, and Bright Focus (☎ 9091639, 9091467).

Photography & Film If you're looking for print film, you could try the shops under the arches just south of Freedom Square, or the photographic shop (☎ 9097850) on Sharia Jamal Abdul Nasser, opposite the back of Funduq Tibesti (look for the Fuji sign). You can also get films developed.

Walking Tour
The best way to see Benghazi is on foot and most of the sights can be seen in a leisurely two- to three-hour ramble.

As good a place as any to start is the **Old Egyptian Consulate**, just off Sharia Jamal Abdul Nasser. The pastel shades and wooden shutters of the exterior has a certain decaying elegance amid the palm trees and is strongly evocative of its Italianate origins.

Head to, and take a left down, Sharia Jamal Abdul Nasser. After about 100m you'll pass a **small square**. The thoroughfare leading north-west behind the square leads into the heart of Benghazi's old city with four- or five-storey buildings crowding over shady alleyways. Watch out for the **Greek Orthodox Church**, distinguishable only by a simple cross above the door; some reports suggest that the last parishioner died in 2000. If you knock loudly enough, someone may appear to let you look inside.

Continue north-west and turn right onto busy Sharia Omar al-Mukhtar and turn right. You'll soon enter an attractive **pedestrian precinct** lined with shops (including a few mediocre handicrafts stores) behind arched porticos. The pedestrian area opens out onto **Freedom Square**, one of Benghazi's most enchanting spots, particularly in late afternoon when Benghazi children play football. Lining the western side of the square is the evocative **Old Town Hall**. Contributing to the delightful facades of Freedom Square, at the northern end, is the **Atiq Mosque** (also known as Al-Jame' al-Kabir, or the Great Mosque). The original mosque on the site was built in the early 15th century, but had many later renovations. At the time of research, it was again being renovated to the point of reconstruction.

Behind the mosque is another square surrounded by modern porticos and off to the north-west is the **Osman Mosque** with its distinctive Ottoman-style minaret. Veering to the north-east, you enter the covered passageway of the **Souq al-Jreed** which winds its way north-east for over 1km, crossed only by Sharia ash-Sharif. At the north-eastern end of the souq you enter a small square, home to the city's micro station. On the north-western corner of the square is a basic **teahouse**, where you can pass the time with a nargileh and take on all-comers in a game of *tawle* (backgammon).

This area stands at the heart of the **Al-Funduq Market**, an very crowded transport hub thick with diesel fumes. The downmarket clamour is in contrast to the vaguely sanitised order of most modern Libyan cities. There is no denying that this is a tough neighbourhood and you should certainly watch your valuables; one local suggested that if you open your mouth you could lose your teeth. Be careful, but don't be paranoid: you're far more likely to encounter smiles and invitations than pickpockets. The area is, however, one of Benghazi's liveliest, especially in the large, walled **vegetable market** immediately east of the micro station. On street corners women from sub-Saharan Africa sell all manner of goods in their brightly colourful wraps.

Return through Souq al-Jreed to Sharia ash-Sharif, which leads north-west towards the **old lighthouse** on the waterfront. The small archaeological excavation by the lighthouse is all that remains of the ancient Greek city of Berenice. Follow the coast road around to the shores of the main harbour. A couple of hundred metres along Sharia al-Corniche, on your left behind the railings, is **Al-Jami' al-Libya**, Libya's first university. From here you should be able to see the twin domes of the **former cathedral** off to the east. This was once the largest church in North Africa. From a distance, its imposing grandeur is impressive; up close, it stands forlorn and disused, its austere beauty made more poignant by the broken, stained-glass windows.

Follow the footpath back around to the waterfront to the Funduq Qasr al-Jezira for Benghazi's best waterfront views; it's especially nice at sunset.

Old Town Hall

Benghazi's Old Town Hall runs along the western side of Freedom Square. Built during the period of Italian occupation, the town hall is now derelict and closed to the public. The passage of time has certainly taken its toll but strong traces of its former elegance remain. The decaying, whitewashed Italianate facade is unmistakably grand, with some lovely arched doorways

and pillars. The large balcony has played host to its share of important orators – Mussolini addressed the crowds, German field marshal Rommel reviewed his troops and King Idris spoke to his subjects from here. The square beneath the balcony is charming.

Souq al-Jreed

The covered market of Benghazi, Souq al-Jreed, stretches for over 1km from Freedom Square to Al-Funduq Market. It's not the most evocative bazaar in the Arab world but its liveliness and colour are nonetheless among the highlights of a visit to Benghazi.

Like any Middle Eastern market worth its salt, Souq al-Jreed offers just about anything you could want and plenty that you don't. This market exists primarily for locals, which is what makes it so worthwhile. There are watches, cheap clothes, elegant gold jewellery, *galabiyyas* (men's robes) of alternately questionable and refined taste, henna, Levis and 'anything you want, one dinar', all displayed to the accompaniment of the music of Umm Kolthum crooning out from the latest Sony sound systems. Also visible through the cloud of overbearing perfumes are pharmacies, felafel stalls, mosques and glossy pictures of Mecca. The nearer you get to Al-Funduq Market, the greater the noise and general clamour, and the more the lines between an Arab bazaar and an African market become blurred. For many reasons, this is a place to wander through slowly, not least because the floor is quite uneven in parts.

Commonwealth War Graves Cemetery

Benghazi is home to a small but well-kept cemetery for Allied soldiers killed in WWII. It contains the graves of Australian, British, Greek, Indian, Jewish, Libyan, Norwegian, South African and Sudanese soldiers. The cemetery is 5km south-east of the city centre. Take the First Ring Road from Funduq Uzu for about 1.5km, passing under the road to Tripoli. The cemetery is on the right behind a fence of iron railings. If you're taking a taxi (3LD), ask for '*maqbara australiya*'.

Places to Stay

Benghazi has a decent range of accommodation, although travellers on a really tight budget will find the options less appealing.

Places to Stay – Budget

Buyut ash-Shabaab (☎ *2234101, Behind the sports stadium)* Beds in dorms for HI members/nonmembers 3/5LD. Benghazi's well-run youth hostel is basic but most rooms are well maintained. Men and women are housed in different parts of the building and there are a few family rooms. It's a popular place, so try to arrive before lunchtime. There's a garden cafe selling cheap food and some parts of the building have views of the harbour.

The remainder of Benghazi's rock-bottom hotels are not for the faint-hearted, light sleepers, lone women or those who consider cleanliness important. Most are in the noisy and polluted Al-Funduq Market area. Typical examples of this particularly grotty genre include **Funduq al-Bahr al-Medoss** (☎ *9090386),* north of the vegetable market and in the heart of the action, and **Funduq Falasteen**, which is quieter than most despite being opposite Al-Itihad al-'Arabi bus terminal. Expect to pay 5LD per person per night or 10LD for a room to yourself.

Funduq al-Anis as-Siyahe (☎ *9093147, Sharia Omar ibn al-Khattab)* Singles/doubles with shared bath 13/18LD, singles/doubles with bath 15/23LD. The reception manager at the Funduq Omar al-Khayyam directed us to this place, obviously seeing it as preferable to his own. The location is good, the rooms spartan, and don't expect things like carpet on the floor, toilet paper in the loo, fluffy towels by the bath or working telephones. Unhelpfully, the lift only works from the 2nd floor and up. On the plus side, there is plenty of hot water.

Funduq al-Khordabiya (☎ *9096997, Sharia Jamal Abdul Nasser)* Singles/doubles with bath 14/18LD. This place is tired-looking, with a ramshackle air, and the rooms are correspondingly run-down. Those rooms at the front are noisy.

Funduq Ifriqiya (☎/*fax 9081738, Sharia al-Jezayir, postal address: PO Box 17419,* *Benghazi)* Singles/doubles/triples with bath, breakfast & air-con 15/20/30LD. Funduq Ifriqiya is streets ahead of the other budget options. Shafi, the friendly owner, used to work at the upmarket Funduq Uzu and it shows. The rooms are good value, well maintained and handy for the bus and shared-taxi stations, but those at the front can be noisy. The restaurant is similarly good value – set meals of couscous, beans, salad, soup and a soft drink cost 6LD; other options cost little over 10LD.

Funduq an-Nama (☎ *89961, Sharia al-Jezayir)* Singles/doubles/triples with shared bath & air-con 15/25/30LD. Funduq an-Nama, nearby, is nowhere near as good value. There aren't too many bathrooms and most rooms are noisy. Staff don't seem able to rustle up breakfast but can sell you an Eminem CD at reception. The entrance is from the back of the building, next to the small **shwarma place**, which isn't a bad option for a snack.

Funduq Qasr al-Jezira (☎ *9096001/8, fax 9095428, Sharia al-Corniche)* Singles/doubles with bath 15/20LD, suites 40LD. In a previous life, this was the old Hotel Berenice (occasional light fittings still bear the old name), one of Benghazi's finest. Now the hotel has fallen on hard times, with some rooms carrying the none-too-faint smell of urine; the bottom two floors are the preserve of prostitutes and their clients who, when things are quiet, take up residence in the ground-floor cafe.

Places to Stay – Mid-Range

Quoted prices in this and the top-end section include breakfast and all rooms come with private bathroom.

Funduq Omar al-Khayyam (☎ *9095101, fax 9096291, Sharia al-Corniche)* Singles/doubles/triples 21/26/31LD, suites 43LD. The rooms are basic; ask to see a few different ones because some are light and airy. The only inhabitants of the huge and over-priced presidential suite (80LD) seem to be hotel staff watching the TV and enjoying the air-con. Air-conditioners in the other rooms seem to date from the Italian era and stopped working a long time ago.

Qaryat Qar Yunis as-Siyahe (Qar Yunis Tourist Village; ☎ *9094594, fax 9095355, Sharia Qar Yunis, postal address: PO Box 2333, Benghazi)* Singles/doubles/suites/ apartments with air-con 20/30/40/50LD. Six kilometres south of Benghazi (opposite the western perimeter of Qar Yunis University), this long-established tourist village still maintains reasonably high standards. The rooms are tidy, though some bathrooms are better than others. You'll need to book months in advance if you want a room in summer. Meals are available in the *restaurant* for 18LD to 25LD.

Funduq an-Nadi Libya (☎ *9088973, Sharia Ahmed Rafiq al-Madawi)* Singles/ twins with air-con 35/50LD. Around 3km north of the city centre, this place is excellent value. The comfortable rooms are quiet and spacious and come with satellite TV. The hotel is in a complex of office buildings behind a large iron gate with a security guard; the sign in Arabic outside reads *Al-Mujame as-Siyahe* (Tourist Complex). Once inside the compound, take the second lane on the left, then the second building on the right. This is also the headquarters for the Automobile Club of Libya.

Places to Stay – Top End
Funduq Uzu (☎ *9095160, fax 9092110, Sharia al-Jezayir, postal address: PO Box 2333, Benghazi)* Singles without/with lake view 50/60LD, doubles 65/75LD, suites from 100LD. One of Benghazi's top hotels, Funduq Uzu has superbly appointed rooms with all the requisite bells and whistles. Suite No 534 wins our vote for the best room in Libya, with its plush leather couches, cosy sitting area and views across the lake to the city centre (especially stunning at night). The buffet breakfasts (included in the room rates) are the best in Benghazi. In the *restaurant*, meals are good value at 17LD to 20LD, although if you choose from the a la carte menu expect to pay at least 30LD.

Funduq Tibesti (☎ *9098029/31, fax 9097160, Sharia Jamal Abdul Nasser, postal address: PO Box 9414, Benghazi)* Singles without/with lake view 65/75LD, doubles 85/100LD, suite singles/doubles 130/140LD.

On the northern side of the harbour, this is another classy hotel with a luxurious ambience; look for the waterfalls adorning the facade. Facilities include expensive boutiques, a patisserie and health club. There are two coffee shops and four restaurants (see Places to Eat); breakfast is included in the rates.

Places to Eat
Restaurants Benghazi has at least two high-quality, reasonably priced Turkish restaurants (the first two in the following listing) – the delicious cheese bread that accompanies the meals is an undoubted highlight. Both are open noon to 4pm and 6.30pm to 11pm Saturday to Thursday and 6.30pm-11pm Friday.

Mat'am al-Kabir (☎ *9081692, Sharia Jamal Abdul Nasser)* Meals 18LD. The friendly service and bright atmosphere complement the excellent banquet-style meals, which have all the usual accompaniments.

Mat'am Gharnata (☎ *9093509, Sharia Jamal Abdul Nasser)* Meals 15-17LD. The food and service here are similarly good, although the banquet includes five salads, fish and a choice of cakes.

Mat'am al-'Arabi (☎ *9094468, fax 909 9522, Sharia Gulf of Sirt)* Meals 16.5LD. Open 12.30pm-4pm & 6.30pm-11pm Sat-Thur, 6.30pm-11pm Fri. This is one of Benghazi's finest restaurants, but with an eminently reasonable price tag. The banquet meals come with flat Arab bread and are excellent value. The upstairs eating area has a delightful atmosphere, with a mosaic floor, tented roof and soft lighting. Not surprisingly, it's a popular place with locals, tour groups and expats alike.

Mat'am al-Asddaf (☎ *2223171, Sharia Qar Yunis)* Meals 19LD. Open 12.30pm-3.30pm & 6.30pm-10.30pm Sat-Thur, 6.30pm-11pm Fri. A bit out of town, right next to Funduq an-Nadi Libya, this specialist seafood restaurant is worth the taxi fare (3LD). After you've been marshalled by the welcoming Mahar, the service is attentive and the food high quality. The fish soup is good, as is the bread, and the hummus dip as good as you'll get in Libya. The enormous seafood platter contains calamari, octopus and a variety of fish, although each of these can be ordered separately. Throw in tea, salad and soft drink and the meal is great value. The restaurant can also pack a picnic lunch for groups.

The restaurants at Funduq Tibesti serve good food with superb views. *Mat'am Sahat (13th floor)* Meals from 25LD, open from 6pm-11pm daily. This place serves good Italian food. *Balad at-Toyoub (3rd floor)* serves reasonable Libyan food, while *Al-Lloaloah Coffee Shop (15th floor)* serves drinks, light meals and desserts.

Self-Catering & Fast Food Self-caterers with an exotic taste may wish to purchase the sheep's stomach hanging by the roadside along Sharia Ahmad Rafiq al-Mahdawi – we don't, so we can't vouch for its quality.

Almost next door to the photographic store (see Information) on Sharia Jamal Abdul Nasser is a well-stocked *supermarket*. For cheap *shwarmas* and sandwiches, there are numerous *cheap restaurants* along Sharia Jamal Abdul Nasser and in the streets surrounding Al-Funduq Market, and next to the Mat'am al-'Arabi (see later). The north side of the vegetable market is one of the few places in Libya where you can get *ta'amiyya* (Egyptian variety of felafel) due to the high number of Egyptians working in the area. There's also a *felafel stand* halfway through Souq al-Jreed on the east side of the lane.

The souq is also one of the rare places in Libya where you'll come across a *juice stand* selling freshly squeezed juices and milkshakes. In the souq and a few doors north of Sharia ash-Sharif, it sells excellent banana milkshakes *(moze halib)* for 1LD, mango shakes *(manga halib)* for 1.5LD and fruit cocktails for 2LD.

Getting There & Away

Air Benghazi's Bernina airport handles both international and domestic flights.

International Swissair (☎ 9094689, fax 9098811), 40 Sharia Omar al-Mukhtar (c/o Horizons Travel), has twice-weekly flights between Benghazi and Zürich. Olympic Airways (☎ 9094937), 31 Sharia Jamal Abdul

Nasser, connects Benghazi and Athens, although schedules were undergoing changes.

Domestic At the time of research, there were flights from Benghazi to Al-Kufra (32/64LD, Monday, Wednesday and Friday), Sebha (36/72LD, Tuesday and Thursday) and Tripoli (28/56LD for economy one-way/return, four times daily).

The entrance to the Libyan Arab Airlines office (☎ 9092064/9) is from Sharia al-Jezayir. If you have a car, you'll need to drive around the back of the building to the car park, which faces the roundabout. The office is open 8am to 7pm Saturday to Thursday and 9am to noon and 3pm to 7pm Friday.

Bus Amid the chaos of Al-Funduq Market, two bus companies operate in relative serenity. You should always book tickets at least one day in advance.

Al-Itihad al-'Arabi (☎ 88186), northeast of Al-Funduq Market, usually has the best buses and is well organised. It specialises in international destinations, including Alexandria (41LD, 21 hours) and Cairo (51LD, 24 hours), both with departures at 7am and 7pm, Damascus (81LD) and Amman (81LD).

It also has a daily bus to Tripoli (15LD, 12 hours) via Sirt (10LD, five hours), which leaves at 8am. The ticket office is on the southern side of the parking bays.

On Sharia Amr ibn al-Ass, government-run An-Nakhl as-Seria (Fast Transport Co;

Benghazi Buses

destination	price (LD)	duration (hrs)
Al-Bayda	2.75	3
Al-Khoms	12	11
Al-Kufra	13	12
Al-Jaghbub	10	7½
Derna	3.75	4
Gialo (Jalu)	5.25	5
Misrata	10.75	10
Sebha	16	15
Sirt	7.25	7
Tobruk	6	7–9
Tripoli	13.5	12
Zliten	11.5	10½

CYRENAICA

☎ 9090460) is also good and covers most Libyan destinations. Its international buses go to Alexandria (35/45LD in summer/ winter) and Cairo (45/55LD). See the table 'Benghazi Buses' for some of the domestic services.

Shared Taxi Micro and shared-taxi offices abound throughout Al-Funduq Market. Shared taxis leave much more frequently, but you're likely to be squeezed into a very small space, making the journey seem longer than it is. Finding a relevant departure point (there is usually more than one) can be a challenge, although if you tell enough people where you want to go, someone's bound to take you by the hand to the exact spot. Most are concentrated outside the An-Nakhl as-Seria bus terminal on Sharia al-Jezayir. Early mornings are best. For shorter journeys, the crush of taxis and people means you'll rarely have to wait long for one to fill.

Destinations include Al-Bayda (5LD), Al-Marj (2.5LD), Derna (7LD), Sebha (23LD), Sirt (14LD), Tobruk (12.5LD) and Tripoli (25LD).

Getting Around
To/From the Airport Bernina Airport is 18km east of the city. There are no regular or reliable micro or shared-taxi services to the airport, although it might be worth turning up at the shared-taxi stations along Sharia Amr ibn al-Ass or the city micro station in Al-Funduq Market the day before you plan to travel to check if any of the drivers think there'll be anything going. A private taxi to the airport costs 10LD.

Taxi & Micro Most micro journeys cost 0.25LD, while a shared taxi costs around 0.5LD. Most private-taxi journeys will cost 2LD to 3LD, although drivers may ask up to 5LD for destinations outside the city centre.

AJDABIYA اجدابـيـا
Ajdabiya was traditionally a key destination for traders arriving from the Sahara. The town was also important during the Fatimid period – you can see the rubble of a Fatimid mosque and fortress (ask for '*qasr Fatimid*'),

which has stones bearing a few Roman inscriptions. Ajdabiya is now the central administrative centre for the region.

Ajdabiya can seem like a welcoming oasis if you've come from the desert. Don't be fooled: If you stay longer than the hour it takes to have some food and fill your car with petrol, you'll soon discover that it's a place of little charm.

There are plans to build a new hotel north of town on the road to Benghazi. Simple *eateries* are dotted around town. Reasonable shared-taxi connections go south, across the desert, to Al-Kufra (23.5LD, 12 hours), Benghazi (4LD, two hours) and Sirt (10LD, five hours). Note that if you are heading to Tobruk from Ajdabiya via the desert route, this is the last petrol stop for 380km.

AWJILA
Awjila, one of the Jalu oases, breaks up the long journey to Al-Kufra (625km). Conquered by the Arab armies of Islam in the 7th century AD, it became an important staging post for caravans travelling between the coast and the oases of the Fezzan. It became a prosperous commercial centre renowned in the 8th century for exporting high-quality dates. These days, Awjila is noted for the **Mausoleum of Abdullah ibn Ali Sarh**, the last resting place of a leader of the Islamic conquest and friend of the Prophet Mohammed. The old **Al-Kabir Mosque** has distinctive conical domes made out of mud brick and limestone. Awjila is also famous as a centre of Berber culture and, rarely for Libya, some people speak only Berber. There's nowhere to stay in town.

SULUQ سلوق
Suluq, 55km south of Benghazi, is where the Italians hanged Omar al-Mukhtar in front of 20,000 of his imprisoned supporters (see the boxed text 'The Capture & Trial of Omar al-Mukhtar' later in this chapter). The great man's body has been buried here since his execution, but the commemorative shrine was not moved from Benghazi to Suluq until early 2001. Occasional shared taxis (1.5LD) to here leave from Benghazi's Al-Funduq Market area.

Northern Cyrenaica

TOCRA   توكرة

Tocra was one of the five cities of the Greek Pentapolis; the site is 70km north-east of Benghazi. This is the least evocative of Cyrenaica's surviving ruins, so if you need to give one ancient site a miss, make it Tocra.

The new village has no facilities for visitors other than the fruit stalls around the charming old village square, which was the centrepiece of an Italian settlement.

History

Founded around 510 BC, Tocra was one of the first ports settled from Cyrene. It was renamed Arsinoe, after the wife of Ptolemy II, and later known as Cleopatris, after the daughter of Cleopatra and Mark Antony. From the time of the Ptolemies, the city shared a similar history with its sister city, Ptolemais, 37km north-east along the coast and known today as Tolmeita. Tocra was built using soft sandstone, which has proved unable to withstand the earthquakes and other vagaries that the centuries have wrought upon the Cyrenaican coast.

Ancient City

After passing through the gate into Tocra (admission 3LD, camera/video 5/10LD; open 8am-5pm daily), you walk between Greek and Roman columns in varying states of disrepair. Over the wall to your right are the excavated remains of **Roman tombs** cut into the rock wall of a sunken pit.

The **fort** itself, no more than 100m from the gate, is compact and attractive; the current structure dates from the Turkish and Italian eras. There was a fort (and possibly a temple) on this site in the Greek period. The structure was later embellished by the Romans and Byzantines, although there are no obvious traces of these buildings. From the watchtower, there are splendid views over the Mediterranean.

Well-signposted behind the castle is the **museum** (admission 3LD, camera/video 5/10LD; open 9am-noon & 3pm-6pm daily Oct-Apr, 9am-noon daily May-Sept). It con-

tains a site map of Tocra, but is probably not worth the expense.

Outside the gate and to the west, a small archaeological railway runs west to the **Eastern Basilica**, in which the skeleton of the main sanctuary, apse and baptistry are visible, as are some ancient Greek inscriptions. Also worth looking out for are the **Greek Gymnasium**, the remains of the **city walls** and **necropolis**, all of which are nearby.

Getting There & Away

You might find a shared taxi or micro heading to Tocra from Benghazi (1.75LD) or, less likely, Al-Bayda (3LD), but you're more likely to need to change in Al-Marj. The driver will take you to the ruins for a small extra charge, but be sure to arrange your return or onward journey, as there is nowhere to stay at Tocra unless you're camping wild.

To get to Tolmeita from Tocra, you could try hitching along the picturesque coast road; hopefully you won't be picked up by the man we saw taking pot-shots with his rifle at birds from his car window.

TOLMEITA (PTOLEMAIS)   طلميتة

North-east along the coast, 37km from Tocra, is the ruined city of Tolmeita (formerly Ptolemais). Tolmeita's attractive palm-fringed setting, and its transition from Greek to Roman occupation, make this a worthwhile excursion. The beaches have good bathing and soft sand, especially to the west of town near the Italian fort.

History

Tolmeita was founded in the 4th century BC and its privileged position as one of the five cities of the Pentapolis continued under the Romans. The city fell into decline with the arrival of the invading Arab armies in the 7th century, with Tolmeita the last city of the Pentapolis to fall.

The excavated areas of the city mostly date from the 1st and 2nd centuries BC, when Tolmeita covered 3 sq km and was a thriving Hellenistic city. Only 10% of the ancient city has been excavated and there are, sadly, no immediate plans for further work.

TOLMEITA (PTOLEMAIS)

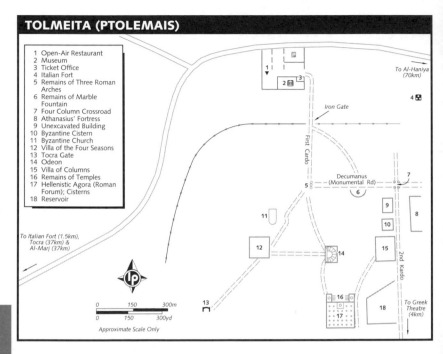

1 Open-Air Restaurant
2 Museum
3 Ticket Office
4 Italian Fort
5 Remains of Three Roman
   Arches
6 Remains of Marble
   Fountain
7 Four Column Crossroad
8 Athanasius' Fortress
9 Unexcavated Building
10 Byzantine Cistern
11 Byzantine Church
12 Villa of the Four Seasons
13 Tocra Gate
14 Odeon
15 Villa of Columns
16 Remains of Temples
17 Hellenistic Agora (Roman
   Forum); Cisterns
18 Reservoir

To Al-Haniya
(70km)

Iron Gate

First Cardo

Decumanus
(Monumental Rd)

To Italian Fort (1.5km),
Tocra (37km) &
Al-Marj (37km)

2nd Kardo

To Greek
Theatre
(4km)

0   150   300m
0   150   300yd
Approximate Scale Only

Ancient City

A dirt track runs up behind the ticket office (*admission 3LD, camera/video 5/10LD; open 7am-5pm daily*) towards the Jebel Akhdar. Tolmeita has an excellent guide, the knowledgeable Abdusalam Bazama (☎ 0685-2124). He worked on the original excavations and his fee of 50LD includes entry to the museum.

From the simple iron gate after about 200m, you can see two **Italian forts** off to the east and south-west and dating from 1923. You may also be able to see the skeletal traces of the ancient **Greek city walls** along the northern face of the Jebel Akhdar.

The trail continues up the hill, shadowed on the left by the rubble of the first **cardo**, which ran from the water's edge to the mountains. After 250m, there are bases of three **Roman arches** which, in the 3rd century AD, stood with four columns each and marked the crossroads of the first cardo (unusually, Tolmeita has two cardos) and the

decumanus, which ran east-west. This was one of the most important crossroads in the city and stood at the heart of ancient Tolmeita. The decumanus, also known as the Monumental Road, was once lined with colonnaded arched porticos running either side along its length.

Off to the south-east is the compact **Byzantine Church**, which dates from the 5th century AD and is notable for the fact that its domed apse remains largely intact, unlike many in Libya. A further 100m south-west are the remains of the **Villa of the Four Seasons**, which was built in the 4th century AD. Belonging to a wealthy Roman notable, it contained the beautiful Four Seasons mosaic, which is in the museum. The north-eastern corner of the villa was a *frigidarium* (cold room). Close to the centre of the villa was a courtyard which was, unusually, semicircular on one side; the floor was covered with mosaics. From the villa, you can see the ancient **Tocra Gate**, about 300m to the south-west.

CYRENAICA

Around 300m to the east is the enchanting **Odeon**, a small theatre, which was once covered by a roof and was large enough to seat up to 500 people. Performances of Greek music were accompanied by dancers in the sunken pit. In the 3rd century AD, the Roman love of water won out and they transformed it into a swimming pool; traces of the pipes running to the nearby cistern are visible on the south-eastern side of the building. The front of the stage was adorned by three statues – Claudius, Marcus Aurelius Antoninus and Archimedes.

A short walk up the hill takes you to the Greek **agora** (marketplace), which later served as the Roman forum. Along the northern side were three temples, each with four Doric columns. The column bases remain and those of the north-eastern temple are particularly fine. As you climb up to the raised area of the agora, be careful of the many small shafts, which drop 6m to the cavernous cisterns beneath the floor – these were the largest **cisterns** in North Africa.

A staircase just off-centre leads down into the cisterns, which received water from mountain springs 25km east of Tolmeita via an aqueduct. The long, eerie caverns with arched ceilings suggest that a sense of style prevailed even for underground water storage. At shoulder height along the walls, note the clearly discernible dividing line between the ceiling height during Greek rule (when stone slabs were used in construction) and that of the 2nd century AD, when the thirsty Romans enlarged the cisterns by raising the ceiling (using bricks and cement).

The path running north-east from the agora skirts the former **reservoir walls**, which also show the transition from Greek to Roman occupation – the bottom half marked with lines is Greek, while the top section is Roman.

After about 300m, you come to the **Villa of Columns**. The original structure was destroyed in AD 115–17 during the Jewish Revolt. The later villa belonged to a wealthy Roman local. One of the rooms on the southern side contained an exquisite Medusa mosaic on the floor. Next to it was the dining room; its floor still contains mosaic fragments and its wall traces of marble. In the centre of the villa is the sunken swimming pool. The pool was lined by two small gardens, while the pedestal in the centre once supported a small animal fountain in granite. On the northern side of the villa was the frigidarium.

Along the eastern side of the villa runs the **second cardo**, which was lined with shops and ran all the way up the hill to the south to the **Greek Theatre**, the remains of which are barely visible halfway up the mountain. Northwards along the cardo is a **Byzantine cistern** and an **unexcavated building** with a mosaic peeping out from beneath the soil. Off to the north-east is **Athanasius' Fortress**, which dates from the 5th century AD.

Continuing north along the cardo, you reach the **Four Column Crossroad**, another significant intersection in the ancient city. Only the bases remain, but the columns once provided an important counterpoint to the three arches that lay west along the decumanus. Halfway between the two junctions are the base remains of a **marble fountain**, which depicted Bacchus. The gate by which you entered the site is not far off to the north-west.

Museum

The museum *(admission 3LD, camera/ video 5/10LD; open 7am-5pm daily)* has uninformative labels in English, so if you've paid for a guide you might as well get your money's worth here, too.

The central room is dominated by the superb Four Seasons mosaic from the villa of the same name; clockwise from the top left is summer, spring, winter and autumn. On the left wall is the wonderful Medusa head mosaic from the Villa of Columns; to the right of it is a plan of the Villa of Columns with explanations in Italian. On the right of the Four Seasons mosaic are the three statues from the Odeon.

The highlights of the western room are the 3rd-century AD tablets of gladiators (found in the theatre) and a mosaic of Orpheus (western wall) taming the wild beasts (2rd to 3rd century AD).

In the eastern room are raised column pieces adorned with the faces of Mars and Jupiter, as well as a number of interesting sarcophagi and grave covers. There are also 6th to 7th century BC statues from the Pentapolis city of Barce (now Al-Marj), and along the northern wall is the granite animal fountain from the Villa of Columns.

Places to Stay & Eat

There is nowhere to stay in Tolmeita. Bringing a picnic lunch can be a good idea; the third Italian fortress (about 4km along the road to Tocra) would be an excellent spot. There is an *open-air restaurant* in the car park in front of the museum, which serves simple food (around 10LD) and drinks.

Getting There & Away

Tolmeita is a sleepy town and shared taxis headed there can take ages to fill. Try in Benghazi or Al-Marj. You may have to pay a few piastres extra to be taken as far as the ruins; otherwise expect a walk of 2km. A good road leads up over the mountains to Al-Bayda, Al-Marj and Qasr Libya.

AL-MARJ   المرج
☎ 067

The ancient city of Barce (one of the cities of the Greek Pentapolis) was founded near here from 560 BC, but there's nothing left to see. The modern town of Al-Marj (which was the centre of much Italian settlement) was destroyed by an earthquake in 1963. The new town, which has sprung up on a nearby site, has reasonable shopping and other facilities. There are a couple of banks on the main street and the main post office is in the centre of town, not far from the big mosque.

The only place to stay is run-down *Funduq al-Marj* (☎ 2700), where double rooms cost 15LD. There's also a *restaurant* and *cafe*.

The micro and taxi station is about 500m from the main mosque. The taxis run all day, travelling both east and west.

QASR LIBYA   قصر ليبيا
Qasr Libya, about 45km west of Al-Bayda and 59km east of Al-Marj, may only be

small but it has one of the best collections of Byzantine mosaics in the country. The mosaics were laid in AD 529–40, during the reign of Justinian I (527–65), in the village of Olbia, which lay in the hinterland of Cyrene. In 1957, Libyan dam workers rediscovered the two Byzantine churches. The ceramic pieces that make up each panel are less than 1cm in diameter and follow the Hellenistic school of mosaic. The craftsmen drew inspiration from natural and folk scenes of daily life with pagan influences being incorporated into the Christian panoply.

Orientation

In the centre of the town of Qasr Libya, opposite a mural of Colonel Gadaffi presiding over a united Africa, is a small service road running parallel to the main road up a slight incline. At the top of the incline take the road leading under the boom gate. After 1.2km you reach a junction with a red, white and green sign in Arabic. Take the road running down the hill to your left; the Turkish fort should be visible on the hilltop to your right. After 200m, a dirt track leads up towards the car park and museum entrance.

Museum

The small museum (*admission 3LD, camera/ video 5/10LD*) is quite breathtaking with all 50 mosaic panels, each covering half a square metre, adorning the walls. Viewed alone each is impressive, but when you realise that all 50 covered the floor of a single room of the Eastern Church it all seems extraordinary. To see them as they appeared, look for the small black-and-white photo reproduction on the wall to the right after you enter, alongside an informative article from the academic who excavated the site.

The panels, which cover a wide range of subjects and seem to have links with early Christian beliefs, are numbered, well-labelled and grouped into often diverse sets of five. Among those depicting the gods, panels seven (the river god Geon), nine (the river god Physon), 17 (the river god Euphrates) and 19 (the river god Tigris) form a set representing the Four Rivers of Paradise, with the mischievous nymph Kastelia of Delphi

(18) in the middle. There are also some fine Nilotic river scenes – panels six and 10 are especially good, with waterfowl, lotus flowers and fish. Some of the animals are also exquisite, especially the snakes (panel 11), deer (five), horses (29) and birds (42). Also stunning are the buildings including a brilliant evocation of the New City of Theodarius (three) and a wonderful church facade with columns (28).

Yet it is **panel 48** that aroused the most excitement when the church was uncovered. It contains one of the few representations of the legendary Pharos lighthouse of Alexandria. Atop the roof on the left is the dark-green (to indicate bronze) figure of the naked Helios with a downward-pointing sword in his right hand. The circular object at the tip of his sword is believed to be the famous iron mirror of the lighthouse. On the right of the panel is another human figure, standing on the mainland and depicted as a naked, bronze colossus. Nicely juxtaposed to the main image is panel 49, which represents a boat with a passenger whose hand is stretched out towards Pharos.

Also of great importance is **panel 23**, a Byzantine inscription stating that the mosaics were laid in AD 339. This panel lay in the centre of the church floor. The much-larger mosaic on the museum floor lay at the eastern end of the church's northern aisle. This mosaic of panoramic scale includes a variety of plants and animals, a hunting scene, and the Nile with crocodiles and lotus flowers in the centre. Two of the three inscriptions are religious, invoking God's protection and referring to Christian martyrs, while the third (closest to the museum door) records the laying of the mosaic.

As you leave the museum, note the mosaic fragment on the wall to the right of the door. This forms part of the mosaic frieze that ran between the evenly spaced panels.

The gatekeeper claims that the museum is open from sunrise to sunset, but it's better not to get there too early.

Western Church

Directly opposite the entrance to the museum is the tranquil Western Church, which is shaped like a cross. Its large, dusty mosaic in the centre of the floor, though reconstructed in keeping with its original state, seems quite dull in comparison to those in the museum.

Turkish Fort

Next to the museum and Western Church is a small Turkish fort which has fine views over the surrounding countryside.

Eastern Church

The Eastern Church, where the mosaics were found, is east of the museum, about 75m down a dirt footpath. Given the splendour of its former contents, the modern building, with its aluminium roof and reconstructed walls, is a disappointment. The now-empty squares do, however, provide some context to the original layout of the mosaics.

Getting There & Away

Shared taxis run quite regularly between Al-Bayda (1LD) and Al-Marj (1.5LD), although check that the route the drivers take passes through Qasr Libya. Most shared taxis only go as far as the main road, so unless you can find a kindly local to give you a lift, you may have to walk; take plenty of water as none is available along the way nor at the site itself. If in doubt as to the direction, ask for 'al-mathaf' (the museum).

WADI AL-KUF   وادي الكوف

Wadi al-Kuf, east of Qasr Libya on the road to Al-Bayda, was the scene in 1927 of some of the most bitter and defining battles between the Libyan resistance and Italian forces. As a result, Wadi al-Kuf holds huge historical significance for many Libyans. It also has some of the finest scenery in the Jebel Akhdar.

One tributary of the wadi is spanned by a striking modern bridge, but try to take the detour that leads down through the wadi proper, rejoining the main road after 8km. If you're in a share taxi, get the driver to let you out at either end of the wadi; the eastern end is much steeper. You can either hitch or walk through the wadi, but to do the latter you would need to be self-sufficient in food and water and, in winter, warm clothes.

Coming from the west, the road twists through the picturesque landscape of wooded areas down through the increasingly towering cliffs. The further you descend, the more the cliffs are pockmarked with caves. The resistance retreated to these caves after each ambush to hide from the retaliatory bombardments of the Italians. The greatest concentration of caves is near the bottom of the valley after about 6km.

Around 7km down into the valley an iron bridge spans the road. Built by the Italian army in an attempt to ferry troops and supplies through the valley, it marks the spot where the forces of Omar al-Mukhtar halted, albeit temporarily, the southwards march of the Italian army, which was on the march from the Mediterranean to Al-Kufra. It was not until the infamous General Graziani surveyed countryside from a cliff-top and pinpointed the caves where the guerillas were hiding that the Italians, supported by targeted bombing, were able to break through. For details, see the boxed text 'The Capture & Trial of Omar al-Mukhtar' later in this chapter.

Throughout Wadi al-Kuf, you may also recognise many scenes from *Lion of the Desert,* the film about the life of Omar al-Mukhtar, which was partly filmed here.

AL-BAYDA   البيضاء
☎ 084 • pop 120,000

Al-Bayda is a pleasant, if unspectacular, city on the northern fringe of the Jebel Akhdar. The area has one of the mildest climates in Libya and is famous for its apples, grapes and, in November, *shmari* (a very sweet berry). While there's little to see in Al-Bayda, the city makes a good base for exploring the ruins of Cyrene, Apollonia, Qasr Libya and Slonta.

Al-Bayda was one of the main strongholds of the Sanusi Movement during the Ottoman period. After the Italians took control of the town, the resistance movement moved south to Al-Jaghbub and to Al-Kufra. In the years after independence, King Idris effectively used Al-Bayda as his administrative capital and spent much of his time here, alienating the powerbrokers in Tripolitania.

Orientation & Information
The easiest landmark in town to use to get your bearings is the telecommunications mast of the main post office. Sharia al-Ruba, Al-Bayda's main thoroughfare, runs straight through the centre of town and continues as the main coastal highway to Shahat (Cyrene) and beyond. About 150m east of the post office along Sharia al-Ruba, a road leads northwards past Libyan Arab Airlines and southwards to an Internet cafe (second street on the left above an arcade of shops).

A further 1km along Sharia al-Ruba, another road leading north boasts banks and the distinctive local parliament building with its large bronze dome. Behind the parliament is a compound of white buildings containing the jawazzat (☎ 633925). Near the intersection are also some hotels and restaurants. Another 1km east towards Shahat, you pass the Masraf Jamahiriya bank and then a roundabout topped by a globe. Less than 100m down the road to the south is the main shared-taxi station on a corner, with a couple more hotels nearby.

Things to See
Al-Bayda's sights are more for admiring as you pass by. On the western edge of town is the huge sandstone clock tower and dome of **Omar al-Mukhtar University**. Formerly an Islamic university, now a multidisciplinary institution, it is not open to casual visitors. West of the main post office, the road is lined with cypress trees, beneath which is a simple white **tomb** topped by a green dome, the last resting place of Rawayfa and Sari (friends of Mohammed).

At the other end of town, you can't miss the striking, white **Bilal Mosque**. This modern mosque has an attractive onion-like dome flanked by four smaller domes, as well as two piercing minarets. The mosque is particularly lovely at sunset.

Otherwise, there are a few colonial-style buildings along the main street, a small marble statue of Omar al-Mukhtar opposite the main post office and an old sheikh in the wadi behind the university who dispenses weird and wonderful medicines for ailments you never knew you had.

Places to Stay

Funduq al-Qahira (☎ 634976, Off Sharia al-Ruba) Singles/doubles from 10/20LD, suites 40LD. In a lane off the main drag in the centre of town, Funduq al-Qahira is run-down, but it's generally clean and certainly better than locals will lead you to believe. The front rooms are noisy and the water often lukewarm.

Funduq al-Jebel (☎ 635126, 70m west of shared-taxi station) Singles/doubles with shared bath 10/15LD. The rooms are a tad basic, but are clean and the location is good for transport.

Funduq Aya (☎ 637258, 75m west of shared-taxi station) Singles/doubles with bath 30/45LD. The friendly management don't quite compensate for the fact that the clean rooms are uninspiring, overpriced and that the plumbing is unreliable. Still, it's preferable to others in this price range in town. The price does include breakfast.

Funduq Qasr al-Bayda (☎ 633455, fax 633459, Sharia al-Ruba) Singles/doubles with bath 35/45LD. This erstwhile favourite of tour groups is living on borrowed time – most people stay here only because of the absence of competition. The rooms (no air-con) in this large, white, Art Deco building in the centre of town are fine, but the staff are sullen to the point of being positively unhelpful. Most odiously, if you don't eat in the **restaurant** (25LD *plus* drinks for very mediocre food) they may evict you from your room. A place to be avoided until they get their act together.

Thankfully a long-overdue new hotel is being built at the western end of Sharia ath-Thawra.

Places to Eat

If you can escape the clutches of the Funduq Qasr al-Bayda, there is a handful of decent restaurants in town, as well as plenty of **snack bars** the length of Sharia al-Ruba for 2km east of the post office.

Sharia ath-Thawra, parallel to Sharia ar-Ruba two blocks to the south, has some decent **grocery stores**.

Mat'am al-Batriq (☎ 638450, fax 636 957, Sharia al-Ruba) Meals 3-10LD. Open noon-11pm Sat-Thur, 2pm-11pm Fri. Right in the centre of town, this place serves great pizzas (if you don't want liver, ask for '*bidoon kibdeh*') for 5LD to 6LD, shwarmas (3LD to 5LD) and chicken dishes; it also does food to take away. Look for the two penguins above the door

Asservium (*Sharia al-Ruba*) Meals from 10LD. Open 11am-11pm Sat-Thur, 2pm-11pm Fri. Opened in April 2001, this cool place has trendy music and great outdoor seating. The upstairs terrace is a great place to watch the world go by with a *shay* (tea, 1LD) or a smoke of the nargileh (1LD). The affable Mustapha will ensure your stay is a pleasant one. It's in the centre of town, on the corner of the street running up to the parliament building.

Mat'am al-Barqa (☎ 635328, Sharia al-Ruba) Meals up to 18LD. Open noon-3.30pm & 6pm-10pm Sat-Thur, 2pm-11pm Fri. At the eastern end of town, right on the roundabout leading to the shared-taxi station, Mat'am al-Barqa serves good-quality banquets in pleasant surroundings.

Getting There & Away

Shared taxis run from the station at the eastern end of town to Al-Marj (3LD), Benghazi (6LD), Derna (2.5LD) and Tobruk (5.5LD). Note that not all Tobruk-bound transport passes through Derna. Shared taxis also leave from here for Shahat (Cyrene; 0.5LD) although it's easier simply to hail one down anywhere along Sharia al-Ruba. You could also try at the shared-taxi station for Susa (Apollonia), but services are infrequent to the point of nonexistent. Often the only option is a private taxi, which costs 10LD one way (25LD return, including waiting time).

AROUND AL-BAYDA

Ras al-Hammamah (known locally as Hammamah) is a tiny village 22km north of Al-Bayda. The beach, which is a mixture of soft sand and rock pools, is a great place to swim although there's no shade. There's a summer-only tourist village.

Further along the coast, south-west from Ras al-Hammamah, are other good beaches. About 5km west of the Hammamah Tourist

The Capture & Trial of Omar al-Mukhtar

In early September 1931, the Italians received word that a party of Libyan rebels were planning a live-stock raid on Cyrene. Not long after, the small raiding party was sighted near Slonta. Italian soldiers closed in and 11 rebels, close to starvation, were killed. The horse of the 12th was shot and its rider overtaken as he tried to escape on foot. He was about to be shot until one of the soldiers recognised him as Omar al-Mukhtar, the leader of the Libyan resistance. Al-Mukhtar was taken to Apollonia and later transported by ship to Benghazi. There was great rejoicing in colonial ranks.

Upon receiving the news, Marshal Badoglio told his underlings to 'make immediate arrangements for a criminal trial which can only end with the death sentence'. Other colonial officials rubbed their hands with undisguised glee at the prospect of a sensational execution. The trial on 15 September was a farce, with the dignified bearing of al-Mukhtar in stark contrast to the unseemly bloodlust of the Italian prosecutor and audience. Al-Mukhtar took full responsibility for his actions and calmly accepted his fate with the words: 'From God we have come and to God we must return'. His Italian defence lawyer was imprisoned for performing his role too sympathetically. The next day al-Mukhtar was hanged in the Suluq concentration camp in front of 20,000 eerily silent prisoners. The Italians had their man, the rebellion petered out and a Libyan legend was born.

Village is **Bst Beach**, a sheltered cove, home to a small fishing community. It's a good place for a picnic or campfire. A further 10km south-west is **Al-Haniya**, another small town with good beaches. The views towards the west are quite picturesque.

You'll need your own vehicle to get to these beaches – you could ask around the taxi station in Al-Bayda in case something's going that way. On Friday, there's plenty of traffic as people flock to the coast, so hitching might be an option. At the turn-off from the main highway (just east of Massah) is a high-walled compound. Inside is the former **Palace of King Idris** – with no doubt a hint of black revolutionary humour, the compound has been turned into a mental hospital.

SLONTA   سـلنطة

About 24km south of Al-Bayda the village of Slonta is home to the only significant pre-Greek Libyan artefact discovered in northern Libya. Of more historic than aesthetic appeal, the **remains of a stone temple** cover a mere 5 sq metres. The style of the often-childlike figures, human faces and animals carved into the rock is unlike anything else in Libya. The site was obviously a place of worship, but very little is known about the cult that gave rise to the temple. Some good examples of the Slonta carvings are on display in the

Tripoli Museum (Gallery 5); it's probably not worth a special effort to get out here.

The site (3LD) is 500m west of the sandstone mosque in the centre of town, behind a green metal gate with chicken wire around the perimeter. Ask for directions at the checkpoint immediately north of the mosque. The gate's usually left open.

Occasionally, shared taxis run from the shared-taxi station in Al-Bayda (0.25LD) or, even less often, Shahat (0.25LD), but they can take an age to fill as demand is minimal. Make sure you arrange return transport to avoid getting stuck.

At the western edge of town, a minor road runs north to the small village of **Omar al-Mukhtar**, so-named because the rebel leader was finally captured by the Italians near here.

SHAHAT   شـحات
☎ 084

The modern village of Shahat, 17km east of Al-Bayda and 74km west of Derna, has nothing of interest but serves as the gateway to the spectacular ancient city of Cyrene. The town stretches from the highway north to the ruins.

Buyut ash-Shabaab (☎ *637371*) Camping 5LD, dorm beds for HI members/ nonmembers 3/5LD. The hostel is opposite the shared-taxi station, behind the petrol station and a stone's throw from the gate leading down to the ruins. It's clean, friendly and has been recommended by a number of travellers; the hot water is reliable. It can fill up quite early in the day and is sometimes closed during Ramadan. You can't get meals but there is a *kiosk* selling snacks (including sandwiches) and drinks.

Shared taxis between Al-Bayda and Shahat (0.5LD) arrive and leave from under the eucalyptus trees, just short of the pillars marking the gate leading down to Cyrene. Taxis also pass by on the main highway from Derna (2LD) or Tobruk (5LD); it's 2.5km from the highway to the pillars.

CYRENE

It's easy to spend a day exploring the ruins of Cyrene, which are worth visiting as much for their spectacular setting as their significance as monuments of the Greek occupation. If your time is limited, it is possible to see most of the site in half a day and combine it with a trip to nearby Apollonia.

Visiting the site *(admission 3LD, camera/ video 5/10LD; open 7.30am-6pm daily May-Sept, 8am-5pm daily Oct-Apr)* is difficult without without a guide. Fortunately, there are plenty milling around the entrance; lone travellers and small groups can usually get in without one or tag along with a larger group. If you do take a guide (50LD), Mahmoud Abu Shreet and Abdul Ghader are among the best in the business, and Fadil Ali Mohamed has also been recommended.

The south-eastern gate is the best place to start as it's closest to Shahat. (The name Shahat is used to describe the site and the town.) From here you can fully appreciate Cyrene's special location and, as the site is set on many levels, it also means a downhill walk!

There are stalls selling snacks, drinks and a moderate selection of expensive books opposite the northern gate (exit).

History

In the early 7th century BC, settlers set out from the Greek island of Thera (modern Santorini). They were led by Battus, a man chosen for the task by the oracle of Apollo at Delphi. The reason for their journey was both demographic and political – the island had

The Founding Myth of Cyrene

Cyrene's founding myth places the gods at centre stage in an epic tale of romance, betrayal and renewal.

Cyrene, a Thessalian nymph known in Greek as Kurana, was a princess and a very modern woman, preferring to hunt animals at Mt Pindus while refusing to undertake the domestic chores, that were the lot of her contemporaries.

One day, Apollo saw her wrestling a lion and immediately fell in love with her. Clearly used to getting his own way, Apollo abducted Cyrene and took her in a golden chariot to the site that would one day bear her name. The Temple of Apollo was founded to commemorate Cyrene strangling a lion to make the region safe for settlers.

But it doesn't end there. When Aristaeus, the beekeeping son of Apollo and Cyrene, pursued Eurydice in a clumsy rite of seduction, the unfortunate woman was killed by a snake. Aristaeus' bees died in a plague of divine retribution. Only after Aristaeus conducted the ceremonies of atonement and the bees were born again from the carcasses of sacrificed animals was Cyrene freed from the titanic struggles of the gods.

limited resources for a growing population, but their departure was also seen as a means of reducing the political tension caused by the prevailing power struggles on Thera. The small band of less than 100 people landed on the island of Platea, south of Crete in the Gulf of Bomba, before landing to the east of modern Derna. They quickly discovered that their new home was not suitable for the colony they hoped to establish. The wily Giligami tribe convinced the Greeks to return the stolen land with a promise to lead them to a more fertile site where there was a 'hole in the heavens'. Cleverly, the tribesmen marched them through the night, concealing the more fertile areas en route. They took them to land occupied by a different tribe and Cyrene was founded, in 631 BC.

Cyrene soon expanded and more settlers arrived from Greece on a promise of prime

CYRENAICA

agricultural land. Not surprisingly, the local tribes resented the intrusion and asked the Egyptian pharaoh for help, but the Greeks won out in 570 BC. The leader of the first colonists, Battus, ruled as king for 40 years. His dynasty lasted from 631 BC to 440 BC – a period of eight kings, great stability and territorial expansion.

During the city's golden age in the 4th century BC it was considered by many as the pre-eminent city of the Greek world. Its wealth and agricultural abundance enabled it to save Greece from famine in 390 BC through a massive export of grain. Plato, who had been sold as a slave by Dionysius, was liberated by a citizen of Cyrene, Annikeris, in 388 BC. Cyrene was at this time a great cultural centre, home to Aristippus (a philosopher of renown who founded the Cyrenaic school of philosophy), Theodorus (a contemporary of Socrates and famous for his skill in arithmetic, geometry, astronomy and music) and Eratosthenes (mathematician, astronomer and the third librarian of the great library of Alexandria).

In 331 BC, Cyrene came under the rule of Alexander the Great. When Alexander's empire collapsed, the Greek world fragmented and the federation of the Pentapolis again became a largely autonomous entity. In the 3rd century BC, Cyrene and the other cities of the Pentapolis fell under the umbrella of the Ptolemies, who ruled Egypt. Instability ensued and Ptolemy I sent his stepson Magas to Cyrene in an attempt to restore their dominance. The ambitious Magas, reading from a different script, severed his ties with the Ptolemaic dynasty which was by then ruled by Ptolemy Philadelphus, son of Ptolemy I. It was not until 260 BC, with the engagement of Magas' daughter, Berenice, to the son of Philadelphus that Cyrene was again incorporated into Egypt and the period of independence came to an end.

In 96 BC Ptolemy Apion generously bequeathed Cyrenaica to the Romans and by 75 BC Cyrene had become an important Roman capital. Successive Roman proconsuls favoured an approach that recognised the Greek heritage of Cyrene and the city re-

mained essentially Greek in character until the 1st century AD. The Jewish Revolt of AD 115–17 saw the destruction of Cyrene. The emperor Hadrian, often referred to as Cyrene's second founder, sought to re-establish the pre-eminence of Cyrene. His rebuilding program gave the city's architecture a more Roman flavour – temples were elevated onto platforms and columns were left smooth and unfluted.

By the middle of the 3rd century AD, the city was in decline, in keeping with the general malaise of the Roman Empire. From then on it was a downward spiral, with a devastating earthquake in AD 262, a shift of the Roman capital from Cyrene to Tolmeita as part of the administrative reforms of emperor Diocletian and another massive earthquake in AD 365. Unfortunately, subsequent restoration work did little more than paper over the cracks.

In the centuries that followed, Cyrene became a Christian city subject to frequent droughts and predatory raids from the nomadic tribes of the interior. Much weakened, Cyrene was in no position to resist the westward march of the Islamic armies of Amr ibn al-Ass in AD 643. There is evidence of ongoing settlement for a few centuries after then, but Cyrene's day had passed.

SUSA
سوسة
☎ 084

The small town of Susa, about 20km from Shahat, is the gateway to another wonderful ancient Greek city – Apollonia. The modern town was first established in 1897 by a group of Muslim refugees from Crete.

The road from Shahat and Cyrene to Susa is shadowed by the ancient road between Cyrene and Apollonia, and deep ruts mark the tracks left by the chariots of old. Halfway between the two sites stands a simple, white monument to the memory of Libyans who died in the war against the Italians. The last part of the journey involves a spectacular descent as the road winds down off the northern rim of the Jebel Akhdar with great views along the coast.

[Continued on page 181]

THE ANCIENT CITY OF CYRENE

The ancient city of Cyrene is one of the undoubted highlights of any visit to Libya. It was the premier city of the Greek Pentapolis and its glorious remains are an enduring testament to the great civilisations that flourished along the northern Libyan coast.

Gymnasium/Forum

The large open square on your right a few hundred metres after passing through the gate was originally built by the Greeks in the 2nd century BC as a gymnasium. As the major sporting building of Cyrene's upper terrace, it was surrounded on four sides by Doric columns and the open palaestra (exercise area) was the scene of races and other sporting contests. In the second half of the 1st century AD, it was converted by the Romans into a forum, or caesareum (Forum of the Caesars), where political meetings were held. The compound contained a civil basilica and a temple. Access was through two monumental gateways with four Doric columns. Now stripped of their main adornments, the open spaces wear a decidedly abandoned air.

Skyrota

The road running along the south western perimeter of the forum was the Skyrota, the main road through the Greek city. It is still lined with impressive columns bearing graven images of Hermes and Hercules. This section was once known as the Portico of the Hermas and the road was to become in Roman times a monumental passageway linking the forum to the agora. Behind the western wall of the gymnasium was the Odeon (theatre) and the Xystos, a track used by athletes training for races. Across the thoroughfare was another small theatre for musical performances, which was probably abandoned after the earthquake in AD 262.

House of Jason Magnus

Also across the path from the Xystos is the impressive private residence of Claudius Tiberius Jason Magnus, high priest of the Temple of Apollo in the 2nd century AD. The floor of the main entrance is covered with marble. A number of rooms, including the large dining room or banquet hall, feed off the main inner courtyard. Around the courtyard are a few Corinthian capitals (one bearing the bearded face of Battus, next to a silphium plant) and there are some well-preserved female figures draped with finely sculpted marble clothes. The best example of the house's mosaics is the superb **Four Seasons mosaic**, which is now kept under an unattractive aluminium roof.

House of Hesychius

On the hill overlooking the agora is the home of Hesychius, a Christian who returned to Cyrene after the AD 365 earthquake in a bid to restore the glory days of the city. Hesychius was a friend of the philosopher and bishop Sinesius. There is a fine mosaic of an angel on

CYRENE

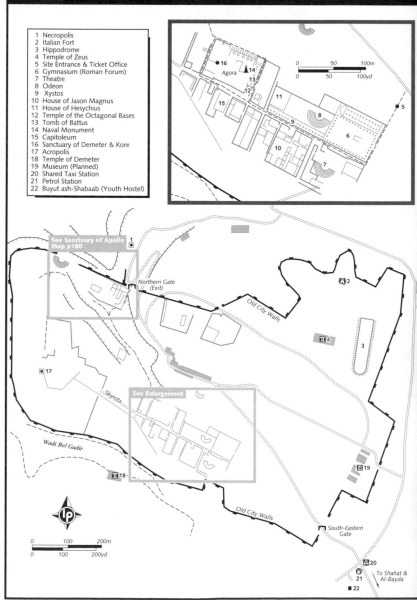

1 Necropolis
2 Italian Fort
3 Hippodrome
4 Temple of Zeus
5 Site Entrance & Ticket Office
6 Gymnasium (Roman Forum)
7 Theatre
8 Odeon
9 Xystos
10 House of Jason Magnus
11 House of Hesychius
12 Temple of the Octagonal Bases
13 Tomb of Battus
14 Naval Monument
15 Capitoleum
16 Sanctuary of Demeter & Kore
17 Acropolis
18 Temple of Demeter
19 Museum (Planned)
20 Shared Taxi Station
21 Petrol Station
22 Buyut ash-Shabaab (Youth Hostel)

Agora

See Sanctuary of Apollo Map p180

Northern Gate (Exit)

Old City Walls

See Enlargement

Skyrota

Wadi Bel Gadir

Old City Walls

South-Eastern Gate

To Shahat & Al-Bayda

the north-western side showing clearly recognisable Byzantine icon-ography, alongside an inscription imploring God to protect the women and children of Cyrene. In the compact, three-sided courtyard are the remains of a small fountain or nymphaeum.

Agora

The agora was the heart of ancient Cyrene, serving as a public square, a forum for orators, a market and a magnet for the powerful people of the day. Many civic and religious buildings were clustered around the agora. Many still bear the traces of Roman influence, superimposed onto the fine monumental constructions started by the Greeks. Under Severus, porticoes were added on three sides in the 3rd century AD.

The **Temple of the Octagonal Bases** (2nd century AD) lies in the south-eastern corner of the agora, with the base of four columns remaining. It may have replaced an earlier Greek temple. However, the Roman temple is believed to have been built in honour of Aesculapius, the god of healing. The rubble also contains a poorly preserved floor mosaic.

The most distinctive of the agora's monuments is the reconstructed **Naval Monument**, originally built by the Ptolemies in the 3rd century BC in celebration of a naval victory. This stunning statue features a wingless (and now headless) Victoria standing on the prow of a ship, flanked by two dolphins and holding the tritons of Neptune. The female form is wonderfully rendered, with clothing elegantly carved into the marble.

The **Tomb of Battus**, the leader of the settlers from Thera and first king of Cyrene, is now thought to lie behind the naval monument on the eastern side of the agora, although there is still some disagreement among archaeologists. The founder of the colony has the rare honour of being buried not only within the city walls but also in the principal square.

The **Sanctuary of Demeter and Kore**, an unusual circular structure, was the scene of a riotous, women-only, annual celebration and feast. As part of the festivities, the women of Cyrene proceeded from here to the **Temple of Demeter** outside the city walls. The statues represent goddesses of fertility. The cavities alongside the statues of the seated goddesses (3rd century BC) were used for offerings to the goddesses; the standing figures were added by the Romans.

Outside the agora's southern wall is the **Capitoleum**, the customary temple to the Greek trinity of Zeus, Hera and Athena (or, if you were Roman, Jupiter, Juno and Minerva).

From the northern side of the agora, a path leads down off the plateau and there are some superb views towards the Sanctuary of Apollo and across the coastal plain to the Mediterranean.

Sanctuary of Apollo

This rich collection of temples, baths and other public buildings sits on a ledge overlooking the plain.

The path down from the agora leads to the **Fountain of Apollo (Baths of Paris)**. This delightful spot under the cliff is a good place to rest in the shade to the accompaniment of a particularly vocal colony of frogs. This small thermal complex at the outlet of a natural spring was built in the 5th century AD. Note that around some of the pools are some small niches used for the personal possessions of the bathers or for oil lamps.

The sanctuary's ancient gateway is marked off to the east by the four Doric columns of the reconstructed **Greek Propylea** or Monumental Gateway (3rd century BC).

The **Temple of Apollo** was one of the earliest temples at Cyrene, with the foundations dating from the 6th century BC. The initial structure was little more than an open courtyard, but was soon enhanced by rows of six columns along two sides and eleven on the other two. Fragments of the temple's pediment suggest a representation of the nymph Cyrene strangling a lion. A statue of Apollo playing the lyre was found and is now in the British Museum. The temple was rebuilt during the 4th century BC, again with 34 columns. It was destroyed during the Jewish Revolt and what you see now is essentially a 2nd-century AD Roman building in the Greek Doric style (the columns are smooth, not fluted).

Immediately in front of the temple is the **monumental altar**, 22m long and made from limestone covered by marble slabs (6th century BC). Religious rites, including animal sacrifices, were carried out here. The great Greek poet of the age, Callimachus, describes in his famous Hymn to Apollo scenes of sacrificing bulls, the altar adorned with flowers and crowds of dancing young people. Note also the reconstructed **Sacred Fountain**, or nymphaeum, with its attractive lions and columns.

SANCTUARY OF APOLLO

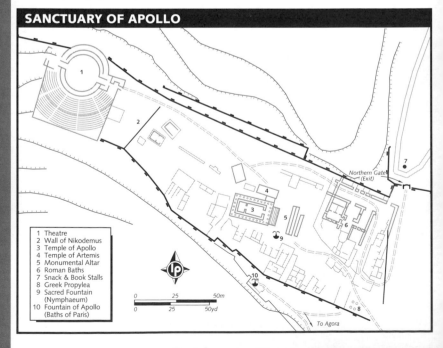

1 Theatre
2 Wall of Nikodemus
3 Temple of Apollo
4 Temple of Artemis
5 Monumental Altar
6 Roman Baths
7 Snack & Book Stalls
8 Greek Propylea
9 Sacred Fountain
   (Nymphaeum)
10 Fountain of Apollo
   (Baths of Paris)

Northern Gate
(Exit)

To Agora

On the northern side of the Temple of Apollo is the **Temple of Artemis**. The foundation was laid in the 6th century BC and is thought by some archaeologists to pre-date the Apollo temple. It consisted of a room, or cella, with columns in the centre. It may once have celebrated both Apollo and Artemis. Most of what you see now, including the marble portal, derives from the temple's rebuilding in the 4th century BC. In the remainder of the sanctuary are the barely visible remains of temples to Isis, Hecate and Latona, and the tomb of Hercules.

Theatre

Just west of the sanctuary is the spectacularly situated theatre, which could once seat 1000 spectators. Its original construction was by the Greeks and probably dates from the 6th century BC although it was much modified in subsequent centuries. In the 2nd century AD, the Romans transformed it into an amphitheatre in which the oval-shaped arena measured 33m by 29m. Seats, supported by struts built into the cliff, were constructed on the Mediterranean side. The slabs down the hillside are all that remains of this ambitious idea. The theatre affords a superb view over the sheer drop, and of the hillsides with occasional glimpses of the old necropolis and the sea.

Wall of Nikodemus

Separating the Sanctuary of Apollo from the theatre and built during the Roman era, this wall protected the much-frequented public buildings in the sanctuary from the wild animals in the amphitheatre. The wall is named after one of the priests of the Temple of Apollo.

Roman Baths

The Roman baths are the last buildings as you leave the site via the northern gate. Built in AD 98–99 under the emperor Trajan and restored by Hadrian, these baths contain some good mosaics and cipolin columns. The frigidarium is the best preserved room of the baths complex and contains a Latin inscription honouring Hadrian. There is also a apodyterium (changing room, where the statue of the Three Graces now in Tripoli's Jamahiriya Museum was found), tepidarium and calidarium. In December 1913, during a violent storm, a famous statue of Venus (or Aphrodite) of Cyrene wringing out her hair was unearthed; it now stands in the Museo Nazionale Romano in Rome.

Necropolis

Cut into cliff face along the old road down to Apollonia are the 2010 tombs of the old necropolis. Originally built by the Greeks in the 6th century BC, they were used and added to by the Romans and Byzantines right up until the 6th century AD. Many of the tombs were later used by nomads for habitation, some of them being quite spacious. Some contain traces of the original architectural facades. The hollows in front of some Greek tombs once held likenesses of Persephone, the goddess of death, while the Roman tombs held carved portraits of the deceased. On the hillside there are also some sarcophagi with lids.

Temple of Zeus

A steepish climb up the hill from the rest of the site is the famed Temple of Zeus, one of the highlights of Cyrene. Reflecting Cyrene's importance in the ancient Greek world, the Temple of Zeus was larger than the Parthenon in Athens. Constructed in the 5th century BC, the sanctuary measured 32m by 70m and was surrounded by two rows of eight and two rows of 17 columns. In the sanctuary itself there were two rows of Doric columns as well as two columns in the porch. On the main platform in the sanctuary was a statue of a seated Zeus holding Victory in his right hand and a sceptre in his left. Animal sacrifices were carried out in the temple; before then they were carried through the peristyle or porticoes. The ancient entrance was from the east. Under the Romans it was used as a temple of Jupiter while it also served the Greek/Libyan hybrid deity, Zeus Ammun.

The temple was restored under the emperor Augustus (27 BC–AD 14), but was then destroyed in AD 115 during the Jewish Revolt. Like many of Cyrene's public buildings, it was rebuilt in AD 120 by the Roman emperor Hadrian. After it was reduced to rubble by the AD 365 earthquake, it was ransacked by Christian zealots who called it a 'den of demons' in reference to the statues to ancient gods.

The temple is being comprehensively and painstakingly reconstructed by Italian archaeologists.

The rubble of the Hippodrome or racetrack area, which once had tiered seating, is on the same plateau nearby.

Museum

At the time of research, Cyrene was badly lacking a museum. That is set to change – a site for a museum has been set aside south-east of the Temple of Zeus.

[Continued from page 174]

Susa has a petrol station and some well-stocked grocery stores along the main street, close to the main post office.

Places to Stay

Qaryat Susa as-Siyahe (Susa Tourist Village; ☎ *636551)* Doubles with bath 30LD. Susa's only place to stay, 4.2km west of the petrol station or 1km west of the checkpoint on the road from Cyrene, has spacious rooms, most with a balcony overlooking the sea. Some of the sheets could be cleaner and the plumbing is notoriously unreliable. For an insultingly small breakfast, you pay an extra 5LD; for dinner, the *restaurant* is slightly better. The beach isn't bad.

While we were in Susa, the *Funduq al-Manara*, superbly located between the museum and the entrance to ancient Apollonia, was under construction and due to open in 2002. Also planned is the ambitious *Susa Beach Resort*, 2.5km west of the town centre.

Getting There & Away

There is little, if any, public transport to Susa. A private taxi from Shahat costs 10LD one way or 25LD return (including waiting time).

APOLLONIA　　　　　سوسه

Apollonia does not, and never did, rival the splendour of Cyrene, but it's still one of the best ancient sites of Cyrenaica and well worth a visit.

History

Apollonia was the harbour for Cyrene, 18km west, and because of this it played a critical role in the prosperity of Cyrene and the other cities of the Pentapolis. Archaeological evidence gathered to date suggests that the city was operating as a port as early as the 7th century BC. It served a similar purpose under the Romans and even came to rival Cyrene in significance in the late Roman period, as it was considered to be less vulnerable to attack than cities further inland. After Diocletian, the city was for a time the seat of Roman Governors in the province of Libya Superior.

Most of what remains today dates from the Byzantine era (from the 5th to 6th century AD) when Apollonia was known as the 'city of churches'. It had five basilicas and 19 towers.

Ancient City

The ruins of Apollonia are strung out along a narrow strip of coastline – they stretch westwards for about 1km from the entrance to the Greek theatre.

Apollonia's ticket office *(admission 3LD, camera/video 5/10LD; open 7.30am-7pm daily May-Sept, 8am-5pm Oct-Apr)* is on the waterfront at the northern end of the modern town. Two excellent guides to the ancient city are Ali Mahmud or Mahmoud Abu Shreet (50LD).

Of the Byzantine city's five churches, four are within the city walls and the fifth is just outside the walls to the south. The **Western Church** is just near the entrance, with the western wall of the city running around the apse. The four green columns in the sanctuary are of Roman origin and, like much of

---

Silphium

The great wealth that fed Cyrene's growth as a metropolis of monumental grandeur was fed in part by its agricultural abundance. Primary among its crops was the indigenous *silphium* plant, which was much sought after in the ancient world. Now extinct, this plant, which is similar to wild fennel, was harvested on the highlands of the plateau inland of Cyrene. The list of claimed properties for silphium is quite extravagant, but there is little doubt that its sap was used as a medicine (a purgative and antiseptic) and as a dressing added to food. There is also some suggestion that silphium was a highly effective aphrodisiac – which may explain its almost-mythical importance. The plant was so highly prized that its image appeared on the city's coinage. Around Cyrene and Apollonia you may see carved representations of the plant. There is a modern drawing in the museum at Susa.

CYRENAICA

Apollonia, were used by resourceful Byzantines in later construction; the four white columns are wholly Byzantine. The church was originally covered with a wooden roof and the floor was entirely marble. The cisterns at the eastern end lead to the baptistry in the north-eastern corner and there are some mosaic fragments on the floor.

A short distance east is the **Central Church**. Its marble floor is better preserved; in the main sanctuary are some fine pillars adorned with Byzantine crosses, the globe of Atlas and representations of the silphium plant. Outside the main sanctuary on the western side, you should note the bench reserved for the bishop to rest on after the strenuous task of presiding over communion and, to the north, the tiny child's baptistry. North of the church is the rubble of **Byzantine baths**.

The **Roman baths** just east of the Central Church date from the 2nd century AD. The columns lining the eastern side have Roman capitols dating from AD 138, while the drums, clearly visible within the columns, are Greek. In the north-eastern corner of the main building is the **gymnasium** – pottery from the Greek (black) and Roman (red) eras is scattered about. Immediately south of the gymnasium is the frigidarium.

Above the baths on the hill is the **Byzantine Duke's Palace**, once one of the biggest palaces in Cyrenaica. The first room after you enter from the north was a waiting room and library; note the huge stone shelves reserved for large books. The western section of the palace was the domain of the duke and his family. The private chapel (one of the city's five churches) is reached by passing under some well-executed stone arches. In the chapel, the elegant curve of the apse is a feature as is the throne room leading off the main room. There were 83 rooms in the eastern wing, used as quarters for servants and soldiers. A small staircase leads up to the highest point, formerly the home of the leading officer, which enabled him to keep an eye on his troops and the remainder of the palace. Close to the foot of the staircase is a large, black stone, once used by the Romans to seal their wells.

The Earthquake of AD 365

If one event signalled the final decline of the Roman Empire in North Africa, it was the earthquake in AD 365. There had been earthquakes before – in AD 306 and AD 262 – but this one brought centuries of civilisation crashing down. With its epicentre in the Mediterranean, near Cyprus, its devastating power wrought havoc from Sabratha in the west to Apollonia in the east. So powerful was the quake that parts of these cities, including Apollonia's entire port, disappeared into the sea and the great cities of Cyrene and Leptis Magna were reduced to rubble. The empire that had conquered the world was brought to its knees and never recovered.

North-east of the palace and down the hill are **Byzantine houses** and the **Eastern Church,** in its heyday the biggest church in Cyrenaica. Huge columns of cipolin marble once divided the nave and aisles, forming transepts; many are still standing. The marble was shipped from the Greek island Paros, while the granite slabs used to close off the knave came from Egypt. Although this was among the earliest of the churches (5th century AD), some mosaics remain. Other features to watch out for are the two sacrificial altars and baptistry.

After you've explored the church, follow the path above the beach to the **storage rooms** cut into the wall – goods being shipped awaited distribution or loading here. In the rock wall are two arched **cisterns**. On the beach itself the two stone-tower bases protruding from the sand were once used as **pottery and amphora stores**. Into the beach's southern wall are wedged hundreds of pottery shards. It is believed that this was the site of a **pottery factory**; the blackened sections indicate that there was a kiln here. The ancient harbour, now underwater, lay out to the north. Visible offshore, Hammam Island was, before the quake, connected to the mainland and home to a lighthouse. The underwater ruins, including a ship of 22 hands, would make for fantastic snorkelling, but the authorities are understandably reluctant to allow it for fear of damage from treasure seekers. The beach is still a good place for a swim, although you should ask your guide before taking a dip; if you don't have a guide, someone will soon turn up if you're doing the wrong thing.

From the small hill above the cisterns, you can see down to the five perfectly circular holes cut from the rock. These were the **olive oil tanks** of the Byzantine city. To their right is an enormous **fish tank** (4th century AD) from where the townsfolk could come to choose their evening meal.

The remains of the Greek **acropolis** (tombs) are to the south-east, and over the hill to the east is the plunging **Greek theatre**, which stood outside the walls of the ancient city. The view is wonderful and somehow rendered more poignant by the lone palm tree standing by the stage. There are also remains of the Roman **necropolis** off to the east and south.

Apollonia Museum

The museum *(admission 3LD, camera/ video 5/10LD; open 7.30am-7pm Tues-Sun Apr-Sept, 8am-5pm Tues-Sun Oct-May)* is a short distance south-west of the site entrance. The dusty exhibits aren't bad but are poorly labelled.

In the centre of the main entrance room is a fragment of a 2nd- to 3rd-century AD Roman tomb, which was found in front of the Western Church. On the left as you enter the main entrance room is a modern drawing of the silphium plant. The room also contains mosaics from the Byzantine church at Ras al-Hillal.

The museum also contains a motley array of Islamic tablets, items of Libyan folklore, marble, alabaster, glass and pottery pieces in desperate need of enlightening labels. In the case of the pottery, the black indicates Greek origin, the red is Roman, while yellow pieces date from the Byzantines.

Among the items of special interest is a line drawing, dating from 1825 and by a French artist, portraying the construction of the Greek Theatre – it can be found in the south-eastern room.

Worth seeking out in the south-western room are the elegant tablet reliefs from L'Atrun Church, the exquisite door frame from the Byzantine Duke's Palace and four mosaics found in the Eastern Church.

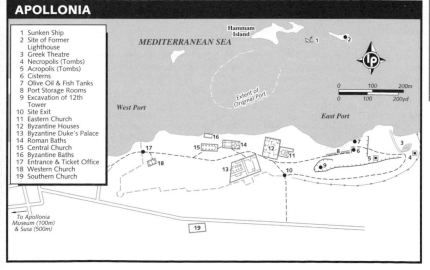

APOLLONIA

1 Sunken Ship
2 Site of Former Lighthouse
3 Greek Theatre
4 Necropolis (Tombs)
5 Acropolis (Tombs)
6 Cisterns
7 Olive Oil & Fish Tanks
8 Port Storage Rooms
9 Excavation of 12th Tower
10 Site Exit
11 Eastern Church
12 Byzantine Houses
13 Byzantine Duke's Palace
14 Roman Baths
15 Central Church
16 Byzantine Baths
17 Entrance & Ticket Office
18 Western Church
19 Southern Church

Hammam Island

MEDITERRANEAN SEA

West Port

East Port

Extent of Original Port

To Apollonia Museum (100m) & Susa (500m)

CYRENAICA

KAF HAWAFTE   كهف الهوافت

Kaf Hawafte is reportedly the largest cave in North Africa and, although containing little of interest, is worth a look if you're a cave enthusiast. The opening is visible 100m south of the road, 8.4km east of Susa.

RAS AL-HILLAL   رأس الحلال

The area around Ras al-Hillal, 30km east of Susa, has the most dramatic scenery along the Libyan coast. For the full effect, Ras al-Hillal is best approached from the west. Coming up over the rise, you are confronted with a beautiful arc of bay, with a backdrop of towering mountains and a canyon-like valley running into the Jebel Akhdar. Knud Holmboe explains the experience well:

It was a marvellous morning, and I have rarely seen anything so beautiful as this mountainous country. Colour was everywhere, from the sky which formed a deep blue arch over my head, to the thousand shades of green in the woods all around. The ground was thickly strewn with all kinds of flowers, and black and brownish-red butterflies fluttered among the gaily coloured blooms. Here the rocks, even where they were bare, were not grey, but displayed a wealth of colour.

Knud Holmboe, *Desert Encounter*

These days, the effect is made more stark by the fact that the hillsides remain scarred by a fire, which swept along the mountains in the mid-1990s.

Ras al-Hillal was, for a time, the second port of Cyrene, after Apollonia, although nothing remains to suggest this. At the eastern end of town is a nice small beach, behind which is a natural fresh water spring – ideal for showers.

The road behind the town climbs into the mountains, with some fine views en route. After 14km, the picturesque **Shallal Ras al-Hillal** waterfall, which flows virtually year-round, is visible on the left. The valley shelves are an excellent place for a picnic. Climbing still further, you reach a plateau, which is also a good place to rest and then to set off exploring the Jebel Akhdar on foot. Around 2.5km beyond the waterfall is a fork in the road. The left branch leads up towards the **Greek Tombs** either side of the road for

about 1km. A few of these lonely sentinels are surrounded by sunken graves as well as ancient wheel ruts hewn into the rock. Near the northernmost tomb are the simple remains of **Ras al-Hillal Church**; its mosaics can now be seen in the Apollonia Museum.

To explore the valley, you'll need your own vehicle or have to rely on very limited hitching opportunities.

At the time of research, the only place to stay in Ras al-Hillal was the run-down, summer-only tourist village. There was, however, a new tourist village nearing completion at the western end of the bay, promising decent bungalow-style accommodation; it could be a great place to relax for a few days.

L'ATRUN   الأثرون

The small town of L'Atrun, 9km east of Ras al-Hillal and 29km west of Derna, contains better-preserved Byzantine churches than Ras al-Hillal. The **Western Church** stands on a bluff above the Mediterranean and must have been a spectacular place to worship. The walls of the church are still intact and the sanctuary is strewn with marble pillars, some of which are marked with a carved Byzantine cross. Just outside the sanctuary walls are abandoned grave covers, with carved cross, snake and other motifs.

The less dramatic **Eastern Church** lies over the hill 150m to the east. To reach it, you skirt a steep, rocky cove with cave tombs gouged into the rock.

The main road runs along the southern side of L'Atrun. A small wadi runs down to the road from the mountains, just west of which is a small road running north (there's a nondescript sand-coloured building with a green roof on the corner). Take this road, which runs towards the sea. After 150m, turn left at the T-junction. A further 100m, opposite the driveway to a house, walk towards the sea by skirting the ploughed fields. It's a further 100m to the Western Church.

DERNA   درنة

☎ 081 • pop 110,000

Derna is situated around the outlet of an attractive wadi. The valley's steep sides are filled with lush vegetation, although most of it has been consumed by Derna's urban sprawl. The city's main attraction is Shallal Derna, a waterfall at the top of the wadi.

The city itself is attractive enough, especially around the older quarter. The waterfront is a bleak place, the preserve of shabby concrete apartment blocks. The main square in the old town is surrounded by small cafes and there is also a covered souq, which is well worth a look around for its local colour.

Orientation & Information

Sharia al-Corniche runs along the waterfront from the western end of town, where there is the Masraf al-Jamahiriya bank, to the harbour. Along this road you'll find a few cheap hotels and Derna's best restaurant. The old town lies about 1km south of the corniche, with the main square and Masjed as-Sahab at its heart; there are more hotels in this area.

Masjed as-Sahab

This mosque, not far from the main square, is a fine example of modern Islamic archi-

tecture. Built largely of sandstone, it has two fine minarets with lattice windows halfway up the tower, a large open courtyard and lovely red calligraphic motifs above the archways.

Shallal Derna

Shallal Derna is 8km out of town and can be reached by the road south, called Bab Shallal, which winds up the hillside behind the town. The wadi is crossed by a bridge, close to which is one of the largest sinkholes in the world. Normally the water is just a trickle. It is a popular walk from the bridge along the floor of the wadi up to the waterfall. The walk takes about one hour and you need good, sturdy boots. The road continues past the bridge up to the waterfall, a further 4km south.

Places to Stay

Funduq al-Bahr (☎ *626506, Sharia al-Corniche*) Singles/doubles with shared bath 10/15LD. From the outside, this grim place seems to be slowly shedding its skin. Inside, the poorly maintained rooms aren't much better. Price is the only virtue here.

Funduq al-Medina (☎ *625401, fax 622463*) Singles/doubles with shared bath from 10/ 15LD, suites 30/35LD. This would be an excellent choice – centrally located, clean rooms and friendly management – if the rooms had private bathrooms. Even the small suite, which comes with satellite TV and a small kitchen, has the toilet outside. The hotel is in a lane west off the main square, 300m west of the Masjed as-Sahab.

Funduq al-Jebel al-Akhdar (☎ *622303, Main Square*) Singles/doubles with bath 15/25LD, suites 65LD. This hotel, 200m west of the Masjed as-Sahab, must have been nice once, but it's now a hoary old place with a distinctly abandoned air. The rooms are plain and a little dusty, while the huge suite is no more luxurious than the other rooms, although it could conceivably sleep eight people. The meals are similarly uninspiring and cost 10LD per person. Entrance is from the square around the back.

Funduq al-Ferdous (☎ *633570, fax 626146, Sharia Rafal Ansari*) Singles/

Round One to Libya

The western entrance to Derna is marked by a huge sign emblazoned with '1805' in big yellow numbers. It symbolises a proud moment in Derna's, and indeed Libya's, history. In 1801, Yusuf Karamanli (the autonomous Ottoman ruler of Libya) tried to coerce the newly independent United States of America into paying an annual tribute (glorified protection money) of US$250,000. When the USA offered just US$18,000 in return, the insulted Karamanli ordered the sacking of the US consulate in Tripoli. The Americans interpreted this as an act of war, and not for the last time, despatched a warship, the USS *Philadelphia*, to the Libyan coast. The ship was overrun and the crew taken prisoner in Derna. Only when US forces, assisted by Arab horsemen, Greek mercenaries and dissident members of Yusuf's own family, captured the town was the confrontation (1801–05) resolved. The Americans paid US$68,000 and Karamanli emerged as something of a local hero.

doubles with bath & breakfast 15/25LD, doubles with bath & air-con 35LD. Funduq al-Ferdous offers the best value for money in Derna and is certainly better than its exterior suggests. The whole place is well run, the rooms are clean and there's a pool table in the reception area. Most rooms have a TV. This hotel is signposted in Arabic at the western end of the Corniche, although it's about 1km inland – ask for *'Nadi Darnus'* (Derna Club), which is very close by.

Places to Eat

There are plenty of **snack bars** along the streets west of the mosque. All do hamburgers (around 1LD) and some also do shwarmas (1LD to 2LD) and pizzas (1LD to 5LD).

Mat'am Sal-Sabil (☎ 624863, Sharia al-Corniche) Meals 8.5LD to 13.5LD. Open noon-11pm Sat-Thur, 2pm-11pm Fri. This restaurant, 450m west of the harbour, serves reasonably priced meals and also makes hamburgers (1LD). Whatever you choose, you'll be served, somewhat incongruously, by bow-tied waiters gliding effortlessly across marble-tiled floors.

Getting There & Away

The shared-taxi station is about 2km east of the town centre. Taxis run east to Tobruk (5.5LD) and on to the Egyptian border (9LD). To the west, shared taxis run to Al-Bayda (2.5LD) via Shahat (2.5LD) and Benghazi (7LD).

Getting Around

Every second car in Derna seems to be a private taxi. Most journeys around town should cost 1LD. A private taxi to Shallal Derna should cost 15LD return, including waiting time; on Friday, when locals flock to the waterfall for a picnic, you may find cheaper shared taxis (0.25LD to 0.5LD).

Eastern Cyrenaica

TOBRUK   طـبـرق

☎ 087 • pop 140,000

Tobruk – 142km west of the Egyptian border and the scene of some of the most im-portant WWII battles – is a household word. Its only drawcard is the war cemeteries.

Apart from that, Tobruk is completely uninspiring – bear in mind that the town was fiercely contested for its strategic significance, not its aesthetic beauty. If you're arriving from Egypt across the desert, the lights of Tobruk can be a welcoming sight. That's about as good as it gets, although while we were there the new governor had, after years of official neglect, instituted a massive public works campaign.

Al-Nahr Sinai (The Great Man-Made River) can't come quickly enough to Tobruk. Until it does, avoid drinking the local water, which is very salty.

Orientation & Information

All roads in Tobruk lead to the harbour. The road from Egypt is lined with WWII sites and enters town at the western end of the harbour, next to Funduq al-Masira. From the west, the main road from Derna cuts through the centre of town to the harbour; the shared-taxi station is near its eastern end. A new ring road encircles the north of the city and runs into the north-western corner of the harbour. The compact city centre, home to Libyan Arab Airlines, the main post office and most of the banks and cheap hotels, is on the hill overlooking the harbour from the north.

Almnahel Cafenet Club (☎ 627206, e almnahel-cafenet@hotmail.com), 3B Sharia Omar al-Mukhtar, is also in the city centre. It's open 10am to 11pm Saturday to Thursday and 2pm to 11pm Friday, and charges 3LD per hour.

WWII Cemeteries

Tobruk's WWII cemeteries *(open 9am-5pm Sat-Thur, 2pm-5pm Fri)* are well maintained. There are cemeteries for most of the major participating nations, except for Italy (its government repatriated all the bodies of slain Italian soldiers).

Cemetery registers are kept in a safe at the gate of the two Commonwealth cemeteries (Knightsbridge and Tobruk); these list the names of fallen soldiers, in alphabetical order, with a corresponding row number and letter to assist in finding a specific grave. Sadly, many Muslim graves are not listed.

Knightsbridge (Acroma) Cemetery The Knightsbridge Cemetery, 20km west of town, is the largest in Tobruk. Contained within its walls are 3649 graves. Of these 2663 are of known soldiers and 986 unknown (most of these have headstones marked 'Known unto God'). The nationalities represented highlight the massive loss of life in this tragic period of history: United Kingdom (1584/703 known/unknown); New Zealand (435/61); South Africa (363/47); Australia (240/63); India (8/3); as well as Canada (15 known), France (two), Greece (12), Poland (two) and Yugoslavia (two). Among the graves are the bodies of two soldiers who were awarded the prestigious Victoria Cross.

Unlike most of the other cemeteries, Knightsbridge is on the site of an actual battleground. The large white cross overseeing the thousands of headstones lends the place an air of tranquillity.

Tobruk (Commonwealth) War Cemetery The Tobruk (Commonwealth) War Cemetery, 6km south of the harbour on the road to the Egyptian border, also has an air of simplicity and dignity. This cemetery contains 2479 graves – not all are from Commonwealth countries, but simply those who fought for the Allied cause. The countries most represented include Australia, India, New Zealand, South Africa, the United Kingdom and Poland. There are also two soldiers buried here who were awarded the Victoria Cross.

French Cemetery Most of the over 300 soldiers buried here died in the Battle of Bir Hakim, 80km south-east of Tobruk, in May and June 1942. The graves are marked with simple crosses inscribed with each soldier's name and regiment. The bodies of Muslim soldiers who fought alongside the French are also buried here.

The French Cemetery is behind a sandstone gate and walls, 8km south of the harbour and on the corner of the road to Al-Jaghbub. If the main gate isn't open, reach through to open the smaller side gate.

German Cemetery The names of 6026 German soldiers are inscribed in mosaic slabs lining the inside walls of the forbidding sandstone fort overlooking the harbour. The fort was built by the Germans although probably not for this purpose. It's often closed but there's usually someone around who can help find the key *(miftah)*. The cemetery is signposted east off the road to the Egyptian border, 3.2km south of the harbour; ask for *'maqbara al-manya'*.

Other WWII Sites

Trenches During the Siege of Tobruk, the city was completely encircled by 25km of defence lines or trenches. The most easily accessible are just north of the road to the Egyptian border, 18.4km from the harbour; the trenches are not signposted and are just past the huge factory to the north, which sends up huge clouds of white dust.

The four lines of concrete trenches were built by Italian and Australian soldiers. The Australians and Germans, who rarely fought in Tobruk itself, faced off in a bloody war of attrition here. The trenches have silted up over the years, but some key elements are still visible, including large, sunken tank platforms as well as smaller Browning gun emplacements. In places, stairs lead to underground bunkers, some of which are still quite deep.

On the north side of the trenches is Wadi Dalia, a shallow valley whose walls are riddled with caves. It was in this wadi that hundreds of Australians died from aerial bombardment.

It's a good idea to wear boots or shoes, rather than sandals, when visiting, as the area is strewn with rusted WWII-vintage barbed wire.

Australian (Fig Tree) Hospital Between the Knightsbridge Cemetery and Tobruk, this former Australian field dressing station is often known simply as the Fig Tree. This shady spot on the now-peaceful plains surrounding Tobruk was an ideal location for a hospital, with its deep natural caves (now heavily silted up) and shelter offered by fig trees a few kilometres from the front line. It was also connected by a ridge to the battlefields of Knightsbridge.

Travel east along the main road to Tobruk from Knightsbridge Cemetery for 11.9km. Take the turn-off to the south for 1.7km.

Rommel's Operations Room This poorly maintained site in the heart of Tobruk, 600m north of the western end of the harbour, includes the bunker (not open to the public) from where Rommel directed operations; the maroon-tiled roof gives an idea of the scale. In the same square are an assortment of WWII memorabilia, including a small tank, anti-aircraft guns, an old cannon and a 40-tonne antiship gun, which once faced the sea from Tobruk's highest point.

Behind the white wall immediately to the east are the rusting remains of the *Lady Bijot*, a US B-24 bomber, which inexplicably disappeared off the radar in June 1942. It was not until 1963 that the wreckage of the plane was discovered in a remote stretch of desert near Sarir. The skeletons of the crew were strung out for 12km around the crash site.

Places to Stay

Funduq al-Jellah (☎ 622310) Dorm beds 7LD, singles/doubles with shared bath 9/14LD. This place is typical of the genre – bare, basic and dusty. If you can afford to stay somewhere else, do so.

Funduq al-Amawi (☎ 622043, Sharia Omar al-Mukhtar) Singles/doubles/triples with shared bath 10/15/22LD. This place, 50m north of the white mosque, is marginally better, though similarly spartan. The highlight is the ice-cream parlour downstairs.

Funduq al-Jebel al-Akhdar (☎ 6261 28/30). Singles with sink & shared bath 15LD, doubles with bath 30LD. These rooms are better but definitely overpriced. Most are pretty simple, many a tad dreary, but the ones with a harbour view are not quite so bad. The hotel's claim to fame is that Rommel stayed in Room 319, report-

The Rats of Tobruk

The Rats of Tobruk are among the best-known soldiers in Australian military history and an integral part of the country's mythology. Some 14,270 Australian soldiers (out of a total 24,000 troops) participated in the Siege of Tobruk, which lasted from 10 April 1941 until 10 December 1941 – 240 days spanning a fierce Libyan summer and inflicting its first major WWII defeat on the German army.

The aim was to halt the advance into Egypt of the German Afrika Korps to buy time for the Allied forces in Egypt to resupply and reinforce their ranks. The besieged Allies were supplied by a motley array of seafaring vessels, known variously as the Tobruk Ferry Service, the Junks or the Scrap Iron Flotilla, which made the highly dangerous Spud Run into Tobruk Harbour.

At the time of the siege, a Radio Berlin announcer denounced the Australians as the 'rats of Tobruk', comparing them to rats burrowing underground and caught in a trap, in a bid to destroy their morale. Instead, the Australians turned the name into a badge of honour and source of amusement. A famous photo shows a Bren gun carrier with the words 'Rats to you' painted on the side and an unofficial medal with a rodent on it was struck from the aluminium of a downed German plane.

Seven months after the Australians were finally evacuated, on 20 June 1942, German field marshal Rommel's army launched a fresh assault and Tobruk fell in a day.

edly for only four hours – he was obviously a man of simple tastes. The *restaurant* serves unexciting meals for 10LD to 15LD.

If you can afford to pay more, the options are much better.

Funduq Qartaj (☎ 623043, 620442, Ring Road, postal address: PO Box 60 Tobruk) Twins with shared bath from 20LD, twins/triples with bath 30/45LD. This is a fine choice, although its location, about 2km north-west of the harbour, leaves it a bit out on a limb. The rooms are clustered in groups of three and open out onto a shared sitting room with a TV. These clusters can easily be transformed into a secure seven-bed apartment (100LD), which is ideal for groups. The cosy *restaurant* serves decent meals for 15LD (drinks are extra).

Funduq al-Masira (☎ 625761, fax 625769, postal address: PO Box 699, Tobruk) Singles/doubles with bath 35/45LD, doubles with fridge 50LD, ground/upper floor suites 55/90LD, villas 70LD. This concrete eyesore on the south-western corner of the harbour also happens to be Tobruk's finest hotel. The rooms, with satellite TV, are semiluxurious, although the concrete struts – supposedly design features – annoyingly rob you of most of the little view Tobruk has to offer (then again, maybe that was the point). The four-bed harbourside villas are ideal for families. Avoid the restaurant, which is completely lacking in atmosphere, overpriced and serves mediocre food in meagre portions.

Places to Eat

The largest concentration of *cheap restaurants* are in the city centre, in the streets fanning out from the main post office. There are also a couple of outdoor *sandwich places* along the western end of the harbour, opposite Nadi Sukkur (Falcon Sports Club).

Mat'am Qartaj (☎ 620136, Tobruk Harbour) Meals 5LD to 15LD. Open 1pm-3.30pm & 6.30pm-10pm daily. Run by the hotel of the same name, Mat'am Qartaj serves good meals at reasonable prices. With all the roadworks, it's hard to tell what will happen to the surrounds, but the outdoor tables by the water should continue to be a good place to spend a summer's evening. Look for the lurid green lighting under the hill on the northern side of the harbour.

Mat'am ad-Dolphin (Shariakat ad-Dolphin; ☎ 625050) Meals 20LD. Open noon-11.30pm daily. This excellent restaurant almost makes the tedium of Tobruk seem worthwhile. Run by the charismatic and hospitable Georgia, this place does Greek cooking with a Libyan flavour. There are outdoor tables by the water or an elevated dining room with modern murals painted by local artists. You get top-notch cuisine and service that doesn't miss a beat.

A delicious and generous banquet of octopus with macaroni, fish, rice, french fries, fish soup, Greek salad and drinks is a bargain at 20LD. The restaurant is at the northeastern tip of the harbour, 3.5km east of the city centre; a taxi there should cost no more than 3LD, although you may have to ask it to return later.

Getting There & Away

Air Given that Tobruk is about as far east as you can go in Libya, those returning to Tripoli may want to consider flying at least one way. There are three flights weekly in either direction between Tripoli and Tobruk (44/88LD one way/return).

The Libyan Arab Airlines office (☎ 622 681) is on the east side of the square, diagonally opposite Funduq al-Jebel al-Akhdar.

Shared Taxi Shared taxis leave from the open parking lot at the eastern end of the main road in from Derna, just before it meets the western end of the harbour. Taxis leave a few times a day for: Ajdabiya (10LD), Al-Bayda (10LD), Benghazi (12.5LD), Derna (5.5LD), the Egyptian border (5LD) and Shahat (for Cyrene; 9LD). Taxis to Al-Jaghbub (6LD) leave infrequently.

Car & Motorcycle If you need to get to Benghazi in a hurry, consider taking the desert road to Ajdabiya. The distance is the same as going around the coast, but the minimal traffic and gun-barrel straightness of the road makes it much quicker. It can also be good for doubling back towards Tripolitania. But be warned: There is no petrol beyond Tobruk's outskirts for a distance of 380km.

Getting Around

If you want to see every one of the WWII sites listed in this section, expect to pay 25LD and take a minimum of three to four hours, depending on your negotiating skills and how much time you plan to spend on a private taxi.

AL-JAGHBUB الجغبوب

The remote desert oasis of Al-Jaghbub is actually closer to the Egyptian town of Siwa

Graziani's Fence

In February 1931, the Italian Government decided to build a barbed-wire fence stretching from the Mediterranean port of Bardia to the oasis of Al-Jaghbub a mere 270km away. Supervised by armoured patrols and the air force, the fence sought to cut off the rebels from their supply sources and contacts with the Sanusi leadership in Egypt. The construction of the fence was begun in April and completed in September. This move, along with the deportation of almost the entire population of the Jebel Akhdar, was decisive and precipitated the end of the rebellion. This extraordinary barbed-wire monstrosity still runs along the Libyan-Egyptian border from near Tobruk, finishing at Al-Jaghbub whereupon the desolate Great Sand Sea begins.

than it is to any Libyan town of note. Supported by reservoirs of fresh underground water and a healthy supply of dates, the town is famous for its hard-won self-sufficiency. Wheat, fruit and vegetables (peppers, tomatoes and potato) are also grown here.

As the once-fiercely defended redoubt of the Sanusi Movement and home of a long-disappeared Islamic university of world renown, modern Al-Jaghbub is a little disappointing. In the centre of town is the unremarkable rubble of the former **Sanusi Palace**. There are also some decaying, largely untouched, two-storey **traditional houses** built of rock and palm trunks. If you do make it this far, you're likely to be the only tourist in town – an increasingly rare event in Libya.

Outside the town are a number of worthwhile natural sites worth visiting, including two **salt lakes** in the desert, namely Fredga (about 8km east of town) and the larger Malfa (about 6km east). Even more impressive, around 4km south of town, is a small forest of **fossilised trees**.

There are no hotels in Al-Jaghbub, although if you ask around for Salheen (everybody seems to know him), he can usually arrange a room for you in town or a place to pitch your tent. The lakes attract swarms of mosquitoes.

If you are heading out this way, let someone know, as this is a border area and your unannounced presence may arouse suspicion. Contact Ali, the public relations manager at Funduq al-Masira in Tobruk and he can usually make the necessary notifications (there are no phone lines to Al-Jaghbub).

There are only occasional shared taxis linking Al-Jaghbub with Tobruk (6LD).

The Jebel Nafusa & Ghadames

The Jebel Nafusa, or Western Mountains, stretch from southern Tunisia in the west to Al-Qusbat, near Al-Khoms, in the east. The most rewarding area for visitors is between Nalut in the west, close to the Tunisian border, and Gharyan.

The landscape includes barren mountains, rocky escarpments and large areas of land suitable for agriculture. In the mountains, the summer climate is less punishing than in the desert or on the coastal plains, although it can get very cold in winter with – believe it or not – occasional snowfalls.

The Berber heartland of the semiarid Jebel Nafusa yields some spectacular scenery, with stone villages overlooking the Sahel al-Jefara (Jefara Plain) from their perch high above. Even more evocative are the vestiges of Berber troglodyte architecture that resemble something from a fairytale.

This is one of the few areas in Libya where Berber culture still thrives and you're likely to hear Berber dialects being spoken, although all signs are in Arabic. The region is known for its social and religious conservatism, which manifests itself in a certain reserve rather than any hostility towards outsiders. The Berbers' history of independence has also fostered a reputation for self-sufficiency that sees them prefer to eke out a hard-won existence over accepting government handouts.

The mountains peter out, giving way to the epic harshness of the Sahara, which stretches from northern Libya to the heart of the African continent. On the northern reaches of the world's greatest desert is the enchanting oasis of Ghadames, one of the most extensive ancient caravan towns anywhere in the Sahara.

The road system in this area is like a horizontal ladder, where north-south 'rungs' connect two main roads that both run from east to west. The fast, northern main road runs from Bir Ayyad to Nalut, and the slower, but more picturesque, southern main road runs from Gharyan to Nalut. Frequent

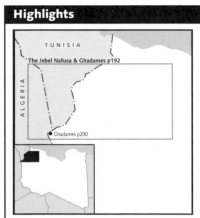

Highlights

TUNISIA

The Jebel Nafusa & Ghadames p192

ALGERIA

Ghadames p200

- Lose yourself in the labyrinthine lanes of the old city in Ghadames.
- Explore the medieval Berber *qasrs* (fortified granaries) of Qasr al-Haj, Nalut and Kabaw.
- Wander through the stone villages of the Jebel Nafusa.

smaller roads run between the northern and southern roads to serve mountain villages.

Infrequent public transport and limited accommodation options mean that it's easier to explore the mountains in your own vehicle. Most places, with the exception of Nalut and Ghadames, can be visited as part of a long day trip from Tripoli or Zuara. If there are enough of you to bring costs down, hiring a car or arranging an expedition with one of Tripoli's or Zuara's tour companies can be the best way to go.

GHARYAN
غريان

☎ 041 • pop 135,000

Gharyan sprawls across the top of a plateau and is one of the last towns of any size before Sebha, 690km south across the desert. By virtue of its elevation above the coastal plain, Gharyan escapes the worst of the

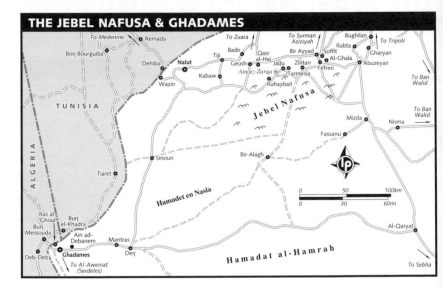

summer heat. Its attractions as a centre of pottery production and underground Berber houses could easily be absorbed in a few hours but most people stay overnight to prepare for, or recover from, the rigours of long-haul desert travel.

Most of the facilities you'll need are within easy walking distance of Funduq Rabta on Sharia al-Jamahiriya. Two blocks east is the post office (look for the usual telecommunications mast), which has a couple of banks nearby. In the same complex as the hotel is an Internet cafe, Al-Fagher Office (☎ 632692), which is open 9am to 1pm and 2pm to 10pm Saturday to Thursday; it charges 3LD per hour. In the same building is a cinema, with sessions (1LD) at 6pm, 7.30pm and 9.30pm, as well as a bank and barber. One of two small gift and handicraft shops in the lobby of Funduq Rabta sells camera film.

Berber Houses

Gharyan's main attractions are its underground houses, built by the ancient Berber inhabitants of the area. Their unique design arose very much from the environment in which the Berbers lived. Underground houses provided a refuge from cold winters,

hot summers and invaders – the houses were invisible to all but those within a few hundred metres. All of Gharyan's houses have been abandoned by their owners for modern housing and some are now used as storage pens for animals.

The most accessible houses are close to Funduq Rabta. Walk 400m south (right as you leave the hotel) and then turn right again. One is about 50m along on the left behind a 3m-high white wall with two large pottery amphorae atop the gate. The site is usually left open (no charge), but you'll have to ask around for the key *(miftah)* to be able to climb down into the house. The living quarters are at the base of a dramatic circular pit, with a radius of about 10m, cut three storeys deep into the earth. Rooms were cut into the base of the walls encircling what must have been a pleasant courtyard to spend a summer afternoon. Houses like this were once home to as many as three families. The wooden door at ground level opens to a tunnel that leads down into the house consisting of living rooms, a kitchen, bedrooms and storage areas.

There are up to four similar houses in the surrounding streets. Most lie hidden in

DOUG MCKINLAY

PATRICK SYDER

ANTHONY HAM

Cyrene is almost worth visiting for its coastal setting alone (top right). The significance of this former Greek outpost is demonstrated by its scale and the quality of its embellishments, eg, the statues of two goddesses in the Sanctuary of Demeter and Kore (top left) and the Temple of Zeus (bottom).

Impressive desert edifices: a covered walkway with an elegant arch motif in Ghadames' old city (top left); exploring the 700-year-old *qasr* (fortified granary) with its 400 chambers in Nalut's old town (top right); and one of seven early Islamic tombs that grace the desert just outside Zueila (bottom).

high-walled compounds and can be difficult to find. Seek directions from your hotel; ask for '*dammous*'.

Pottery

Gharyan is famous throughout Libya for its pottery. Stalls line the road in from Tripoli selling everything from huge serving bowls to small storage jars at reasonable prices (not much more than 10LD). To see the pottery (*fakhar* or *gilal*) being made, head to the **crafts school** in the small street south of the Funduq Rabta. You should be able to see pottery-making and carpet-weaving demonstrations.

Places to Stay & Eat

Like many throughout Libya, the *buyut ash-shabaab* (youth hostel) was closed for renovations when we visited, leaving the town without any budget accommodation.

Funduq Rabta (☎ *631970, fax 631972, Sharia al-Jamahiriya*) Singles/doubles 35/45LD. This place is expensive for what you get – uninspiring rooms (with bath), some of which are cramped and a touch run-down but otherwise fine. Most rooms come with a TV. There's a mediocre *restaurant* that lacks atmosphere and the meals (10LD) are unlikely to inspire, but in Gharyan you're not exactly spoiled for choice.

There are *cheap restaurants* dotted around town, especially lining the main roads into town.

Getting There & Away

The shared-taxi and micro station is 500m south of Funduq Rabta. Little public transport leaves or arrives after early morning or early evening. Shared taxis to/from Tripoli (2LD, two hours) leave throughout the day from 6am, although they take longer to fill as the day wears on. There are also irregular shared taxis to Yefren (1.5LD, 1½ hours), early morning or evening shared taxis to Sebha (10LD, eight hours) and a micro to Nalut (around 4LD, four hours) at 7am most days. As always, ask around at the taxi station the day before you wish to travel to make sure something's heading your way.

BUGHILAN   بوغيلان

The small village of Bughilan, 17km north of Gharyan on the road to Tripoli, is, like Gharyan, famous for its pottery and stalls that line the main road through town.

YEFREN   يفرن
☎ 0421

Yefren is one of the more appealing towns in this mountainous region. It sits high on a series of rocky bluffs, overlooking the flat coastal plain, and is surrounded by attractive wooded areas. It's a relaxed place and nothing happens here in a hurry.

The deserted, old part of town is over 500 years old and there are a few ruined remains scattered around the hillsides. The largest concentration of old houses is on the hilltop overlooking the town, which is also home to a **mud-brick mosque** that has a short minaret with large openings on the sides of the tower. To gain an appreciation of Yefren's remarkable location, wander out to the abandoned shell of the old **Funduq as-Siyahe**, a graceful building that once had superb views from its back terrace, overlooking the plains below. It's at the western end of town (look for the green-domed mosque nearby). This vantage point is also *the* place to watch the sunset.

There were no hotels in Yefren at the time of research. The pleasant *buyut ash-shabaab* was closed for renovations but should have opened by the time you read this. It's behind the police station, up the hill from the post office.

Shared taxis run reasonably regularly between Gharyan and Zintan and beyond. Many of these don't pass through Yefren but will drop you off at the turn-off to Yefren. From here it's a further 9km or so into town and while you might find a shared taxi, the wait can be a long one and you may have to hitch. Occasionally there are shared taxis direct from Tripoli to Yefren (two hours) or Gharyan (one hour).

AROUND YEFREN

South of town in a delightful valley of palm trees is an unusual dark **sandstone mosque** with a small dome and an ochre-and-green topped minaret.

Around 4km east of Yefren is the attractive village of **Al-Ghala** while 18km north of Yefren is the Roman mausoleum of **Soffit**, which is of minor interest.

ZINTAN   الــزنــتــان

The inhabitants of this pleasant but unspectacular town, 34km west of Yefren, are renowned throughout Libya for their quick wit – they're certainly a friendly lot. There's nothing to see in town but, with a couple of petrol stations (one in the centre of town and another on the road from Nalut), a *buyut ash-shabaab* and well-stocked *grocery stores*, it's a reasonable place to break up a journey. The main Gharyan-Nalut highway runs through the southern outskirts of town, and the surrounding fields are covered with olive and almond groves. Zintan really starts to bustle around sunset.

QASR AL-HAJ   قصرالحاج

The village of Qasr al-Haj has the largest, and arguably Libya's most spectacular, example of Berber architecture. The circular and completely enclosed fortified granary is worth the difficulty of getting here. But note that there's no accommodation.

Qasr

This extraordinary structure *(admission 2LD)* was built as a place to store the harvests of the surrounding area in the second half of the 12th century by the formidably named As-Sheikh Abd-'Allah ibn Mohammed ibn Hillal ibn Ganem Abu Jatla (Sheikh Abu Jatla).

Despite its name (*qasr* means castle), this structure was rarely used as a form of defence. Instead it offered protection for the local crops necessary for the community's survival. Constructed entirely from local rock and gypsum, the cool storage areas, sealed with doors made of palm trunks, warded off insects, thieves and inclement weather alike. Its purpose was akin to a modern bank, with the system of enforced saving and stockpiling preventing the crop-holders from squandering their resources.

When the qasr was first built, Sheikh Abu Jatla, a deeply religious man, extracted rent from each interested party in the form of barley and wheat, then distributed it among the poor and haj pilgrims or sold it for money for the upkeep of the mosque and to pay Quranic teachers in the madrassa.

The crumbling old part of town, which the last inhabitants left in the 1950s, surrounds the qasr. There is a small mosque and tomb on the track up from the main road. This modern structure replaces an earlier mosque that housed the tomb of Sheikh Abu Jatla.

Today, the site is usually kept closed, not least because many of the storage rooms are still in use. The caretaker, the amiable Ali Abd-'Allah al-Hars, is always happy to open it for travellers – the revenue from travellers goes towards efforts to preserve the qasr from heavy rains and vagaries of time. Ali doesn't live on the site but his house is just 500m south of the qasr on the other side of the main road, just after it turns to the west. Everyone in town seems to know Ali.

You enter the qasr from the eastern side. After passing through the main door, the passageway is flanked by two spacious alcoves. They were once used by gatekeepers guarding the entrance and are now used for a good display of agricultural and household items; note in particular the huge latches for securing the doors.

The main courtyard is breathtaking and like wandering into a self-enclosed, man-made canyon. The walls are completely surrounded by cave-like rooms. In all, there are 114 storage rooms in the qasr – exactly the same number as there are *suras* (verses or chapters) in the Quran – although many are now subdivided into pens for different crop types or for various families who share the same space. The qasr's area is 1188 sq metres, with each storage area about five metres 'deep' from the door to the back wall. There are three storeys of rooms above the ground and another storey underground. The basement rooms, of which there are 30, were once used for the preservation of oil, while the rooms above ground stored barley and wheat.

If you arrive after good rains, many of the stores may be filled to overflowing, although those on the top floor are no longer in use. When we visited, some crops had been stored for as long as 12 years and looked as fresh as if they had been harvested the day before. Please remember, however, that these crops represent people's livelihoods, so don't venture inside without permission.

Some of the rooms still boast the original palm-trunk doors, which have aged remarkably well. Note also the holes on either side of each door for threading the latch (usually made from the wood of olive trees).

Viewed from any angle, the qasr is spectacular. For a different perspective, climb the stairs leading up above the entrance. A ledge (1m wide in most places) circles the qasr's top level. The animal horns high on the ramparts served as amulets of good fortune. At a couple of points around the top level there are the remains of ancient winches used for hoisting produce from ground level to the upper storage rooms.

Getting There & Away
You'd be lucky to find a shared taxi heading to or from Qasr al-Haj, so travellers with their own vehicle are obviously at an advantage. Take any shared taxi or micro heading along the road between L'Aziziyah (or Tripoli) and Nalut, and ask to be let out at the turn-off to Qasr al-Haj. From there, the village is clearly visible from the road; you can either walk or hitch the 2.2km to the town. About 300m after entering town, take the track leading right up an incline, just after the forlorn (and teasing, if you've walked) bus shelter. The qasr is about 200m away, beyond the mosque and remains of the old town.

JADU   جادو
The modern hilltop town of Jadu is another Berber settlement overlooking the Sahel al-Jefara from the barren escarpments of the Jebel Nafusa. Built on the site of an older town, Jadu has lost much of its charm and the few old buildings that remain are in a sorry state. The post office and petrol station are both on the road running southwards out of town and there are no banks that change money.

Museum
The museum *(admission 3LD, camera/video 5/10LD; open 9am-1pm & 3pm-6pm Tues-Sat)* contains an oil press, a model reconstruction of Qasr al-Haj, examples of building materials traditionally used in the area, local costumes and agricultural implements. You'll often find the museum closed on Friday morning and on summer afternoons, but if you ask around for the key, someone will usually let you in, except at prayer time. The museum is in the stone building 100m north of the main roundabout in the centre of town (ask for *al-mathaf*).

Places to Stay & Eat
Jadu's only hotel is the simple *Funduq Jadu as-Siyahe (Sharia al-Jamahiriya)* in the pink building just east of the main roundabout. Expect to pay 10LD per person in basic, but habitable, rooms.

For food, take what you can get in Jadu. There are the usual grocery stores selling biscuits and tins of tuna, as well as a few *cheap restaurants* that do hamburgers and liver sandwiches for 1LD to 2LD each.

Getting There & Away
The shared-taxi station is by the roadside on the main road into town. You may find shared taxis running directly to/from Tripoli or Nalut, but your best chance is early in the morning. Some shared taxis between Gharyan and Nalut make the small detour to Jadu if there are enough passengers. The occasional shared taxi shuttles between Jadu and Kabaw or Yefren.

AROUND JADU
Ain az-Zarqa
This is one of many natural springs or wells dotted throughout this stretch of mountains. This small, crystal-clear pool fringed by palm trees is stunningly located at the bottom of cliffs that surround it on three sides. It's a great spot for a picnic and particularly popular with locals on Friday.

To get there, take the road southwards out of Jadu for 4.5km, from where a dirt track runs off to the right (west). The turn-off is marked with a maroon-and-blue sign in Arabic. The road deteriorates significantly to become a deeply rutted track that can't be good for your car and, after about 1km, you come to an open picnic area. For those with limited time, a short walk takes you to the edge of the cliffs that overlook the pool far below; please be careful of loose stones, as it was here that one Lonely Planet author nearly took a high dive. Alternatively, follow the road down the canyon – about a one-hour walk going down and almost twice that coming back up. A taxi from the centre of Jadu to the turn-off, from where you'll have to walk, shouldn't cost more than 4LD. Alternatively, you could hitch.

Tarmeisa

This abandoned and ancient stone village, 10km south-east of Jadu, is perched on a narrow, rocky outcrop overlooking the Sahel al-Jefara. It is one of the most evocative of the ancient Berber settlements in the Jebel Nafusa.

The only entrance to the town is from the car park at the road's end across a dirt 'bridge' with a deep trench on either side. This was once the town gate with a drawbridge that was opened every morning at 6am and closed again at 6pm, effectively sealing off the town, surrounded on three sides by plunging cliffs. The first house you come to on your left was one of the last to be abandoned in the late 1950s. Look for the **tunnels** leading underground to the houses, one of which contains a huge oil press.

Entering the village proper, there are plenty of small doorways and passageways to explore. About halfway through the village, one house on the eastern side contains a well-preserved **bridal room** (for use on the wedding night), which has traces of relief-carving patterns and attractive storage alcoves. Elsewhere, note the roofs reinforced with a multitude of palm or olive tree trunks. The buildings at the northernmost (and narrowest) end of the village include a **mosque** with a squat, pyramidal minaret. Most of the structures in this section were rebuilt in 1205, suggesting that the original construction of the village took place much

earlier. There are fantastic **views** from here, and a stunning vista down off the escarpment over the Sahel al-Jefara, with its hundreds of snaking wadis heading northwards. Be *very* careful as there are no rails to prevent unsuspecting travellers from falling and it's a long way to the bottom of the sheer cliffs.

There are no places to stay or eat in Tarmeisa, nor any public transport. Your best bet is to either hitch from the main road or arrange a taxi from Jadu (it should cost no more than 15LD, including the return journey and waiting time at the site).

KABAW   كاباو

The pleasant Berber town of Kabaw, 9km north of the Gharyan-Nalut road and around 70km west of Jadu, is set among rolling hills and is home to another superb qasr. This stretch of countryside is one of the more fertile areas of the Jebel Nafusa and the sight of shepherds with their flocks in the surrounding fields is not uncommon.

There are no hotels or restaurants in Kabaw.

Qasr

The qasr (also known locally as the *ghurfas*) is over 700 years old and, while smaller and less uniform than the one at Qasr al-Haj, is still captivating, with a wonderful medieval charm. None of the storage rooms remain in use and the door is permanently left open. The qasr's impregnable hilltop position highlights how, in such an unforgiving landscape, the protection of grains was almost as significant as guarding water.

The rooms surround an open courtyard, with some sections climbing four- or five-storeys high. Many of the doors are made of palm trunks and most of the structure is a combination of rock, gypsum and sun-dried mud bricks. In the centre of the courtyard is a white tomb belonging to a local religious notable. Pottery storage jars are scattered around the courtyard's perimeter. Most of the time, you're likely to have the place to yourself except on Thursday afternoon and Friday, when it comes to life as a favourite picnic spot for local families.

Outside the qasr's walls, the ruins of the old town tumble down the hillside. Most of the houses are sadly derelict while some are filled with rubbish.

The qasr is about 500m west off the main road through town; the turn-off is in a dip in the road about 2km from the start of the town if you're coming from the south.

Qasr Festival

In April every year, Kabaw hosts the Qasr Festival. The festivities celebrate the unique heritage of the Berber people of the area, with particular emphasis on Berber folklore. Important local ceremonies (weddings, funerals and harvests) are re-enacted by people in traditional dress. For exact dates of the festival, contact any tour company (see Organised Tours in the Getting Around chapter).

Getting There & Away

There are no regular buses or shared taxis to Kabaw. If you don't have your own vehicle, any shared taxi or micro between Nalut and Yefren (or Zintan) will drop you at the turn-off to Kabaw. From there, hitching or the occasional taxi is your only option – ask around at the restaurant at the turn-off to Kabaw on the main (southern) Nalut-Gharyan road.

NALUT   نالوت

☎ 0470 • pop 55,000

At the western end of the Jebel Nafusa, the regional centre of Nalut is home to yet another exceptional Berber granary. With a slightly wider range of accommodation and eateries than other towns in the Jebel Nafusa, Nalut is a decent place to break up the long journey between Ghadames and Tripoli.

The road from Tripoli winds up off the plain to the east and meets the Ghadames road (which approaches across the plateau from the south) at the main roundabout in the centre of town. The large white *baladiya* (municipal or town hall) and post office are just west of the roundabout; along this road are a number of shops and a mosque. The town's only bank, sometimes reluctant to change money, is on the road up the hill to the Funduq Nalut. There is a petrol station along the road to Ghadames.

To reach the old town and qasr, visible on a hill to the east from the main roundabout, take the small road that runs from the Tripoli and Ghadames roads to the car park near the entrance to the old town. The car park is around 200m from the main roundabout. From the car park, a walking track runs along the ridge to the qasr.

Old Town

The qasr was once the old town's centrepiece and is now almost completely surrounded by the uninhabited remains of the village that cling to the edge of the steep hillside. The views over the mountains and plains from any of the elevated areas around the qasr are superb.

Mosques There are three mosques, only one of which (the white mosque) is still in use. The white mosque between the car park and the qasr is the most recent mosque; it's closed to visitors and rarely used. Down the hill immediately behind the white walls is Nalut's oldest mosque, **Alal'a Mosque**. Its low arches and stone mihrab suggest that it was once a fine, if simple, place of worship. There is also a functioning well in one of the rooms off the compact main sanctuary. The walls just inside the entrance are marked with Arabic relief inscriptions stating that the mosque was rebuilt in 1312. Old Nalut's third mosque is beyond the qasr on the eastern end of the outcrop.

Oil Presses Also near the qasr are two old olive oil presses. One is about 30m back towards the car park from the caretaker's tent, off the northern side of the path; look for the huge circular platform and crushing stone. There's another, equally impressive example of an oil press around 150m west of the qasr, off the southern side of the path. In use until 2000, this one is kept locked so you'll need to ask the qasr's caretaker for the key – ask to see the '*ma'sered zeytoun*' (olive press).

Qasr Like the other qasrs of the Jebel Nafusa, the main section of this ancient troglodyte granary *(admission 1LD)* is reached through a covered tunnel that used to regulate entry to the inner sections. The door is usually kept locked, but the caretaker resides under a semipermanent Berber tent just outside the walls. The walls of the entrance tunnel are lined with Arabic inscriptions carved in relief, which record that the qasr was rebuilt over the ruins of an earlier structure in AD 1240.

The qasr of Nalut is unlike those at Kabaw and Qasr al-Haj. While the same principles are in evidence – small rooms used for storage, carved into the rock and self-enclosed within high walls from a perch on a rocky bluff – the qasr at Nalut has the feel of a small, fortified village. Rather than facing onto an open courtyard, the rooms with their palm-trunk doors are tightly packed and overlook two narrow thoroughfares without any hint of uniformity.

The structure's interior is strewn with old pieces of pottery once used to store dates, wheat, oil and barley. As well as the palm-trunk doors and holes used for latches to seal the rooms, look for the small wooden struts protruding from the walls – these provided reinforcement to the walls, which look fragile but have proved remarkably resilient. The larger rooms belonged to richer merchants or farmers, while some were subdivided for families unable to justify a room all to themselves. There were 400 chambers, but the keeper always knew how much each family had in storage at any given time. The last rooms fell vacant in 1960.

Places to Stay

Buyut ash-Shabaab (☎ 2858, Sharia Ghadames) Dorm beds for HI members/ nonmembers 3/5LD. Close to the petrol station, this small hostel is basic but as cheap as you'll get in Nalut.

Funduq Nalut (☎ 2204) Singles/doubles 10/20LD. Wonderfully located on the hill across the valley from the old town, Funduq Nalut has deteriorated significantly since it was built by the Italians in 1933. Many of the bathrooms don't seem to have been cleaned since then and the basic rooms (with shared bath) are only marginally better. There has been talk for years of this place being renovated; the day can't come

soon enough. The *restaurant* isn't bad and serves meals for around 12LD. The view of sunsets from the balcony are some compensation for the quality of the rooms.

Funduq Nasim (☎ 2816) Singles/doubles 10/20LD. Another unappealing option, this hotel is similarly in need of a good spring-clean; rooms have shared bath. It's west off the road to Ghadames, about 1.5km from the town centre.

Places to Eat

There are small *sandwich bars* along the road in from Ghadames. One of them about 1km north of the roundabout stays open from late morning until late evening; it's on the right-hand side if you're coming from Ghadames.

On your right on the road to Tripoli, just down the hill from the roundabout (next to a post office), is a small, unnamed *mat'am* (restaurant), which is very clean, sells a variety of soft drinks and whips up a hearty meal of soup and chicken for around 15LD (including drinks). Almost opposite, a little farther down the hill, is *Mat'am Taghalis (☎ 2437)*, which serves similar fare.

Getting There & Away

Few buses originate in Nalut and those that pass through town, travelling between Ghadames and Tripoli, are often full. The bus stop is almost next to the baladiya and the buses pass through in either direction any time between 11pm and 2.30pm. At the time of research, there was a 7am bus service to Tripoli but there was talk of it changing, so check when you arrive.

You're far more likely to find a shared taxi heading in either direction with your best chance being early in the morning (between 6am and 7am). The taxi station is on the main roundabout.

NALUT TO DERJ

At the checkpoint on the outskirts of Nalut you may be asked to pay 15LD per vehicle if you're heading to Ghadames – a most brazen example of cashing in on tourism by the Nalut municipal authorities. Shortly after you leave Nalut, the landscape loses the last tinges of green. After you've travelled for around 50km, make sure you drive particularly carefully as there are frequently free-ranging camels wandering by the road-side. About 125km from Nalut is the unattractive town of **Sinoun**, a bleak settlement that is only partially redeemed by the tiny stone-and-mud-brick old town with a crumbling fort by the roadside.

After Sinoun, the low, barren hills disappear to be replaced by the vast emptiness of the desert. Just before reaching the checkpoint outside Derj, a turn-off to the east leads to Al-Qaryat (312km) and Sebha; this road shares the prize with the road from Tobruk to Ajdabiya for Libya's most unexciting road. Note that if you're arriving from Al-Qaryat, you'll have to pay the 15LD 'tourist tax' at the checkpoint.

DERJ درج

The sleepy town of Derj, 210km south of Nalut, is little more than a place to stop, refuel and stretch the legs. The road bypasses much of Derj itself, which has a post office and a mud-brick **old city** that is rarely visited but worth exploring. If old cities are your thing, it's at its atmospheric best around sunset.

Back on the main highway, at the cross-roads 150m south of the checkpoint, is where you'll find the newish-looking *Tsawa Company for Tourism* (☎ *021-3610167*), which has a clean restaurant selling snacks; it's a favoured stopping-off point for tour groups. There are also basic rooms available in the rudimentary mud-brick building out the back for 5LD to 8LD; the plumbing is problematic. Also near the junction is a petrol station and, on the right-hand side, the shack of *Cafe Derj* selling tea. At the cross-roads, a particularly garish poster of the Colonel reminds you that in Libya you need never be alone.

DERJ TO GHADAMES

The road to Ghadames is quite bumpy in patches. While we were there one of the small bridges was being repaired. You may also see people clearing sand dunes from the road. Wandering camels can be a hazard.

About 10km west of Derj is the small mud village of **Mantras** with a small, crumbling mud fortress visible from the road. There is a checkpoint about 50km before Ghadames.

GHADAMES غدامس
☎ 0484 • pop 10,000

Don't come to Libya without seeing Ghadames. The tourist cliches – 'the jewel of the Sahara' – are not that wide of the mark. The Unesco World Heritage-listed old city is by far the largest and best preserved in Libya. Although the old city is virtually deserted, it is easy to imagine it as a thriving city and one of the most significant trading towns of the northern Sahara. The oasis is surrounded by the Hamada al-Hamra (Red Rocky Desert), which stretches away to the south.

Not surprisingly, Ghadames receives large numbers of visitors, yet when you're lost among the labyrinthine alleys it can feel at times like you're the only person in a city of ghosts. On summer afternoons, Ghadames shuts down, usually from around 1pm to just before sunset, as the inhabitants retreat from the punishing heat.

How Ghadames Got Its Name

An ancient caravan of travellers and merchants from the Nemrod tribe stopped for lunch at a tiny oasis to break up the arduous desert crossing. With the sun beating down, the oasis was a welcome sight although they thought it didn't have enough water to warrant a lengthy stay. As they continued their journey the next day, they realised that they had left behind a cooking pot, so one of the men was sent to retrieve it. As he was about to leave the oasis, his horse pawed the ground and fresh water rose to the surface. In honour of the occasion, but with a little less romance than some of us would have liked, the party combined the words *ghad* (which means 'lunch') and *ames* (which means 'yesterday') to produce the name Ghadames, or 'lunch yesterday'. The other traditional name of Ghadames is Ain al-Faras (the Well of the Mare or Horse Fountain). This spring formed the foundation of the original oasis and subsequent settlements.

THE JEBEL NAFUSA & GHADAMES

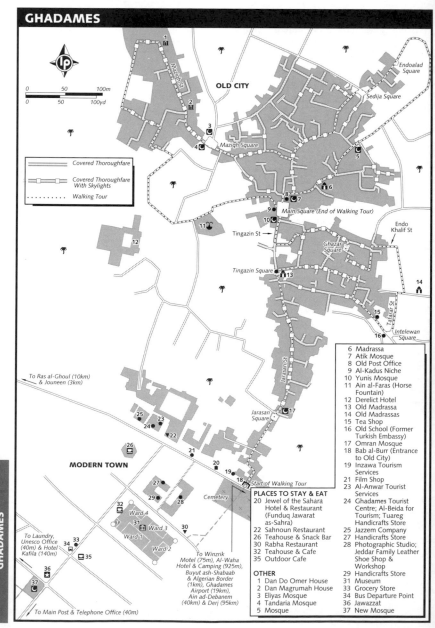

GHADAMES

OLD CITY

Endoalad Square

Sedija Square

Mazigh Square

0   50   100m
0   50   100yd

Covered Thoroughfare

Covered Thoroughfare
With Skylights

Walking Tour

Main Square (End of Walking Tour)

Endo
Khalif St

Tingazin St →

Ghazar
Square

Tingazin Square

Intelewan
Square

To Ras al-Ghoul (10km)
& Jouneen (3km)

Jarasan
Square

MODERN TOWN

Ward 4

To Laundry,
Unesco Office
(40m) & Hotel
Kafila (140m)

Ward 3

Ward 1

Ward 2

Cemetery

To Winzrik
Motel (75m), Al-Waha
Hotel & Camping (925m),
Buyut ash-Shabaab
& Algerian Border
(1km), Ghadames
Airport (19km),
Ain ad-Debanem
(40km) & Derj (95km)

Start of Walking Tour

To Main Post & Telephone Office (40m)

PLACES TO STAY & EAT
20 Jewel of the Sahara
   Hotel & Restaurant
   (Funduq Jawarat
   as-Sahra)
22 Sahnoun Restaurant
26 Teahouse & Snack Bar
30 Rabha Restaurant
32 Teahouse & Cafe
35 Outdoor Cafe

OTHER
1 Dan Do Omer House
2 Dan Magrumah House
3 Eliyas Mosque
4 Tandaria Mosque
5 Mosque

6 Madrassa
7 Atik Mosque
8 Old Post Office
9 Al-Kadus Niche
10 Yunis Mosque
11 Ain al-Faras (Horse
   Fountain)
12 Derelict Hotel
13 Old Madrassa
14 Old Madrassas
15 Tea Shop
16 Old School (Former
   Turkish Embassy)
17 Omran Mosque
18 Bab al-Burr (Entrance
   to Old City)
19 Inzawa Tourism
   Services
21 Film Shop
23 Al-Anwar Tourist
   Services
24 Ghadames Tourist
   Centre; Al-Beida for
   Tourism; Tuareg
   Handicrafts Store
25 Jazzem Company
27 Handicrafts Store
28 Photographic Studio;
   Jeddar Family Leather
   Shoe Shop &
   Workshop
29 Handicrafts Store
31 Museum
33 Grocery Store
34 Bus Departure Point
36 Jawazzat
37 New Mosque

The downside of Ghadames' popularity is that it can be expensive. Bargaining in the shops can be a frustrating experience of hard work for little gain – shopkeepers know that if you won't pay the asking price, there are plenty who will. That said, the persistence of traders who pursue you down the street in tourists hotspots elsewhere is thankfully lacking here. Unusually for Libya, many signs are in English.

History

The stories of Ghadames' past are safeguarded by the old men of the community who keep the oral history alive.

It is believed that there was a town near Ghadames' current site around 3000 BC, but little is known of the area's history prior to Roman occupation in 19 BC. The Romans fortified the town, which they called Cydamus, and turned it into a regional centre that provided the coastal cities with olive oil. But with their attention focused on their city strongholds along the Mediterranean coast, the Romans maintained a loose control over the town, just enough to keep open the trans-Saharan supply routes. Under the reign of Septimus Severus (AD 193–211), Ghadames became a garrison town for the Third Legion. The Roman occupation of Ghadames lasted for over two centuries, during which time the ancient idols of the traditional religions lost influence in Ghadames life.

In the 6th century AD, the Byzantine armies of Justinian I brought Ghadames under the empire's jurisdiction while Greek missionaries who followed in the army's wake effectively turned the town into a Christian settlement. With the arrival of the Islamic armies in Libya in the 7th century AD, the town was overrun in 46 AH (AD 668) and most of the Berber inhabitants converted to Islam (see Ras al-Ghoul under Around Ghadames later in this chapter).

Although dates of any precision are difficult to come by, it is believed that the site of the old city was founded around 800 years ago. It is the third town in the area now known as Ghadames. The town remains largely unchanged in design since that time and, although restoration work has been regularly required, the Islamic and Turkish character of the architecture remains intact.

In AD 1228, the Hafsid dynasty extended its control southwards to Ghadames. The imposition of taxes by far-distant rulers caused tension and in the 18th century AD, with the Ghadamsis' taxes unpaid, the rulers in Tunis sent an army of some 10,000 men to collect their dues. Met by a force of Ghadames men outside the town, a terrible battle ensued in which, according to one chronicler of the day, the fighting 'raised such a black dust that the sky could not be seen'. Remarkably, the Ghadamsis won the battle and, their point made, duly paid their taxes. Not long afterwards, the town became largely independent. Ghadames remained one of the most important caravan towns of the northern Sahara until the 19th century.

Relying so heavily as it did on the lucrative trade in human slaves, Ghadames' fate was sealed when the movement to abolish slavery gathered pace. As the colonial powers began to assert their control over the Sahara, the slave trade was abolished first in Tunis and then French Algeria in the 1840s. The Ottomans loosely administered Ghadames after 1810. When squabbles broke out between the semiautonomous families of the city in 1874, the town was occupied by a full Ottoman garrison that stayed until the Italians arrived.

When the Allied forces sought to eject the Italians from Libya during WWII, even Ghadames was not spared. On 11 November 1943, French pilots flew US-registered B-17 bombers in an assault on Ghadames, launched from neighbouring Algeria. Although lasting for only 10 minutes, the intense bombardment killed 39 Ghadamsis (their names are listed in Arabic in the museum), including 12 children, destroyed 70 houses and damaged a further 200. The Atik Mosque, which had stood for almost 1300 years, was destroyed and the neighbouring Yunis Mosque (the second oldest in Ghadames) was significantly damaged. No Italians, the supposed targets of the raid, were killed.

In recent decades, Libya's old cities, including the ancient houses of Ghadames,

The Great Caravans of Ghadames

Remarkably, for one of the principal trading centres of the Sahara, Ghadames produced only one product of note and a not very lucrative one at that – embroidered slippers. Instead, Ghadames became one of the great entrepot towns for goods from all over Africa and, unusually for a town with few locally produced products, the merchants of Ghadames made up their own caravans of merchants. The reach of Ghadames' commerce and the sheer volume of trade that passed through its gates was so great that when caravans arrived in towns across the Sahara, they were assumed to be Ghadames caravans.

The town was also unique in that the main traders rarely travelled themselves but relied on a network of agents across Africa who, when a Ghadames caravan arrived, would check loads and undertake transactions on behalf of the real owners, the entrepreneurs of the desert. The influence of the agents stretched from Mauritania to Egypt, from Lake Chad to the Mediterranean – and their descendants can still be found living across Africa. Interestingly, Ghadamsis are disproportionately over-represented among the ranks of drivers of long-distance haulage lorries.

In ancient times, goods from the interior of Africa that passed through the gates of Ghadames en route to the coast included an exotic array of precious stones, gold and silver, ivory, Tripolitanian horses, dates and ostrich plumes. Most goods were carried to be sold in the souqs of North African coastal cities, while the more precious items were loaded on boats to Europe and Palestine. In the other direction, glass necklaces and paper for use in religious texts from Venice, pearls from Paris and linen from Marseille passed through en route south.

The arrival of a caravan in town was quite an event. The camels bearing great chests were unloaded and the goods almost immediately offered for sale in the markets of the town. The world that many Ghadamsis would never see for themselves was brought to life in the perfumes from Timbuktu, spices from the Maghreb and precious metals from central Africa. These were heady days in Ghadames, with the caravans also bringing loved ones and news from across the sands. Their arrival was marked with celebrations and endless stories of desert adventure (sandstorms, pillage and tragic loss of life) told around the campfire, the caravaneers knowing that they would soon have to set out again.

have fallen victim to the revolutionary government's push towards modernisation.

In 1973 there were around 3700 people living in Ghadames' old city, with a few Tuareg living in the area west of the city walls. In 1982–83, the Libyan government began building a new town beyond the walls and new houses were given to Ghadamsis to encourage them to leave the homes of their ancestors. In 1984, there were 6666 people living in the old town; four years later there was just one family left. Although some families move back into their old houses within the cool walls of the old town during summer (especially during Ramadan), the old city is effectively deserted, save for that one family that continues to hold out against the rejection of traditional ways of living.

Fortunately, the potential windfall from tourism and the involvement of Unesco

since 1999 has helped to assure the future of old Ghadames. For more information on Unesco's efforts to preserve the old city, contact the Unesco office (☎ 63303), a small block north-west of the New Mosque.

Orientation

Ghadames is an easy place to find your way around. All but the most ambitious exploring can be done on foot. Entering town from the east, the road forks just before entering the built-up area. The left branch leads up to the buyut ash-shabaab and the Algerian border, while the right fork takes you into the town. This latter road runs past the cemetery on your left while the old city fans out beyond the walls on your right. About 1.5km after the fork, the other main road of Ghadames runs off at right angles to the south. Most, if not all, of the sights and facilities are on or just off these two roads.

Information

The *jawazzat* (passport office; ☎ 62437) is almost opposite the New Mosque; it's open 9am to noon Saturday to Thursday.

Post & Communications The post office, open 8am to 1pm Saturday to Thursday, is south of the New Mosque – look for the usual telecommunications mast. This is the place to make telephone calls and international connections are generally good; take your passport, although it's rarely asked for.

Many businesses in Ghadames boast a fax number, most of which are, upon closer examination, all identical and carry a Tripoli area code. Faxes in Ghadames itself are rare, so many businesses have an arrangement with the post office in Tripoli to receive faxes there. The faxes are then forwarded by road or mail to Ghadames – don't expect an immediate reply.

At the time of writing, there were no Internet facilities in Ghadames.

Travel Agencies Travel agencies are scattered around the main intersection. All can arrange day trips to some of the surrounding sand dunes (100LD per 4WD vehicle) and most can also muster a more serious three- to four-day expedition across the desert to Al-Aweinat (see Al-Aweinat in the Fezzan & the Sahara chapter) in south-western Libya (150LD to 200LD per day). To make the same journey by camel takes around 24 days (100LD to 150LD per day).

Al-Anwar Tourist Services (☎ 62450) The office is almost on the main intersection.

Al-Beida for Tourism (☎ 63205, fax 021-3601374) The office is almost on the main intersection. The owner, the amiable Mustapha, can arrange hotel or home-stay reservations, guides, visa registration at the jawazzat (10LD) and meals in some of the traditional houses that have been restored in the old city (13LD per person).

Ghadames Tourist Centre (☎/fax 62533, e gha dames_tour@hotmail.com) Also almost on the main intersection, this centre's postal address is PO Box 878, Ghadames.

Inzawa Tourism Services (☎ 62962) The office is just west of the entrance to the old town.

Jazzem Company (☎ 62153, fax 62979) The office is just north-west of the main intersection.

Winzrik Tourism Services (☎/fax 62485, e wts@winzrik.com, w www.winzrik.com) In the Winzrik Motel, 75m east of the entrance to the old town, this is a branch of Libya's largest tour company.

Guides A guide can be invaluable for your first visit to the old city. The standard charge is 35LD for a morning or 60LD for the day (including a trip to Ras al-Ghoul at sunset – see Ras al-Ghoul under Around Ghadames later in this chapter). It may seem like a lot to pay, but they know their stuff and if you can get a few people together individual costs soon start falling.

Highly recommended guides include: the hugely knowledgeable At-Tayeb Mohamed Hiba (☎ 62300, fax 021-3601374), at Hay al-Salam, whose love of the old city is infectious; the indefatigable Mohamed Ali Kredan (☎ 62190, fax 021-3601374) and Bilal S Aghali (☎ 62073), a friendly Tuareg from the Fezzan whose postal address is PO Box 844, Ghadames. Each of these guides speaks good English.

Laundry If your clothes are in danger of exploring the old city without you, there is a good laundry a small block west of the New Mosque. Your clothes will be dry-cleaned and ironed (sometimes including your underwear!) and the owners are friendly and obliging. Shirts and pants cost 1.5LD each, and underwear is 0.5LD each. If you're having trouble finding it, ask for '*Ash-Sharouk Maasella*' or '*Launderie*'. It's open 9am to 1pm and 6pm to 9pm Saturday to Thursday.

Photography & Film Taking photos anywhere in Ghadames is usually not a problem although you should always ask permission before taking anyone's photograph, especially in the old city. You should also be careful about straying into border areas if you venture west of Ghadames.

There is an unnamed photographic studio next to the Jeddar leather-shoe shop. It sells Konica print film for 5LD. Out the back is a traditional Ghadames room in which you can pose in traditional costumes – the whole thing is pretty tacky but it doesn't cost much (1LD), and you can pick up the photos two days later.

There is also a small shop selling film along the main road into town, west of the entrance to the old city.

Old City

The original families still retain ownership over the **houses** in the old city *(adult/child 3/1LD, camera/video 5/10LD)* and many return regularly to carry out maintenance. Many of the gardens surrounding the covered areas of the city are still in use. There's no ticket office but the man in charge of tickets will soon be notified of your presence; tickets are valid for 24 hours.

The covered alleyways rely entirely on natural light and in most places there are evenly spaced skylights – some are as high as 10m – which can be surprisingly effective. Areas where the skylights are not as prevalent can be quite dark, so it's worth bringing a torch (also remember that there are no toilets in the old city). Almost every thoroughfare is lined with sitting benches that are good places to rest – even on the hottest summer day the covered areas are remarkably cool. Most of the houses and other buildings are not open to the public (except at festival time), although a couple (see under Walking Tour later in this section) are set up to receive visitors. But you can usually find a caretaker willing to let you have a look around the mosques.

The old city of Ghadames was a city of loosely configured concentric areas. The inner circle consisted of residential and commercial districts and covered around 10 hectares. As you moved further away from the city's heart, the densely packed houses gave way to gardens. Beyond the gardens was the city wall.

The built-up areas of old Ghadames were divided into two main sections to represent the two major families or tribes of the region: the Bani Walid and the Bani Wazid (named after the sons of one of the first Berber leaders of Ghadames). The Bani Walid occupied the quarters north of the

main square, with their sector subdivided into three sub-groupings of families, while the Bani Wazid area to the south was home to four distinct sub-families or tribes.

Each of these seven sections were known as 'streets'. There are, therefore, seven main streets in old Ghadames and there were once seven gates into the city that were closed at sunset each night. Each 'street' was like a self-contained town, with a mosque, houses, schools, markets and a small communal square. The square was used for weddings, celebrations and funerals.

Although the rhythms of daily life were largely played out within the seven streets and conflicts between the different quarters were frequent, there was also a strong sense of belonging to a wider Ghadames community. Whenever the whole town was under threat from an external enemy or a collective decision was needed, the families of the seven streets would congregate in their respective squares to agree on a response. The oldest man or most respected elder from each of the seven families would then be sent to the central square of the whole town where the seven representatives would organise a communal defence or come to a collective decision. These councils of elders would also handle internal community disputes, discussions of whether to maintain ancient customs, criminal issues and irrigation. Punishment for indiscretions often comprised of exclusion from festivities or market activities.

All events of city-wide importance took place in the central square. At other times, it was where news was passed from one sector of the city to another. The main square also reflected Ghadames's position as a trans-Saharan caravan town – caravans from throughout Africa would enter the city through here, bringing news of tribal allegiances, battles and the wellbeing of loved ones far away. Staring off at each other across the main square are the two main mosques, one for the Bani Walid (the Atik Mosque) and one for the Bani Wazid (the Yunis Mosque).

In addition to the two primary subdivisions of the town, a third (outside the old

The Old Houses of Ghadames

Ghadames houses were deceptively big and had to fulfil a multitude of social purposes. Town builders made maximum use of vertical space to create splendid houses of gypsum and sun-dried mud brick, which had ceilings reinforced with palm trunks.

Behind the street-level, palm-trunk doors was invariably a small reception or entrance room where guests were greeted. A short corridor ran past a storage room on the same level. A staircase led up to the next level, at the top of which was often a 'dry toilet'.

The small landing at the top of the stairs also led onto the main living room. This large room (generally around 3m by 4m) was where a family would take its meals, entertain guests and spend most of their time. It was also the centre of the social life of the women of the house. The ceiling could be as much as two-storeys high with a skylight at the very top. Some houses contained strategically placed mirrors throughout the house to reflect the only source of external light. At night, oil lamps were used. Adorning the walls were painted decorations, including the four-fingered hand of Fatima that was believed to ward off evil. The painting and intricate carvings were done largely by women, often as a means to prepare the house for married life.

Another feature of the living room was the large number of decoratively painted cupboards, each serving a specific and carefully demarcated purpose – cooking implements, women's clothes, the father's possessions, a toy cupboard or gifts for a boy on reaching manhood. Smaller niches were repositories for sugar and tea, while the small, circular hole at ground level was the place to throw date seeds when you had finished with them (like most things in Ghadames, these were later recycled for animal feed). Every border of even the smallest architectural feature was brightly painted. Cushions and carpets were always laid out on the floor for meals.

On the same level as the living room were two smaller rooms. One was simply a bedroom but the other room had an arched doorway with the Al-Qubba canopy, formed by two pillars with a pointed roof. This was where a woman received her husband on their wedding night (see the boxed text 'A Woman's World' later in this chapter).

Two sets of stairs usually led up from the living room to more bedrooms, and storage and food preparation rooms. One staircase ultimately led to the roof. In the wall of an upper room there was often a small door that connected to a neighbouring house. This door served a dual purpose of being a fire escape and a pathway for women passing from house to house. This way, Ghadames women could conceivably walk across the entire city without being seen by men. Five or six houses were often joined in this way and neighbouring houses often belonged to close relatives.

The roof area often contained the kitchen and more storage areas reached via more stairs – Ghadames houses were clearly not for the infirm. The flat, open rooftop had fine views over the local houses.

city walls) began to spring up to the west of the old city in the 1960s. This area, known as *fogas*, was home to the Tuareg who had started to move away from a purely nomadic lifestyle and chose to settle in Ghadames.

Walking Tour To see it at its best Ghadames should be explored on foot and the following walking tour takes you through the seven sectors of the city. If you want to fully explore the old city, you could easily take an entire day, although this walking tour can be completed in a minimum of three to four hours.

The best place to start is at the main gate of the old city, **Bab al-Burr**. This was once used by the city's inhabitants; strangers usually entered the main square via Ain al-Faras (Well of the Mare or Horse Fountain), meaning that the residential districts were spared from the arrival of unwanted intruders. Bab al-Burr fronts onto the main road into Ghadames and is entered through the sunken arched gateway opposite the western end of the cemetery. Immediately after passing under the arches, you find yourself in a cavernous covered passageway lined with benches.

Continue to the end of the passageway, turn left and then right. This is the start of one of the seven major streets, **Jarasan Street**, which runs deep into the heart of the city. The lovely whitewashed walls are a taste of things to come and, during the time when the city was inhabited, their height must have offered residents significant privacy. A short distance further on is **Jarasan Square**, entered through an attractive archway framing the minaret of the white Omran mosque. This compact square was the meeting place for one-seventh of the city's men and, as such, is surprisingly small. Note that in the four corners are the remains of Roman pillar bases – these were taken from the old Roman city nearby and used for building materials by residents of the later Islamic city.

The continuation of Jarasan Street leads into the covered section of the city, where the cool walls can provide welcome respite from the heat. Note the **skylights** that climb up in narrow shafts between the houses. The natural light enables you to both find your way and admire the distinctive **Ghadames doors**. Made of sturdy palm trunks split in half to form planks, the larger doors lead into houses while the smaller ones indicate chambers used for storage. Note also the improbably large padlocks used to secure the rooms. Another feature of the doors are the small leather studs in bright red, green and yellow (the colours of Ghadames), which partially cover some doors; these indicate that the owner has made the haj pilgrimage to Mecca.

After about a 300m walk north of Jarasan Square, you reach **Tingazin Square** which also represents the start of **Tingazin Street**. Although similar in size to the earlier square, the feel is entirely different. This delightful square is completely covered from the sun and is lit by a soft light from nearby skylights. On the western wall are some **decorative patterns** carved in relief. Taking the road running east off the square, you pass the shell of an old **madrassa** on the right. Head east for approximately 200m,

then turn right and then left. The covered area continues for a short distance before you again come out into the open air – the start of the garden area.

Almost as soon as you come out into the light, there is a teahouse on the left. It has excellent local tea served with mint and peanuts (0.5LD).

A little further along the same street, you come to another open area, **Intelewan Square**. On the right as you enter is a whitewashed building that was the first non-Quranic **school** in Ghadames. Modern sciences were studied in the building, which was later used as the Turkish embassy. If you turn north (left), the path is lined with gardens enclosed behind walls. This thoroughfare is **Tafarar Street**, another of the seven main streets. At the next junction, look to your right to see the towers of two old **madrassas**. Continuing east (right) and then north (left), you come to **Endo Khalif Street** where a path leads, again, undercover and turns left. The roof is, typically, covered by palm leaves with struts made from palm trunks. Winding your way left, right, right again and then left brings you into **Ghazar Square**. This lovely uncovered square is surrounded by alcove niches and a balcony encircling the square on the 1st floor. This balcony enabled children to watch the public ceremonies played out in the square below; wedding festivities sometimes lasted for up to 14 days!

The paths heading west soon leads to the main square. Just before entering the square, you can visit the **Yunis Mosque**, the main mosque of the Bani Wazid part of town. This simple mosque makes use of pillars from the old Roman triumphal arch. Upon entering the square, you leave the Bani Wazid part of town.

The **main square** of Ghadames is, like the seven tributary squares, surprisingly small in size given its importance in the public life of the city. With two mosques overlooking its open courtyard, the square is simple and lacks the charm of some of the smaller squares. In a niche on the northwest wall of the square, built into the back wall of the Yunis Mosque, is Al-Kadus, the

Al-Kadus & the Art of Water Management

Ghadames was renowned on the caravan routes for the plentiful water from its well. The city authorities recognised the need to carefully manage their most precious resource. The egalitarian system they devised was ingenious.

The main water supply was connected to all points in the city via a network of underground canals. By controlling supply close to its source, the town was able to ensure that every section of the city received its fair share of the water. Water users were divided into three categories: private homes were the first to be supplied; followed by the mosques; and then the gardens. Not only did mosques need water for the requirements of ablutions for prayers, they also functioned as public water outlets from which members of each family could also collect a set quantity of water.

To precisely calculate and distribute the water, a man would occupy the niche in the main square into which water was fed from the spring and into canals. This man, charged with the task of water distribution for the entire city, would ensure that the large bottle (*al-kadus*) that hung underneath the outlet was filled each time. A hole in the bottle then released the water into the canal. The time it took to empty (approximately three minutes) represented a unit of measurement – one *kadus*. Each kadus was noted by making a knot in a palm leaf. Two men helped the main regulator by telling him how much water each district or garden was permitted. Each garden was fed off the main canals – when they had received the correct amount, a stone was placed over the opening to ensure that no-one took more than their fair share.

So regular was this process that time was measured for the whole city by calculating how many kadus had passed since sunrise. Nine kadus were equivalent to one *dolmesa*. Anyone could find out the time by visiting the main square and asking in the al-kadus niche, thereby making Ghadames one of the few places to have devised its own independent system of time and water management.

unlikely headquarters of Ghadames' water supply regulator.

If you exit the main square under the northern arch, you enter the **Bani Walid** districts of Old Ghadames. If you turn right at the first opportunity, the **Old Post Office** is on your right. Above the path immediately outside the door hangs a chain from one of the palm struts. This is where bags of mail were hung. The appointed man from each departing caravan could sort through the bag to see whether any letters could be delivered along his caravan route, while arriving caravans could check whether any mail had been sent to them during their long absences. By all accounts, the old men who loitered around the main square made a point of knowing everybody's business, so it usually wasn't necessary to check the mailbag.

Next door to the post office is the **Atik Mosque**. This was once the oldest mosque in Ghadames, if not all of Libya. The original mosque on this site was built in 44 AH (AD 666) and survived incredibly until 1943, when it was destroyed by the Allies. The re-

built mosque is presided over by an old, Italian-speaking caretaker who shows visitors around for a small tip. Your best chance of finding him nearby is in the morning. The sanctuary is off-limits to non-Muslims but from the door you can see the attractive row of arched pillars, running across the centre of the rectangular hall, and the mihrab.

To get to the women's section of the mosque, return to the main thoroughfare outside the door and take the door immediately to the east. The next opening, again, leads into the **public well**, which served as a public water-gathering point.

After leaving the well, follow the covered street to the east for about 400m. The uncovered path running east through the gardens is divided by a shallow canal which still serves as an irrigation channel. Winding your way north and then west between more gardens, you re-enter the built-up areas of the old city at the very small and partially covered **Endoalad Square**.

To the south-west is **Sedija Square** (pronounced 'se-de-ha'), which is surrounded

A Woman's World

In Ghadames, women led a life of concealment in keeping with the dictates of traditional Islamic society. The woman's domain was the house and she determined how a family lived. One of the central features of any traditional Ghadames house was *Al-Qubba*, a canopy set up in a room where a wife received her husband on their first night of marriage.

When her husband died, the wife was confined to the house for four months and ten days (a Quranic principle known as *Ar-Ridda*), after when she was free to remarry and resume a normal life as there would be no doubt as to who was the father of any children. The husband was, of course, free to remarry immediately. Although the mourning woman was free to move within the house, tradition demanded that she receive any visitors in Al-Qubba.

Men would attend the funerals in the public squares, while women performed the mourning ceremonies, attended only by women, inside the house. (Other public ceremonies were similarly held in the town squares for men and either in the houses or on the rooftops for women.) In matters of inheritance, a wife received one-eighth of her husband's property and her daughters half that of her sons.

Whenever a decision was made or judgement passed down by the town's elders, the women of the city were informed by two specially appointed, freed, female slaves. A weekly women-only market was held on the interconnected rooftops of the old city.

by some superb three-storey, mud-brick Gha- dames houses. Note also the pattern of alternating upright and inverted triangles running along the top of one of the walls. The design is found across the Sahara of western Libya (as far south as Ghat) – one legend claims they represent the crown of an ancient Berber queen who ruled over the desert. Taking the right fork of the two lanes running south-west, you soon return to the covered lanes, where you can fully appreciate the value of skylights (and a torch), as there are fewer of them. At the T-junction,

turn right, follow the curving arc of a lane to the south-west and then turn right again; watch out for jutting walls in the darkness. Continue west then north-west through a light passageway that is one of the most lovely in the old city. The benches along its side are a nice place to sit and rest.

The passage leads into **Maziqh Square** (also known as Al-Touta Square or Indentuman Square). This open courtyard has a tree just off-centre; if you're game, try one of the small white berries that are tasty, not to mention perfectly safe. On the western side of the square is **Tandaria Mosque**, while **Eliyas Mosque** fronts onto the eastern side. The perimeter is lined with the usual arched alcoves.

Maziqh Street continues across the square. Not long after leaving the square, just after veering to the right, is **Dan Magrumah House**, a traditional Ghadames house open to the public; you need to make a prior appointment (see Travel Agencies under Information earlier in this chapter for details on arranging entry and even lunch here). A further 250m, at the far north-western end of the city, is **Dan Do Omer House** (see Places to Eat later in this chapter).

Maziqh Street continues to the outer reaches of old Ghadames. At the end, turn left where a few twists and turns between walled gardens and mud-brick houses take you to **Ain al-Faras** (Well of the Mare or Horse Fountain), the site of a deep well that gave birth to the creation myth of Ghadames (see the boxed text 'How Ghadames Got Its Name' earlier in this chapter).

Immediately west of the well is the place where caravans and other outsiders could come to tether and water their camels; they could gain access to the town via the nearby main square to receive mail, news and provisions. Also nearby is the elegant facade of a derelict old hotel; Sophia Loren twice slept in Room 10. This was the area for strangers who were not to be privy to the secrets of the magical old town.

New City

Modern Ghadames has few obvious attractions but is a pleasant town nonetheless. It is difficult to miss the attractive **New Mosque**, along the main street, with its marble pillars and towering minaret; non-Muslims are not generally allowed inside. The **old cemetery** opposite Bab al-Burr, the main gate to the old city, is filled with thousands of what appear to be unmarked gravestones. However, true to the Ghadames tradition of oral history, the precise identity and location of each grave is passed down from father to son.

Ghadames Museum Ghadames Museum (☎ 62225; adult/child 3/1LD, camera/video 5/10LD; open 9am-1.30pm Sat-Thur) is worth a quick look, although it's not up to the standard of some other museums in Libya. Although it's officially closed on Friday, staff often open the doors if there are enough tourists in town. The fort-like building in which it is housed began life as a police station under the Italians. The ticket office is in the northern gate and the camera-video ticket man loiters with intent just inside. Most items are labelled only in Arabic.

Ward One contains some informative posters about Ghadames' history and a range of ethnographic exhibits. Highlights include the famous embroidered slippers of Ghadames made by the Jeddar family, huge copper keys and padlocks, the like of which are still used in the old city, and a large selection of folk medicines; the remedy for constipation (top row on the left) looks particularly nasty. There are old black-and-white photos of Ghadames throughout.

Ward Two contains artefacts from the Roman era, including the remains of Roman pillars from the town's Triumphal Arch.

Ward Three has a decent collection of Tuareg items, including a reconstructed desert tent, goatskins for carrying water, wooden spoons (the Tuareg are unique among desert people in that they use spoons for eating) and the distinctive camel saddles and platforms for carrying brides on camels to their desert wedding.

Ward Four has architectural drawings from a Libyan-Italian archaeological team, building materials, fossils and a few stuffed animals. The photos of the old town are

good and there is a counter selling a decent selection of postcards.

Ghadames Festival
In October every year, Ghadames' annual three-day festival brings the old city alive in a riot of colour and activity. Ghadamsis return to their family homes in the old town and throw open the doors for singing, dancing and public festivities, most of which are performed in traditional dress. It's a great chance to see re-enactments of ancient celebrations in their traditional environment.

On the first day of the festival, some public events are held in the modern city. On the morning of the second day, the festivities move to the old city, with weddings and ceremonies to celebrate the rite of passage of young men to adulthood. Up to thirty of the old houses are used – where some events would once have lasted seven days, seven houses are used to represent each day. On the third day, the festival moves to the Tuareg part of town (west of the old city) and into the desert, concluding in the evening in a Tuareg camp amid the sand dunes.

Ghadames is not blessed with an abundance of hotel rooms at the best of times and finding a bed during the festival can be difficult; arriving without a reservation would be unwise. Most hotels are booked out months in advance but home-stays with local families can usually be arranged to meet the extra demand. See Places to Stay for advice on making a reservation.

Places to Stay
There is a shortage of accommodation in Ghadames and quality places are even more scarce; it pays to book ahead. Many Ghadamsis rent out rooms in their second homes – if there wasn't this option, many times there wouldn't be anywhere to stay at all. These home-stays are known locally as 'villas' and, though most are spartan, they're fine provided you're not expecting five-star comfort. The going rate is 15/20LD without/with breakfast. Contact any of the travel agencies in Ghadames (see Travel Agencies under Ghadames earlier in this chapter) or Tripoli (see Organised Tours in the Getting

Around chapter) to make a booking. Hotels have signs in English.

Youth Hostel *(☎ 62023)* Dorm beds for HI members/nonmembers 3/5LD. The location is not ideal (a 15- to 20-minute walk to the old city) and the rooms are very small, but it is cheap. It's the first building on the left that you come to (if travelling from the east) after the junction on the road to Algeria.

Jewel of the Sahara Hotel & Restaurant *(Funduq Jawarat as-Sahra; ☎ 62015, fax 021-3601374)* Beds in 4-bed/2-bed room 5/7LD. Run by the avuncular Ahmed at-Tunisi, this small hotel is a stone's throw from the entrance to the old city and has basic rooms.

Winzrik Motel *(Funduq Winzrik; ☎/fax 82485)* Camping 5LD, singles/doubles 30/35LD. About 75m east of the entrance to the old city, this comfortable place has 16 spotlessly clean rooms with bath and air-con. You can also pitch a tent in the hotel's walled compound; the cost includes use of the shower and toilet. There's a pleasant *restaurant* (meals 15LD to 20LD). The company has reportedly purchased the adjacent block and has plans to open a 100-room hotel in late 2002.

Al-Waha Hotel & Camping *(Funduq al-Waha; ☎ 62569-70, fax 62568)* Camping 5LD, singles/doubles 30/40LD. The simple but comfortable rooms with bath and air-con are favourites of tour companies, so it can be difficult to get a room. You can also camp on their grounds and use the showers and toilets. There's a fine view over the desert from the roof and often local dance performances are held in the evening (from around 8pm).

Hotel Kafila *(Funduq Kafila; ☎ 62991)* Singles/doubles 30/40LD. In the streets behind the New Mosque, this characterless place has rooms (with bath) of a similar standard to the others in this price range.

Places to Eat

The restaurants in Ghadames also aren't fantastic.

Jawharat as-Sahra Restaurant *(☎ 620 15, fax 021-3601374)* Meals 15LD. Open noon-2.30pm & 6.30pm-10pm Sat-Thur, 6.30pm-10pm Fri. Arguably the best restaurant in Ghadames, this place is friendly with a chilled-out atmosphere. The music is unintrusive, the service attentive and the food is quite tasty. There's also a coffee machine that churns out good macchiatos (espressos; 1LD) and thick Arabic coffee (*qahwa*; 1LD).

Sahnoun Restaurant *(Couscous Restaurant; ☎ 62533)* Meals 10LD. Open noon-3.30pm & 6pm-9.30pm daily. Also signed as 'Couscous Restaurant', this place right on the main intersection is laid-back to the point of somnambulence. While it's more basic than its neighbour, Jawharat as-Sahra, it's friendly. The dishes owe much to a preoccupation with couscous and rice.

Rabha Restaurant *(☎ 62960, fax 021-3601374)* Meals 15LD. Open 12.30pm-3pm & 6.30pm-10pm Sat-Thur, 6.30pm-10pm Fri. Perhaps they were having an off night when we visited, but the rice and tea were cold and the main meal contained more fat than meat. Other travellers have enjoyed their meal here far more than we did, so if you give it a try let us know what you think. It's opposite the entrance to the museum.

Undoubtedly the best eating experience in Ghadames is lunch in one of the traditional houses of the old town. The most frequently prepared meal is the delicious *fitaat* (lentils, mutton and buckwheat pancakes cooked together in a tasty sauce in a low oven and eaten with the hands from a communal bowl). Eating this wonderful meal amid an evocative atmosphere is a highlight. ***Dan Do Omer House*** *(☎ 62300, fax 021-3601374)* does this to perfection – ask for At-Tayeb Mohamed Hiba. Alternatively, any of the travel agencies around town should be able to arrange an experience like this.

In the modern town, outdoor *cafes* and *teahouses* abound. While some may do the occasional snack, most are for tea or coffee drinkers only. The greatest concentration is along the road running between the main intersection and the new mosque. They're particularly good on a warm summer evening. For self-caterers, there is a grocery store with a limited but reasonable selection of items just north-east of the New Mosque.

Shopping

The handicraft stores of Ghadames have a wide selection of items on sale although prices are generally higher than Tripoli or further south in the Fezzan. Most of the shops sell a reasonable range of Tuareg handicrafts, especially leather items, replica camel saddles, cloth for Tuareg turbans and some silver pieces. For more details of what to look for, see the boxed text 'Tuareg Handicrafts' in the Fezzan & the Sahara chapter. You can also pick up palm-woven products and tacky items such as long-dead desert scorpions and snake skins in glass cases.

There are a number of distinctive Ghadames items worth seeking out. Most famously, the striking embroidered slippers in bright colours are unique to Ghadames and have been produced by the Jeddar family for centuries. The family has a shop and workshop in the block north of the museum. They're not cheap (most 50LD and upwards) but do make a wonderful souvenir. Huge copper keys (mostly replicas) used in the old city are also a good buy.

Getting There & Away

Air At the time of research, there were no scheduled flights to Ghadames but that may change in the post-embargo era. Libyan Arab Airlines (no office in town) lists the prices for the Tripoli-Ghadames service as 20/38LD for one-way economy/1st class, so flights may be close to recommencing. The airport is 19km east of town.

Bus & Shared Taxi A large government bus (An-Nakhl as-Seria) leaves for Tripoli (via Nalut; 8LD) at between 5.30am and 6am, while a private micro starts out for Tripoli (8LD) at 6pm. Both leave from the main street, 50m north-east of the new mosque; book tickets at the small ticket window a day in advance. A more comfortable 'Iveco' micro also leaves at 6pm (15LD), starting at the buyut ash-shabaab and stopping at the new mosque just after sunset.

Shared taxis leave for Tripoli and the towns of the Jebel Nafusa from the same place as the government bus a few times a day, if demand requires; your best chance of getting one is from 7am. To get to Gharyan, you'll probably need to change in Nalut.

Getting Around

You're unlikely to need a taxi in Ghadames, but, if you do, no journey within the town is likely to cost more than 2LD.

Getting around by bicycle is not a bad option – you could even use a bicycle to meander through the lanes of the old town if you're going for a second visit. Ghadames Tourist Centre, at the main intersection, hires them out for 2.5LD per hour.

AROUND GHADAMES
Ras al-Ghoul

About 10km north-west of Ghadames is the lonely desert castle of Ras al-Ghoul (Mountain of Ghosts), perched on a rocky bluff rising up from the plains. This dramatic fort predates the arrival of Islam and was once part of a chain of desert castles across North Africa which communicated with each other through messengers and smoke signals. When the forces of Islam swept through Ghadames in 668, the majority of Ghadamsis converted. Those who didn't were driven from the town and took refuge at Ras al-Ghoul. The Islamic soldiers encircled the castle and placed it under siege, not realising that a secret well within the remote redoubt could keep the rebels alive indefinitely. After negotiations took place, a compromise was reached and the siege was lifted.

The castle originally consisted of three concentric walls – the stone skeletons of the castle's rooms are still visible. Be very careful when climbing up as the deep shaft of the ancient well is uncomfortably close to the top of the path. From the eastern side you can see, about 100m away to the east, the barely visible low remains of a camp used by Islamic fighters during the siege; a further 100m east are the remains of the camp's cemetery, containing 13 graves. Perhaps not surprisingly, given their losses, the Arabs also called the site Jebel ash-Shohada (Mountain of the Dead). It was from the camp that the ghostly legend of Ras al-Ghoul was born. The soldiers reported seeing strange lights coming from the castle.

Elsewhere from the summit, the views are superb. The undulating sand dunes to the north and west lie within Algerian territory while just 7km away to the north-east is the Tunisian town of Burj el-Khadra. It's one of the most accessible places in Africa to watch the sunset in three countries.

To the west, you can see a sandy track running over a low ridge of uniform hills, along which are a series of Algerian border posts. Beyond the ridge, the track leads to a large sand dune (about 4km away) which is in a small finger of Libyan territory surrounded by Algeria. The sunsets here can be the stuff of legend.

Ras al-Ghoul can be difficult to reach without a guide, as the tracks leading westwards from the town soon peter out to just two tyre tracks in the sand. If you've hired a guide for Ghadames, the full-day service includes a sunset trip to Ras al-Ghoul. The other reason why a guide is necessary is that they'll stop you straying inadvertently into Algeria, whose border guards reportedly do not take kindly to even innocent incursions. Taxi drivers may refuse to do the journey because the terrain is quite rough.

Jouneen

The small village of Jouneen, 3km west of Ghadames, has a mud-brick old city. A return taxi trip from Ghadames (including waiting time) should cost no more than 7LD.

Ain ad-Debanem

About 40km east of Ghadames are the two salt lakes of Ain ad-Debanem (Mjezzem). There is something quite romantic about swimming so buoyantly in lakes surrounded by the desert. The lakes in the Idehan Ubari in the Fezzan are more beautiful but if you won't be venturing that far south, this may be your only opportunity to swim in a salt lake. The turn-off to the lakes is 35km east of Ghadames on the road to Derj.

A taxi will charge at least 20LD, but you'd be better off negotiating a price with one of the travel agencies in town and combining it with visits to some of the other sights around Ghadames.

GHADAMES TO AL-AWEINAT

The desert expedition from Ghadames to Al-Aweinat is not to be undertaken lightly and definitely not without an experienced local guide (for more information, see Travel Agencies under Ghadames earlier in this chapter or Organised Tours in the Getting Around chapter). See also Al-Aweinat in the Fezzan & Sahara chapter. By 4WD, the journey takes three to four days while by camel it stretches to over three weeks. One traveller, who made the journey in reverse, described the journey in the following terms:

The sand is orange pink, the mountains high and out of HG Lovecroft's books. Out of this world. After three days of Garamantian graffitis...and caves containing drinkable rainwater, on to Al-Aweinat. Four days pass as we drive northwards along the Algerian border. The medina of rocks and sand, with streets and avenues made by solid high rocks takes our breath away. The Tuareg call it Madrgat. Teas in the desert, bread baked in the sand, the full moon. At the end we reached Ghadames, the jewel of the desert.

Christina Koutoulaki, Greece

Fezzan & the Sahara

The Fezzan region of southern Libya (Phasania in Roman times) is completely engulfed by the Sahara and is home to some of the most spectacular (and most diverse) desert scenery in the world.

The majestic dunes of the Idehan Murzuq and Idehan Ubari (Murzuq and Ubari Sand Seas) cover thousands of square kilometres. Deep valleys within the deserts conceal idyllic, palm-fringed lakes. In the Jebel Acacus, in the extreme south-west, formerly volcanic mountains with breathtaking rock formations rise starkly from the sands. Many of these formations have rock walls adorned with carvings and paintings dating as far back as 12,000 years. Elsewhere, particularly in the northern Fezzan, the landscape can be one of unrelieved monotony, with featureless plains stretching towards a horizon that never seems to end.

It is also a land with a fascinating human history. The trade routes of the Libyan Sahara had strong links to the great empires of central and West Africa. The oases of the interior – small explosions of fertility in the midst of great expanses of desert wasteland – spawned towns, such as Ghat, which endure to this day, holding out as enchanting redoubts against the vast Sahara. Improbably it was in the Fezzan, close to the modern settlement of Germa, that the great civilisation of the Garamantians flourished and, for almost 1400 years, made the desert bloom.

The Sahara is also the land of the Tuareg, the former nomads of the central Sahara. This proud and hardy people, once the feared protectors and pillagers of caravans, continue to inhabit the remotest of areas, eking out a harsh existence from animal husbandry, small crops and, increasingly, tourism.

These days, the caravan routes have been replaced by the well-worn tracks of 4WD enthusiasts. That said, there are plenty of places where you can feel like there are no other human beings in existence. For that

Highlights

Fezzan & The Sahara p214

Ubari Lakes & South-Western Fezzan p223

Sebha p217●

●Ghat p230

NIGER   CHAD   EGYPT   SUDAN

- Swim, surrounded by sand dunes, in the idyllic Ubari Lakes.
- Follow the caravans of old to the medina in Ghat.
- Marvel at the skill of the ancients in the Rock Art of the Jebel Acacus and Wadi Methkandoush.
- Be awestruck by the silent majesty of the Idehan Murzuq.
- Go in search of the crater lakes of Waw al-Namus.
- Learn about the desert from the Tuareg.

reason, never travel too far off the beaten track without an experienced local guide (compulsory in some places).

Choosing when to go is also important. Any time after mid-May at the latest or before September can be fiercely and debilitatingly hot. At other times, the days are generally warm and the nights surprisingly cold, especially on clear nights when sleeping out under the countless stars requires a good-quality sleeping bag. For those used to cool, northern-European temperatures, taking a couple of days to acclimatise before scrambling up your first sand dune is

FEZZAN & THE SAHARA

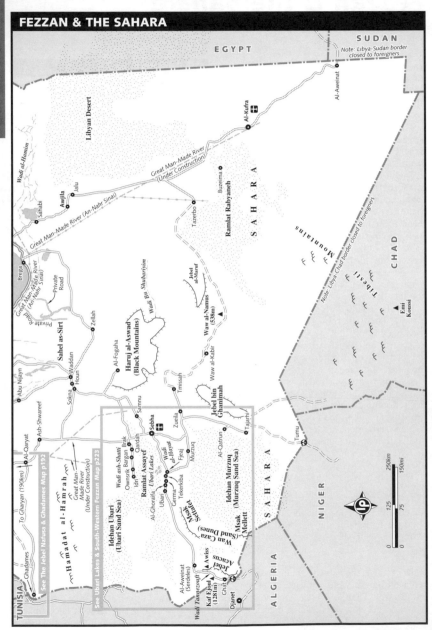

The Era of European Exploration

From the late 18th century onwards, the Libyan Sahara saw a steady stream of European explorers. The motivations ranged from geographical expeditions in search of the true course of the Niger River or the source of the Nile, to a romantic desire to be among the first Europeans to reach the fabled Saharan city of Timbuktu. European governments also funded antislavery expeditions as well as those with far from benign aims – a forerunner to the unseemly scramble for Africa. Tripoli was seen as the gateway to Africa and the Old British Consulate in Tripoli was the scheming hub out of which many of the following explorers radiated.

Frederick Hornemann A theological student from Germany, Hornemann left Cairo in 1798 posing as a Muslim in a caravan of merchants. He proceeded to Tmissah before reaching Murzuq on 17 November 1798, about 10 weeks after leaving Cairo. He became very ill and was forced to stay in Murzuq for seven months as he sought safe passage through the little-known kingdoms south of Murzuq. He finally joined a caravan to Katsino (Nigeria). He wrote a letter to the Africa Association on 6 April 1799 in which he told them not to begin searching for him for three years. He was never heard from again and is believed to have died soon after writing the letter.

Hugh Clapperton This naval lieutenant from Edinburgh set out from Tripoli in early 1822. Accompanied by Walter Oudney and Dixon Denham, their plan was to reach the kingdom of Bornu (Lake Chad). Clapperton was laid low by malaria in Murzuq but during his recovery made forays to Germa and Ghat. The party laboured on to Lake Chad and two of them returned to tell the tale of a journey that was 'distressing beyond description to both camels and men'. Oudney died while trying to reach the Niger River.

Major Alexander Gordon Laing Laing started out from Tripoli in 1825 headed for Timbuktu. His route took him through Ghadames and then across the Algerian Sahara. He is believed to have reached (and been disappointed by) the former city of riches, making him one of the first Europeans to do so. He was murdered on the return journey and his notes were never found.

James Richardson Travelling under the banner of the British Bible Society, Richardson left Tripoli in August 1845 and, unusually, travelled openly as a European and a Christian. His journey took him from Ghadames due south to Ghat, where he was warmly welcomed by the sultan who presented him with gifts for Queen Victoria. His second expedition, in 1850 on behalf of the British Government, included a young Heinrich Barth (see following) and was one of the best-equipped Saharan expeditions in history; it even carried a wooden boat in order to cross Lake Chad. Richardson was a difficult man and the party members travelled separately and slept in separate camps. Barth and Richardson travelled to Murzuq and Ghat before going their separate ways.

Heinrich Barth Arguably the doyenne of European Saharan explorers, most of his travels took him beyond Libya, especially to Agadez and the Aïr Mountains of Niger. He was one of the first Europeans to report rock carvings in the Tassili-n-Ajjer, very close to the Jebel Acacus.

Alexandrine Tinné One of the more grisly stories of exploration involves this wealthy Dutch heiress who, in 1869, arrived in Murzuq with a large caravan (she travelled in style) and a bodyguard of two Dutch sailors. An Ahaggar Tuareg chieftain promised to escort her from Murzuq to Ghat, but a few days into the journey, he attacked her, slashed off her hand and left her to slowly bleed to death.

a good idea. Still, it isn't quite as bad as the 18th-century German explorer Frederick Hornemann claimed:

The climate of Fezzan is at no season temperate or agreeable. During the summer the heat is intense; and when the wind blows from the south it is scarcely supportable, even by the natives. The winter might be moderate were it not for the prevalence of a bleak and penetrating north wind during that season of the year, and which chilled and drove to the fire not only the people of the place, but even myself, the native of a northern country.

The Journal of Frederick Hornemann's
Travels from Cairo to Mourzouk 1797–8

One thing to watch out for is the difficulty of changing money throughout Fezzan. Although you should be able to find a bank or someone in most towns willing to swap US dollars for dinars, you'll save yourself wasting a lot of time looking around if you come prepared.

Maps

Navigating the Sahara requires good maps and an experienced local guide. A satellite-generated Global Positioning System (GPS) can also come in handy, but is not a substitute for good local knowledge – a GPS can point you in the right direction but can't tell what lies in between and hence the most appropriate route.

Maps of the Sahara are notoriously inexact and only by using a combination of maps can you gain a vaguely accurate picture. Even then, some tracks, and even some topographical features, may not be shown. The better of the easy-to-find maps include *Sahara and Environs* by International Travel

Maps (1:2,200,000), *Africa North and West (Map 953)* by Michelin (1:4,000,000) or the *Djanet – NG-32* by Carte Internationale Du Monde (1:1,000,000). The Carte Internationale Du Monde map covers only the extreme south-west of Libya and is good for topographical features, but not tracks. You may also come across Russian maps (1:200, 000) from the 1970s, which are still the best maps for Saharan navigation, even though they're in Cyrillic (see Maps in the Facts for the Visitor chapter).

One very useful companion for Sahara expeditions is *Sahara Overland – a route and planning guide* by Chris Scott. Its section on Libya includes five detailed route descriptions (including GPS coordinates).

Sebha Region

Sebha is an important transit point for travel in the Sahara, though the only reason to visit the featureless plains between Sebha and Gharyan is on your way somewhere else.

SEBHA   سبها
☎ 071 • pop 75,000

Sebha is the largest settlement in the Libyan Sahara and now serves as a sprawling garrison town. It's a bit too far from the action to make a convenient base for exploring the south-west of the country, but overnighting here enables you to break up the long journey to or from the coast. It's not a particularly attractive town but, if you're arriving from the desert around sunset, the main thoroughfare of Sharia Jamal Abdul Nasser can be quite pleasant.

From Naughty Schoolboy to Leader of the Masses

Many myths surround Colonel Gaddafi and the origins of his political awakening, but there are a few facts of which historians are certain. After completing primary school in Sirt, he began his secondary school in Sebha. At the age of 14, he was expelled from school, probably for organising demonstrations against government inaction during the 1956 Suez crisis. The young Mu'ammar went on to strut his political stuff on a much larger stage, but the Point of Light School (Gaddafi is seen as the 'point of light' for the masses) is now part of the Gaddafi legend. It's at the eastern end of Sharia 5 October and, as it's still in use, not open to visitors. Local students are, however, constantly reminded of their famous forerunner by oil paintings depicting scenes from his life in his old classroom.

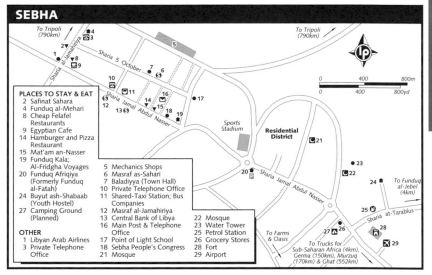

SEBHA

PLACES TO STAY & EAT
2 Safinat Sahara
4 Funduq al-Mehari
8 Cheap Felafel
   Restaurants
9 Egyptian Cafe
14 Hamburger and Pizza
   Restaurant
15 Mat'am an-Nasser
19 Funduq Kala;
   Al-Fridgha Voyages
20 Funduq Afriqiya
   (Formerly Funduq
   al-Fatah)
24 Buyut ash-Shabaab
   (Youth Hostel)
27 Camping Ground
   (Planned)

OTHER
1 Libyan Arab Airlines
3 Private Telephone
   Office

5 Mechanics Shops
6 Masraf as-Sahari
7 Baladiyya (Town Hall)
10 Private Telephone Office
11 Shared-Taxi Station; Bus
    Companies
12 Masraf al-Jamahiriya
13 Central Bank of Libya
16 Main Post & Telephone
    Office
17 Point of Light School
18 Sebha People's Congress
21 Mosque

22 Mosque
23 Water Tower
25 Petrol Station
26 Grocery Stores
28 Fort
29 Airport

To Tripoli (790km)
To Tripoli (790km)
Sharia 5 October
Sharia Jamal Abdul Nasser
Sports Stadium
Residential District
Sharia Jamal Abdul Nasser
Sharia at-Tarablus
To Farms & Oasis
To Funduq al-Jebel (4km)
To Trucks for Sub-Saharan Africa (4km), Germa (150km), Murzuq (170km) & Ghat (552km)

Sebha is an important transit point for Sahara travel, and heavily laden trucks deposit and collect human and other cargo for destinations as far afield as Chad, Niger and Algeria. Sebha is awash with cheap (often smuggled) goods, particularly cigarettes, which come from across the desert. The area around Sebha is quite fertile with barley, wheat and onions the main crops.

The Italian-built **fort** that overlooks the town doubles as a military base and anywhere in town you should be very wary of pointing a camera in its direction.

Orientation & Information

It's unlikely that you will need to stray beyond the two main streets, Sharia Jamal Abdul Nasser and Sharia 5 October (formerly Sharia Mohammed Megharief), which run parallel to each other through the heart of town. Sharia Jamal Abdul Nasser is the extension of the road in from Murzuq and Germa.

If you need to change money, the Masraf al-Jamahiriya (Bank Jamahiriya) can be found along Sharia Jamal Abdul Nasser, while Masraf as-Sahari (Bank as-Sahari) is on Sharia 5 October.

Post & Communications The post office is situated in a small street connecting the two main streets not far from Funduq Kala; look for the huge telecommunications tower. There are also a number of private telephone offices, which can be convenient when the post office is closed; most are expensive and charge a three-minute minimum.

Travel Agencies One of the better travel agencies in town is Al-Fridgha Voyages (☎ 631434, fax 630433, e afri.vog@hotmail .com, w www.afrivog .bizland.com), which has an office in the lobby of Funduq Kala.

Places to Stay

Sebha has a reasonable range of accommodation although, typically, budget travellers don't exactly have a lot of choice. Service with a smile is difficult to find at any of the hotels in town; staff are usually civil at best, but don't expect to be bowled over by the warmest of welcomes.

Buyut ash-Shabaab (Youth Hostel; ☎ 621178, off Sharia at-Tarablus) Dorm beds for members/nonmembers 3/5LD. After a bright start a few years back, this hostel has not been very well maintained and can be quite grubby. It's often filled with dusty sub-Saharan Africans recovering from their ordeal of crossing the Sahara.

There is a *camping ground* being constructed at the south-eastern end of town with rooms around a high-walled compound where you can park a vehicle or pitch a tent. Expect to pay 15LD per person in rooms or 5LD per tent. It's south off Sharia Jamal Abdul Nasser at the eastern end of town.

Funduq Afriqiya (Funduq al-Fatah; ☎ 623951/4, fax 631550, Sharia Jamal Abdul Nasser) Singles/doubles 15/20LD. Easily recognisable by the row of flags from African and other Muslim states out the front, this hotel seems to be run entirely by women. The rooms (no air-con), with private bathroom, are a tad faded, but otherwise reasonable value and some on the upper floors have good balcony views over the town. The water supply is erratic. There's an OK restaurant (meals 10LD to 15LD).

Funduq Kala (☎ 623106, fax 627670, Sharia Jamal Abdul Nasser) Singles/doubles with breakfast 20/25LD, suites 35LD. The comfortable and clean rooms (no air-con, with private bathroom) here are slightly better value if you can overlook the 1970s feel. There's a swimming pool out the back, but it was in desperate need of water when we were there. The restaurant serves reasonably priced lunch or dinner for 13LD.

Funduq al-Jebel (☎ 629470/9) Singles/doubles 25/35LD. This fully renovated hotel of long-standing occupies a hilltop location, which is great at sunset. The rooms have a private bathroom and air-con. This is probably the best value accommodation in Sebha, but it's miles from anywhere and it can be difficult to find a taxi, a fact the owner exploits by insisting (even upon threat of eviction) that you eat in his restaurant. As hotel restaurants go, it isn't bad, but it's still a Libyan hotel restaurant; meals cost 17LD.

Funduq al-Mehari (☎ 631910/3, fax 631914, Sharia al-Jamahiriya) Singles/doubles 35/50LD. This is Sebha's most expensive hotel, but if you're not here on government business or for a conference, the service can range from indifferent to downright surly. The rooms, with private bathroom, are very comfortable if a tad sterile (some are better than others). The price of a room includes breakfast. Most of the bathrooms are of a high standard with instant hot water. There's also an expensive restaurant (15LD to 25LD) and 24-hour room service, which is somewhat reluctant after 10pm.

Places to Eat

Aside from the hotels, most eating places are along Sharia Jamal Abdul Nasser or Sharia al-Jamahiriya, or in the streets around the Libyan Arab Airlines office. Don't expect fine dining, but at least Sebha is generally cheaper than other Libyan cities.

Mat'am an-Nasser (☎ 628220, Sharia Jamal Abdul Nasser) Meals 10LD. Open 12.30pm-3.30pm & 6.30pm-11pm daily. It serves a range of sweets, such as baklava (4LD per kilogram), and snacks such as chicken shwarma (meat sliced from a spit and stuffed in pita bread; 1LD) in the bright and breezy downstairs dining area. The atmosphere in the upstairs, air-con dining room is a bit sterile with an eerie blue aviary, but it does good food at a reasonable price. The service is well-intentioned if a little quirky at times. There are a couple of other similar restaurants nearby along the main street.

Egyptian cafes (Sharia Jamal Abdul Nasser) Open 11am-1am daily. On the corner opposite Libyan Arab Airlines are two wildly busy cafes that attract a lively group of Egyptian and Libyan workers in the evenings. It's an all-male crowd; Western women will attract initial looks but little else. Options include *tawle* (backgammon; free), nargileh (1LD to 2LD), tea (0.5LD) and oily ta'amiyya (felafel; 1.5LD). The cafe closest to the corner is the more appealing. As Sebha's only real nightlife, it's a good earthy place to spend an evening, although your conversation will have to compete with Egyptian movies blasting from the TV.

Safinat Sahara (Sharia al-Jamahiriya) Hamburgers 1LD. Open 11am-3pm & 6pm-1am daily. Also open late, Safinat Sahara is usually filled with locals. It's more a tea and tawle kind of place but they do snacks.

Getting There & Away

Air The Libyan Arab Airlines office (☎ 623875) is open 7am to 2pm Saturday to Thursday in summer (May to September) and 8am to 3pm in winter. It's in the large building on the corner of Sharia Jamal Abdul Nasser and Sharia al-Jamahiriya. There are flights to Tripoli (28/56LD for one way/return, Monday to Saturday) and Benghazi (36/ 72LD, Tuesday and Thursday).

Bus & Shared Taxi The shared-taxi station is along Sharia Jamal Abdel Nasser in a small yard about 400m south-east of the Libyan Arab Airlines office. Shared taxis usually start the long journey north to Tripoli (25LD, 12 hours, 930km) early in the morning (5.30am to 7am) and early in the evening (5pm to 6pm), but departures depend on the supply of passengers. These are also the best times to find taxis heading for Ubari (6LD, three hours, 190km); if you're only heading as far as Germa, you may still have to pay the full 6LD. For Ghat, you'll need to change in Ubari. For the smaller towns of Fezzan, there's sometimes one each day for places like Murzuq or Idri.

A few bus companies have offices around the shared-taxi station. There is usually (depending on demand) at least one bus or Iveco micro each day for Tripoli (15LD to 20LD, 12 hours) and Benghazi (16LD, 16 hours). Again, they generally leave early in the morning (7am) or late afternoon (6pm) and you should make a booking as soon as you arrive in town as they can fill up a day in advance. When we were there, there was talk of a daily 6am bus to Ghat but it was only talk. Some readers have said it operates on occasion.

Truck Approximately 4km south-east of the airport and just north of the highway to Murzuq and Germa, is an open patch of ground where trucks wait and load up for the seriously long-haul journeys to Agadez (Niger) or northern Chad. Impossibly laden down and uncomfortable, these epic trans-Saharan journeys are not for the faint-

A Grim Road to Nowhere

The most common tracks across the Sahara are not those left by well-equipped 4WDs or by the camel caravans of the nomadic Tuareg. They are left instead by immigrants from sub-Saharan Africa desperate for work and a better life for their families in the Libyan El Dorado. Sadly, many do not make it. In mid-May 2001, a Niger-registered truck, which crossed into Libya on 8 May, was found in a remote stretch of the Libyan Sahara; alongside it were the bodies of 93 people who had died of thirst. An astonishing 26 people who were also on the truck made it to safety. In winter 2000, a lorry was found by a group of tourists in the Idehan Murzuq with the bodies of those who had died a horrible death clustered nearby. For those of us who visit the desert for pleasure, it is worth remembering that crossing the vast Sahara is a matter of life and death for some. Before joining one of the trucks lumbering south from Sebha, remember that if you make it, you are one of the lucky ones.

hearted. Usually the preserve of immigrants from sub-Saharan Africa, there's nothing romantic about them; they can take weeks to arrive at their destination, if indeed they arrive at all.

Getting Around

To/From the Airport Sebha airport is 4km south-east of the town centre and reached by a small road that runs north off Sharia Jamal Abdul Nasser. Private taxis into town shouldn't cost more than 2LD to 3LD, but their drivers often ask for, and won't budge from, 5LD. If there are enough passengers, a seat should cost around 0.5LD.

Taxi

Sebha has a dearth of taxis but most shared-taxi journeys (from one end of Sharia Jamal Abdul Nasser to the other) should be no more than 0.5LD; most trips in a private taxi cost 2LD to 3LD.

WADI ASH-SHATTI وادى الشاطىء

This rarely visited wadi is 139km long and has no tourist facilities. Some of the wadi's small villages contain some interesting deserted mud-brick houses, although most have been reduced to rubble, and some locals claim to be descended from the ancient Garamantian people. The south side of the wadi is lined with the massive dunes of the Idehan Ubari (also known here as the Ramlat Assayef), which separate the wadi from Germa and the Wadi al-Hayat. On the north side of the road barren plains stretch all the way to the Jebel Nafusa. The road is surfaced as far as **Qattah** and then a rougher track continues on to Idri.

Idri, at the far western end of the wadi, was once a beautiful place of gardens, springs, date trees and a dramatic castle. Things have definitely changed. The town was destroyed in 1836 by the chiefs of the Awlad Suleiman tribe and the town now has an abandoned, end-of-the-road feel to it. The castle exists only as rubble and all the rubbish from the wadi seems to have blown here.

Expeditions south across the dunes to the Ubari lakes are possible from the villages of **Missaan** or **Al-Gurda**. You would, however, need to arrange this trip in advance with one of the travel agencies in Tripoli or Sebha.

BRAK براك

The dusty settlement of Brak is unlikely to detain you for long. Situated almost at the start of Wadi ash-Shatti, Brak's small **museum** *(admission 3LD; open 9am-1pm & 3pm-6pm Tues-Sun)* is in the town's decaying 19th-century Turkish fort. It contains some examples of prehistoric carvings and local ethnographic exhibits. Despite the official opening hours, you may need to ask around for the key *(miftah)*. Beyond the museum are palm groves and the old part of town. The **Italian fort**, in the centre of the modern section of town, is now a police station, complete with a collection of old firearms.

There is a basic but friendly *restaurant* on the highway from Tripoli, 2km north of the turn-off into the wadi; simple meals cost 7LD and there's a reasonable grocery store next door.

BRAK TO GHARYAN

There is very little to break the monotony of the road north of Brak. Crossing the road at two points and running alongside it in several places is the Great Man-Made River (An-Nahr Sinai) – a decidedly unremarkable bump in the landscape. Elsewhere only the cursory checkpoints relieve the boredom.

The nondescript town of **Ash-Shwareef**, 277km north of Brak, has petrol and eating facilities. *Mat'am Al-Qala'a* isn't a bad restaurant for couscous and chicken (10LD).

Al-Qaryat, a further 90km to the north, is similarly uninspiring. At the checkpoint just south of town is the turn-off for the desert road that leads across the plains to Derj (313km) and Ghadames (408km). South of the checkpoint is a petrol station and two unnamed *restaurants*; the southernmost one is better and serves simple meals with a limp salad for 6LD. Across the road is *Desert Coffee*, a shack serving hot drinks.

The town of **Mizda**, 130km north of Al-Qaryat (about 70km south of Gharyan), also has a petrol station.

AL-JUFRA الجفرة

Halfway between Sebha and the coast, east of the Tripoli-Sebha Highway, are the three adjacent Al-Jufra oases of Houn, Sokna and Waddan. Bizarrely, Al-Jufra was announced as the capital of Libya in 1987, but the idea never caught on. The road north from Sebha to Sirt passes through the **Jebel as-Sawda** – a wild, rocky landscape of black basalt with marvellous formations.

Houn هون
☎ 057

Houn, 345 km from Sebha, is the main town in Al-Jufra. The modern town is the fourth settlement in an area that has been occupied for the last 700 years. Not surprisingly, Houn has been called the migrating town.

The original town, called Miskan, is buried under the dunes 4km to the north-west of town and the second town, about 500 years old, is nearby although next to nothing remains. The third city is the medina of the current town and is 150 years old; it was abandoned for modern housing during the

1950s and 1960s. There is one large, typical **Medina House** that was built in 1842 and has been restored.

If you happen to be in Houn at the end of February or beginning of March, you may happen upon the annual **Sweet-Making Festival**. The celebrations to herald the end of winter see the town's best cooks vie to make the most outlandish sweets and cookies. The results are later consumed by all and sundry in a wonderfully indulgent way to mark the beginning of Spring.

The bank, post and telephone offices are along Sharia al-Jamahiriya, Houn's main street, as is the museum.

Museum This sweet little museum, **Thakirat al-Medina** *(admission 3LD; open 9am-1pm & 3pm-6pm Tues-Sun),* has a collection of local artefacts and memorabilia. It's the warehouse-like building opposite the turn-off to the old medina; ask for *'al-Mathaf'*.

Places to Stay *Buyut ash-Shabaab (Youth Hostel; ☎ 2040)* Dorm beds for members/nonmembers 3/5LD. Next door to the school and run by one of the teachers, this small hostel is about 500m from the highway. The place is simple and friendly, though a bit noisy when school's in.

Funduq al-Haruj (☎ 3067, 3381) Singles/doubles 25/40LD. This oasis of relative comfort, on the main highway near the Houn hospital, is the only hotel for hundreds of kilometres in any direction. The rooms are enormous and the private bathrooms are good; price includes breakfast. Lunch or dinner costs 10LD to 20LD.

Sokna & Waddan
Sokna is a few kilometres south of Houn. In the early 19th century, the Arabs of Sokna were particularly active as traders and financiers in Murzuq and the central Sahara, forming allegiances with the powerful tribes of the Awlad Suleiman and Al-Qaddhafa. The landscape around Sokna is very attractive, with palm trees and sand dunes.

Waddan, north of Houn at the crossroads where the highway splits to Misrata and Sirt, is a small and quite charming town with a picturesque ruined castle on the hill in its centre; it provides a panoramic view over the town and oasis. Close to the castle are some old mosques built in the local style.

Getting There & Away
Public transport is more occasional than regular. You might find the occasional bus passing through en route between Sebha and Benghazi, but they're often full. You're best bet is a shared taxi to either Sirt or Sebha; get there early in the day and be prepared to wait.

OTHER EXPEDITIONS
If you're in search of a desert expedition where you're unlikely to encounter any other tourists, there are a few remote stretches of the Libyan Sahara where tourist expeditions have yet to commence, but which have great potential. These include striking out south from Zellah (161km south-east of Waddan) to the **Haruj al-Aswad** (the Black Mountains), which reportedly contains some prehistoric Egyptian paintings. **Wadi Bu Shubariyim**, which runs from the east into the Haruj al-Aswad, is another alternative and home to some remarkable volcanic scenery as well as one of the largest **petrified forests** in world. We were not able to visit these sites but it is worth discussing the possibility with any Libyan tour company – Robban Tourism Services (see Organised Tours in the Getting Around chapter) is a good place to start.

Idehan Ubari & Wadi al-Hayat

The Idehan Ubari (also known as the Ramlat Dawada) is a dramatic sea of towering sand dunes. Along the southern border of the sand sea runs the Wadi al-Hayat. Once the domain of the Garamantian empire, the Wadi al-Hayat has always inspired strong feelings and was formerly known as Wadi al-Ajal (the Valley of Death); Wadi al-Hayat means the 'Valley of the Value of Life'. The valley is 2km to 12km wide and bordered to the south by the forbidding ridges of the Msak Settafet (Msak Setthaf).

The wadi is one of the most fertile (and hence habitable) areas of the Fezzan. The underground water table lies close to the surface, allowing palms to flourish unirrigated, while other crops can be watered from shallow wells and *foggaras* (layers of rock separated by channels that hold water). There is also good grazing for camels. As a break in the long trans-Saharan journey from the southern Sahara to the Mediterranean Coast, Wadi al-Hayat was also traditionally an axis of communications along the caravan routes.

The main highway from Tripoli to Ghat runs through the heart of the wadi. It's quite easy to pick up shared taxis anywhere along the road between Fjeaj and Ubari.

FJEAJ   الفجــيع
☎ 0728

Fjeaj, 133km south-west of Sebha, has a **weekly market** every Thursday, which can be colourful. There is a prehistoric **rock-carved giraffe** on the rocky wall opposite the hostel.

The only claim to fame of this otherwise nondescript town is that it has a *Buyut ash-Shabaab (Youth Hostel;* ☎ *2827, Main Highway)*. Right on the main highway (look for the HI sign), the friendly youth hostel, with its basic though clean rooms, has been popular with travellers for years (some of the staff speak French). However, its star does seem to have waned since the shift towards group tourism. We visited during a sandstorm, which made it look bleaker than it probably is. Shared rooms cost 5/7LD for members/nonmembers and a tent costs 5LD to pitch. Guests can use the kitchen, and meals are available for 7LD to 10LD. The hostel can also arrange excursions to the lakes.

About 300m west along the highway from the hostel is a bakery, and there are the usual small grocery stores around town.

TEKERKIBA   تكركيبة
Tekerkiba, the gateway to the Ubari Lakes, is one of many towns along the Wadi al-Hayat, hard up against the sand dunes of the Ubari Sand Sea. There is little of interest

along the main highway, but its profusion of palm trees set against the backdrop of the towering dunes is quite attractive.

When Hugh Clapperton passed through Tekerkiba in the 1820s he remarked that 'We found a great deal of trouble getting anything to eat'. There are no such problems these days provided you're not expecting *haute cuisine*.

Two camping grounds are signposted in English off the highway and are reached via a 1km dirt road that leads between palm trees, houses and small farms. They both charge 5LD to pitch a tent, and 10LD to park your car (5LD per motorcycle). There are also a few thatched huts (15LD per person). Meals cost 10LD to 15LD. *Fezzan Tours Camping (☎ 021-3335556, fax 3339438)* is the quieter of the two, and tends to avoid the convoys that stream off the dunes during peak season. The very busy *Camping Africa Tours (☎ 071-625594, fax 621778,* e *africa tours_libya@hotmail.com)* stands at the base of the main entry/exit point to the Idehan Ubari. It's run by the alternately funky and offhand Abdul Aziz who serves Pepsi (1.5LD), cappuccino (1LD) and basic meals from the thatched bar area in the centre of the main compound. There's usually no charge to use the shower or toilets, although the flimsy curtains don't offer much privacy and the dodgy plumbing can create quite a smell if business has been brisk.

Come here if you're craving Western company. If you prefer the solitude of the desert, you're better off heading into the dunes to camp for free, and just head down to the camping ground for a shower or food.

THE UBARI LAKES   بحيرات أوبارى
The lakes of the Idehan Ubari are among the many highlights of the Libyan Sahara. In a country devoid of permanent rivers and thousands of kilometres from the nearest ocean, the lakes of the Idehan Ubari are nothing short of a miracle. Many oases of the Sahara have been consumed by sprawling towns, which overwhelm the romantic ideal of a remote and idyllic palm-fringed pool. Even given the increasing numbers of tourists visiting the lakes, these oases are

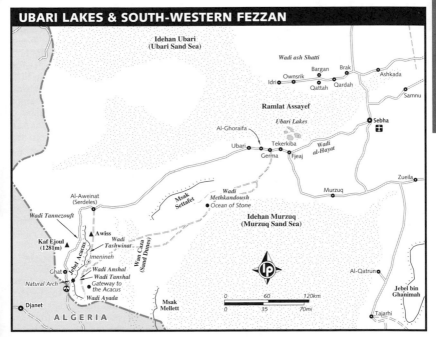

UBARI LAKES & SOUTH-WESTERN FEZZAN

the exception as they still provoke that sense of awe that only water in the desert can inspire. All of the lakes have a high salt content (reportedly as high as the Dead Sea) and swimming in the buoyant waters surrounded by sand dunes is one of *the* great desert experiences (unless, of course, you shaved that morning).

There are at least 11 lakes in the area, although many have dried up as a combined result of evaporation and lowered water tables from intensive agriculture in the nearby Wadi al-Hayat. Some reports suggest that the Great Man-Made River project also hasn't helped, although this link has yet to be confirmed. Nonetheless, the four main lakes – Mavo, Gebraoun, Mandara and Umm al-Maa – are still usually filled with water for most of the year.

Mavo   مافو

This lake, the closest to Tekerkiba (about 40km), nestles against a high ridge-line of

sand, overlooking countless small undulations off to the north. The water's edge is surrounded by reeds, and there are plenty of palm trees. The other lakes are probably more picturesque but it is still a superb spot and an excellent place to start. The *Mafaw Camp* has some thatched huts just off to the northeast, but you'd be better off camping a short distance away in the dunes as the plague of mosquitoes that appears at sunset can be most unpleasant. Mavo has not entirely avoided the long arm of globalisation – there's a shack selling the ubiquitous Pepsi and other soft drinks. Somewhat more indigenous are the small number of unintrusive Tuareg silver merchants who offer a decent array of jewellery for sale and will gladly help dig you out if you get bogged.

Gebraoun   قبر عون

Gebraoun (Grave of Aoun), around 3km east of Mavo, is one of the largest of the Saharan lakes, measuring about 250m by 300m.

The Worm-Eaters

The inhabitants of Old Gebraoun were members of the Dawada tribe who went by the none-too-charitable name of 'Worm-Eaters'. The epithet has been in use since the British explorer, Walter Oudney, became the first European to visit the lake in 1822. The reason for the name is that their diet once included tiny red shrimp-like creatures that were found in the lake's shallows and that thrived in the high salinity levels. Fishing for the shrimps was the preserve of women who pounded their catch into cakes, which they sun-dried. Surplus cakes were exchanged, along with dates and other fruits of the oasis, for the tobacco and olive oil of passing Tuareg.

Locals proudly proclaim that the lake is 'very deep'. Again the lake is surrounded by reeds and palm trees.

The ruins of the town of Old Gebraoun lie on the lake's western shore. With gaping doorways and generally abandoned air, the deserted town has an eerie, evocative feel. In 1991, after centuries of habitation, the population of Old Gebraoun was forcibly relocated by the Libyan Government to the bleak settlement of Gebraoun al-Jadid (New Gebraoun), which is on the main highway in Wadi al-Hayat. Many of the town's inhabitants were reportedly (and not surprisingly) very reluctant to move from the home of their ancestors. Among the recognisable buildings, most of which have deteriorated rapidly without regular maintenance, are two mosques, with squat minarets, and a school. On the dune overlooking the town and the lake is a small tomb marked with a flag; this is the last resting place of the local notable Aoun, who gave the area its name.

Gebraoun lake is one of the best places for a swim and there are plenty of access points around the shore-line (the water gets very hot the deeper you go). Although the few locals that live here are possibly becoming used to travellers stripping down to practically nothing, as a mark of respect you should try and be as discreet as possible, especially when families are about. However, unless you want to spend the rest of the day caked in salt, you should end up at **Camp Winzrik** (☎ 021-3611124-5, fax 3611126) where there is a well with fresh water (no charge). You could also camp here (10LD per person in thatched huts or your own tent), although, again, mosquitoes are a problem. The plumbing in the toilets is pretty ordinary. Inside the camp, **Restaurant des Daouda** serves couscous, salad and soup for an expensive 15LD.

If you've always wanted to try your hand at dune skiing, the camp has available a pair of rickety old skis for which it charges 5LD for an unlimited number of goes. If it's your first time, practise on some of the smaller dunes nearby before attempting the main hurtling descent behind the lake.

Umm al-Maa   أم الماء

Arguably the most picturesque of the Idehan Ubari lakes, Umm al-Maa has a narrow, elongated stretch of water surrounded by closely packed palm trees. As a smaller lake and much less open-sided than the others, it has an intimate feel to it and is an idyllic spot. Umm al-Maa, which means the 'Mother of Water', is a wonderful place for a picnic and a swim (there are rudimentary bucket showers nearby). The landscape is also wonderful with small clusters of palm trees petering off to the horizon. A couple of Tuareg handicraft sellers spread out their wares not far from the lake shore.

Mandara

Mandara, once one of the most stunning of the lakes, has begun to suffer an alarming drop in its water level and there is a danger that the water may disappear entirely within a couple of years. Like Gebraoun, it used to be surrounded by a small village, but the inhabitants were forced to leave in 1991. The buildings are now derelict and, with the receding water line, contribute to a sad shadow of its former beauty. If there is enough water, watch out for Mandara's famous changes in water colour with brilliant shades of green, blue and even red making for a superb spectacle. If you're keen to camp in the area,

The romance of the Libyan Sahara: a Tuareg camel driver and his mount (top left); traversing rolling sand dunes in the modern alternative (top right); and the palm-fringed Umm al-Maa (bottom) in the heart of the Idehan Ubari (Ubari Sand Sea), an idyllic respite from the hardships of desert travel.

The Jebel Acacus (bottom) is the haunting backdrop to some of the world's most extraordinary ancient rock art. Rock paintings depict hunting scenes and people in a time before desert sands encroached on verdant plains and waterways (top left & top right).

you'll need to watch out for snakes, scorpions and, of course, mosquitoes.

Exploring the Lakes

The best bases for exploring the lakes are Germa, Fjeaj and Tekerkiba. Mavo and Gebraoun, approximately 3km apart, are the closest to Tekerkiba and there are a further three dry lakes in the same wadi. Mandara and Umm al-Maa, also 3km apart, lie further to the north behind a towering ridge of sand dunes; the dry lakes of Umm al-Mahsan and Atroun are in the same area.

The ideal way to explore the lakes is with your own vehicle, which will enable you to seek out the least frequented camping spots and to visit each lake at your own pace. The round-trip from Tekerkiba to the four lakes and back is just over 100km. For Mavo and Gebraoun, follow the 4WD tracks leading north over the ridge of sand dunes from the Africa Tours camping ground in Tekerkiba and then east along the valley. Note that there are a number of smaller ridges that you have to cross en route, as this is an area of surprisingly heavy traffic, you should approach each ridge-line with caution in case something is coming the other way. Umm al-Maa and Mandara are reached via a hair-raising descent over very high dunes. From Umm al-Maa and Mandara, trails lead back to Wadi al-Hayat near Germa.

If you don't have your own vehicle, the hostel at Fjeaj, some of the hotels in Germa, and the tour-company-run camping grounds in Tekerkiba can arrange **excursions** for up to 200LD per 4WD for the day (up to four persons) – expensive, but there is usually no requirement of two 4WDs as there is in more remote stretches of the Libyan Sahara.

GERMA   جرمة
☎ 0729

Germa, 150km from Sebha, is one of the largest settlements in Wadi al-Hayat and carries with it a wealth of historical associations. The modern town lies near the ancient city of Garama, which was once the capital of the Garamantian empire (see History in the Facts about Libya chapter) and is well worth visiting. All along the high-

way on either side of Germa (particularly to the east) are the remains of pyramid-style burial sites, cemeteries and other funerary buildings; all are marked with a yellow Department of Antiquities sign. As you come over the brow of the Msak Settafet from Wadi Methkandoush to the south, you can see more Garamantian burial tombs.

Orientation & Information

The residential area of Germa lies north of the Tripoli-Ghat Highway, although most of the facilities are along the highway. At the turn-off to the paved road running south over the Msak Settafet to the desert is a petrol station and nearby are a couple of hotels, basic restaurants and the museum. Germa is not a good place to change money.

Ancient Garama

Garama *(adults/children 3/1LD, camera/video 5/10LD; open 8am-7pm May-Sept & 9am-5pm Oct-Apr)*, the ancient city of the Garamantians, is one of the most significant archaeological sites in Libya.

The initial Garamantian settlement was at Zinchecra, high on the hills of the Msak Settafet overlooking the Wadi al-Ajal (as the wadi was then called), 2km south of Germa. Zinchecra was thereafter used as a place of burial and the tombs there are among 50,000 that once dotted the area. In the 1st century AD, the Garamantians moved to Garama, a new city made of stone, clay and animal dung at the foot of the sand dunes. After Rome had sent several (often unsuccessful) punitive expeditions in an attempt to pacify the troublesome Garamantians, a treaty formed a commercial and military alliance between the two civilisations at around the same time. This new location also took full advantage of the natural fortifications offered by the Idehan Ubari and the mountains of the Msak Settafet and it is believed that there was a lake and natural spring nearby. There were originally six towers within the city walls. Most of the buildings that remain were added in subsequent centuries.

About 50m after entering the site is an open **square** on the left where wild horses were brought from the desert to be domesticated and then exported to Rome; the Garamantians were famous as horse breeders and herders of long-horned cattle. The square also functioned as a starting point for caravans, which carried dates, barley and wheat to exchange for Roman goods such as wine. In their heyday, the voracious Garamantian traders controlled most central Saharan caravan routes from this base in the Wadi al-Ajal.

The newer-looking sandstone structure on the south-west side of the square was the **home of a wealthy merchant**. When the forces of Islam arrived in Libya, Muslims moved into the old town and remodelled it. The buildings behind the merchant's house made up the **Islamic Quarter**. In this section is the modern reconstruction of the mosque and madrassa.

The **western sector** of the ruins is the oldest part of town and at least some of the buildings are believed to show traces of the original settlement. The rubble immediately north-west of the junction was once thought to be the remains of a bath built in the Roman style, but the British archaeologists excavating the site now believe it was more likely an ancient **temple**. The ramshackle **lanes** that twist out from behind the temple through the old quarter were built just wide enough to enable camels laden with saddle bags to pass through.

The old city is dominated by the large castle-like structure at the western end. This building may once have been a **Garamantian palace** containing a harem section on the far western side of the enclosed compound. When the Byzantines moved in, it was inevitably converted into a church. Little remains of either manifestation, but there are good views over the old town from the walls and of palm trees that still flourish in the immediate surroundings.

Old Garama is about 1km north of the main highway. There is a sign in English pointing to the 'Old City' opposite the petrol station on the highway.

Museum

Germa's small museum (admission 3LD, camera/video 5/10LD; open 9am-1pm &

3pm-6pm Tues-Sun) is situated 50m west of the petrol station on the Tripoli-Ghat Highway. It contains some photos of the prehistoric carvings from Wadi Methkandoush, a map of the region carved in rock, skeletons from Garama, a number of old Qurans, a model of the cemetery of Mohammed's followers in Zueila, a few broken ostrich eggs from the Jebel Acacus and a display of gifts given to Colonel Gaddafi (where would a Libyan museum be without such a display?).

Special Events

Every year in March the town hosts the **Germa Festival**, which is a colourful occasion. Inhabitants of the Wadi al-Hayat don traditional dress and perform local dances, all contributing to a highly festive atmosphere. Many of the children from Germa and the surrounding areas also dress up and in some performances occupy pride of place. Check with any of the tour companies (see Organised Tours in the Getting Around chapter) for the exact dates.

Places to Stay

Germa has a decent range of accommodation, and its camping grounds are signed in English.

Eirawan Camping (☎ 2413, fax 021-3601362) Huts 10LD per person. Located 250m north of the Tripoli-Ghat Highway and 1.5km west of the petrol station, this camping ground consists of whitewashed mud huts with thatched roofs. It isn't a bad choice, although it's a fair hike into town. There are shared showers (with geyser-sourced hot water), squat toilets and a kitchen for use by guests. The covered eating area is quite pleasant (breakfast 5LD, dinner or lunch 10LD).

Tassilie Tourism Camping & Restaurant (☎ 2299, Tripoli-Ghat Highway) Singles/doubles 10/20LD. The location here is better although the accommodation is a tad run-down and there are only seven rooms (with private bathroom) set around a compact courtyard. The owner is friendly and, as it was full when we visited, displayed an admirable concern for security by not allowing us to see the rooms. It's a couple of hundred metres east of the museum. There's a small restaurant doing simple meals.

Funduq Germa (☎ 2276, Tripoli-Ghat Highway) Singles/doubles 15/30LD. The friendly management of Funduq Germa has gone for the utmost simplicity in its pricing system – the price is the same whether or not you have a room with air-con or a private bathroom (some with mosaic tiled floor). It's not bad value if you can get both. For those with a shared bathroom, there is one toilet for every two bedrooms. The rooms are otherwise jaded. The air-con sitting area in the lobby is most welcome in summer.

Funduq Dar Germa (☎ 2396) Singles/doubles 30/40LD. If you're arriving in Germa from the desert, the Funduq Dar Germa will feel like the Garden of Eden. The 30 rooms are very comfortable and the squeaky clean private bathrooms come with, wait for it, a bathtub. The restaurant is very nice if expensive (lunch or dinner 25LD). They can also arrange a picnic lunch for excursions to the lakes or elsewhere for 15LD. Breakfast is included in the price of the room. There is a gift shop, a small teahouse and the front terrace is most pleasant, especially when bedecked with sunflowers. Best of all, the staff are hospitable. Worst of all, you'll need to book ahead as it is frequently filled with tour groups. It's the maroon building 50m south of the petrol station on the road to the desert.

When we were in Germa, there was a *camping ground* under construction just as you come over the brow of the Msak Settafet as you're coming from Wadi Methkandoush.

Places to Eat

Apart from the hotels and camping grounds, there are a couple of basic restaurants along the highway. *Tourist Restaurant* is opposite the museum, while the just-as-imaginatively-named *Tourist Restaurant* is at the eastern end of town on the south side of the road, next to a very colourful and well-stocked fruit stall. Both places do basic meals (couscous and chicken) for 5LD to 10LD.

Getting There & Away

The best place to pick up shared taxis is on the highway outside the petrol station, al-though you should be able to flag something down anywhere along the road. At Ubari (1.5LD, 30 minutes) you'll have to change if you're heading on to Ghat. In the other direction, there are taxis to Sebha (4.5LD, 1¾ hours) while Fjeaj or Tekerkiba costs from 0.5LD to 1LD.

Around Germa

The small town of **Al-Ghoraifa** is little more than an adjunct to Germa, but it does have a post and telephone office that is about 100m past the *El-Ghoraifa Restaurant*. Simple meals go for around 10LD.

UBARI أوبارى
☎ 0722 • pop 60,000

The friendly town of Ubari has little of interest to travellers, but you're likely to pass through here en route to the Jebel Acacus. It's also the only town of any size between Al-Aweinat (Serdeles) and Germa.

The valley here is broader than further east. The mountains to the south of town are known as the Jebel al-Aswad (Black Mountains). In the 1820s, Hugh Clapperton found Ubari to be 'situated amidst well-cultivated fields and gardens surrounded by a higher wall and in better condition than any other town in Fezzan' before concluding that 'the inhabitants appear to be more plentifully supplied with the good things of this world than the rest of their countrymen'.

Clearly this is no longer the town it once was. Water shortages are a periodic problem and you may even encounter water rationing.

Orientation & Information

Ubari sprawls either side of the highway, but most of the facilities you'll need are along the main road. There is a bank just east of the fort, almost opposite the road to Ghat. The petrol station is at the eastern end of town. The Methkandoush Travel & Tourism Company (☎ 2731) is located in the fort and can arrange excursions to the neighbouring burial ground of Hatya (see Around Ubari) and further afield. Ubari Tourism (☎ 2950), near the main roundabout, also may be able to help out.

Post & Communications The main post and public telephone office is at the western end of town. Take the highway until it reaches a T-junction (100m west of where it branches off towards Ghat); it's along on the right.

Remarkably, Ubari has joined the cyber revolution with *two* Internet cafes. Internet and General Services (☎ 2845) is on the Ghat road just south of where the highway turns south, while Al-Mustaqbal Internet (☎ 2767) is on the main roundabout. Both are signposted in English and charge 4LD per hour.

Things to See

If you're here in the morning or late afternoon, there's a good **old market**, which is still in use and can get quite colourful; it's just north of the main roundabout. The hybrid Turkish-Italian **fort**, 50m west of the Ghat turn-off, is worth a quick look, as is the **Tuareg Mosque**, which dates from the 19th century and is named in honour of the town's Tuareg heritage.

Places to Stay & Eat

Funduq Ubari was closed when we visited, but check it in case it's reopened; it's 1km south of town on the road to Ghat.

Just east of the main roundabout, the *Belket Tourist Rest House* was under construction with a camping ground out the back; expect to pay 15LD per person in thatched huts or 5LD to pitch a tent. There's also a restaurant (meals 10LD).

Simple food is the order of the day in Ubari with basic restaurants along the highway serving couscous and chicken and not much else. *Tourist Africa Restaurant*, right on the main roundabout and next to Al-Mustaqbal Internet, is probably the pick of the bunch (10LD). There is also the usual array of small grocery stores.

Getting There & Away

The shared-taxi station is about 100m east of the fort. Taxis run to Ghat (6LD, four hours, 362km) via Al-Aweinat (4LD, three hours, 262km) and to Sebha (6LD, 2½ hours, 190km) via Germa (1.5LD, 30 minutes, 40km) and the other towns of Wadi al-Hayat.

AROUND UBARI

Around 15km east of Ubari is another Garamantian cemetery called **Hatya**. Most of the graves are still covered by the sands and are yet to be excavated but some of the tombs are quite elaborate. They are just visible from the highway, around 200m south of the road.

South-West Fezzan

Libya's extreme south-west is the second most popular area (after the Ubari lakes) for excursions into the desert. The old caravan town of Ghat has its own appeal, but is also an excellent base for exploring the wonderful landscapes and prehistoric Saharan rock paintings of the Jebel Acacus.

AL-AWEINAT العوينات

☎ 0716

The pleasant, small oasis town of Al-Aweinat (also known as Serdeles) lines the highway with its trees and houses. Al-Aweinat can make an alternative base to Ghat for exploring Jebel Acacus. Another alternative is the challenging route from Ghadames to Al-Aweinat (see Ghadames to Al-Aweinat in the Jebel Nafusa chapter for details) to the north.

Al-Aweinat has a decaying **fort** that is built on the spring of Al-Aweinat. The castle was built during the Arab/Islamic period but, according to Hugh Clapperton writing in the 1820s, the local Tuareg believed it to be inhabited by ghosts and, as a result, wouldn't enter the site. There's a small *handicraft shop*, run by Youssef, that sells Tuareg handicrafts; it's about 300m beyond Aflaw Camp (see following) on the main road.

Aflaw Camp (☎ 32040, fax 0724-2828, mobile 091 2140678, Tripoli-Ghat Highway) has beds in good mud-thatch cottages for 15LD per person. This well-run place also has a delightful open-sided dining area where reasonable chicken, couscous and salad is served for 10LD. It's an excellent place to break up the journey between Germa and Ghat. There's an Aflaw Tours branch office on site, which can arrange camel or 4WD excursions, although it's better to set something up with its Tripoli office (☎ 021-4802881) before arriving to avoid waiting around.

KAF EJOUL كهف الجنون

A number of ancient paths once led south to Ghat, but most took the less perilous and longer route via Wadi Tannezouft, which the modern road follows. About 40km north of Ghat (60km south-west of Al-Aweinat) is the legendary Kaf Ejoul or Kaf al-Jinoun (Cave of Ghosts). It is less a cave than an unusually shaped mountain (a couple of kilometres west of the highway and visible from the road), which is the subject of a treasure-trove of Tuareg ghost stories. It is possible to camp close by, if you dare – it's an eerie place and there are those who claim to have heard strange night-time noises (see the boxed text 'The Legends of Kaf Ejoul').

GHAT غات

☎ 0724 • pop 16,000

The ancient trading centre of Ghat is one of the most attractive of the Libyan oasis towns. A highlight is the well preserved, enchanting mud-brick medina in the heart of town. It is also one of the few permanent Tuareg settlements in the Sahara. The setting is superb: a backdrop of stunning sand dunes, the dark ridges of the Jebel Acacus to the east and the distant peaks of the Tassili-n-Ajjer (in Algeria) to the west.

Unlike many of the old Fezzan centres of trade whose time seems to have passed, Ghat is a living town with a bustling energy that's hard to resist. Nearby borders have not been an impediment to the town forming strong links with the oases of neighbouring Algeria and Niger. As a result, this is one place where you're more likely to come across French being spoken rather than English.

The Legends of Kaf Ejoul

The ghost stories of Kaf Ejoul lured many a sceptical European explorer. The site was once known among the Tuareg as the Devil's Hill, a 'mountain hall of council where djinni meet from thousands of miles around'. With total disdain, Hugh Clapperton claimed that 'we had been told many wonderful stories about this hill, that there were people with red hair living in it, that at night when encamped near it you would hear them beating on their drums, see their fires and hear them firing on their musquets'. Marabout Sidi Mohamed of Al-Aweinat, a respected local notable (whose claims Clapperton felt free to dismiss without investigation), claimed to have visited Kaf Ejoul and saw people with red hair and beards. Clapperton's disrespectful air of superiority perhaps goes some way to explaining why white strangers were feared as the potential children of Idinan (Kaf Ejoul).

Sniffling with patronising outrage, he told the story he had heard about a merchant travelling from Ghadames to Algeria. The traveller had been stopped by one of these red-haired djinns (in Muslim belief, a spirit who could assume human form) who then demanded a gun for which it paid with a piece of paper inscribed with writing the merchant could not understand. The djinn told the merchant that on arriving in a town in Tuat (Algeria), the paper was to be given to a black dog that would come to meet him at an appointed place. The merchant was surprised to receive the payment from just such a dog at the appointed place in exchange for the paper; he was blessed with riches for the rest of his life.

Perhaps knowing something that Clapperton didn't, no Tuareg would climb the hill or get too close. Walter Oudney climbed the hill without any adverse effect, but before you dismiss the stories as superstition and set off to climb to the top, remember the difficulties of two other explorers. Heinrich Barth, one of the greatest Saharan explorers, reached the summit, but was completely exhausted and thirsty by the time he got there. On the way down, he lost his way and collapsed. To stave off thirst he cut open a vein to drink his own blood. A mere 27 hours after setting out, he was found by a local Tuareg man, feverish and close to death. James Richardson also became lost and was unwell for days after his own ordeal. Hugh Clapperton never chanced his luck.

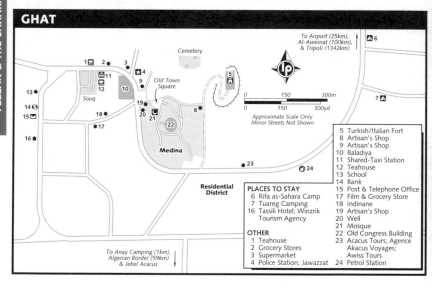

GHAT

To Airport (25km),
Al-Aweinat (100km),
& Tripoli (1342km)

Cemetery

Old Town
Square

Souq

Medina

Residential
District

To Anay Camping (1km),
Algerian Border (59km)
& Jebel Acacus

0   150   300m
0   150   300yd
Approximate Scale Only
Minor Streets Not Shown

PLACES TO STAY
6 Rifa as-Sahara Camp
7 Tuareg Camping
16 Tassili Hotel; Winzrik
   Tourism Agency

OTHER
1 Teahouse
2 Grocery Stores
3 Supermarket
4 Police Station; Jawazzat

5 Turkish/Italian Fort
8 Artisan's Shop
9 Artisan's Shop
10 Baladiya
11 Shared-Taxi Station
12 Teahouse
13 School
14 Bank
15 Post & Telephone Office
17 Film & Grocery Store
18 Indinane
19 Artisan's Shop
20 Well
21 Mosque
22 Old Congress Building
23 Acacus Tours; Agence
   Akacus Voyages;
   Awiss Tours
24 Petrol Station

History

The medina was built at the end of the 1st century BC on top of the ruins of an earlier settlement known as Rana, although it has been much modified and most of what is visible originated in the 12th century. First built by the Garamantians, Ghat was one in a chain of fortified oases that afforded protection to Garamantian merchants as they crossed the desert in their caravans. It also served as part of the defence system of Garama, as a bulwark and early warning system against hostile forces from the south. Although it never rivalled Ghadames in size, its strategic location as the only significant town in the region ensured that it played a critical role in the ebb and flow of Saharan conflicts and the pursuit of trade. This function as a natural hub of Saharan communications brought it considerable prosperity.

The Tuareg used to call the area the 'Land of Peace', while it was known in the old Libyan language as the 'Land of the Sun'. It was not until the 14th century that the name of Ghat began to appear in the accounts of geographers and travellers. Throughout this period and until relatively recently, the town came under the aegis of the Tuareg of the Tassili-n-Ajjer. They used their influence to set up a free-trade zone of sorts, although caravans only remained free of peril if they paid protection money to the local Tuareg tribes. In this way, they were able to control access to the Hausa states, including Timbuktu, along the Niger River. By the early 19th century, Ghat was said to be on the verge of supplanting Ghadames and Murzuq as the principal town of the Libyan Sahara.

The Sultan of Ghat (a hereditary position passed down through the female line) was subservient to the sultans of the Ajjer Tuareg, but enjoyed a significant degree of autonomy, including considerable freedom of action as regards the external affairs of the oasis. In the 19th century, the Ottomans extended their reach into the Sahara and the period of autonomy came to an end in 1875 with the first full-scale Ottoman occupation of the town. This, combined with the decline of the slave trade and the shift away from trans-Saharan trade routes, saw Ghat fall into decline and the French and Italians ruled from afar. Cross-border trade ensured that the town did not disappear entirely and non-Muslim visitors were rare. Ghat has quite recently reinvented itself as a gateway to the Jebel Acacus ensuring that tourism has become the town's lifeblood.

Orientation & Information

Ghat is a compact town with one main street. The highway in from Tripoli enters the town from the north, and then sweeps west, past a number of travel agencies and then the medina. The road then turns north and then west, passing the police station, *jawazzat* (passport office; ☎ 2308) and souq. Turning south, the road runs past the main post office, bank and Ghat's only hotel of note.

The bank is sometimes reluctant to change money; you're better off asking around the souq. There is a small shop, in behind the souq, which sells rolls of 36-exposure Konica print film for 6LD, as well as drinks and basic groceries. The petrol station can sometimes run low on supplies for a day or two so it's worth carrying extra with you to avoid having to backtrack from the Acacus.

Permits for the Jebel Acacus You're not permitted to visit the Jebel Acacus without a permit (120LD for the minimum two-car convoy). At the time of writing, permits had to be arranged through the travel agency responsible for your tour. Even when the restrictions on travelling in Libya are lifted, you will still need to be accompanied by a guide (30LD to 40LD per day) and the permit should be arranged through one of the agencies in town – the desecration of the rock art of the Acacus is still a sensitive issue here (see the boxed text 'The Day the Vandals Came to Libya' in the Facts for the Visitor chapter). Unless it's part of your tour fee, most will charge 10LD for piloting the process through to successful completion. If you don't have your own vehicle, you'll have to add the cost of at least two 4WDs (90LD to 150LD each) and the drivers (generally included in the 4WD price).

Travel Agencies There are a few tour companies on the main road just east of the medina. Among those who have come recommended by travellers are Acacus Tours (☎ 2318), the highly experienced Agence

A Glossary of Tuareg Terms

In this land of the Tuareg, many features of the landscape are known by their Tuareg names. The Tuareg language is known as Tamashek or Temissa, while the letters or script of Tamashek are called Tifinagh. Alongside many of the rock paintings are ancient inscriptions in an ancient Berber/Tuareg alphabet that was the forerunner of Tifinagh.

Tamashek words for 'mountain' are many, including *adrar*, *msak* or *tadrart*.

When it comes to the niceties of social contact, it will often bring a smile to the face of your guide if you greet him with *labas* (hello), *djordaed* (how are you?) or *matigum* (what's your news?). If he tells you that he is *mellet* (good), then chances are he's a happy man (or just being polite). If you want to say thank you, it's *taanomerd*.

Akacus Voyages (☎ 2804) and Awiss Tours (☎ 2396). Also good are Indinane (☎ 2460, postal address: BP 60), 500m west of the entrance to the medina in the streets behind the Baladiya, and Winzrik Tourism Agency (☎ 2604), which has an office in the Tassili Hotel (see Places to Stay later in this chapter). Increasingly, tour companies from Tripoli are setting up branch offices in Ghat.

Medina

Ghat's medina is a fine example of an ancient Saharan oasis and some of the lanes and roofscapes are reminiscent of the much larger Vieux Quartier in Agadez (Niger). The medina is compact but you could easily spend a couple of hours wandering through this well-preserved outpost of Libyan history.

The city has become, like many of its kind, deserted in revolutionary Libya (see the boxed text 'Out with the Old' in the Facts about Libya chapter). The nationwide policy of resettlement from medinas to modern houses reached Ghat in the 1970s and the last of the medina's old inhabitants moved out in 1991. There are 10 families now living again in the medina although few of the traditional inhabitants have re-turned; those living on the medina's fringe are mostly immigrants from Niger.

The **main entrance** to the medina *(admission 3LD, camera/video 5/10LD)* is from the small open square opposite the Baladiya. There's no ticket office, but once you've entered, word will get around and the friendly Tuareg ticket seller will soon find you. On the square are several artisans selling Tuareg

Tuareg Handicrafts

Tuareg jewellery and leatherwork are very distinctive and make a wonderful gift or souvenir of your time in the Libyan Sahara.

The most unusual item is the *croix d'Agadez* (Tuareg cross of stylised silver with filigree designs) named after the ancient town in Niger. However, every town and region with a significant Tuareg population has its own unique version of the cross. Although European explorers saw the design as evidence of prior Christianity, traditional Tuareg see them as powerful talismans designed to protect against ill-fortune and the evil eye. Some also serve as fertility symbols. The crosses are still used by Tuareg men as currency (eg, for buying camels), although these days this is rare in Libya. At other times, the crosses are worn by their wives as a sign of wealth.

Other silver items include: a wide range of silver necklaces (those containing amber are generally from across the border in Niger); striking square, silver amulets that are worn around the neck by elders as a symbol of status (some are also used in weddings by women); and ornamental daggers made of silver with leather hilts.

Leather items include tasselled pouches worn around the neck by men for carrying tobacco or money when out on the desert trails (some contain a surprising number of pockets) and saddlebags or cushions. The strong odour of camel comes at no extra cost.

The best places in Fezzan to find these items include small shops in Ghat and Al-Aweinat and around the lakes (the itinerant sellers at Mavo and Umm al-Maa had the best selection when we visited).

jewellery and daggers. By the roadside just outside the square is a wonderfully well-preserved ancient well.

In the medina proper, the first square you come to after passing under the low arch was used for weddings and is still used for festivals (see Special Events later in this chapter). This western area of the medina *(agrum wusharan)* is the oldest part of town.

The town's **mosque** (not generally open to the public), with its distinctive white, squat **minaret** in the Sudanic style, was built in AD 900, although next to nothing remains from this time. Given the hotch-potch of alterations, it shows a surprising unity of style.

The ziggurat-like structure in the heart of the old town served as the **old congress building**, where public meetings were held and from where the people of the town could be addressed. Climbing to the top affords excellent views over the roofs of the medina.

Around the town, there are a number of features to watch out for. Some of the doors (many are made from palm trunks) are very small – the passing centuries have seen the level of sand rise, raising the ground level of the town. Visitors are free to wander into the disused houses although many are filled with rubbish. The roofs are supported by wooden beams and laced with palm fronds for added protection. The houses, and indeed most of the public buildings of the medina, were built from a durable mixture of animal dung, sundried clay, mud-brick and straw. Atop some houses are mud adornments of alternately upright and inverted triangles. While no-one is certain, one local legend (which is also believed in Ghadames) claims that its resemblance to a crown is to remind the inhabitants of a much-loved Berber queen who ruled the desert. Another theory is that it is a representation of the goddess Tarnit.

Carved into some internal walls are nice relief facades. On some of the small flat platforms surrounding the lanes are indentations caused by the ancient process of crushing date seeds.

Overlooking the medina is the **fort**. The Turks started its construction, but it was not finished until Italians arrived and converted it into barracks. There are some superb

Tying a Tuareg Turban

The Tuareg turban (known as *ashaersh* or *tagelmoust*) has puzzled ethnographers for centuries. The Tuareg are one of the few people in the world for whom men, but not women, must wear the veil. One functional purpose is as protection against wind and sand. However, it also serves a social purpose in the rigid hierarchy of social relationships. A Tuareg man is not supposed to show his face to one of higher status, and Tuareg who still follow the traditional way of life will rarely expose the lower half of their face in company. When such men drink tea, they are supposed to pass their glass under their tagelmoust so as not to reveal the mouth.

There are many ways of tying the tagelmoust. Although it's likely to take a while for you to muster the casual ease with which Tuareg men accomplish the daunting task, one relatively easy way to do it is as follows:

Step 1 Fold the cloth so that it remains the same length but half the width.

Step 2 Drape the folded cloth flat over your head so that three-quarters of its length hangs down in front of your right arm and the shorter length over your left.

Step 3 With your right hand, hold the cloth about halfway down its length.

Step 4 Place your left hand across your body, tense it so that your four fingers are pointing out to your right and your thumb is pointing to the sky.

Step 5 Holding your left hand just below your right shoulder about chest high and about six inches out from your body, rest the nearest fold of the long length of cloth on your left hand between the thumb and flattened forefinger.

Step 6 With your right hand, quickly take the length of cloth in a full circle in front of your face and around the back of your head until you return to where you started.

Step 7 Repeat as many times as necessary.

Step 8 Tuck any remaining strands of cloth into the folds on the top or back of the head.

Step 9 Ask your Tuareg guide to sort it out.

There, we told you it was easy.

views from the roof. The best views over the medina itself are from the path that climbs up to the fort from behind the old town.

Special Events
New Year is a great time to visit Ghat. The **Acacus Festival** sometimes includes a spectacular sunset concert amid the cathedral-like Jebel Acacus. It's also an excellent (and possibly the only) opportunity to see performances of Tuareg dancing (see Dance in the Facts about Libya chapter). Check with any tour company (see Organised Tours in the Getting Around chapter) or with the local Ghat agencies mentioned earlier for exact dates and to arrange accommodation.

Souq
Ghat's open-air souq is small, but it has a delightful feel, and you can hear a mix of Arabic, Tuareg and French being spoken. It's a good place to browse and to soak up the atmosphere. Most of the stalls are given over to clothes, but there are also watches, sunglasses and fruits on offer. This is the place to purchase your Tuareg turban *(ash-aersh)* for protection against the sun and sand of the Sahara. The standard cost is 3LD

per metre and although some Tuareg take up to 10 metres, three should be sufficient. Another good buy are Tuareg pants *(aker-bai)*, with their exquisitely brocaded hems. These loose-fitting pants are very comfy and ideal for minimising the chafing of riding a camel; expect to pay around 25LD.

Places to Stay & Eat

Ghat is not blessed with an abundance of accommodation but many of Libya's larger tour companies are setting up camps in town where you will be able to pitch a tent (5LD) or sleep in a simple thatched hut (15LD per person including breakfast).

Anay Camping (☎ 2622, fax 2479) Thatched huts 15LD per person with breakfast; camping with your own tent 5LD. Just 1km south of town off the main road to the Jebel Acacus, this place has the usual cute, simple thatched huts. The shared showers don't have much water pressure, but the hot water usually arrives if you're patient. Inside the compound is a small artisan's shop with a selection of Tuareg souvenirs. The kitchen can be used by guests (please clean it after use), and tea and coffee (and sometimes simple meals) are available.

Rifa as-Sahara Camp *(Tripoli-Ghat Hwy)* Thatched huts 15LD per person with breakfast, camping with your own tent 5LD. This camping ground, near the north-eastern side of town, is not quite as good as Anay Camping, but still fine.

Tuareg Camping Thatched huts 15LD per person with breakfast, camping with your own tent 5LD. This camping ground, in the residential area east of the highway into town, is also OK.

Tassili Hotel (☎ 2560) Singles/doubles 25/30LD. On the western side of town on the main road, Ghat's only hotel has seen better days and is in need of renovation. Too cold in winter and too hot in summer, the rooms (with private bathroom) are overpriced and you'd be better off staying at one of the camps until it gets its act together. It does, however, have the town's only restaurant to speak of (meals 15LD).

The decision of where to eat simply does not arise in Ghat. Apart from the hotel, self-

How Times Have Changed

While we were in Libya, we were told the story of a Tuareg man who was still living a nomadic lifestyle in the Jebel Acacus in 1974, long before the tourist invasion. While travelling with his family along one of the sandy wadis, he came across a single set of tyre tracks left by a 4WD vehicle. He was astonished by what he saw and wondered what great animal it was that could leave such a trail. He refused to continue his journey and cross over the tracks until he had erased them. Only then would he continue his journey.

catering is the order of the day. There are a number of small *supermarkets* along the main road between the souq and the medina, which are good places to pick up last-minute rations for your desert expedition. Directly opposite the souq is a more sturdy-looking teahouse, which is an OK place to drink tea (0.5LD) and smoke nargileh, (1LD) and it occasionally serves snacks.

Getting There & Away

Shared taxis congregate at the entrance to the souq on the main road. Most taxis only go as far as Ubari (6LD, four hours) via Al-Aweinat (4LD, 1½ hours). For Sebha, Germa and the other towns of the Wadi al-Hayat, you'll need to change at Ubari. In the past there was one air-conditioned bus daily in either direction between Sebha and Ghat so with any luck it will be running again when you visit.

After wonderful roads from Tripoli all the way south and elsewhere in Libya, the last 20km into Ghat is surprisingly rutted. Locals blame a particular type of sand that expands and contracts in extreme weather underneath the asphalt.

There haven't been regular air services to Ghat since the embargo, but quoted one-way fares to Tripoli were 44/79LD for an economy-/1st-class ticket. The airport is 25km north of town.

[Continued on page 239]

ROCK ART OF THE LIBYAN SAHARA

The other-worldly landscape of the Libyan Sahara provides a perfect gallery for viewing one of the finest collections of rock art on earth.

These ancient art forms have proven astonishingly enduring. Their whimsical beauty reflects an almost child-like simplicity in the conception of the natural world, but they have been created by extremely skilful artists. Some rock walls in isolated wadis are covered to magnificent effect and in extraordinary detail. Indeed, it can be a good idea to bring a magnifying glass for bringing out many of the finely wrought elements.

The rock art's appeal is also enhanced by an understanding of what it represents. The local Tuareg believe that the ancient artists saw their art as a school for their descendants, a record of what they saw and how they lived.

It is not known who was responsible for the art. Some archaeologists attribute the images to the ancestors of the modern Tuareg, a people who remained in the Sahara as the climate dried and the remainder of the previous inhabitants migrated south around 4000 years ago. Others claim that the Garamantes people, who inhabited Wadi al-Ajal to the north, were responsible. Both claims may indeed be true, but the fact that much of the art predates these groups suggests that they were merely following a tradition set in motion by earlier indigenous inhabitants of the region.

The Discovery of Saharan Rock Art

Although the indigenous Tuareg inhabitants of the Sahara have known about the rock art in their midst for centuries, it has only recently captured the attention of the outside world. The German explorers Heinrich Barth and Gustav Nachtigal reported their findings and even made sketches of some of the pieces. On 6 July 1850, Barth wrote: 'No barbarian could have graven the lines with such astonishing firmness, and given to all the figures the light, natural shape which they exhibit.' This view partially reflected the prevailing belief that only Europeans could have produced such fine images. It was not until 1955 that a team from the University of Rome, led by Professor Fabrizio Mori (whose name has become synonymous with the rock art of the Acacus), undertook a serious study of the art. This tradition continued through the 1990s when another Italian team recorded over 1300 sites in the Acacus alone. Their findings, and the modern threats to the art, have contributed to the area being added to Unesco's World Heritage List of Endangered and Protected Sites.

The Climatic Context

When the Ice Age peaked in the northern hemisphere around 20,000 years ago (18,000 BC), it ushered in a period of low rainfall and barren landscapes across the Sahara – much the same as prevails today. With the thaw of the Ice Age 12,000 years ago (10,000 BC), the climate of the Sahara again became temperate and animals and people returned to occupy most of the region. Another possible dry spell approximately 8000 years ago (6000 BC) saw the introduction of domesticated cattle from the West, but for the next 3000 years the Sahara was covered with savanna, year-round lakes, pastureland and acacia trees. The temperate, often humid climate continued until 4500 years ago (2500 BC) when the last transition commenced and the Sahara began to become the vast, arid desert it is today, a process that was drawn out over 1500 years. Perennial lakes were replaced by more-seasonal water sources and as the region became progressively drier, oases replaced lake side and mountain villages as the sites of settlements and agricultural or pastoral activity. It was also the period in which trans-Saharan trade became the dominant economic activity fostered by an increased reliance on chariots, then horses and finally camels that were introduced to the Sahara 2200 years ago (200 BC).

The rock art from these periods is an invaluable resource depicting humankind's changing relationship with nature. There is some evidence of symbolic and religious inspiration. Professor Mori's tracing of the transition from the dominance of animals over human beings towards domestication and a taming of the natural environment through food production still holds true. Indeed, it remains the most enduring legacy of the art – a deeper understanding of the ancient world.

Types of Rock Art

The two main types of rock art in the Libyan Sahara are paintings and carvings (also known as petroglyphs). The paintings were usually made by a brush made of feathers or animal hair, a spatula made of stick or bone or the fingers of the artist. To ensure accurate proportions, the artists are believed to have painted the images in outline and then coloured them in. Most of the paintings in the Jebel Acacus are red, which was achieved through the use of a wet pigment thought to have been derived from ground-and-burned stone; the colouration came from soft rock containing oxidised iron (hematite or ochre). A liquid binder was then applied, most often egg white or milk, although urine, animal fat and blood were also used on occasion. It is to these binding agents that we owe the remarkable longevity of the paintings.

The carvings or petroglyphs are concentrated in the Msak Settafet, especially Wadi Methkandoush, although there are some examples in the Acacus. The engravings were achieved through a method known as 'pecking', which involved the use of a heavy, sharp stone. A second stone was sometimes used to bang the sharp stone like a pick. Like the paintings, the outline was usually completed first, often by scratching. Upon completion, some of the lines were ground smooth and, on occasion, the rock face was smoothed first as a form of preparation. After metal was introduced to the Sahara around 3200 years ago (1200 BC), a metal spike may have been used.

Periods of Saharan Rock Art

The rock art of North Africa is thought to have its origins almost 12,000 years ago (10,000 BC) in the central Sahara. There is also a belief among some archaeologists that it was from here that such art spread to Ethiopia, Kenya and Egypt, the latter possibly drawing on the Saharan art for inspiration in the great subsequent flourishing of Egyptian art. Although centuries of exposure to the elements have made it difficult to precisely date much of the rock art, most of the examples to be found in the Libyan Sahara fall within five relatively discrete historical periods.

The first of these is most commonly known as the **Wild Fauna Period** (10,000–6000 BC) but the period is also called the Early Hunter Period and the Bubalus Period after a species of giant buffalo that became extinct 5000 years ago. This era is characterised by the portrayal of elephants, giraffes and Barbary sheep from the time when the Sahara was covered by the plentiful savanna.

The **Round Head Period** (8000–6000 BC), overlapping for a time its forerunner, is known for human figures with formless bodies and painted, circular heads devoid of features. During this period, the people of the central Sahara are believed to have been foragers in the era prior to the appearance of domesticated stock. Its later stages feature more decorative figures adorned with headdresses and unusual clothing.

The next era was the **Pastoral Period** (5500–2000 BC) or Bovidian Period, which coincides with the gradual transition from a temperate to arid climate. Accordingly, human figures are shown in positions of dominance over the natural world, with spears, domesticated cattle and ceremonies in keeping with more settled communities. Experts also believe that this was when the skill of the artists began to show a decrease in quality.

The **Horse Period** (1000 BC–AD 1) followed, with many images of horses or horse-drawn chariots, some seemingly propelled through the air, reflecting the fact that transport and movement became more sophisticated and enabled relatively long-distance travel. Cattle are by far the dominant forms. Human figures from this period are represented by two triangles, one upright and one upside down, joined at the apex with a circular head on top. Much of the Tuareg writing (Tifinagh) alongside the paintings is from this period.

The final era of Saharan rock art was the **Camel Period** (200 BC–present). Camels became the Sahara's beast of burden and they are shown in abundance during this period. Paintings from the earliest part of this period are of the highest quality while more recent ones are nowhere near as finely conceived.

The Protection of Rock Art

While there are few laws on the books designed to protect Libya's rock art, the Libyan government has long recognised the need to protect its unique heritage. For many years, visits to the Acacus have only been possible with the accompaniment of local guides, and bags are generally searched upon leaving Libya for stashes of stolen treasure. The local Tuareg also proudly seek to safeguard the art forms and have lived alongside them for millennia. Although oil companies have caused some damage through their prospecting, one company has set up plans for the art's preservation.

Sadly, tourists pose the greatest threat to the survival of this priceless storehouse of ancient life (see the boxed text 'The Day the Vandals Came to Libya' in the Facts for the Visitor chapter). Whatever you do, please leave the paintings and carvings as you find them. That seemingly obvious point is lost on a small minority of travellers whose greed to take home the perfect gift or photograph has placed in jeopardy the survival of art forms that have existed for over 12 millennia. These actions have included chipping away sections of the rock wall or throwing water on the paintings to enhance the light for taking photographs, to complex silicon processes designed to copy the paintings.

If you want to learn more about Saharan rock art or about efforts being undertaken to preserve rock art across Africa, contact the Trust for African Rock Art (TARA; ☎/fax 254-2-884467, e tara@swiftkenya.com, postal address: PO Box 24122, Nairobi, Kenya). In Italy, you could try contacting the Archaeology Department at the University of Rome, while in Germany try the Heinrich-Barth-Institut (☎ 0221-556680, fax 5502303, e fst.afrika@uni-koeln.de) at the University of Cologne.

[Continued from page 234]

THE JEBEL ACACUS جبل اكاكوس

The Jebel Acacus (pronounced A-ka-**kous**) is an other-worldly landscape of dark basalt stone monoliths rising up from the sands of the central Sahara. This Unesco World Heritage–listed area is home to some wonderful scenery with a number of unique natural rock formations enhanced by the ever-shifting sands of the desert. Concealed within many of the Acacus wadis are prehistoric rock paintings and carvings, some dating back at least 12,000 years, which rank among Libya's principal attractions.

This was once purely the domain of the Tuareg; settled and nomadic Tuareg families ranged across the whole Acacus region. Most of the Tuareg families have in recent years moved to the towns, especially the oases around Ghat, and there are only 10 families left living in the Acacus Mountains. Many of those who remain work as guides and drivers for the tour companies, who are keen to utilise the Tuareg's intimate knowledge of the landscape.

Exploring the Jebel Acacus can be done by camel or 4WD vehicle. A permit and guide are compulsory (see Permits for the Jebel Acacus under Ghat earlier in this chapter). Even if a guide was not officially required, the dearth of accurate maps mean that it would be an unwise, even foolhardy traveller to set out without one. More than that, the experience of spending time with a Tuareg guide brought up in the desert is an essential part of the desert experience.

Some visitors to the Jebel Acacus are initially disappointed by the large numbers of tourists visiting the area. Indeed, this is not the place to come if you're in search of an isolated desert experience – hundreds of tyre tracks, which mark the most popular routes, can resemble a desert highway during peak season. Still, you would be missing a very special place (it's not without reason that these mountains are so popular with travellers) if you decided not to come, and there are plenty of isolated spots that you can visit to the east and south after visiting the mountains.

Exploring the Jebel Acacus

The possible routes for exploring the Acacus region are endless and the description that follows is designed to give some idea of how much time is needed to see the main attractions.

Day One The road to the Acacus leads south from Ghat. The paved road continues as far as **Ehsayir**, literally the town at the end of the road. From here the trail descends into a rocky and sandy series of tracks for which a 4WD is essential and where the going is much slower. Soon after Ehsayir, a track branches off to the Algerian border from where the track continues south around the Tassili-n-Ajjer and then north again to the Algerian oasis town of Djanet, 80km away as the crow flies but closer to 300km by 'road'.

Approximately 5km past Ehsayir is a white **monument** to Libyan and Algerian mujaheddin who died fighting the French. Right next to the main trail are a number of **overturned French military vehicles** marking the spot where the French occupying army lost a battle. Buffeted by desert winds devoid of moisture, they remain rust-free and are likely to remain here for centuries.

Thereafter, the road runs roughly parallel to the Algerian border as it heads south and then east. The border is marked by evenly spaced white markers and you must be careful not to stray into Algerian territory – even in this remote area, a border is still a border.

Entrance into the canyons and wadis of the Jebel Acacus is to the north via **Wadi Ayada** (Tuareg for 'leg'), a broad wadi lined with uneven cliffs rising to towering rocky bluffs. This is the start of the ridge of mountains that runs all the way to just south of Al-Aweinat. If you've spent the morning exploring Ghat and not set out until close to midday, it's a good place to pause for lunch.

The trails lead north into the wadi with some sections climbing up onto the minor bluffs. They offer fine vantage points for views back down the wadi, but be careful of loose stones close to the edge. A short distance further on is an army checkpoint – one of the most remote postings on earth. It is here that your permit and passports will be

Taajeelah (Tuareg Bread)

An essential part of the desert experience are nights spent under a million stars around a campfire. If you can, get your guide to talk about his desert experiences. Some will break into the raw songs of the desert as you sit by the fire surrounded by moonlit peaks or sand dunes. To complete the experience, ask if you can make *taajeelah* (Tuareg or desert bread). The bread is prepared from flour, water and a little salt. After the fire has been burning for some time, it's cleared away. The dough is laid on the hot sand and then covered with more hot sand. It's cooked beneath the sand for 15 minutes, uncovered, turned over, covered again and cooked for a further 15 minutes. It makes a meal on its own or can be added to stews. Either way, this delicious damper-like bread is at its best while still warm.

checked. This checkpoint marks the official **Gateway to the Acacus**. Soon after, the route becomes more sandy and drivers have to take care because the sand is soft and made up of very fine particles – the dreaded *fish-fash*. A few kilometres after the checkpoint, the trail leads over a deceptive ridge that is followed by an exhilarating descent of almost 100m. This is the point of no return – it is almost impossible for vehicles to climb the soft sand going the other way and the only exit points from the Acacus lie a considerable distance to the north and north-west.

The trail continues to descend, passing some minor examples of rock art nowhere near as impressive as those that lie ahead. The path winds between forbidding and magnificent moon-like rocky outcrops and across a stony plain before the valleys narrow and the trail becomes more sandy with sand hills pushing up against the rock faces. Although it is possible to reach the towering Natural Arch (see Day Two) by sunset, it's a favourite camping ground for 4WD convoys. You are far better off camping in one of the stunning wadis en route.

Day Two The wadis twist between the cliffs and continue to the awe-inspiring Natural Arch, which stands at the junction of three valleys about 100km along the trail from Ghat. Towering at least 150m high, this huge stone gateway is one of the most spectacular natural rock formations in the Acacus. Although there are others, none are as impressive as this one.

Not far after the arch are many of the finest examples of prehistoric **rock art** in the area. **Wadi Anshal** is one of two parallel wadis running north-south and contains at least three sites worth visiting. The **first site** you come to is on the left (west) cliff face and includes a cow, camels and a number of ancient Tuareg letters, most of which date from the time when domesticated beasts of burden had replaced wild animals as the predominant wildlife of the Sahara. There is also a very faint giraffe from an earlier period. The **second site**, also on the west side of the wadi also shows cows as well as a fine, stylised human figure. From here, a cave leads into the rocks and comes out on a ledge affording fine views back down the wadi.

The **third site** is on the other side of the valley. It involves a bit of a climb, but is definitely worth it. There is a very faint image of an elephant, of which the top half is missing. However, the highlight is a superb representation from an unknown period of three women dancing; it stands almost half a metre high. At the base of the climb are numerous pottery shards laid out for display and some remarkably smooth and circular holes once used by the ancients for pounding date seeds.

Wadi Tanshal is the parallel wadi that has more rock paintings at its far (northern) end.

Returning to the starting point of these two wadis, the trail winds gradually north in the course of which the valley broadens out. You'll likely pass through **Wadi Wan Millal** (Wadi of the White Sand), which offers some extraordinary mountain scenery, but is also very exposed during sandstorms. Here, as elsewhere in the Jebel Acacus, you may come across young children or women shepherding their goats in search of pasture among the scrubby bushes. At the northern end of Wadi Wan Millal is **Imenineh**, one of the Acacus' most popular wells where water is pumped out in generous quantities whenever a group arrives. If you're struggling with the heat and sand, this well will supply welcome relief. Situated on a broad, barren plain, Imenineh strongly highlights the miracle of water in the desert. You can have a bucket shower and give those clothes a much-needed wash; drying is not a problem.

After the well, a trail leads west over a low ridge and across a desolate black-shale wasteland, which the Tuareg don't consider worthy of a name. This leads directly to **Wadi Tenghliga**, which runs onto the prolific Wadi Tashwinat (see Day Three).

Day Three You could easily devote an entire day to exploring the 101 wadis that make up the main valley of **Wadi Tashwinat** (also known as Wadi Tashween).

Close to the entrance of Wadi Tashwinat is **Awanini**, a small mountain whose name means 'Go Up and See', so named after a legendary figure did precisely that, but was unable to climb down and so died there. On a wall facing Awanini to the south are more fine **paintings** showing giraffe, fighting and hunting scenes, a chariot and horned cattle. This wonderful collection spans a number of periods, ranging from around 10,000 BC (the giraffe) to the more recent chariot. Sadly, the best giraffe has been defaced by souvenir hunters.

Approximately 300m around the corner to the west is a superbly carved **elephant** or mammoth represented in a skilled line-carving of perfect proportions. Next to it is a smaller elephant, which has been less well preserved due to water damage. These carvings are unusual for the Acacus, which is dominated by paintings.

Not far into the main wadi, a series of tablets, sheltered by an overhang of rock, show remnants of what must have been an enormous and ancient **rock-carved map** of Wadi Tashwinat. The tributary wadis are marked by lines and the wells by small depressions in the rock. Next to the map are some more paintings and Tuareg letters.

One of the 'minor' offshoots of Wadi Tashwinat is **Wadi Inferden**, which contains some good paintings. Look for the **desert**

An Encounter with the Tuareg

Wadi Tashwinat is home to one of the few Tuareg families that remain living in the Acacus. The old man or elder of the family worked with Professor Mori in uncovering the sites of Wadi Tashwinat and he has since set up a semipermanent camp with his extended family. Most of the guides will take you on a visit to the family but, before you go, it might be worth bearing in mind our experience. The old man greeted us and showed us a small number of souvenirs for sale (one of which we bought). When we asked if we could take his photograph, he proclaimed himself heartily sick of tourists who come, take a photograph and leave without purchasing anything.

His anger was understandable. This family lives in the Acacus because it chooses to pursue a traditional lifestyle, not for the benefit of tourists. An increasingly exploitative relationship threatens that choice. This and other similar Tuareg families are in danger of becoming a tourist sideshow as foreigners seek to meet an 'authentic' Tuareg family. It is a difficulty faced by indigenous peoples the world over; if you do visit, please treat the family with the utmost respect and discretion. To avoid it becoming a one-way encounter, consider making a small contribution to their fuel or firewood stocks, or purchasing one of the small items they offer for sale.

mosque, which consists of a collection of stones facing Mecca that have served desert travellers for centuries. High above the mosque is a rock ledge, the walls of which have great **hunting scenes** with human figures pursuing animals with bows and arrows, as well as **giraffe** and a faint representation of what may be a **panther**. Above the ledge and visible from the 'mosque', there is a rock formation shaped like a camel.

Nearby, in the main Wadi Tashwinat, is one of the Acacus' famed painted **wedding scenes**. Also worth seeking out are the **excavation pits** of Professor Mori where a child's skeleton (now in Tripoli's Jamahiriya Museum) from 5400 years ago was found. There is also a smaller **natural rock** arch at the entrance to a small valley, at the end of which are some more paintings. Near the southern end of Wadi Tashwinat is a narrow, steep-sided canyon, which you can only explore on foot. This used to contain three natural springs *(gillta)*, which provided an invaluable water source for the Tuareg. Only one, at the furthest end of the canyon, still contains water.

Day Four Leaving Wadi Tashwinat, there are two main options. One is to continue to the northern reaches of the Jebel Acacus. This journey takes in the spectacular area of the **Awiss**, with its deep golden sands, small natural arches and black rocks in precariously balanced finger-like protrusions. It's a very long day from Wadi Tashwinat to Al-Aweinat, which should take you past the well of Bir Telouait, around 280km from Ghat and 80km from Al-Aweinat.

The alternative is to travel east towards the dunes of Wan Caza, the Idehan Murzuq and the exceptional rock carvings in Wadi Methkandoush. To visit these sites in conjunction with the itinerary outlined above would involve a minimum of six days (five nights), which would enable you to rejoin the highway at Germa.

WADI TASHWINAT TO WAN CAZA

One of the eastern tributaries of Wadi Tashwinat is **Wadi Tin Lallal**, which is one of the last wadis before commencing the crossing of the Murzuq Plateau. The wadi's main attraction is a **lovemaking scene** carved into the rock in enviously large proportions. It dates from the pastoral period (up to 7500 years ago) and of special interest is the figure with the dog or jackal mask – some experts believe it to be an invocation of the Saharan fable of a jackal's wedding, which symbolises fertility and rain.

To reach the golden sand dunes of **Wan Caza**, the trails lead east, leaving the Jebel Acacus behind. It's a full day's drive across the uninteresting plains between the **Msak Mellet** (a mountain range running off to the south) and **Msak Settafet** (east-west). You can either drive along the northern rim of

the Idehan Murzuq (Murzuq Sand Sea), which is more picturesque, though the soft sand will use up more petrol, or you can take the parallel route to the north, crossing plains of unrelieved monotony, completely devoid of vegetation or landmarks. It can be slow going, especially across the stretches of sharp, black rocks where you'll have to proceed at walking pace. If you take this route, it's about four hours from Wadi Tin Lallal to a windswept wadi of scrubby trees running due north from the Idehan Murzuq. This wonderfully remote spot makes a good lunch stop; keep your eye out for gazelle, which sometimes shelter here. The trails continue east within sight of the dunes of the Idehan Murzuq.

IDEHAN MURZUQ   أدهان مرزق

For many travellers the Idehan Murzuq is the desert of which they have always dreamed. This incomprehensibly vast mountain range (over 35,000 sq km and not much smaller than Switzerland) made entirely of sand is simply breathtaking. It's home to as beautiful desert scenery as you'll see anywhere – dunes rise hundreds of metres high. The northern face of the sand sea rises up from the impossibly barren Murzuq Plateau; myriad wave-like ridges, sculpted by the wind, ascend to razor-sharp summits. From a distance during the heat of the day, the Idehan Murzuq shimmers pale yellow in the heat haze. In the midst of the dunes as the sun lowers, the undulations change into subtle yet magical plays of light and shadow.

The sand here is lighter and lacks the reddish tinge of the Idehan Ubari. The Idehan Murzuq is also far less frequented. It's possible in this stretch of the Sahara to go for an entire day without seeing another vehicle and the choice of sand valleys in which to camp are seemingly endless. This is a place to soak up the solitude of the desert, sleeping under the stars and surrounded on all sides by moonlit sand dunes.

Ask your Tuareg guide to tell you stories about one of the north-eastern valleys of the sand sea. It is said that at night those camping there will hear the sounds, carried eerily by the wind, of ghosts at a wedding party, singing and dancing in order to lure the inquisitive to their deaths.

WADI METHKANDOUSH
وادى متخندوش

Wadi Methkandoush lies along the southern side of the Msak Settafet. It has one of the richest concentrations of prehistoric rock carvings in the world. Most of the carvings in the soft sandstone date back at least 12,000 years, making this one of the oldest rock-art sites in Libya. This open-air gallery contains hundreds of carvings of animals, which include wild cattle, giraffe, hippopotamus, elephant, ostrich and rhinoceros. There is also carving of a herd of giraffe scarred by bullet holes.

The proliferation of animals is all the more remarkable because of the barrenness of the surrounds. The carvings run for around 12km. You can ask your driver to drop you at the western end of Wadi Methkandoush at a place called Wadi Hin Patra and walk the length of the wadi, arranging to be picked up at the other end. This latter point is the favourite camping site for a number of groups as there are plenty of high-quality carvings in the vicinity.

Although it depends upon which aspect of desert life interests you, the more visually stunning Idehan Murzuq is an arguably preferable campsite, but if you do camp at Wadi Methkandoush, make sure you zip up your tent as snakes abound in the rocky clefts.

The wadi is separated from the Murzuq Sand Sea by the Ocean of Stone (named by the Tuareg), a large undulating plain covered with black stones, which looks like a post-apocalyptic vision of the end of the earth; it makes for slow going. If you're not coming from the Acacus, the carvings can be visited on a much shorter excursion from Germa (just over 150km away). Of the two trails from this direction, the southernmost route high on the plateau is preferable, although you'll still need to traverse part of the Ocean of Stone.

MURZUQ
مرزق

Murzuq, 170km south of Sebha, is historically one of the great Saharan towns. How-

The Formation of Sand Dunes

Sand dunes are among the great mysteries of the Sahara. In the desert, sand particles are relatively heavy so even the strongest winds can rarely lift them much higher than an adult's shoulders. The slightest bump in the landscape can cause a phenomenon known as cresting, where an accumulation of drifting sand builds up. The slopes facing the wind are generally more compacted and less steep than those that lie on the other side of the ridge-line. Individual or small groups of dunes inch forward with time, pushed by consistent winds. Sand seas are relatively stable, having formed over millennia as rock is scoured and worn down to individual grains of quartz or sand. The actual formation takes place where there were originally favourable land formations (often surprisingly small) and a constancy in the direction of the winds. Over time, with a base of ever more densely compacted sand, they become a 'permanent' feature of the landscape.

One of the most common types of dune are barchan or crescent dunes (the shape of the ridge-line), *seif* (Arabic for sword) which have long, sweeping ridges and *akhlé*, a haphazard network of dunes without any discernible pattern. Unique combinations of all of these can be found in both the Idehan Ubari and Idehan Murzuq.

ever, it's now greatly reduced in stature and wealth, a town whose time has past. Murzuq was once maligned as one of the most dangerous and unhealthy places in the Sahara but was nonetheless the capital for the chieftains of the powerful Awlad Suleiman tribe, which ruled Fezzan for almost four centuries, losing power in the 19th.

Although the highlight of the town remains the open-air **market**, Murzuq is a sleepy town of few charms. The **castle** (*admission 3LD; open whenever the caretaker can be found*) is still intact and open to the public as a museum. It was home to the Sultan of Fezzan and his considerable household and later to a Turkish garrison of 500 men. Next to the castle is one of the most charming **vernacular-style mosques** in Libya. The

FEZZAN & THE SAHARA

prayer hall is vividly painted in Fezzan colours and the mud-brick minaret curves unusually.

The modern town is downright ugly, but it does house a petrol station (which often runs out of supplies) and the odd grocery store whose stocks are similarly limited. Unless the *Buyut ash-Shabaab* (*Youth Hostel*) has reopened, there is nowhere to stay in town and camping is the only option. Nor are there any restaurants to speak of, although the occasional *cafe* serves chicken and couscous.

There are infrequent shared taxis between Murzuq and Sebha (4LD, one to two hours) and Zueila (3LD, 130km, two hours).

AL-QATRUN القطرون

This remote settlement, 310km south of Sebha, is little more than a few shacks, houses and a checkpoint. This impoverished region has always been home to a floating Toubou population (see Toubou under Population & People in the Facts about Libya chapter). Located on Wadi Ekema, it was historically Fezzan's most southerly town on the trade route to the kingdom of Bornu at Lake Chad. It is now the last town of any size en route to the Niger border and the end of the tarmac road. The authorities at the checkpoint will be keen to scrutinise your papers before allowing you to pass and, depending on whether the border post at Tumu is manned, may even require that you complete Libyan exit formalities here.

The Eastern Sahara

ZUEILA زويلة

Zueila is another former home of the Fezzan sultans (the town used to be called Balad ash-Shareef or Town of the Chiefs) and a rendezvous point for caravans, although it never rivalled Murzuq as a centre of trade. When the Arab traveller Al-Bakri visited in the 11th century, he described seeing a cathedral, mosque, bath and markets.

The **fort** overlooking the old town is quite impressive. Around 10km east of town is Zueila's main attraction – a set of **seven tombs**, known as As-Sahaba, belonging to a group of Mohammed's contemporaries who died here in a battle to defend the town in the 7th century. The tombs, comprising two storeys made of sun-dried bricks and stone and each topped with a dome, have been restored to something like their original appearance; ask for '*maqbara Sahaba*'.

There is a handy petrol station at the eastern entrance to town although, as always, supplies can be unpredictable. The only place to stay in town is *Winzrik Camping* (☎ 021-3611123), where huts are 15LD per person, and it costs 5LD to pitch a tent at the small campsite. You could also ask whether the *Funduq Hamera*, in the village of Hamera, 30 km west of Zueila, has reopened.

As for food, take what you can find in Zueila, which hopefully will be better than that Frederick Hornemann found in the 18th century when the food was 'apt to produce flatulencies and diarrhoea'.

There are occasional shared taxis to Sebha (5LD, 200km, three hours) and Murzuq (3LD, two hours).

TMISSAH TO WAW AL-NAMUS

The road east from Zueila goes as far as the tiny town of **Tmissah** (76km). Thereafter, it is unsurfaced for about another 100km to Waw al-Kabir. There is a *rest house* (15LD per person) and checkpoint (around 150km from Tmissah) on the track close to Waw al-Kabir where you must register your presence and show your permit.

WAW AL-NAMUS واو النامؤس

Few Libyan destinations require such an effort to visit as Waw al-Namus and, for the most part, the journey is one of unrelieved monotony. Waw al-Namus must rank among the most remote places in the world, standing as it does at the centre of the Sahara, just under 300km from Tmissah and even more from Tazerbo to the east. The lakes in this crater formed by a now-extinct volcano are superb, surrounded as they are by high reeds and fine black and white volcanic sand.

Travelling to Waw al-Namus is a major undertaking. You'll need reliable vehicles, an experienced local guide and to be entirely self-sufficient in food and water;

you will also need a good sleeping bag (especially in winter). Not for nothing is Waw al-Namus known as the Crater of the Mosquitoes, so bring repellent.

You'll also need to obtain a permit. At the time of writing, this could be obtained for 120LD (two vehicles) from the jawazzat in Zueila. You can hire a guide in Zueila but you'd be better off organising it through a tour company in Tripoli (see Organised Tours in the Getting Around chapter). In Waw al-Namus, be sure to use the existing track up the mountain to avoid scarring the landscape for others.

You may be thinking that this is a lot of trouble and expense just to see a mountain, but many people think it is well worth the effort.

TIBESTI MOUNTAINS   جبال تيبيستي

Libyan guides to whom we spoke claim this breathtaking chain of extinct volcanic mountains to have Libya's most superb desert scenery of dramatic cliffs, curious rock formations and deep ravines; it is also home to more fine examples of prehistoric rock art. Most of the range lies across the border in Chad, including the highest peak in the Sahara, Emi Koussi at 3415m.

Sadly, the area is presently closed to tourists. The main reason for this decision is the presence of thousands of unexploded mines left over from Libya's border conflict with Chad in the 1980s, as well as continuing unrest across the border in Chad.

TAZERBO   تـــازربو

Most people turn back from Waw al-Namus, but a hardy few continue eastwards towards Tazerbo, skirting the northern reaches of the **Ramlat Rabyaneh**, home to some splendid sand dunes. The ramlat itself can be difficult

to traverse because of the very fine sand; a guide is essential.

Tazerbo is a small place, significant because it is a source of water for the Great Man-Made River project. South of the town are the well fields. There are the remains of an old **Toubou fort** in the town. There's nowhere to stay and only the occasional grocery store.

The desert route to Al-Kufra passes through the oasis of Buzeima, which has very hot spring water, supposedly good for rheumatism. This spa town, also once famous for its dates, has long been deserted.

AL-KUFRA   الكفرة

Rather than being just one town, Al-Kufra is more a group of oases clustered together and a centre of the government's efforts to develop large-scale agriculture in remote areas. Many farms have closed due to a lowered water table with the Great Man-Made River the most likely culprit.

Al-Kufra was once an important staging post for trans-Saharan trade and, from the 19th century, it was an important centre of the Sanusi Movement. After strong resistance, it was finally occupied by the Italians in the 1930s. During WWII the oasis became a base for the Long Range Desert Group under the British.

There's nothing really to see here, apart from the **camel market**, and only the *Hotel Sudan* has beds (15LD per person). There are a few cheap *restaurants* dotted around the centre of town.

There are weekly flights to/from Tripoli (51/102LD one way/return) and three flights weekly between Al-Kufra and Benghazi (32/64LD, three hours). There are a couple of buses a week to Tripoli (45LD, 32 hours) and Benghazi (13LD, 12 hours).

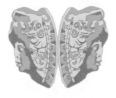

Language

Arabic is the official language of Libya and the government has decreed that all street and business signs and radio programs must be in Arabic. Generally, the Arabic spoken in the east of the country is more akin to that spoken in Egypt, while to the west it's closer to the Tunisian variety. If you can speak either of these dialects, you'll encounter few problems – and with the popularity of group tourism, an interpreter is never likely to be too far away if you do get stuck.

All publications and signs are written in Modern Standard Arabic (MSA), which is the common written form in all Arabic-speaking countries. Unusually, however, both Western and Arabic numbers are used almost universally in Libya (eg, for road distances).

Although Libya has its own distinct culture, hundreds of thousands of Egyptians and Tunisians live and work there, and their presence has served to lessen the differences between the dialects. The dominance of the Egyptian film and music industries as the entertainment of choice among many Libyans has also worked to minimise the differences.

There are nonetheless some subtle differences in pronunciation that are worth noting, though they're unlikely to impact upon beginners. These include a tendency towards more guttural pronunciations, especially in Cyrenaica, and some of the long vowel sounds are discernibly shorter than in other dialects. The words and phrases included in this chapter are predominantly in Egyptian Arabic, but Libyan variants are given where important differences occur.

If you take the time to learn even a little of the language, you'll discover and experience much more while travelling through the country. For a comprehensive guide to Arabic, get hold of Lonely Planet's *Egyptian Arabic phrasebook*.

Pronunciation

Pronunciation of Arabic can be somewhat tongue-tying for someone unfamiliar with the intonation and combination of sounds. Pronounce the transliterated words and phrases slowly and clearly.

The following guide should help, but it isn't complete because the myriad rules governing pronunciation and vowel use are too extensive to be covered here.

Short Vowels

a   as in 'had' (sometimes very short)
e   as in 'bet' (sometimes very short)
i   as in 'hit'
o   as in 'hot'
u   as the 'oo' in 'book'

Long Vowels

Long vowels are indicated by a macron (stroke above the letter).

ā   as the 'a' in 'father'
ē   as the 'e' in 'ten', but lengthened
ī   as the 'e' in 'ear', only softer
ō   as the 'o' in 'four'
ū   as the 'oo' in 'food'

You may also see long vowels transliterated as double vowels, eg, 'aa' (ā), 'ee' (ī) and 'oo' (ū).

Diphthongs

aw   as the 'ow' in 'how'
ay   as 'y' in 'why'
ei   as the 'a' in 'cake'

These last two are tricky, as one can slide into the other in certain words, depending on who is pronouncing them. Remember these rules are an outline and are far from exhaustive.

Consonants

Pronunciation for all Arabic consonants is covered in the alphabet table on page 247.

The Arabic Alphabet

Final	Medial	Initial	Alone	Transliteration	Pronunciation
ـا			ا	ā	as the 'a' in 'father'
ـب	ـبـ	بـ	ب	b	as in 'bet'
ـت	ـتـ	تـ	ت	t	as in 'ten'
ـث	ـثـ	ثـ	ث	th	as in 'thin'
ـج	ـجـ	جـ	ج	j/g	as in 'jet'; as the 'g' in 'go' in Egyptian Arabic
ـح	ـحـ	حـ	ح	H	a strongly whispered 'h', almost like a sigh of relief
ـخ	ـخـ	خـ	خ	kh	as the 'ch' in Scottish 'loch'
ـد			د	d	as in 'dim'
ـذ			ذ	dh	as the 'th' in 'this'
ـر			ر	r	a rolled 'r', as in the Spanish word caro
ـز			ز	z	as in 'zip'
ـس	ـسـ	سـ	س	s	as in 'so', never as in 'wisdom'
ـش	ـشـ	شـ	ش	sh	as in 'ship'
ـص	ـصـ	صـ	ص	ş	emphatic 's'
ـض	ـضـ	ضـ	ض	ḍ	emphatic 'd'
ـط	ـطـ	طـ	ط	ţ	emphatic 't'
ـظ	ـظـ	ظـ	ظ	ẓ	emphatic 'z'
ـع	ـعـ	عـ	ع	'	the Arabic letter 'ayn; pronounce as a glottal stop – like the closing of the throat before saying 'Oh oh!' (see Other Sounds on p 248)
ـغ	ـغـ	غـ	غ	gh	a guttural sound like Parisian 'r'
ـف	ـفـ	فـ	ف	f	as in 'far'
ـق	ـقـ	قـ	ق	q	a strongly guttural 'k' sound; in Egyptian Arabic often pronounced as a glottal stop
ـك	ـكـ	كـ	ك	k	as in 'king'
ـل	ـلـ	لـ	ل	l	as in 'lamb'
ـم	ـمـ	مـ	م	m	as in 'me'
ـن	ـنـ	نـ	ن	n	as in 'name'
ـه	ـهـ	هـ	ه	h	as in 'ham'
ـو			و	w	as in 'wet'; or
				ū	long, as the 'oo' on 'food'; or
				aw	as the 'ow' in 'how'
ـي	ـيـ	يـ	ي	y	as in 'yes'; or
				ī	as the 'e' in 'ear', only softer; or
				ay	as the 'y' in 'by' or as the 'ay' in 'way'

Vowels Not all Arabic vowel sounds are represented in the alphabet. See Pronunciation on p 246 for a list of all Arabic vowel sounds.
Emphatic Consonants To simplify the transliteration system used in this book, the emphatic consonants have not been included.

Note that when double consonants occur in transliterations, each of the two consonants is pronounced. For example, *al-hammam*, (bathhouse), is pronounced 'al-ham-mam'.

Other Sounds

Arabic has two sounds that are very tricky for non-Arabs to produce, the 'ayn and the glottal stop. The letter 'ayn represents a sound with no English equivalent that comes even close – it is similar to the glottal stop (which is not actually represented in the alphabet), but the muscles at the back of the throat are gagged more forcefully and air is allowed to escape – it has been described as the sound of someone being strangled! In many transliteration systems 'ayn is represented by an opening quotation mark, and the glottal stop by a closing quotation mark. To make the transliterations in this language guide (and throughout the rest of the book) easier to use, we have not distinguished between the glottal stop and the 'ayn, using the closing quotation mark to represent both sounds. You'll find that Arab speakers will still understand you.

Transliteration

Converting what for most outsiders is just a bunch of squiggles into meaningful words (ie, those written using the Roman alphabet) is a tricky business – in fact no really satisfactory system of transliteration has been established, and probably never will be. For this edition, an attempt has been

The Transliteration Dilemma

TE Lawrence, when asked by his publishers to clarify 'inconsistencies in the spelling of proper names' in *Seven Pillars of Wisdom* – his account of the Arab Revolt in WWI – wrote back:

'Arabic names won't go into English. There are some 'scientific systems' of transliteration, helpful to people who know enough Arabic not to need helping, but a washout for the world. I spell my names anyhow, to show what rot the systems are.'

made to standardise some spellings of place names and the like. There is only one word for 'the' in Arabic: *al*. (Before certain consonants, it modifies: in Arabic, Saladin's name is *Salah ad-Din*, meaning 'righteousness of the faith'; here, 'al' has been modified to 'ad' before the 'd' of 'Din'.) Sometimes the 'al' also appears as 'el'. Whichever way you see these little blighters spelled, remember that they are all the same word.

The whole business is fraught with pitfalls, and in a way there are no truly 'correct' answers. The locals themselves can only guess at how to make the conversion – and the result is often amusing. The fact that French and English have had a big influence in many Arabic-speaking countries has led to all sorts of interesting ideas on transliteration. Don't be taken aback if you start noticing half a dozen different spellings for the same thing.

For some reason, the letters 'q' and 'k' have caused enormous problems, and have been interchanged willy-nilly in transliteration. For a long time, Iraq (which in Arabic is spelled with what can only be described in English as the nearest equivalent to 'q') was written, even by scholars, as 'Irak'. Other examples of an Arabic 'q' receiving such treatment are *souq* (market), often written 'souk'; *qasr* (castle), sometimes written 'kasr'; and the Libyan town *Murzuq*, often written as 'Murzuk'. It's a bit like spelling English 'as she is spoke' – imagine the results if Australians, Americans, Scots and Londoners were all given free rein to write as they pronounce!

In some instances in this book, however, we have used the forms of common words and place names as most people know them (eg, Tobruk rather than 'Tubruq').

Greetings & Civilities

Arabic is more formal than English, especially with greetings; thus even the simplest greetings, such as 'hello', vary according to when and how they are used. In addition, each greeting requires a certain response that varies according to whether it is being said to a male, female or group of people.

Hello.
salām 'alēkum
(lit: peace upon you)
(response)
wa 'alēkum es salām
(lit: and peace upon you)
Hello/Welcome.
ahlan wa sahlan
(response)
ahlan bīk (to m)
ahlan bīkī (to f)
ahlan bīkum (to group)
Pleased to meet you. (when first meeting)
tasharrafna (polite)
fursa sa'īda (informal)
Good morning.
sabāH al-khēr
(response)
sabāH an-nūr
Good evening.
misa' al-khēr
(response)
misa' an-nūr
Good night.
tisbaH 'ala khēr (to m)
tisbaHī 'ala khēr (to f)
tisbaHu 'ala khēr (to group)
(response; also used as 'Good afternoon' in
the late afternoon)
wenta bikhēr (to m)
wentī bikhēr (to f)
wentū bikhēr (to group)
Goodbye.
ma'as salāma (lit: go in safety)

Essentials

There are three ways to say 'Please' in
Arabic, each of which is used somewhat
differently:

When asking for something in a shop, say:
min fadlak (to a male), *min fadlik* (to a
female), *min fadlukum* (to group).

Under similar, but more formal, circumstances (eg, when trying to get a waiter's
attention), say: *law samaHt* (to m), *law
samaHtī* (to f), *law samaHtu* (to group).

When offering something to someone, for
example, a chair or bus seat, or if inviting

someone into your home for a meal, say:
tfaddal (to m), *tfaddalī* (to f), *tfaddalū* (to
group). When preceded by 'i' (eg, *itfaddal*),
these words can be used to mean much the
same thing, as in 'Please, go ahead' (and do
something).

Excuse me.
'an iznak, esmaHlī (to m)
'an iznik, esmaHīlī (to f)
'an iznukum, esmaHūlī (to group)
Thank you.
shukran/
shehaet (lit: 'good health')
bari kelorfik (a blessing, but used widely)
Thank you very much.
shukran jazīlan
No thank you.
la' shukran
You're welcome.
'afwan
Yes.
aywa
na'am (more formal)
No.
la'
Sorry.
'assif
OK/Alright!
bahi!

One of the most useful words to know is
imshī, which means 'Go away'. Use this at
at tourist sites when you are being besieged
by children. Do not use it on adults; instead,
just say, *la' shukran* ('No thank you').

Small Talk

How are you?
kief halak/kief ul-halk? (to m)
kief halik? (to f)
kief halakum? (to group)
I'm fine.
kwayyis ilHamdu lillah
(to m, lit: fine, thanks be to God)
kwaysa ilHamdu lillah (to f)
kwaysīn ilHamdu lillah (to group)

(On their own, *kwayyis*, *kwaysa* and
kwaysīn literally mean 'good' or 'fine', but

they are rarely heard alone in response to 'How are you?')

What's your name?	*ismak ēh?* (to m)
	shin ismak? (informal)
	ismīk ēh? (to f)
	shin ismik? (informal)
My name is ...	*ismī* ...

America	*amrīka*
Australia	*ustralya*
Canada	*kanada*
England	*inglaterra*
France	*fransa*
Germany	*almanya*
Italy	*itāliyya*
Japan	*al-yaban*
Netherlands	*holanda*
Spain	*isbanya*
Sweden	*as-swīd*
Switzerland	*swīsra*

Language Difficulties

I understand.	*ana fāhem/fahma* (m/f)
I don't understand.	*ana mish fāhem/ fahma* (m/f)
Do you speak English?	*enta bititkallim inglīzī?* (to m)
	entī bititkallimī inglīzī? (to f)

Getting Around

bicycle	*'agala/darrāja*
boat	*markib*
car	*sayyāra/'arabiyya*
ferry	*ma'atiya*

Where is the ...?	*'ayna/fein ...?*
airport	*matār*
bus station	*maHattat al-otobīs*
railway station	*maHattat al-'atr*
ticket office	*maktab at-tazāker*
street	*ash-shāri'*
city	*al-medīna*
village	*al-qarya*
bus stop	*maw'if al-otobīs*
station	*al-maHatta*

How far is ...?	*kam kilo li ...?*
I want to go to ...	*ana 'ayiz arūH ...*

Signs

Entrance	مدخل
Exit	خروج
Toilets (Men)	حمام الرجال
Toilets (Women)	حمام النساء
Hospital	مستشفى
Police	الشرطة
Prohibited	ممنوع
Hotel	فندق
Restaurant	مطعم
Youth Hostel	بيوت الشباب
Bank	مصرف
Street	شارع
City Centre	المركز المدينة

When does the ... leave/arrive?	*emta qiyam/wusuul...?*
bus	*al-otobīs*
train	*al-'atr*
boat	*al-markib*

Which bus goes to...?	*otobīs nimra kam yerūH...?*
Does this bus go to ...?	*al-otobīs da yerūH ...?*
How many buses per day go to ...?	*kam otobīs fil yōm yerūH...?*
Please tell me when we arrive in ...	*min fadlak, ullī emta Hanūsel ...*
What is the fare to ...?	*gedaesh/bikam at-tazkara li ...?*
May I/we sit here?	*mumkin eglis/neglis hena?*
Stop here, please.	*wa'if/hassib hena, min fadlak*
Please wait for me.	*mumkin tantazarnī*
Where can I rent a bicycle?	*'ayna/fein e'ajjar 'agala/darrāja?*
Wait!	*istanna!*

Directions

Where is the hotel ...?	*'ayna-l-funduq ...?/ fein al-funduq ...?*
Can you show me the way to the hotel ...?	*mumkin tewarrīnī at-tarīqlil-funduq ...?*
Where?	*'ayna/fein?*
here	*hina*
there	*hināk*
this address	*al-'anwān da*
north	*shimāl*
south	*janūb*
east	*shark*
west	*gharb*

Around Town

Where is the ...?	*'ayna/fein ...?*
bank	*al-bank/al-masraf*
beach	*al-plā/ash-shaata*
embassy	*as-sifāra*
female toilet	*twalēt al-Harīmī*
market	*as-sūq*
male toilet	*twalēt ar-ragel*
mosque	*al-jāme'*
museum	*al-matHaf*
old city	*al-medīna/al-'adīma*
police station	*al-bolīs*
post office	*al-bōsta/ maktab al-barīd*
restaurant	*al-mat'am*

Accommodation

I'd like to see the rooms.	*awiz ashūf al-owad*
May I see other rooms?	*mumkin ashūf owad tānī?*
How much is the room per night?	*gedaesh/kam ugrat al-odda bil-laila?*
Do you have any cheaper rooms?	*fī owad arkhas?*
It's too expensive.	*da ghālī 'awī*
This is fine.	*da kwayyis*
air-conditioning	*takyīf hawa*

Shopping

Where can I buy ...?	*'ayna/fein mumkin ashtirī ...?*
I'd like ...	*nebbi ...*
How much is this/that ...?	*gedaesh/bikam da ...?*

Numbers

Arabic numerals are simple to learn and, unlike the written language, run from left to right. Pay attention to the order of the words in numbers from 21 to 99.

0	٠	*sifr*
1	١	*wāHid*
2	٢	*itnein*
3	٣	*talāta*
4	٤	*arba'a*
5	٥	*khamsa*
6	٦	*sitta*
7	٧	*sab'a*
8	٨	*tmanya*
9	٩	*tis'a*
10	١٠	*'ashara*
11	١١	*Hidāshar*
12	١٢	*itnāshar*
13	١٣	*talattāshar*
14	١٤	*arba'tāshar*
15	١٥	*khamastāshar*
16	١٦	*sittāshar*
17	١٧	*saba'tāshar*
18	١٨	*tamantāshar*
19	١٩	*tisa'tāshar*
20	٢٠	*'ishrīn*
21	٢١	*wāHid wi 'ishrīn*
22	٢٢	*itnein wi 'ishrīn*
30	٣٠	*talatīn*
40	٤٠	*arba'īn*
50	٥٠	*khamsīn*
60	٦٠	*sittīn*
70	٧٠	*sab'īn*
80	٨٠	*tamanīn*
90	٩٠	*tis'īn*
100	١٠٠	*myya*
101	١٠١	*myya wi wāHid*
200	٢٠٠	*mītein*
300	٣٠٠	*talāt mia*
1000	١٠٠٠	*'alf*
2000	٢٠٠٠	*'alfein*
3000	٣٠٠٠	*talāttalāf*

Ordinal Numbers

first	*'awwal*
second	*tānī*
third	*tālit*
fourth	*rābi'*
fifth	*khāmis*

It costs too much. *da ghālī 'awī*
Do you have ...? *fī 'andak ...?*

Money
I want to change ... *ana 'ayiz usarraf ...*
  money *fulūs*
  travellers cheques *shīkāt siyaHiyya*

US$	*dolār amrikānī*
UK£	*guinay sterlīnī*
A$	*dolār ustrālī*
DM	*mārk almānī*

Time & Dates
What time is it?	*sā'ah kam?*
When?	*emta?*
day	*yom*
month	*shaher*
today	*el nharda*
tomorrow	*bokra*
week	*esbuwa*
year	*sana*
yesterday	*mberrah*
early	*badrī*
late	*mut'akhar*
daily	*kull yōm*

Sunday	*(yōm) al-aHadd*
Monday	*(yōm) al-itnīn*
Tuesday	*(yōm) at-talāt*
Wednesday	*(yōm) al-arba'a*
Thursday	*(yōm) al-khamīs*
Friday	*(yōm) al-jum'a*
Saturday	*(yōm) as-sabt*

In Libya the names of the months are virtually the same as their European counterparts and are easily recognisable. For a list of Hjira calendar months, see the Public Holidays & Special Events section in the Facts for the Visitor chapter.

January	*yanāyir*
February	*fibrāyir*
March	*māris*
April	*abrīl*
May	*māyu*
June	*yunyu*
July	*yulyu*

Emergencies
Help!	*el-Ha'nī!*
Call a doctor!	*itassal-ī bi-doktōr!*
Call an ambulance!	*ittasal-ī bil-is'āf!*
Call the police!	*itassal bil-bolīs!*
I've been robbed.	*ana itsara't*
Thief!	*Harāmi!*
I'm lost.	*ana tāyih/tāyha.*
Go away!	*imshī!*
Where are the toilets?	*'ayna/fein al-twalēt?*

August	*aghustus*
September	*sibtimbir*
October	*'uktoobir*
November	*nufimbir*
December	*disimbir*

Health
I need a doctor.	*'awiz doktōr*
Where is the hospital?	*'ayna-l-mustashfa?/ fein al-mustashfa?*
My friend is ill.	*sadīqi 'ayan*
I'm allergic to antibiotics/ penicillin.	*'andī Hasasiyya dodd el entībiyotik/ el binisilīn*

I'm ...	*'indī ...*
asthmatic	*hasāsiyya fi sadri*
diabetic	*sukkar*
epileptic	*sar'*

antiseptic	*mutahhir*
aspirin	*asbirin*
Band-Aids	*blāstir*
condoms	*kabābīt*
diarrhoea	*is-hāl*
fever	*sukhūna*
headache	*sudā'*
hospital	*mustashfa*
pharmacy	*agzakhana*
pregnant	*Hāmel*
prescription	*roshetta*
sanitary napkins	
stomachache	*waga' fil batn*
tampons	*hifāz al-'āda al-shahriyya*

Glossary

acanthus – stylised leaf used in Greek and Roman decoration

adrar – Tuareg for mountain; see also *msak* and *tadrart*

agora – main public square of ancient Greek cities

ain – well or spring

akerbai – loose-fitting Tuareg pants

akhle – haphazard network of sand dunes without discernible pattern

'alaam – traditional music form

An-Nahr Sinai – The Great Man-Made River

apodyteria – changing rooms in a Roman baths complex

aquifers – layers of rock that hold underground water

ashaersh – Tuareg turban

aysh – soft, unleavened bread

bab – gate or door

bahr – ocean

baladiya – municipal or town hall

barchan – crescent-shaped sand dune

basilica – court or assembly building; under the Byzantines, the word referred to a church

bazin – hard, unleavened bread made from barley

bey – junior officer in Ottoman army

bseesa – dish of crushed seeds mixed with oil

burnous – white robe worn by women; it exposes only one eye

buyut ash-shabaab – youth hostel

calidarium – hot room in a Roman baths complex

caliph – Islamic ruler

Camel Period – the period of Saharan rock art from 200 BC to the present

capital – decorated top part of a column

cardo – road running north-south through a Roman city

castrum – Roman fortified camp

cavea – seating area in a Roman theatre

cipolin – white marble with veins of green or grey

croix d'Agadez – Tuareg cross of stylised silver with filigree designs

cryptae – promenade corridors or underground galleries in Roman times

curia – senate house or municipal assembly in ancient Rome

cuzca – Tripolitanian dance

dammous – underground, troglodyte (Berber) houses

decumanus – road running east-west through a Roman city

divan – council of senior officers who advised the pasha in Ottoman times

djinn – a genie in Muslim belief; a being that can assume human or animal form

dolmesa – unit of measurement in old Ghadames

emir – Islamic ruler, military commander or governor

exedra – semicircular recess, frequently used for games in Roman times

fakhar – pottery

fish-fash – very soft, fine sand found in southern Libya

fitaat – dish from Ghadames of lentils, mutton and pancakes

foggara – underground channels leading to water

forica – latrines in ancient Rome

frigidarium – cold room in a Roman baths complex

funduq – hotel

galabiyya – full-length loose-fitting robe worn by men

gheeta – clarinet-like musical instrument from north-western and southern Libya

ghibli – hot, dry wind of northern Libya

ghurfas – Berber fortified granaries

gilal – pottery

gillta – natural springs

haj – pilgrimage to Mecca; one of the five pillars of Islam

hamada – plateaus of rock scoured by wind erosion
hammam – bathhouse
haram – prayer hall of mosque
harathin – ploughers and cultivators
Horse Period – the period of Saharan rock art from 1000 BC to AD 1

idehan – a vast area of shifting sand dunes known as sand seas
ijtihad – individual interpretation of sacred texts and traditions
ikhwan – followers of the Grand Sanusi
imam – man schooled in Islamic law; religious leader of Muslim community

jamahiriya – in post-Revolutionary Libya a 'state of the masses'
jammour – crescent atop a minaret
janissaries – professional soldiers committed to a life of military service and who in effect became rulers of Ottoman Libya
jawazzat – passport office
jebel – mountain range

al-kadus – literally, bottle; system of water regulation in Ghadames
khutba – sermon delivered by imam, especially at Friday noon prayers
kishk – a dance from eastern Libya

laconica – sweat baths in a Roman baths complex
Lebdah – Arabic name for Leptis Magna

madhhab – school of Islamic law
madrassa – school where the Quran and Islamic law are taught
maidan – square or large intersection
majruda – a dance from eastern Libya
malouf – musical form that originated in Andalusia played at Tripolitania
maqbara – cemetery
masabiyah jamaica – cocktail of 7-Up, Mirinda and Coke
ma'sered zeytoun – olive-oil press
masraf – bank
mat'am – restaurant
matruda – dish from eastern Libya of bread, milk, butter, dates and honey
Mazir – Berber dialect of Jebel Nafusa

miftah – key
mihrab – vaulted niche in wall of a mosque indicating direction of Mecca
minbar – pulpit that stands beside the *mihrab* in a mosque
mriskaawi – a musical form that is the basis for the lyrics of many Libyan songs
msak – Tuareg for mountain; see also *adrar* and *tadrart*
muezzin – man who calls the faithful to prayer from the minaret

naayi – flute-like musical instrument
nargileh – water pipe or *sheesha* for smoking
natatio – entrance hall to a Roman baths complex
nymphaeum – a building with fountains; dedicated to nymphs

osban – dish of sheep's internal organs

palaestra – exercise area or sporting ground in Roman times
pasha – Ottoman governor appointed by the sultan in Constantinople
Pastoral Period – the period of Saharan rock art from 5500 BC to 2000 BC, also known as the Bovidian Period
Pentapolis – ancient federation of five cities (Barce, Cyrene, Eusperides, Tocra and Apollonia) in Greek Libya
peristyle – colonnade or portico of columns surrounding a building or courtyard
Punic – ancient Phoenician people

qahwa – thick Arabic coffee
qaryat as-siyahe – tourist village
qasr – castle or palace; sometimes used to describe Berber fortified granary stores
Al-Qubba – canopy for women in some Ghadames houses

Ramadan – ninth month of the lunar Islamic calendar during which Muslims fast from sunrise to sunset
ras – headland
Riconquista – 1922 policy of reconquest of Libya by the Italians under Mussolini

Ar-Ridda – Islamic principle of confinement for women after husband's death
rishda – noodle dish with chickpeas, tomatoes and onions
Round Head Period – the period of Saharan rock art from 8000 BC to 6000 BC

saadi – tribes with lineage from Bani Hilal and Bani Salim
sabkha – low-lying area of marshland or salt pans
sahn – courtyard of mosque
Sanusi Movement – organised Islamic opposition to Ottoman and Italian occupation
scaenae frons – facade behind the stage in a Roman theatre
seif – Arabic for sword; also the name of sand dunes with long, sweeping ridges
serir – basins, formed by wadis, in which salt is left after water has evaporated
sharia – street or road
shay – tea
shay na'ana – mint tea
sheeshah – water pipe or *nargileh* for smoking
sheikh – tribal chief
shmari – a type of sweet, edible berry from around Al-Bayda
As-Sida – flour-based dish eaten to celebrate the birth of Mohammed
souq – market or bazaar
Sufi – follower of any of the Islamic mystical orders that emphasise dancing, chanting and trances in order to attain unity with God
suras – verses or chapters in the Quran

taajeelah – Tuareg bread cooked on hot sand
tadrart – Tuareg for mountain
tagelmoust – Tuareg veil
tajeen – lamb dish with tomato and paprika
Tamashek – Tuareg language
tarbuni – date juice
tawle – backgammon
Temissa – Tuareg language
tende – Tuareg dance
tepidarium – warm room in a Roman baths complex
tifinagh – letters of the Tuareg alphabet
Tripolis – literally Three Cities; referred to Leptis Magna, Oea and Sabratha in Roman Libya

wadi – a watercourse that is dry (except after rains)
Wild Fauna Period – the period of Saharan rock art from 10,000 BC to 6000 BC

zawiya – religious college or monastery especially under the Sanusis
Az-Zlabin – Tripolitanian dance performed at weddings
zukra – bagpipe-like musical instrument
zumeita – dish of wheat and small yellow seeds

Lonely Planet Guides by Region

Lonely Planet is known worldwide for publishing practical, reliable and no-nonsense travel information in our guides and on our Web site. The Lonely Planet list covers just about every accessible part of the world. Currently there are 16 series: Travel guides, Shoestring guides, Condensed guides, Phrasebooks, Read This First, Healthy Travel, Walking guides, Cycling guides, Watching Wildlife guides, Pisces Diving & Snorkeling guides, City Maps, Road Atlases, Out to Eat, World Food, Journeys travel literature and Pictorials.

AFRICA Africa on a shoestring • Botswana • Cairo • Cairo City Map • Cape Town • Cape Town City Map • East Africa • Egypt • Egyptian Arabic phrasebook • Ethiopia, Eritrea & Djibouti • Ethiopian Amharic phrasebook • The Gambia & Senegal • Healthy Travel Africa • Kenya • Malawi • Morocco • Moroccan Arabic phrasebook • Mozambique • Namibia • Read This First: Africa • South Africa, Lesotho & Swaziland • Southern Africa • Southern Africa Road Atlas • Swahili phrasebook • Tanzania, Zanzibar & Pemba • Trekking in East Africa • Tunisia • Watching Wildlife East Africa • Watching Wildlife Southern Africa • West Africa • World Food Morocco • Zambia • Zimbabwe, Botswana & Namibia
Travel Literature: Mali Blues: Traveling to an African Beat • The Rainbird: A Central African Journey • Songs to an African Sunset: A Zimbabwean Story

AUSTRALIA & THE PACIFIC Aboriginal Australia & the Torres Strait Islands •Auckland • Australia • Australian phrasebook • Australia Road Atlas • Cycling Australia • Cycling New Zealand • Fiji • Fijian phrasebook • Healthy Travel Australia, NZ & the Pacific • Islands of Australia's Great Barrier Reef • Melbourne • Melbourne City Map • Micronesia • New Caledonia • New South Wales • New Zealand • Northern Territory • Outback Australia • Out to Eat – Melbourne • Out to Eat – Sydney • Papua New Guinea • Pidgin phrasebook • Queensland • Rarotonga & the Cook Islands • Samoa • Solomon Islands • South Australia • South Pacific • South Pacific phrasebook • Sydney • Sydney City Map • Sydney Condensed • Tahiti & French Polynesia • Tasmania • Tonga • Tramping in New Zealand • Vanuatu • Victoria • Walking in Australia • Watching Wildlife Australia • Western Australia
Travel Literature: Islands in the Clouds: Travels in the Highlands of New Guinea • Kiwi Tracks: A New Zealand Journey • Sean & David's Long Drive

CENTRAL AMERICA & THE CARIBBEAN Bahamas, Turks & Caicos • Baja California • Belize, Guatemala & Yucatán • Bermuda • Central America on a shoestring • Costa Rica • Costa Rica Spanish phrasebook • Cuba • Cycling Cuba • Dominican Republic & Haiti • Eastern Caribbean • Guatemala • Havana • Healthy Travel Central & South America • Jamaica • Mexico • Mexico City • Panama • Puerto Rico • Read This First: Central & South America • Virgin Islands • World Food Caribbean • World Food Mexico • Yucatán
Travel Literature: Green Dreams: Travels in Central America

EUROPE Amsterdam • Amsterdam City Map • Amsterdam Condensed • Andalucía • Athens • Austria • Baltic States phrasebook • Barcelona • Barcelona City Map • Belgium & Luxembourg • Berlin • Berlin City Map • Britain • British phrasebook • Brussels, Bruges & Antwerp • Brussels City Map • Budapest • Budapest City Map • Canary Islands • Catalunya & the Costa Brava • Central Europe • Central Europe phrasebook • Copenhagen • Corfu & the Ionians • Corsica • Crete • Crete Condensed • Croatia • Cycling Britain • Cycling France • Cyprus • Czech & Slovak Republics • Czech phrasebook • Denmark • Dublin • Dublin City Map • Dublin Condensed • Eastern Europe • Eastern Europe phrasebook • Edinburgh • Edinburgh City Map • England • Estonia, Latvia & Lithuania • Europe on a shoestring • Europe phrasebook • Finland • Florence • Florence City Map • France • Frankfurt City Map • Frankfurt Condensed • French phrasebook • Georgia, Armenia & Azerbaijan • Germany • German phrasebook • Greece • Greek Islands • Greek phrasebook • Hungary • Iceland, Greenland & the Faroe Islands • Ireland • Italian phrasebook • Italy • Kraków • Lisbon • The Loire • London • London City Map • London Condensed • Madrid • Madrid City Map • Malta • Mediterranean Europe • Milan, Turin & Genoa • Moscow • Munich • Netherlands • Normandy • Norway • Out to Eat – London • Out to Eat – Paris • Paris • Paris City Map • Paris Condensed • Poland • Polish phrasebook • Portugal • Portuguese phrasebook • Prague • Prague City Map • Provence & the Côte d'Azur • Read This First: Europe • Rhodes & the Dodecanese • Romania & Moldova • Rome • Rome City Map • Rome Condensed • Russia, Ukraine & Belarus • Russian phrasebook • Scandinavian & Baltic Europe • Scandinavian phrasebook • Scotland • Sicily • Slovenia • South-West France • Spain • Spanish phrasebook • Stockholm • St Petersburg • St Petersburg City Map • Sweden • Switzerland • Tuscany • Ukrainian phrasebook • Venice • Vienna • Wales • Walking in Britain • Walking in France • Walking in Ireland • Walking in Italy • Walking in Scotland • Walking in Spain • Walking in Switzerland • Western Europe • World Food France • World Food Greece • World Food Ireland • World Food Italy • World Food Spain **Travel Literature:** After Yugoslavia • Love and War in the Apennines • The Olive Grove: Travels in Greece • On the Shores of the Mediterranean • Round Ireland in Low Gear • A Small Place in Italy

Lonely Planet Mail Order

onely Planet products are distributed worldwide. They are also available by mail order from Lonely Planet, so if you have difficulty finding a title please write to us. North and South American residents should write to 150 Linden St, Oakland, CA 94607, USA; European and African residents should write to 10a Spring Place, London NW5 3BH, UK; and residents of other countries to Locked Bag 1, Footscray, Victoria 3011, Australia.

INDIAN SUBCONTINENT & THE INDIAN OCEAN Bangladesh • Bengali phrasebook • Bhutan • Delhi • Goa • Healthy Travel Asia & India • Hindi & Urdu phrasebook • India • India & Bangladesh City Map • Indian Himalaya • Karakoram Highway • Kathmandu City Map • Kerala • Madagascar • Maldives • Mauritius, Réunion & Seychelles • Mumbai (Bombay) • Nepal • Nepali phrasebook • North India • Pakistan • Rajasthan • Read This First: Asia & India • South India • Sri Lanka • Sri Lanka phrasebook • Tibet • Tibetan phrasebook • Trekking in the Indian Himalaya • Trekking in the Karakoram & Hindukush • Trekking in the Nepal Himalaya • World Food India **Travel Literature:** The Age of Kali: Indian Travels and Encounters • Hello Goodnight: A Life of Goa • In Rajasthan • Maverick in Madagascar • A Season in Heaven: True Tales from the Road to Kathmandu • Shopping for Buddhas • A Short Walk in the Hindu Kush • Slowly Down the Ganges

MIDDLE EAST & CENTRAL ASIA Bahrain, Kuwait & Qatar • Central Asia • Central Asia phrasebook • Dubai • Farsi (Persian) phrasebook • Hebrew phrasebook • Iran • Israel & the Palestinian Territories • Istanbul • Istanbul City Map • Istanbul to Cairo • Istanbul to Kathmandu • Jerusalem • Jerusalem City Map • Jordan • Lebanon • Middle East • Oman & the United Arab Emirates • Syria • Turkey • Turkish phrasebook • World Food Turkey • Yemen **Travel Literature:** Black on Black: Iran Revisited • Breaking Ranks: Turbulent Travels in the Promised Land • The Gates of Damascus • Kingdom of the Film Stars: Journey into Jordan

NORTH AMERICA Alaska • Boston • Boston City Map • Boston Condensed • British Columbia • California & Nevada • California Condensed • Canada • Chicago • Chicago City Map • Chicago Condensed • Florida • Georgia & the Carolinas • Great Lakes • Hawaii • Hiking in Alaska • Hiking in the USA • Honolulu & Oahu City Map • Las Vegas • Los Angeles • Los Angeles City Map • Louisiana & the Deep South • Miami • Miami City Map • Montreal • New England • New Orleans • New Orleans City Map • New York City • New York City City Map • New York City Condensed • New York, New Jersey & Pennsylvania • Oahu • Out to Eat – San Francisco • Pacific Northwest • Rocky Mountains • San Diego & Tijuana • San Francisco • San Francisco City Map • Seattle • Seattle City Map • Southwest • Texas • Toronto • USA • USA phrasebook • Vancouver • Vancouver City Map • Virginia & the Capital Region • Washington, DC • Washington, DC City Map • World Food New Orleans **Travel Literature**: Caught Inside: A Surfer's Year on the California Coast • Drive Thru America

NORTH-EAST ASIA Beijing • Beijing City Map • Cantonese phrasebook • China • Hiking in Japan • Hong Kong & Macau • Hong Kong City Map • Hong Kong Condensed • Japan • Japanese phrasebook • Korea • Korean phrasebook • Kyoto • Mandarin phrasebook • Mongolia • Mongolian phrasebook • Seoul • Shanghai • South-West China • Taiwan • Tokyo • Tokyo Condensed • World Food Hong Kong • World Food Japan **Travel Literature:** In Xanadu: A Quest • Lost Japan

SOUTH AMERICA Argentina, Uruguay & Paraguay • Bolivia • Brazil • Brazilian phrasebook • Buenos Aires • Buenos Aires City Map • Chile & Easter Island • Colombia • Ecuador & the Galapagos Islands • Healthy Travel Central & South America • Latin American Spanish phrasebook • Peru • Quechua phrasebook • Read This First: Central & South America • Rio de Janeiro • Rio de Janeiro City Map • Santiago de Chile • South America on a shoestring • Trekking in the Patagonian Andes • Venezuela **Travel Literature:** Full Circle: A South American Journey

SOUTH-EAST ASIA Bali & Lombok • Bangkok • Bangkok City Map • Burmese phrasebook • Cambodia • Cycling Vietnam, Laos & Cambodia • East Timor phrasebook • Hanoi • Healthy Travel Asia & India • Hill Tribes phrasebook • Ho Chi Minh City (Saigon) • Indonesia • Indonesian phrasebook • Indonesia's Eastern Islands • Java • Lao phrasebook • Laos • Malay phrasebook • Malaysia, Singapore & Brunei • Myanmar (Burma) • Philippines • Pilipino (Tagalog) phrasebook • Read This First: Asia & India • Singapore • Singapore City Map • South-East Asia on a shoestring • South-East Asia phrasebook • Thailand • Thailand's Islands & Beaches • Thailand, Vietnam, Laos & Cambodia Road Atlas • Thai phrasebook • Vietnam • Vietnamese phrasebook • World Food Indonesia • World Food Thailand • World Food Vietnam

ALSO AVAILABLE: Antarctica • The Arctic • The Blue Man: Tales of Travel, Love and Coffee • Brief Encounters: Stories of Love, Sex & Travel • Buddhist Stupas in Asia: The Shape of Perfection • Chasing Rickshaws • The Last Grain Race • Lonely Planet … On the Edge: Adventurous Escapades from Around the World • Lonely Planet Unpacked • Lonely Planet Unpacked Again • Not the Only Planet: Science Fiction Travel Stories • Ports of Call: A Journey by Sea • Sacred India • Travel Photography: A Guide to Taking Better Pictures • Travel with Children • Tuvalu: Portrait of an Island Nation

LONELY PLANET

You already know that Lonely Planet produces more than this one guidebook, but you might not be aware of the other products we have on this region. Here is a selection of titles that you may want to check out as well:

Middle East
ISBN 0 86442 701 8
US$24.95 • UK£14.99

Cairo
ISBN 1 86450 115 4
US$15.99 • UK£9.99

Healthy Travel Africa
ISBN 1 86450 050 6
US$5.95 • UK£3.99

Egypt
ISBN 1 86450 298 3
US$19.99 • UK£12.99

Morocco
ISBN 0 86442 762 X
US$19.99 • UK£12.99

Tunisia
ISBN 1 86450 185 5
US$16.99 • UK£10.99

Africa on a shoestring
ISBN 0 86442 663 1
US$29.99 • UK£17.99

Read This First: Africa
ISBN 1 86450 066 2
US$14.95 • UK£8.99

West Africa
ISBN 0 86442 569 4
US$29.95 • UK£17.99

Available wherever books are sold

Index

Text

Bold indicates maps.

Boxed Text & Special Sections

MAP LEGEND

CITY ROUTES

Freeway .... Freeway	⊐ ⊐ ⊐ ⊐ ...... Unsealed Road
Highway .... Primary Road	──→── ...... One-Way Street
Road .... Secondary Road	──────── ...... Pedestrian Street
Street .... Street	⊞⊞⊞⊞⊞ ...... Stepped Street
Lane .... Lane	⊃= = = ... Tunnel
═══════ .... On/Off Ramp	═════════ .... Footbridge

REGIONAL ROUTES

═══════ ...... Tollway; Freeway
═══════ .... Primary Road
═══════ .... Secondary Road
─────── .... Minor Road

BOUNDARIES

─··─··─··─ .... International
─··─··─·· .... State
─ ─ ─ .... Disputed
━━━━━ .... Fortified Wall

HYDROGRAPHY

.... River; Creek	⬭ ⬭ ...... Dry Lake; Salt Lake
─·─·─·─ .... Canal	⊙ ⤳ ...... Spring; Rapids
⬬ .... Lake	◐ ⤙ ⤞ .... Waterfalls

TRANSPORT ROUTES & STATIONS

─────⊙── .... Train	─────🚉 .... Ferry
·········· ...... Underground Train	─ ─ ─ ─ .... Walking Trail
──Ⓜ── .... Metro	·········· .... Walking Tour
▪▪▪▪▪▪▪▪▪ .... Tramway	▭▭▭▭▭ .... Path
╫─╫─╫─╫ ...... Cable Car; Chairlift	──────── .... Pier or Jetty

AREA FEATURES

▬▬▬ .... Building	.... Market	∴∴∴ .... Beach	.... Campus
❀ ...... Park; Gardens	⬭ ...... Sports Ground	+ + + ... Cemetery	⌐⌐ .... Plaza

POPULATION SYMBOLS

✪ **CAPITAL** .... National Capital	● **CITY** .... City	● Village .... Village	
◉ **CAPITAL** .... State Capital	● **Town** .... Town	▬▬▬ .... Urban Area	

MAP SYMBOLS

◆ .... Place to Stay	▼ .... Place to Eat	● .... Point of Interest

✈ .... Airport	🏛 ...... Classical Temple	☪ .... Mosque	🍺 .... Pub or Bar
⊖ .... Bank	✚ .... Hospital	🏛 .... Museum	⊠ .... Ruins
🚌 .... Bus Terminal	🖥 .... Internet Cafe	🕌 .... Oasis	⊗ ...... Shopping Centre
⌂ .... Cave	⛪ ...... Islamic Monument	🅿 .... Parking	⊠ .... Synagogue
⛪ .... Church	☀ .... Lookout	★ .... Police Station	☎ .... Telephone
🎬 .... Cinema	⚱ .... Monument	✉ .... Post Office	❶ ...... Tourist Information
			🐾 .... Zoo

Note: not all symbols displayed above appear in this book

LONELY PLANET OFFICES

Australia
Locked Bag 1, Footscray, Victoria 3011
☎ 03 8379 8000 fax 03 8379 8111
email: talk2us@lonelyplanet.com.au

USA
150 Linden St, Oakland, CA 94607
☎ 510 893 8555 TOLL FREE: 800 275 8555
fax 510 893 8572
email: info@lonelyplanet.com

UK
10a Spring Place, London NW5 3BH
☎ 020 7428 4800 fax 020 7428 4828
email: go@lonelyplanet.co.uk

France
1 rue du Dahomey, 75011 Paris
☎ 01 55 25 33 00 fax 01 55 25 33 01
email: bip@lonelyplanet.fr
www.lonelyplanet.fr

World Wide Web: www.lonelyplanet.com *or* AOL keyword: lp
Lonely Planet Images: www.lonelyplanetimages.com